MODERN KOREAN DRAMA

MODERN KOREAN DRAMA

AN ANTHOLOGY

Edited, with an introduction, by Richard Nichols

COLUMBIA UNIVERSITY PRESS   NEW YORK

COLUMBIA UNIVERSITY PRESS WISHES TO EXPRESS ITS
APPRECIATION FOR ASSISTANCE GIVEN BY THE PUSHKIN FUND
TOWARD THE COST OF PUBLISHING THIS BOOK.

 Columbia University Press
Publishers Since 1893
New York   Chichester, West Sussex

Copyright © 2009 Columbia University Press
Paperback edition, 2011
All rights reserved

Library of Congress Cataloging-in-Publication Data
Modern Korean drama : an anthology / edited, with an introduction,
by Richard Nichols.
    p. cm.
  Includes bibliographical references.
    ISBN 978-0-231-14946-4 (cloth : alk. paper)—ISBN 978-0-231-14947-1
(pbk. : alk. paper)—ISBN 978-0-231-52038-6 (e-book)
  1. Korean drama—20th century.   2. Korean drama—21st century.
I. Nichols, Richard.   II. Title.

PL979.7.M63 2009
895.7'25—dc22   2009019566

TO SHARLEEN...

CONTENTS

Preface ix
Acknowledgments xiii
Editor's Notes xv

INTRODUCTION   1

CH'A PŎMSŎK   13
BURNING MOUNTAIN (SANBUL)   15

PAK CHOYŎL   77
O CHANG-GUN'S TOENAIL (O CHANG-GUN ŬI PALT'OP)   79

YI MANHŬI   117
PLEASE TURN OFF THE LIGHTS (PUL CHOM KKŎ CHUSEYO)   119

O T'AESŎK   167
BELLFLOWER (TORAJI)   169

YI KANGBAEK   201
A FEELING, LIKE NIRVANA (NŬGGIM KŬGNAK KAT'ŬN)   203

PAK KŬNHYŎNG   245
IN PRAISE OF YOUTH (CH'ŎNGCH'UN YECH'AN)   247

PAE SAMSHIK   271
CH'OE SŬNGHŬI (CH'OE SŬNGHŬI)   273

Appendix: Theater in Seoul   311
Bibliography   319
Translators   327

PREFACE

Many modern Korean novels, short stories, and poems have been translated, and some Korean plays also have been translated into a number of European languages. But until recently, *modern* Korean dramatic literature has received only scant attention from English-language translators. In the introduction, I examine the term *modern* in more detail, but briefly, modern Korean drama refers to those plays written since 1960. This collection is the first general anthology of such works to be published since 1983 and, I hope, offers some sense of the extensive array of modern Korean drama as well as offering, as in Sŏ Chi-mun's *The Rainy Spell and Other Korean Stories*, glimpses into the "full and true record of a nation's life." Put another way, this anthology gives generalist readers insights into Korean culture through its dramatic literature and introduces students of theater or literature to Asian works.

Here, Korean drama refers to South Korean drama, written by and performed by South Koreans for South Koreans, generally in Seoul. To be sure, many dramas are written by those not residing in Seoul (Yi Yunt'aek's early plays, for example, were written and performed in Pusan), and theater performances may be found in Inchŏn, Pusan, Taegu, and other cities throughout South Korea. But just as in the United States where the mecca for theater artists is New York City, sooner or later South Korean theater artists must make their mark in Seoul.

Dramas from North Korea are not included in this limited definition of "Korean" because information regarding North Korean drama is scarce and because the North

Korean theater has been dominated by epic music and dance performances in service of the people's revolution. The "five great revolutionary operas," such as the 1971 *Sea of Blood* (*P'ibada*) and *A True Daughter of the Party* (*Tang ŭi ch'amdoen ttal*), glorify the proletariat struggle. As spectacles, they may be dramatic—that is, emotionally riveting—but these quasi ballet operas seem inappropriate for inclusion in this collection of dramas.

What, then, is meant by "drama"? It does not mean the ubiquitous Korean "soap operas" that, along with cinema and popular contemporary music, have fueled the advance of the Korean "New Wave" (*hallyu*) throughout much of Asia and major cities in the West. Instead, in this volume, drama is a form of written art intended to be performed in or on some kind of performance space, for an audience, and by actors (or, in some instances, puppets) behaving as if they were someone else. The unfolding of the drama's story, whether in the reading of the text or the performance of it, takes place in the virtual present, driven by the characters' thoughts and external actions, expressing the author's "voice" not in omniscient narrative but through the characters' behaviors. Clearly, the dramas in this collection take many forms, suggesting a variety of theatrical performances. Whatever the dramas' literary value, collectively they signal a tendency in the Korean theater away from the early Western-influenced, word-based realistic form toward complex and genre-blurring dramaturgy and theater performance, communicating universal human behaviors as much through images, music, dance, and ritual as through the printed word.

Ch'a Pŏmsŏk's *Burning Mountain* intertwines the fate of a wavering Communist guerrilla and the barren lives of village women, all trapped by the shift of ideology and front lines during the Korean War. In its depiction of the death of a naïve farm boy mistakenly called to duty, *O Chang-gun's Toenail*, by Pak Choyŏl, satirizes recognizably overbearing bureaucrats and warped military thinking. *Please Turn Off the Lights* is Yi Manhŭi's dissection of sexual relations, politics, and ambition when a powerful politician's guilty past intrudes into the present. O T'aesŏk's *Bellflower* depicts the Korean court's moral decay at the close of the Chosŏn dynasty (1392–1910) as Korea declined from a sovereign nation into a pawn in East Asian geopolitics from around 1880 to 1910. The fate of two historical figures in O's tale questions the place of loyalty and human bonds in contemporary Korea. Buddhist icons and perspectives inform Yi Kangbaek's *A Feeling, Like Nirvana*, a highly imagistic fantasy that explores the dynamics of surface form and inner truth , questions master–apprentice relationships, and illuminates the bond between mother and male child yet unborn. Pak Kŭnhyŏng's *In Praise of Youth* provides an antidote to stereotypes of Korean students as polite, hardworking, academic drones. Sparsely and unrelentingly, the play depicts the dark side of Korean education, alcoholism, spousal abuse, and the marginalization of "un-normal" people, but—without sentimentality—it also offers hope through the healing power of love and concern for others. Finally, Pae Samshik's *Ch'oe Sŭnghŭi* questions the role of art in human relationships and politics, using a controversial figure in Korean history, a world-renowned entertainer who chose North Korea over the South, ultimately to be disowned by her daughter and stripped of political status by the North Korean government. (She was posthumously "rehabilitated" at Kim Jong-il's direction in 2006.)

Readers familiar with the Korean theater well may wonder why Yi Yunt'aek, Cho Kwang-hwa, Kim Kwang-lim, Ch'oe Inhun, and other writers, such as the female playwright Kim Ch'a-rim, are not represented in this volume. Time constraints, publication costs, and, most especially, the availability of interested, capable translators were limiting factors. Thus a number of deserving Korean plays—especially those written by younger playwrights since 2004—still await translation into English.

ACKNOWLEDGMENTS

A Korea Foundation research grant supported my initial theatergoing in Seoul during the summer of 2000, when this anthology was conceived. The collection took basic form in 2002/2003 when I was a Fulbright Senior Research Scholar in Seoul, during which time Professor Horace Underwood, executive director of the Korea-American Education Commission (Fulbright), generously shared his insights and advice. Supplemental travel grants from The Pennsylvania State University's Institute for the Arts and Humanities and the College of Arts and Architecture enabled me to do research in Seoul in the years preceding and following my Fulbright year.

Since 1999, numerous Korean theater artists, critics, and scholars have patiently provided advice and insights, and my gratitude to all of them is immense. At the risk of slighting some, others require specific recognition: First and foremost is the doyen of contemporary Korean playwrights, Yi Kangbaek, who graciously agreed to meet me in July 1999 and who has been a friend and wise mentor ever since. Among those who contributed generously to this book are Chŏng Chinsu, Son Chinch'aek, Yi Yunt'aek, Kim Yunch'ŏl, Kim A-jŏng, Hŏ Sunja, Kim Bang-ok, Kim Ch'unhŭi, Kim Hyŏnggi, Kim Mihŭi, Yi Chaemyŏng, and Shin Suk-wŏn. Kim Dong-uk unstintingly tutored me in the ways of contemporary Korean history, culture, and theater as we prepared our *Four Contemporary Korean Plays by Lee Yun-Taek* (2007). Alyssa Kim and Yi Hyŏngjin shared their intelligence, enthusiasm, and pride in things Korean with boundless generosity over the past eight years or more. In addition to her translations of two plays in this volume,

Alyssa Kim wrote the author's background for Pae Samshik. Yi Hyekyŏng, Yi Hyŏngjin, and Yi Sŭng-ŭn generously provided research assistance in regard to Pak Kŭnhyŏng. The introduction to this text was shaped by the work of many scholars, most notably Chŏng Chinsu, Kim A-jŏng, Kim Chinhŭi, Cho O-kon, and Yu Minyŏng.

Brother Anthony of Taizé, the English adviser of *Korean Literature Today*, and Shin Chongbŏm, associate editor of the *Korea Journal*, were encouraging and helpful during my pursuit of the various permissions required to compile and publish this volume.

Special thanks go to the playwrights, to Ch'a Pŏmsŏk's estate for granting permission to publish his work, and to the translators of the works in this anthology, for their good humor, patience, and perseverance.

Finally, to the anonymous readers of the draft manuscript whose insights and advice were invaluable, to Margaret B. Yamashita for her editing, and to Jennifer Crewe and Columbia University Press for supporting Korean studies: Thank you.

EDITOR'S NOTES

In this volume, a *play* refers to the written script or to the performance of the script on stage; *drama* or *dramatic literature* refers to the text itself. *Theater* refers to a type of building or a performance art.

The McCune–Reischauer system of romanization generally is used throughout this work, with some exceptions, especially for earlier common usages (as in Syngman Rhee, rather than Yi Sŭngman). Conversely, commonly used romanizations of Korean names, such as Hur, Lee, Oh, Park, and Sohn, are rendered according to the McCune–Reischauer system: Hŏ, Yi, O, Pak, and Son. Apologies are offered to those mentioned in the acknowledgments, all of whom prefer a romanization of their respective names very different from McCune–Reischauer.

Korean names generally have three syllables, beginning with the surname. A long-established and frequently preferred personal practice places a hyphen between the second and third syllable. The McCune–Reischauer system, however, suggests removing it unless the meaning or pronunciation would be affected. Thus I have used hyphens sparingly here, only when their omission might lead to a misreading (for example, the character name Chŏngim is hyphenated as Chŏng-im). But the bibliography presents names and titles generally as they appear in print, which in many instances leads to the use of hyphens and various romanizations of names.

Because plays are meant to be read aloud, rather than silently, the pronunciation of Korean words should be a concern, especially if a scene is to be used for acting-studio lessons or if the entire work is to be staged. Pronunciation guides for the McCune–Reischauer system—and others—are readily available on the Internet. Of course, as with any language, the preferred guide to appropriate pronunciation is a native speaker.

Although the critical commentary on each play is minimal, certain aspects seem to require some explanation, which appear as either observations in the short biography of the author that precedes each play or my own brief comments included in the notes. The notes to the scripts are minimal as well, providing only enough information to make sense of the dialogue, characters, and situation. General readers wishing more detailed interpretations of Korea and Koreans are referred to the bibliography at the end of this anthology.

One characteristic of Korean and Japanese play scripts is the ellipses used in the dialogue to indicate indirect expression, tentativeness, or an inconclusive thought. Conversely, in English-language scripts, ellipses are usually used to indicate incomplete dialogue and appear as . . . , whereas Korean playwrights prefer . . . . . . I generally have retained the ellipses in the original text to offer a visual impression of that text but have shortened them to save space.

Finally, some scholars use south Korea and north Korea (rather than the usual capitalized South Korea and North Korea) to suggest one people divided geographically. A discussion of the political ramifications of such usage seems beyond the scope of this volume. In this book, though, when "Korea" or "Korean" is used in a context that predates the official 1948 partition of the peninsula, the terms refer to Korea or the Korean people as a whole. In a postpartition context, however, "Korea" or "Koreans" refers specifically to the Republic of South Korea.

MODERN KOREAN DRAMA

INTRODUCTION

The history of Korean dramatic literature spans less than a century. Put another way, before the first decade of the twentieth century, there is *no* history of a complete, written play script serving as the source of a Korean theater performance. True, proto-theatrical aspects of ritual and shamanistic rites (*kut*) date back at least two thousand years, and more recognizably theatrical forms, such as the puppet theater and mask dance (*t'alch'um*) performances, have centuries-old roots, but they were essentially orally transmitted traditions until the scenarios were transcribed in the 1930s and after. During Korea's Chosŏn dynasty (1392–1910), during which significant forms of dramatic literature developed in neighboring China and Japan, a variety of factors joined in Korea to preclude the development of drama: a dominating, conservative noble class whose Neo-Confucian values relegated theater and its performers to the lowest stratum of society; an agrarian economy and the absence of a sizable, financially secure merchant middle class; the absence of large urban populations; touring companies of farmer-performers that could not perform year-round; the popularity of traditional theater forms among the lower classes; and the lack of buildings specifically designed for theater performance.

In this environment, in which scholarship was an important means to social and political advancement, scholar-authors created venerable traditions in poetry and fiction, written in either classical Chinese or vernacular Korean. *Sijo*, for example, a lyrical three-stanza poetic form, emerged in the thirteenth century and flourished throughout the Chosŏn dynasty. But without patronage from the noble class or a wealthy middle class, dramatic literature did not evolve during that era. Thus dramatic literature, the written text that inspires and shapes theater performance, was, perforce, modern for Koreans at its inception around 1910 because it had no "classical" forebears. This simplistic explanation does not, however, sufficiently incorporate salient aspects of Korean history, so it may be useful here to provide a context for the genesis of Korean dramatic literature.

The ruggedly mountainous Korean Peninsula is home to one of the most homogenous peoples on earth, now some seventy million inhabitants with a common language and a common culture but since 1948 politically divided into two antipathetic nations: the Democratic People's Republic of Korea in the north and the Republic of Korea in the south. The twentieth century was especially turbulent for Koreans, as the peninsula was occupied by foreign powers, was partitioned into two nations, was devastated by civil war, and became home to repressive military regimes (in both North and South Korea). During this time, North Korea became isolated, and in the second half of the century, South Korea metamorphosed from an impoverished, agrarian, third-world nation into an urban economic power of international stature. But even long before the twentieth century, jutting as it does like the thumb of East Asia into the seas separating China and Japan, the peninsula endured recurring foreign incursions and invasions, events reflected in the Korean aphorism "The shrimp caught between two whales gets hurt."

Kim Yong-ok's play *Fire* (*Kŭ, Pul*, 1999) depicts the kidnapping and transportation of a village of ceramics makers to Japan, only one of the many insults to Korean pride inflicted by pillaging Japanese in the 1590s and early 1600s. Following conflicts with Manchu China in the 1620s and 1630s, Korea turned inward, its self-protective isolationism earning it the sobriquet the "Hermit Kingdom." Then, during the last decades of the nineteenth century, Russia, Japan, and various Western powers insisted that Korea open its doors to trade. After Japan and the United States coerced favorable trade treaties from Korea in 1876 and 1882, respectively, ideas and technologies related to the West's industrial revolution increasingly threatened Korean isolationist conservatives and fueled reformers' zeal. The Sino-Japanese War (1894–1895), which took place on Korean soil, demonstrated how quickly Japan had advanced by adopting Western technologies since the Meiji Restoration (1868). Accordingly, Japan became a model for Koreans seeking reform and modernization, both up to and after Japan's annexation of Korea in 1910. It is ironic that today's internationally recognized Korean drama and theater grew not from roots in the revered and emulated Chinese culture but from seeds planted during the early years of the Japanese colonial era, a time in which authorities went to great lengths to suppress Korean theater and drama.

To make sense of the nascent drama's place in a rapidly changing Korea at the turn of the twenty-first century, we need to consider some of the characteristics of late-nineteenth-century Western drama, the drama studied and imitated by Japanese writers and theater artists and transmitted—albeit not always accurately—to Korea.

Modern Western drama was an artistic reaction to the early-nineteenth-century Romantic movement, influenced by the Industrial Revolution's technological advances and works by Darwin, Freud, and others that shrank the Romanticist's "noble savage" into a mere subject of scientific analysis. Émile Zola called for a drama that would analyze the behavior of each subject and class depicted on the stage. The form of theater he proposed came to be known as naturalism, a *tranche de vie* (slice of life), like a slide under a microscope, in which the subject's behavior was described in minute detail. The naturalist playwright was like a doctor presenting symptoms, but unlike the physician, deterministic naturalism suggested no remedy. In the hands of dramatists later in the century, naturalism evolved into realism, a more optimistic form because unlike naturalism and its deterministic perspective, realism denotes potential progress. It suggests that once a problem is presented and analyzed, a solution or cure can be pursued.

Henrik Ibsen's critique of Norwegian society, *The Doll's House*, was translated and staged in Japan in 1911, and other translations of Western realistic plays soon followed. The Japanese perception of the application of empirical science to theater, a view of drama and theater as useful vehicles of social criticism, and the aping of the superficial aspects of realistic acting were transmitted to Korea by Japanese during the early colonial period and then by Koreans studying in Japan. In the years surrounding the 1910 annexation, there were no indigenous dramas on which to build a "modern" Korean version. Instead, the model had to be imported.

Theater artists in the latter part of the twentieth century embraced the incorporation of traditional Korean forms to create "modern" Korean drama. But for reformers in the first decades of the century, incorporation of traditional elements was problematic because as part of policies designed to obliterate Korean culture, Japanese authorities sternly repressed indigenous Korean theater forms, such as *p'ansori* (a solo, sung narrative supported by a drummer) and *t'alch'um*. Japanese performances, however, were encouraged, and touring commercial performers introduced two theater forms that influenced the later development of Korean drama and theater.

The first was *shinpa* (literally, new wave), which appeared in Japan about 1880 as an amalgam of the Japanese kabuki and what the Japanese perceived to be Western realism. In these early efforts to modernize the feudal kabuki, *shinpa* dealt with themes related to modernization but soon acquired melodramatic qualities. The Korean version became the short-lived *shinp'agŭk* (new school drama), initially performed in 1911 by Im Sŏnggu's Hyŏkshindan company. Melodramatic, actor-centered plays appealed to a broad spectrum of the populace, set as they were in contemporary times and often depicting families in duress and beset by ill-fated or unrequited love. Some later works added nationalistic elements to the mix, but the goal—as it was in Western melodrama in the same period—was to move the audience to tears. Early *shinp'agŭk* was not a literature-based form; rather, the scenarios were fleshed out through the actors' improvisation, much in the tradition of the Japanese kabuki's *kuchidate* (improvised conversation based on a predetermined scenario). Although Cho Ilje is deemed by some to be Korea's first playwright, based on his play *Three Patients* (*Pyŏngja*, 1912), Pak Sŭnghŭi also is noted as the first to abandon improvisation and write complete play scripts. Whichever the case, a number of *shinp'a* companies were established, and *shinp'agŭk* became a commercial success until its gradual demise in the 1930s.

The second Japanese model was *shingeki* (new drama), a text-based form modeled on Western realistic drama and theater. *Shingeki* was committed to realism, to a theater performance created by actors and a director working from a script, and to theater that educated the audience about some socially relevant issue.

A major architectural and aesthetic component of European realism was the proscenium arch, which, despite the construction of Korea's first indoor theater, Hyŏmnyulsa (1902–1906), and the Western-style Wŏngaksa (1908–1909), did not appear in Korea in significant form and numbers until the 1980s, a delay that may well have influenced Korean dramaturgy and theater performance to the present day. In any event, the Korean version of realistic drama became known as *shin-gŭk* (new drama), early versions of which are Cho Myŏng-hŭi's *The Death of Kim Yŏng-il* (*Kim Yŏng-il ŭi chugŭm*, 1923) and a pioneering attempt at naturalism, one with a prostitute as the protagonist, Kim U-jin's *A Woman, Yi Yŏngnyŏ* (*Yi Yŏng-nyŏ*, 1925). Both plays were staged by the influential amateur theater group Tongwuhoe (Society of Comradeship).

As the 1920s and 1930s advanced, playwrights experimented with other forms, such as expressionism. Kim U-jin, for example, wrote *Shipwreck* (*Nanp'a*, 1926), subtitled in German as *Expressionist Story in Three Acts*. In general, however, *shin-gŭk* playwrights were drawn to the more realistic works of European dramatists such as Anton Chekhov, August Strindberg, Ibsen, and others in their desire to use theater realism as a vehicle for modernization and social change, but they especially imitated works by Irish playwrights like John Millington Synge and Sean O'Casey. Common people's lives were portrayed through logical plot development and cause–effect relationships. The structure of the Western "well-made play" (exposition, inciting action, complicating actions, reversals, climax, and denouement) was perceptible. Although realistic drama in this period was perhaps less melodramatic than earlier works, it was not commercially successful. Some scholars have suggested that drama and theater imitating Western models—without sufficient adaptation to Korean taste—appealed only to the intellectual elite. Because they were of little interest to the general public, they were limited in their popularity and potential development. Too, the emphasis in some companies, such as Sawŏlhoe, on staging Western translations, rather than indigenous works, and the absence of performance venues appropriate to the performance of realistic plays must have been detrimental. Moreover, colonial law and Japanese censors during the 1930s increasingly made difficult, if not impossible, an accurate dramatic portrayal of Korean life under Japanese rule, effectively stunting the early development of a native realistic drama. From this point until 1988, censorship remained a formidable, repressive force opposed to a freely developing dramatic literature and theater.

One of those forced to choose between writing to please the censors or retiring from the theater was Yu Ch'ijin, "the father of Korean theater," who studied in Japan and identified with Irish writers depicting the plight of their repressed countrymen under British occupiers. Performed by the research association of university intellectuals, Kŭgyesul Yŏnguhoe (Dramatic Arts Study Society), Yu's plays, along with those of Ch'ae Minshik, attempted to incorporate social issues of the 1930s into the new dramatic form, portraying the suffering of the Korean people, especially the farmers, during the Japanese occupation. Yu's *The Shack* (*T'omak*, also translated as *The Hut*, 1932) was followed by other sociopolitical dramas, such as *The Ox* (*So*, 1934), all attempting to raise Korean national consciousness. The colonial authorities took exception, however, to *The Ox*, as it depicts the suffering of a farmer deprived of his land and his son killed by Japanese police. Not surprisingly, Yu had to stop writing plays about the reality of Korean life under Japanese rule. Moreover, by the mid-1930s, if they wished to write for the theater at all, playwrights were forced to write histories or romances in a Japanese style, with a pro-Japanese viewpoint and at least one-third of all dialogue in Japanese. The nascent art of playwriting was, not surprisingly, stifled by such conditions. As the colonial authorities imposed ever more severe policies designed to obliterate Korean culture and as World War II advanced, theater and playwriting in Korea were in severe straits, but Ham Se-dŏk's play *Trip to Muŭi Island* (*Muŭido kihaeng*, 1940), concerning an island's residents living under colonial rule, is a noteworthy *shin-gŭk* drama still performed by the National Drama Company.

Thirty-five years of Japanese censorship ended with the 1945 armistice. Yu Ch'ijin's one-act play *Fatherland* (*Choguk*, 1946) is a melodramatic, patriotic depiction of Korean youth and the March 1, 1919, independence movement, which demonstrates the depth of lingering anti-Japanese sentiments. With the departure of the Japanese, a maturing Korean dramatic art once again seemed possible. Unfortunately, however, the nation soon was caught up in political turmoil, with the conflict between rightist and leftist forces no longer checked by the colonial authorities. From Korea's liberation through (and after) the partitioning of the peninsula, nationalist and Communist groups fervently used the theater as propaganda in their struggle for political hegemony. On the left, the Yŏngŭk Kŏnsŏl Ponbu (Theater Rehabilitation Headquarters) produced historical or political plays, but its activities were limited by a U.S. military command directive. On the right was the Kŭgyesul Hyŏphoe (Theater Arts Association), for which Yu Ch'ijin wrote antileftist works. After the establishment of the Republic of Korea and the Democratic People's Republic of Korea in 1948, many playwrights fled either north or south, depending on their allegiances. The ideological conflict, chaotic political environment, and subsequent Korean War brought theater production to standstill, except for a few performances of Shakespearean plays staged in Pusan. Playwriting as an art was moribund.

After the Korean War, interest in Western culture and theater intensified. Seventy-eight foreign plays were staged in South Korea during the 1950s, about 25 percent of which were American, with works by Tennessee Williams, Eugene O'Neill, William Inge, and Arthur Miller among the most popular. The presence of such high-quality American dramas in wartorn Seoul would seem to indicate a healthy theater, but such was not the case. When the leading theater company, Shinhyŏp, was not staging Western plays, it opted to stage older Korean plays rather than developing young playwrights. Moreover, government policies to promote motion pictures attracted talent away from drama and theater into the film industry. Finally, to end a difficult decade, the 306-seat Wongaksa Theater, built with government subsidies in 1958 and the only viable theater space at the time, burned down in 1960. Nonetheless, when conditions seemed bleakest, hope was on the horizon.

Yu Minyŏng's penetrating essay "Fifty Years of Korean Drama Since Liberation" (1996) suggests that until the 1970s, the major themes of national division, internecine war, ideological strife, and memories of the colonial era were tackled by realist writers. That noted, a significant body of realistic Korean plays never accumulated, for a variety of artistic and sociopolitical reasons. Without a long history of dramatic literature from which realism as an art, not just a dramatic form, might evolve, Korean playwrights in the 1950s and 1960s had neither the necessary training to consistently create meaningful realistic drama nor a significant body of Korean models to emulate.

Realism, Yu observed, "demands an exploration and objective representation of the essence of contemporary social and historical phenomena." But the painful postliberation experience was difficult to objectify; pre- and post–Korean War era ideologies required commitment, not questioning; and under the military governments between 1961 and 1988, the objective depiction of social conditions could result in imprisonment—or worse. Thus as the decade of the 1960s began and advanced, pictorial realism reflecting a Western aesthetic started to fade.

One of the events marking the advance of a sea change from a Western-modeled Korean dramatic literature to a Korean-centered, nonrealistic dramatic literature was the establishment in 1960 of the Shilhŏm kŭktan (Experimental Theater), a company founded by the first generation of Korean theater artists to be educated *by* Koreans *in* Korea.

Other theater companies soon followed, in what is called the little (or coterie) theater movement. Scrambling to find performance space in a Seoul still recovering from the Korean War, they moved into basements around universities, thereby establishing the many small theaters in Seoul's Taehangno theater district and other areas of the city (see the appendix). This no-frills physical environment may have been an unexpected liberating catalyst in the search for subject matter, aesthetics, and dramatic form that were at once modern (not necessarily Western) and Korean. For some observers, it was in this search for an essentially Korean, rather than Western, dramaturgy and theater that the *modern* Korean theater took root in the 1960s and 1970s.

In those decades, in a Pan-Asian movement, theater artists began to shake off colonial vestiges of Western dramatic literature and performance and to look with renewed appreciation and pride to indigenous forms for inspiration. More than a few Korean theater artists energized this trend, looking not only westward but also inward, seeking a drama with a Korean "DNA," a drama modern because it was maturing, a drama no longer reliant solely on Western models. In a sense, "modern" was equated with experimentation in dramaturgy and performances utilizing Korean mask dance, folklore, *p'ansori*, and shamanistic rituals. Traditional drama and theater from other Asian nations, as well as from the Western avant-garde, provided inspiration.

With confidence in their own artistry and Korean traditions, playwrights and directors did not hesitate to borrow selectively from Western absurdists whose view of the Cold War world mirrored their own. Max Frisch, Friedrich Dürrenmatt, Samuel Becket, and even Fernando Arrabal were welcomed influences. While it is true that a kind of modified theatrical realism (a vestige of *shin-gŭk*) remained popular in the early 1960s, represented by Ch'a Pŏmsŏk's *Burning Mountain* (*Sanbul*, 1962) many among the 1960s generation of playwrights and directors were increasingly impatient with realism of any ilk. O T'aesŏk, for example, insisted—and still insists—that Western pictorial realism is inimical to Korean character. He expressed his skepticism about copying Western realism, doubted that a play needed to unravel in a logical order toward a clear-cut goal, and began his quest for new forms of theater based on Korean traditions and culture. O's playwriting and directing are inextricably linked. His script is not a finished piece of literature; rather, it is a kind of scenario awaiting completion through rehearsals. In O's work, latent images are more important than literal text, a trait increasingly seen in the work of other writers in the last decades of the twentieth century, Yi Yunt'aek not least among them.

The 1970s have been called "the dark ages" of Korean cinema, but for drama and theater this period was one of political engagement and artistic experimentation in dramaturgy and performance techniques. In addition to Yi Kangbaek, whose first play opened in 1971, five other playwrights are of note here: O Yŏngjin, Yi Kŭnsam, Hŏ Kyu, Ch'oe Inhun, and Pak Choyŏl.

O Yŏngjin is a representative comedy writer of the era, also credited with incorporating traditional Korean culture into *shin-gŭk*. His high comedies satirized the upper class for its exploitation of the masses (just as traditional mask dance drama criticized the noble class and lascivious monks). His representative play *Wedding Day* (*Maengjinsadaek kyŏngsa*, 1972) centers on a social climber's greed (he bought his social status), juxtaposing the harshness of old marriage customs with marriage for love.

Contemporary with O Yongjin was Yi Kŭnsam, who wrote fifty-two plays between 1960 and 1998, including *A New Common Sense* (*Kugmul issa omnida*,

1966), in which a "new common sense" based on avarice, amorality, and self-advancement at any cost replaces the common sense of the past. In other works, Yi's dark satire utilizes flashbacks, soliloquy, and fluid time, anticipating the dramaturgical devices in some of the plays in this anthology.

In his groundbreaking work *A Born-Again Child* (*Tashiragi*, 1979), Hŏ Kyu used shamanistic ritual and folk elements to engage the audience and lead them to actively participate. In contrast, Ch'oe Inhun, a leading fiction writer, also stands out as the writer of highly literary drama, known for his melding of Korean legends with superior poetry and prose, as in *Wha . . . i, Whai, a Long Long Time Ago*, also translated as *Shoo-oo Shoo Once upon a Time* (*Yennal yejŏk e hwŏŏ'i hwŏ'i*, 1976), a dramatization of a North Korean tale about a couple so beaten down by the realities of life that they take refuge in fantasy.

Pak Choyŏl holds a special place in the history of this decade, as his works are a voice longing for Korean unification. His *O Chang-gun's Toenail* (*O Chang-gun ŭi palt'op*, 1974), an absurdist "fable" indicting the division of Korea and wasted human life in military regimes, was censored in 1974 and suppressed until 1988 when the theater-licensing act was liberalized, bringing an end to some seven decades of theater censorship.

In the 1980s, a decade marked by unrelenting martial law and the bloody Kwangju incident of May 27, 1980, in which Republic of Korea troops beat civilians, theater and dramatic literature were powerful weapons in the people's struggle against totalitarian regimes. Yi Kangbaek was especially active in this period, writing seven works, maintaining the objectivity of his earlier "theater of allegory" but focusing on issues of the 1980s, including the government's rigid anti-Communist stance and right-wing ideology. O T'aesŏk added some dozen plays in the 1980s to his already sizable oeuvre, many of those portraying in some way the cruelty of humanity and the unhealed psychic wounds resulting from Korea's history, which O saw as tragic. *Bicycle* (*Chajŏn-gŏ*, 1983) is an acknowledged masterpiece of the Korean theater, reflecting O's personal experiences in the Korean War and urging forbearance and reconciliation.

It would be remiss of me not to mention one other playwright-director whose works bridge the 1980s and 1990s and have been among the most influential of his generation: Yi Yunt'aek. Like O T'aesŏk, Yi's plays often are little more than scenarios, using masks, puppets, traditional dance, ritual elements, and Brechtian theatricality, but they occasionally surprise with their poignant, affective scenes of profound emotional truths.

Yi's debut play, *Citizen K* (*Shimin K*, 1989), excoriates intellectual cowardice and the government's torture of suspected dissidents. *O-Gu: A*

Ceremony of Death (*O-Gu: Chuggŭm ŭi hyŏngshik*, 1989) uses shamanistic rituals from southeastern Korea in its parody of family life in a time of mourning. *Mask of Fire: A Ceremony in Power* (*Pul ŭi kamyŏn: Kwŏllyŏk ŭi hyŏngshik*, 1993) interrogates the abuse of governmental power. And in *A Dummy Bride: Ceremony of Love* (*Pabo kakshi*, 1993), Yi's talent is brought to bear on some of the troublesome aspects of contemporary Korean life, including the despoiled environment, loss of pure love, sexual degradation, and religious fakery.

A signal event for South Korea as a nation was the 1988 Seoul Olympics, accompanied by a relaxation of governmental controls in everyday life. Especially relevant to drama and theater was the rescission of repressive theater-licensing laws and the onset of a kind of "open door" policy in politics and the arts that permitted greater artistic freedom for domestic playwrights and the introduction to South Korea of hitherto banned dramas from the Communist bloc—plays by Bertolt Brecht perhaps foremost among them.

By the early 1990s, the economic "miracle on the Han" was impressive in its scope. In less than three decades, Korea had risen from its status as a third-world nation to one of the world's major economies. The first peaceful, nonmilitary transition between elected governments had taken place, and government controls over citizens' lives had been eased. Artists in the theater, literature, cinema, and art worlds who had been outspoken social critics during the two preceding decades now found that many of the societal problems earlier energizing their work had either diminished or disappeared. For years, they had written plays that opposed something, and now many of them were affected by the absence of opposing forces. Kim Chiha, a poet openly critical of the military regimes in the 1970s and early 1980s, wrote the following in response to the post-1988 era:

> The iron shackles are broken,
> In the aloneness of freedom
> I long for your oppression.
> I shall have no dreams;
> I will not stop this business of
> Bearing pain with dreams.
> I will live from day to day without feeling
> This life I cannot bear.
>
> *Anonymous translator*

As South Korean society changed during the 1990s, Korean drama and theater reflected many of those changes, transformed from a chronicle of a society repressed by authoritarian regimes into a reflection of a materialistic society with diminished traditional values and all the problems inherent in the rapid transition from an agrarian to an urban nation. The plays in this anthology suggest only some of the major themes occupying playwrights, such as relations between Korea and Japan, diminished and disappearing traditional values, the need to deconstruct and reconstruct history, both the national and individual cost of success, the changing relationships between men and women, obsessive materialism, dysfunctional families, directionless youth, problematic educational practices, and the lingering, painful memories resulting from the partition of Korea. These plays also suggest an evolving dramaturgy, an evolution in which any previous clear distinction between drama (that is, literature) and theater (that is, performance) has been blurred, if not disregarded.

In less than a hundred years, Korean drama's journey progressed from an imitative, Western-style drama at its inception, to inner-directed, Korean-focused experimental dramas, and finally to a mature Korean drama exhibiting universal qualities and appeal. That journey has three major characteristics.

First, Korean dramatic literature and theater in the twentieth century always have contended in some way with pervasive Western influences, whether imported through Japan, absorbed by Koreans studying in the West, or, later, introduced by the sheer number of Western (especially American) dramas translated into Korean and staged in commercial theaters or on college campuses. In recent years, even though the ratio of foreign to indigenous plays produced now favors domestic works, one-quarter or more of the approximately 140 productions staged in Seoul each year are translations of Western works or adaptations of Western works (including those by Shakespeare and the ancient Greek playwrights).

Second, for most of the period between 1910 and 1988, theater artists faced repressive censorship, initially at the hands of the Japanese colonial government, then by the American military provisional government, and finally by a succession of near-dictatorial Korean governments. The upside of such repression was the creation of inventive ways to circumvent the censorship. The downside was the fettering of dramatic imaginations over seven decades. The number of those who left the theater or who never wrote for the theater because of the oppression is inestimable.

Third, the drive to create dramatic literature and performance forms that were *Korean* in essence—not Japanese or Western—gained momentum and potency as the century wore on, motivated by the continuing large presence of Western dramas performed in Seoul and buoyed by the international success of the Korean musical *The Last Empress* (*Myŏngsŏng hwanghu*, 1995). Performances on foreign stages of works by O T'aesŏk, Yi Yunt'aek, Yi Kangbaek, Kim Kwang-lim, Yi Manhŭi, and Son Chinch'aek's Mich'u Drama Company, among others, were a growing sign of Korean artists' international stature.

The internationalization of dramas has continued in the early years of the twenty-first century, but musicals, both foreign and domestic, are now the most popular and greatest economic force in the Korean theater. At a juncture where Korean drama and theater have matured and attained acclaim outside Korea, the theater—and thus the drama that sustains it—must compete for diminishing entertainment dollars with the skyrocketing cost of living in Seoul and other socioeconomic factors, not the least of which is media competition, including the immensely popular Korean television dramas. Korean musicals, no longer knockoffs of American and British hits, have found their own style and seem to have a promising future. Given their economic and artistic clout in the Korean theater world, it is impossible to know how many potentially influential young dramatists will elect to write musicals rather than dramas. Fortunately, some of Korea's finest playwrights are teaching in universities, and their graduates have occasionally produced high-quality work, but will television and film lure them away from writing dramas for the theater? What will be the impact of the ongoing theatrical experiments with ritual, traditional folk performances, Pan-Asian aesthetics, and electronic media, among others? The shape, tone, and promise of Korean drama and theater in the next two or three decades are difficult to discern, a script yet to be determined.

BURNING MOUNTAIN (SANBUL)

CH'A PŎMSŎK

Ch'a Pŏmsŏk (1924–2006), his career spanning more than fifty years, is recognized as a pioneer and leading light in the modern Korean theater. A firm believer in the theater of realism, he sought to show life as it is. Known for acutely observant, emotionally powerful, realistic dramas, frequently depicting the lives of the poverty stricken and the politically repressed, Ch'a also valued a progressive Korean drama, and his Sanha Theater Company (founded in 1963) developed new Korean plays and audiences. His wide-ranging output includes film scripts and television dramas; stage adaptations of novels, such as *Gone with the Wind* (1978); dance scenarios; theater history and criticism; translations of Japanese plays, such as Kobe Abe's *Friends* (*Tomodachi*, 1967); collections of essays; two memoirs; and more than forty plays, many of which received prestigious awards. Beyond his calling as a writer, Ch'a served as president of the Korea Theater Association, the Korean Culture and Arts Foundation, and the Korean National Academy of Arts and taught at the Seoul Art Institute and Ch'ŏngju University, where at the latter he also served as dean of its school of arts.

Burning Mountain (*Sanbul*) premiered in December 1962 at the National Theater in Seoul, staged by the Shinhyŏp Theater Company. It is regarded as the second of three related plays. The first play, *Every Night the Stars* (*Pyŏl ŭn pam mada*, 1951), depicts the conflicts of an intellectual who becomes disillusioned with Communist partisans. The third play, *Forest of Massacre* (*Haksal ŭi sup*, 1977), is, in a sense, a story about what happened before *Burning Mountain*, the play that, over time, has become

Ch'a's signature piece. Ch'a wrote a film version of *Burning Mountain* (English title, *Fires in the Mountains*, 1977); the National Drama Company made *Burning Mountain* a recurrent offering in its 2004 repertoire; and a musical adaptation, entitled *Dancing Shadows*, with a book version by Ariel Dorfman and music by Eric Woolfson, premiered at the Seoul Performing Arts Center in July 2007.

BURNING MOUNTAIN (SANBUL)

TRANSLATED BY JANET POOLE

CHARACTERS

OLD KIM, 78 years old, deaf, and slightly senile
MRS. YANG, 55 years old, Old Kim's daughter-in-law, a widow
CHŎMNYE, 28 years old, Mrs. Yang's daughter-in-law, a widow
KWIDŎK, 18 years old, Mrs. Yang's daughter, mentally disturbed
SAWŎL, 27 years old, Chŏmnye's friend, a widow
MRS. CH'OE, 45 years old, Sawŏl's mother, a widow
SSALLYE'S MOM, 30 years old, a widow
CHŎNG-IM, 22 years old, a widow
NEIGHBOR KAP'S WIFE, 50 years old
NEIGHBOR ŬL'S WIFE, 40 years old
KKŬTSUNI, 17 years old
LADY FROM PYŎNGYŎNG, 45 years old, a fabric peddler
KYUBOK, 30 years old, Communist guerrilla, former teacher
WŎNT'AE, 45 years old, captain of a Self-Defense unit
CAPTAIN, 40 years old, Communist guerrilla in charge of food procurement
COMMUNIST GUERRILLAS, KAP, ŬL, SOLDIERS A and B, WOMEN A and B, and VARIOUS OTHER WOMEN

ACT 1

(Date: winter 1951 through the following spring. Setting: a village in the Sobaek mountain range.[1] *"P" village is surrounded*

by mountains. Act I is set in **MRS. YANG**'s *house, which has a fairly large yard. On the right side of the stage is a thatched, L-shaped house, consisting of a kitchen, two rooms, and an open shed. The thatch roof looks as if it has not been replaced for at least three years; it has turned gray and caved in. The earthen walls also have collapsed in places. There is a wood floor about nine feet wide between the inner room and the side room, which has only three walls so that the audience can see inside. A low wooden door hangs toward the back of the floor and leads out to the back garden. In order to collect rainwater, an old earthenware jar has been placed under the eaves in the corner where the kitchen joins the inner room. The shed has earthen walls and no door, so that it is open on the side facing the audience, who can see everything inside.*

Inside the shed are scattered straw sacks, sheaves of straw, and several farming implements. In the center of the stage is a mud hut that can barely seat one person. This functions as a privy and also as a marker separating the yard belonging to this house from the path. A straw rope, which is rotting from exposure to the elements, joins this hut to the back of the kitchen and partitions off part of the stage. At the side of the hut is a hill path that leads to the back of the stage and crosses another path, which traverses the stage. When standing on the path, one can look down into the yard of this house, and in the distant background, one can see the Sobaek mountain range and the rugged Ch'ŏnwang Peak. Below the path to the left side of the stage is the thatched house belonging to **MRS. CH'OE**. *It is rectangular, with two rooms on either side of the kitchen, and hardly anything else visible either inside or out. A spindle tree stands conspicuously where a gate should be. The characters can enter the stage from all sides.*

It is a winter evening sometime before the lunar New Year. The scene looks cozy with mountains on all sides, but it actually is a hollow where the snowfall is heavy and the cold is severe. As the curtain rises, crows caw noisily in the mountains behind. In the distance, the sun is about to set, although mountain shadows and darkness have long since fallen on the house. A straw mat has been spread out in the center of the yard, and the village women are standing around it, each holding bundles of food supplies. **MRS. YANG** *is sitting on the straw mat, examining the grain or potatoes that the women offer her one by one, separating them according to kind. Beneath a lamp to one side,* **CHŎMNYE** *enters the amounts in a notebook while several others put the food into bags. They all are women, except for a baby carried on someone's back and* **OLD KIM**, *who is smoking a pipe in the inner room, the upper part of his body leaning outside the door. It is cold; everyone's clothes are ragged and dirty. The old women sit on the floor while the younger ones stand in the yard. Groups of people are crouching and whispering to one another under their breath.)*

MRS. YANG (*measuring rice*): This doesn't even come to one *hop*![2] (*She stares at* MRS. CH'OE.)

MRS. CH'OE (*haughtily*): And I thought a lot before I brought that! Where's a *hop* going to come from the way things are . . . (*She looks away.*)

MRS. YANG: Who said rice wasn't precious? We agreed at the meeting to deliver our quota, so you have to bring a full *hop* . . . Come now, Mrs. Ch'oe!

MRS. CH'OE (*in a bad humor*): How can I bring something I don't have?

MRS. YANG (*with a sour smile*): We're all equally hard up, aren't we? Why don't you just bring the rest of your share? If you don't have any more rice, then barley will do, and if you don't have any barley, then even potatoes . . .

MRS. CH'OE (*bursting with anger*): Are you telling me to go steal grain that I don't have?

MRS. YANG (*losing her patience*): Mrs. Ch'oe . . . Now you're going too far. Who told you to steal?

MRS. CH'OE: Well, you keep on insisting even when I've already told you that I can't give you what I don't have.

MRS. YANG: What are you talking about? Those of us with less than you have paid up without complaining. Go and get the rest!

MRS. CH'OE (*standing up suddenly*): If this isn't good enough, then forget it! I crossed the river and went all the way to the village to harvest that rice! (*She snatches the measure from* MRS. YANG'*s hands, pours the rice into the pleats of her skirt, and throws down the measure in front of* MRS. YANG. *The measure hits* MRS. YANG *on the hand.*)

MRS. YANG: Ow! (*She instinctively rubs her hand.*) Is this woman mad? (*She glares at her angrily.*)

MRS. CH'OE (*also glaring fiercely*): What did you say?

MRS. YANG: What are you staring at like that? (*By this point, everyone is watching the two women.*)

MRS. CH'OE: What brought it into your thick head to pick a fight, eh?

MRS. YANG: Since when did I pick a fight? (*She stands. Now* CHŎMNYE, *who has been watching silently, moves to stand between them.*)

CHŎMNYE: Mother, just let it go.

MRS. YANG: Chŏmye! You were watching, weren't you? What did *I* do, eh?

MRS. CH'OE (*with a sneer on her face*): Huh! You think you can boss us around just because you're our great village leader or section leader or whatever you call yourself. Anyone would think you're a queen the way you carry on . . . (*She laughs scornfully.*)

MRS. YANG (*launching an attack*): Since when did I boss you around? Eh? Since when . . .

MRS. CH'OE (*glaring fiercely*): Who said you can talk to me like that, eh? You think I'm going to let your mouth get away with that?

MRS. YANG (*attacking*): So what will you do? Tear it out? Eh? I'm talking to you the way you deserve to be talked to. Anyway, I'm ten years older than you, so what's wrong with that?[3]

CHŎMNYE (*looking at the two of them in turn*): Why are you two behaving like this? Please, can't you just put up with each other? (*Clucking her tongue.*) The sun's already gone down . . . how are we going to collect all the grain?

MRS. YANG: Who's doing this because they want to? It's the Self-Defense army that makes us . . .

CHŎMNYE: Well, even if you don't want to, since you've been given the responsibility, we'd better deliver on time. Or you'll have done the work and still get in trouble.

MRS. YANG: Is it our fault that it's not all ready? When the Self-Defense troops get here, I'll tell them the truth—that we can't do this because the others won't cooperate!

MRS. CH'OE: I see! So you're going to tell on me in secret then? If you're going to tell on me, go ahead! Let's see which one they believe.

MRS. YANG: What?

CHŎMNYE (*trying to suppress her anger*): Don't be so unreasonable, Mrs. Ch'oe. We're not children. Who said they were going to tell on you?

MRS. CH'OE (*exploding with anger*): She did! Everyone here heard her. Didn't you? (*She looks at everyone standing nearby.*)

CHŎMNYE: I've heard everything now. Who would do this job because they want to?

MRS. CH'OE (*sarcastically*): Huh . . . so you took on a job you didn't want?

MRS. YANG: What, are you saying that I volunteered for this job? (*She begins to argue again.*)

MRS. CH'OE: Huh! You think we don't know what you're doing? Well, however cunning you are, you won't escape being called a reactionary! You won't! (*At these words, the other villagers become agitated.* **OLD KIM** *is still smoking, unaware of what is going on.*)

CHŎMNYE (*becoming serious*): Have you finished now?

MRS. CH'OE: Chŏmnye! Aren't your family reactionaries? Eh? Why did your husband run away if he wasn't a reactionary? Didn't you say he ran away because if he was caught by the People's army he'd be killed? (*She tries to trap* **CHŎMNYE** *with her own words.*) If that's not true, why don't you say so!

CHŎMNYE (*trying to control her anger*): What's this got to do with whether my husband was a reactionary or was dragged away and killed?

MRS. YANG: Why do you keep bringing up my dead son?

CHŎMNYE: Mother, please be quiet.

MRS. CH'OE (*audaciously*): There's no connection? . . . Your mother-in-law says she's the village leader because Self-Defense forces made her, but the truth is she had to pretend she was loyal in order to survive. Isn't that right?

MRS. YANG: Oh! You can talk! Whose fault was it that my son was charged as a reactionary?

MRS. CH'OE: Huh! Well, life is full of ups and downs! Everyone who got my son-in-law killed as a Red is my enemy now! Why should I leave be the bastards who made my daughter Sawŏl a widow before her time? Times have changed, and the two of us deserve some comfort now.

MRS. YANG: Huh! And wasn't your son-in-law a model of virtue! He drank like a fish and spent more time playing cards than working in the threshing yard! Ha, ha . . .

MRS. CH'OE: And what about your son? Huh . . . what gives you the right to criticize? Have you forgotten all the trouble he caused as the leader of some youth group? At least my son finished middle school!

MRS. YANG: That new studying ruined everyone who tried it! (*At this, some of those watching burst into laughter.*)

MRS. CH'OE (*glaring at those laughing as she gets even angrier*): Oh, that's great, isn't it! So you're saying that when the reactionaries killed my son-in-law, it was just like having a rotten tooth pulled out? Well, you're all reactionaries, aren't you? Ssallye's Mom, Kapdol's Mom, Sŏngman's Mom![4]

SSALLYE'S MOM: So we're reactionaries because we laughed. What does that make us if we don't laugh? Ha, ha . . . (*Everyone laughs again.*)

CHŎNG-IM (*taking* MRS. CH'OE's *side*): Watch your words! Remember, thieves are apt to give themselves away!

SSALLYE'S MOM: What's that got to do with me? . . . (*As if singing a ballad.*) My only crime was to be born under an unlucky star, to have met the wrong husband and been widowed too young. Oh, my fate . . . (*Everyone laughs.*)

OLD KIM (*he laughs out loud with no idea of what is going on*): Oh, good, good . . .

NEIGHBOR KAP'S WIFE: What you say is true, of course, but are there really any Reds and Yellows here? Our only fault is that we can't feed ourselves and haven't been to school . . . For us stupid poor people, it doesn't matter how the world changes. They say come and we're dragged along; they say go and we're pushed away . . . isn't that the way it goes? (*She looks at the crowd and they all nod to one another.*)

CHŎMNYE: Can't we stop this now, please? We could go on like this forever, but we have to finish up quickly, don't we? It's already time for them to come for the grain. And the people who are on night watch tonight have to get ready.

NEIGHBOR ŬL'S WIFE: You're right. Village leader! Let's finish up. (*Stamping her feet.*) My feet are freezing. Shit . . . when will I be able to sit on a warm floor . . .[5]

CHŎMNYE (*to* MRS. YANG): Mother! There are only a few people left now . . . (*She looks in her notebook.*)

MRS. YANG: Why should I do something I don't want to do? Tell whoever wants to do it to do it. (*She blows her nose and steps up onto the wood floor of her house.*)

MRS. CH'OE (*getting angry again*): What did you say?

CHŎMNYE (*angrily*): Why are you behaving like this, for heaven's sake? Women with daughters and sons-in-law behaving like little children . . . Have you forgotten what will happen to us if we don't have the grain ready on time? Our village will become a sea of flames.

MRS. CH'OE: I was keeping quiet, and then she started up again, didn't she?

SSALLYE'S MOM (*tsk-tsk-ing*): What the old people used to say was right. If there's not a man in the house, even stray dogs put on airs! (*The crowd bursts out laughing again.*) Why are you laughing? (*Starting to complain.*) If there was just one real man in our village, things wouldn't be like this!

NEIGHBOR KAP'S WIFE: She's right. Since liberation, first the police and then the People's army have come and swept them away . . . Now every man who could be called a man in this valley has been exterminated. (*Weeping.*) If only they had taken the old ones . . .

OLD KIM: Baby . . . isn't it dinner time yet? Why are they all standing around here making a fuss? I'm starving.

MRS. YANG (*in a loud voice*): Just wait a minute! How can I make dinner in the midst of this commotion? Oh . . .

NEIGHBOR KAP'S WIFE: Aah, instead of taking the old ones who should have gone first, they took our precious, innocent young . . . Even the gods must be blind.

NEIGHBOR ŬL'S WIFE (*blowing her nose*): You're right. What can possibly go right when women have to do everything that the men should do? They say the house goes to ruin when the hen crows.[6] (*During this time* CHŎMNYE *beckons to several of the women and starts to collect the grain that her mother-in-law was supposed to. But the atmosphere in the house is gloomy. The crows begin to caw even more noisily.*)

SSALLYE'S MOM (*facing the path to the left*): Damn crows, why are you making such a fuss again? Whenever I hear that noise, my insides turn upside down. Shoo, shoo!

NEIGHBOR ŬL'S WIFE: Ssallye's Mom, why are you so upset again? (*She moves toward* **SSALLYE'S MOM**.)

SSALLYE'S MOM: It's just . . . last winter, when I went to look for my husband's body. I crossed Munemi Hill, and I could hear those crows crying, couldn't I? I suddenly remembered what they say about crows seeking out the dead and went to see what was going on. Right at the bottom of Rabbit Rock there was a black mass of crows picking at something. So I went closer, and it was him . . .

NEIGHBOR ŬL'S WIFE: Really!

SSALLYE'S MOM: All the flesh of his face and hands had been eaten away by the crows, and only white bones remained . . . (*She grimaces as if recalling that harrowing scene.*)

CHŎNG-IM: But how did you know it was him?

SSALLYE'S MOM: I saw his clothes, didn't I? His dark brown jacket and gray, cotton-padded trousers . . . There was no doubt, because I even saw the holes burned in his trousers from when he put out the mountain fire on the first full moon, the year before last . . . (*She sighs.*)

CHŎNG-IM: You should be thankful to those crows for finding his body for you.

SSALLYE'S MOM: But if they hadn't been cawing, I wouldn't have seen that awful sight, would I? No eyes, no nose, just his white teeth and cheekbones were left . . . (*She begins to cry, unable to control her emotions. Several of the others rub her back and comfort her.*)

NEIGHBOR KAP'S WIFE (*as if speaking to herself*): Oh, I feel sorry for the young ones! The old ones have already lived their lives, but the young ones who used to leap about like silverfish in late spring . . . (*Rubbing her sleep-filled narrow eyes.*) Killed if they even once gave food to the National army, tortured if they curried favor with the Reds . . . (*Sighs.*) I know a man's life is worth no more than a fly's, but it's too sad . . . oh, it's sad . . .

MRS. YANG (*holding her hand*): Saying things like that will get you into trouble. What kind of world do you think we're living in? Be careful what you say.

(*The crows caw again, and* **SSALLYE'S MOM** *jumps up shouting as if she's gone mad.*)

SSALLYE'S MOM: I hate you! Can't you go away?!

(*At this moment* **WŎNT'AE** *walks down the mountain path to the right of the stage, leading the* **CAPTAIN** *and three Communist* **GUERRILLAS**. *The* **GUERRILLAS** *are dressed in tattered rags, but the* **CAPTAIN** *is wearing cotton-padded trousers and a winter cap.*)

WŎNT'AE (*looking at* **SSALLYE'S MOM**): What's the meaning of this display?

CAPTAIN: Is this on our account, comrade? (*Referring to* **SSALLYE'S MOM**.)

WŎNT'AE: No, no . . . Well . . . Let's go on down.

(*At these words* **SSALLYE'S MOM** *is struck by fear as if she's just woken from a dream and runs back to hide between the other women. The crowd huddles together near the mud hut, unable to stand straight, like mice in front of a cat. Unwillingly,* **MRS. YANG** *and* **CHŎMNYE** *bow subserviently. The* **GUERRILLAS** *stand on the path and watch.*)

WŎNT'AE (*with a salute*): Comrade Yang, thank you for your hard work. (*To the* **CAPTAIN**.) Please take a seat. (*He points to the wood floor.* **MRS. YANG** *hurriedly dusts the floor with a cloth.*)

MRS. YANG: It's not very clean, but if you'd like to sit down . . .

WŎNT'AE (*sitting down*): So, is everything ready?

MRS. YANG (*in an uneasy voice*): Yes, yes . . .

CAPTAIN: How much did you collect?

MRS. YANG: Uh . . . uh . . . (*To* **CHŎMNYE**.) What does it all come to?

CHŎMNYE (*avoiding eye contact with the men*): Well . . . there is one *mal* and four *toe* of rice[7] . . . three *mal* and two *toe* of barley, and four *mal* and six *toe* of potatoes . . . all together, that's what there is.

CAPTAIN (*facing* **WŎNT'AE** *and filling up the bags with a satisfied smile*): That's better than I expected . . . um . . .

WŎNT'AE (*obsequiously*): Ha, ha . . . I warned them in no uncertain terms, but still I was worried something might go wrong . . .

CAPTAIN: Since you were in charge, that's to be expected, isn't it? Ha, ha . . . (**WŎNT'AE** *rubs his hands together and laughs with him.*)

CAPTAIN: Now, gather them all together . . . I will speak first, and then . . .

WŎNT'AE (*quickly*): Yes . . . please do.

(*He takes a whistle out of his pocket and blows it loudly. Everyone looks at one another; a disorderly commotion follows.*)

CAPTAIN (*trying to look dignified*): What are you all doing? Come and stand over here. Quickly, quickly . . . (*Frowning at* **MRS. YANG**.) How will it look if the village leader stands there doing nothing?

MRS. YANG (*not knowing what to do*): Oh, I'm sorry . . . I'm sorry. (*To the crowd.*) All right! Everyone gather over here, quickly. Don't stand over there.

(*The crowd shuffles closer. Standing on the path in the middle of the stage and rolling cigarettes, the three* **GUERRILLAS** *look at one another and laugh. It looks as if they might be laughing at the* **CAPTAIN**.)

WŎNT'AE (*deliberately trying to assume a dignified air, he speaks in a rambling voice*): Well . . . The reason why we have asked you all to gather here today is because the captain here has kindly come from headquarters to deliver some very important instructions to you in person. So you must listen quietly to everything he has to say. As your Self-Defense captain, I hope you won't hurt the reputation of our village. Finally, I'd like to add one more thing . . .

(*At this point, the* **CAPTAIN** *whispers something in* **WŎNT'AE**'*s ear, as if he can't bear to listen to any more*.)

WŎNT'AE (*bowing obsequiously*): Yes . . . yes, I understand. Yes . . . so you would like to speak now, Captain? Yes, please do.

(*During this, the crowd begins to stamp their frozen feet as the tension dissipates*.)

WŎNT'AE (*solemnly*): Quiet! Now we will hear from our comrade from headquarters.

(*He salutes and moves to one side. The* **CAPTAIN** *places one hand on his pistol belt and salutes firmly with the other hand. He looks intently at the crowd. Everyone swallows and pays close attention*.)

CAPTAIN: Comrades! Thank you for coming out in this cold weather. When we cross this final peak, there will be a world in which laborers and peasants will all be able to live in comfort together. According to a wireless message that our Defense Section received day before yesterday, our nation's leader, Premier Kim Il-sung, admonishes those of us waging war in the south to fight courageously to the end against that agent of American imperialism, Rhee Syngman.

(*After saying all this in one breath, he pauses to take a deep breath*. **WŎNT'AE** *starts to applaud and looks at the crowd as if prompting them to join him. The sound of clapping hands breaks out here and there*.)

CAPTAIN: Rumors have been spreading that the UN army and Rhee Syngman's puppet army have had many victories, but don't forget that we have the support of the huge and heroic Chinese and Soviet armies.

WŎNT'AE: Yes! (*He applauds, and the others have no choice but to follow with applause, too*.)

CAPTAIN (*taking a notebook out of his top pocket*): Now I'll tell you about the new task assigned to you.

OLD KIM (*throwing open the door of his room*): Isn't it dinnertime yet?

MRS. YANG (*startled*): Oh! Don't you have any sense of timing? Shut the door. Please! (*She shuts the door from outside, and a grumbling sound can be heard* *from inside the room.* **MRS. YANG** *turns uneasily back to the captain and* **WŎNT'AE**.)

CAPTAIN: Since you've already received these instructions from the captain of your Self-Defense unit, you will know this already, but . . .

WŎNT'AE: Yes, I already told them at the village leaders' meeting and at the section meeting.

CAPTAIN: Starting today you will again have night watch duty . . .

(*There is a stir in the crowd.*)

CAPTAIN: Surrounded as we are by mountains on all sides, this is a natural fortress, which the enemy forces cannot penetrate easily. Therefore, even though they're only 150 *li*[8] away, Rhee Syngman's gang is scoring victories, but this side of the Nam River is still our glorious People's Republic. But the enemy is putting up a last-ditch fight, and with the absurd idea of upsetting the people, they are foolishly sending out scouts. Therefore, we've decided to start the night watch again.

(*The sound of whispering gradually spreads throughout the crowd.*)

CAPTAIN: I have heard that since liberation, our many comrades in this area have battled heroically against the American imperialists and Rhee Syngman's puppet regime. So if you follow my instructions strictly, you will also avenge your sons, your husbands, and your brothers. First, if you see a suspicious person, immediately report that to your village leader or Self-Defense unit. Second, those caught giving food or anything else to the enemy will be severely punished. Third, those neglecting their night watch duties will be severely punished too. (*Putting his notebook in his pocket.*) Don't forget that if even one person is caught violating these instructions, then the whole village will be reduced to ashes. Over on that mountain we hear about everything that is going on.

WŎNT'AE: Did everyone understand? One person from each family must take part.

(*There is another stir. Then* **MRS. CH'OE** *steps forward.*)

MRS. CH'OE: Sir. I would like to say something . . .

(*Everyone focuses on* **MRS. CH'OE**.)

WŎNT'AE: What is it?

MRS. CH'OE: People like us do not have to do night watch duty, do we?

CAPTAIN: Don't have to?

MRS. CH'OE (*glancing at* **MRS. YANG**): It's bad enough that both my son and son-in-law were killed at the same time by the reactionaries' police, but to ask me to do night watch duty in this terrible cold . . .

WŎNT'AE: Are you the only comrade who has lost a son and a husband?

MRS. CH'OE: That's my point. Surely this kind of work should be done by those who were loyal to the Republic of Korea in the old days. Isn't it their turn to suffer? Huh?
(*Agitation spreads throughout the crowd.*)
SSALLYE'S MOM: Who says so? Everyone in the village should have to do these things . . .
CHŎNG-IM (*taking* **MRS. CH'OE**'s *side*): Since when have you been so righteous?
MRS. CH'OE: Surely those who prospered while the Republic of Korea was in power shouldn't be in power now that we have a people's republic?[9]
CAPTAIN: That's right. So you mean there are still some reactionaries among you?
MRS. CH'OE (*wavering*): Well, we can't say that there aren't, can we?
NEIGHBOR KAP'S WIFE: Why don't you just forget about it, Mrs. Ch'oe?
MRS. CH'OE (*getting excited*): It's bad enough that my son-in-law died, but to see those good-for-nothings in power now! (*She glares at* **MRS. YANG**, *and the crowd splits into two groups during the commotion.*)
WŎNT'AE: Qui . . . quiet! What is going on?
MRS. YANG (*stepping forward*): Let me explain. None of us has food to spare now. But when I said that we all have to contribute since we decided to collect grain, Mrs. Ch'oe, well, she . . .
CAPTAIN (*asserting his dignity*): I see! Quiet! At headquarters we all know that you comrades are putting up with great difficulties in order to battle on. But if you once thought of our situation fighting day and night up there on that rugged Ch'ŏnwang Peak, you wouldn't be complaining. (*Becoming more and more threatening.*) Don't you know for whom and for what we are suffering like that up in the mountains? Don't you realize that we're doing this so you comrades can live in comfort? (*The crowd looks completely dejected. The sound of gunfire can be heard faintly in the distance, and the* **CAPTAIN** *looks tense.*) Do you understand? Don't forget that we are at war. Remember that if there is one reactionary or one rebel among you, then all of your houses and lives will be in the hands of that person! (*He shakes his fist threateningly and then speaks to the* **GUERRILLAS**.) Comrades! Let's take this food and go! (*At this, each of the* **GUERRILLAS** *puts a sack on his back and begins to climb the mountain path. The* **CAPTAIN** *whispers something to* **WŎNT'AE** *and then quickly disappears.*)
WŎNT'AE (*after watching the* **CAPTAIN** *leave*): Everyone who is on night watch duty should meet at the tree by half past seven. Got it? (*He leaves to the left.*)
(*The crowd scatters in twos and threes.* **MRS. CH'OE** *goes into her kitchen.* **MRS. YANG** *is left standing vacantly in the yard as* **CHŎMNYE** *clears away the mat and*

the measure. The stage is darker than before, and the early evening stars can be seen far away in the dark sky. An unspeakable silence and emptiness presses down even more heavily here than on the mountaintops.)

MRS. YANG (*mumbling*): Now what will I live on? . . . Since they keep taking our food . . . Damn people. So that we can live in comfort?

CHŎMNYE (*looking around carefully*): Mother! Be careful what you say. Didn't you hear what they just said?

MRS. YANG (*wiping away her tears with the back of her hand*): I really don't think I can go on any more. (*She throws the mat down in the shed.*) What did he say about living a comfortable life? Better to die than to live like this, not able to breathe freely or to eat what is our own. Oh! (*She sits down on the end of the wood floor. The door opens and* **OLD KIM** *appears.*)

OLD KIM: Isn't it dinnertime yet? My stomach's stuck to my backbone. Aren't you going to feed me? Eh?

MRS. YANG (*getting angry*): Who said I wasn't going to feed you? (*Grumbling.*) Old people should go and die, oh . . . what kind of fate is this?

CHŎMNYE: Please wait just a bit, Grandfather. (*Tying a towel around her head as she goes out to the garden.*) What's happened to Kwidŏk? She should've been back by now . . .

MRS. YANG: Damn girl! Instead of gathering wood, she's probably off somewhere eating roasted magpie eggs.

(**CHŎMNYE** *returns from the back garden carrying an armful of firewood and goes into the kitchen.*)

MRS. YANG: How many potatoes are left?

CHŎMNYE (*breaking up the wood into small pieces in the kitchen*): The small crock's about half full.

OLD KIM: Can't we have rice tonight? Don't boil potatoes!

MRS. YANG (*in a bad mood*): Where's the rice going to come from in the middle of this commotion? We give you enough to live on, so you must have worms or something!

(**KWIDŎK** *comes running down the mountain path as if she's being chased, with an A-frame piled with wood on her back. In the distance laughter and the sound of children teasing her can be heard.* **KWIDŎK**'s *hair is tangled and her clothes are messy, giving the impression that she is somehow mentally disturbed. But her breasts reveal that she is a fully grown woman. She jumps down with an angry look and throws stones back toward the path.*)

KWIDŎK: Kwidŏk granddad's balls, soft as ripe persimmons! Hee, hee . . .

MRS. YANG (*a violent look in her eyes*): Now, what is that girl . . . Kwidŏk! Kwidŏk!

KWIDŎK (*like a man*): What?

MRS. YANG: What kind of nonsense is that, when you should have come straight back with the wood? Heh, girl?

KWIDŎK (*coming into the yard*): Those brats just pulled my skirt off! (*Children can be heard playing in the distance.* **KWIDŎK** *puts down the A-frame in front of the shed.*)

KWIDŎK (*trying to shout at the children again*): Granddad's . . .

MRS. YANG (*grabbing* **KWIDŎK**'*s hair*): Can't you shut that mouth of yours? You're an embarrassment! (*She hits her several times in the back.*)

KWIDŎK: Aagh, aagh . . . (*She tries to run away, but* **CHŎMNYE** *comes out of the kitchen and shields her.*) Sister, sister!

CHŎMNYE: Mother, please leave her alone! She can't even understand what you're saying . . . Just stop.

KWIDŎK (*clinging to* **CHŎMNYE**): Sister! Save me!

CHŎMNYE: All right, go inside.

MRS. YANG: Agh, you're seventeen now, and still behaving like this . . . Why don't you drop dead, just drop dead! (*She goes to grab her, but* **KWIDŎK** *shrieks and runs inside, crying.*)

CHŎMNYE: Mother! She's just a poor child!

MRS. YANG: Poor child? She's no child of mine any more; she's my enemy. My enemy! If I'd known she'd turn out like this, I would have left her for dead back then . . .

CHŎMNYE: Mother! (*She takes down the dried radish leaves from where they are hanging on the kitchen wall.*) She wasn't like that before the war, was she? After the shock of that attack, she lost her senses . . . She seems sort of crazy, but inside she's all right. She's grown up, I'm sure.

MRS. YANG: Shut up! If she'd been like her brother, she wouldn't have gone mad like that. (*Staring into empty space.*) If we only knew where he died or if he's still alive, then we would be able to forget him, wouldn't we?

CHŎMNYE (*letting out a heavy sigh and trying hard to control her emotions*): If he were still alive, we would have heard from him by now. It's been two years . . .

MRS. YANG: Stupid child! He should have lived on the land his ancestors left him. What did he think he was doing with his youth group and . . . (*Tsk-tsk-ing.*) If he had given his mother just a little consideration, things wouldn't be like this.

CHŎMNYE: But he was the best son that could be, Mother . . . I know that better than anyone.

MRS. YANG (*suddenly feeling sorry for her daughter-in-law*): That's true, you knew him well, didn't you? If he knew this was going to happen, couldn't he at least have left behind his seed? If only I had a grandson, I'd feel less lonely. He must have frozen to death somewhere.

(*For some time, three shadows have been visible eating dinner under a kerosene lamp in the inner room of* **MRS. CH'OE**'s *house. Finally, a baby starts to cry, and* **SAWŎL**'s *angry voice can be heard.*)

SAWŎL (*only her voice can be heard*): Can't you just stop that! You start crying every time dinner is ready. (*She hits the child, who then cries even more loudly.*)

MRS. CH'OE (*only her voice can be heard*): Why are you hitting her? . . . She's too young to understand. Can't you just tell her—

SAWŎL (*only her voice can be heard*): Mother, please keep out of this. She'll get even worse if you take sides like that. Damn you! You brat!

(**SAWŎL** *opens the door noisily and comes outside.* **MRS. CH'OE**'s *sad voice tries to placate her granddaughter.* **SAWŎL** *looks disheveled, as if she'd just gotten up from her sickbed. She tries to swallow the tears welling up inside and leans against the spindle tree, sobbing.* **CHŎMNYE** *has just come out from the kitchen to fetch some unripe persimmons and walks up to* **SAWŎL**.)

CHŎMNYE: Sawŏl . . . what's wrong?

SAWŎL (*still sobbing silently*).

CHŎMNYE: Have you gotten over your cold yet? What are you doing outside when it's this cold, eh?

SAWŎL: I . . . I . . . I wish I were dead. It'd be better than living like this . . . (*She cries even more plaintively.*)

CHŎMNYE (*smiling sadly*): What, everyone says they want to die . . . Is dying so easy? Why don't you come over later, eh? Your mother's going out on night watch duty, right?

SAWŎL: Um . . .

CHŎMNYE: Be sure to come. Ssallye's Mom says she's coming too. We can talk while we mend socks or something . . .

SAWŎL (*dropping her head*): OK, I'll be there.

CHŎMNYE: Go inside now. (**OLD KIM** *comes outside and asks for dinner again.*)

OLD KIM: Isn't it dinnertime yet? Eh? Have you forgotten you live with an old man? Haven't they learned anything! (*He hits the floor with his pipe.*) Have you forgotten about the Way of Heaven?[10] (*Both* **MRS. YANG**, *sticking her head out of the kitchen, and* **CHŎMNYE**, *rushing in from outside, reply at the same time.*)

MRS. YANG and **CHŎMNYE:** All right . . . we're coming.

Curtain

ACT 2

(*Same as the previous scene. About three hours later. A new moon hangs in the night sky. Wild dogs can be heard barking far away. As the curtain rises,* CHŎMNYE, SAWŎL, *and* SSALLYE'S MOM *are mending socks.* CHŎMNYE *quickly turns up the oil lamp, and the room brightens. The room is almost empty except for an earthen fireplace and a chest.* SAWŎL *leans against the wall, lost in thought.* CHŎMNYE *looks at her, at a loss for something to say.*)

CHŎMNYE: Aren't you going to eat your burned rice?
SAWŎL (*sighs*): No—my tooth hurts.
CHŎMNYE (*breaks the piece of burned rice in two, which looks as if it has frozen, and offers half to her*): Try it. It's hard to chew at first, but once it softens up in your mouth it's OK. It's pretty good. Go on.
SAWŎL (*with no choice but to put it in her mouth*): Um . . .
SSALLYE'S MOM (*with a sweet smile*): Do we have any choice? This is life. Isn't that right? (*She smiles, as if her words have great meaning.*)
CHŎMNYE: Isn't what right?
SSALLYE'S MOM: It's just that I feel sorry for Sawŏl, looking so empty.
CHŎMNYE: Does anyone who's just been sick ever look lively?
SSALLYE'S MOM: No . . . Mm . . . (*With a meaningful smile.*) We all know why young widows are sick, so there's nothing to worry about. Ha, ha . . .
CHŎMNYE (*laughing as if she has just realized what* SSALLYE'S MOM *is talking about*): Oh, it's a good thing you can diagnose our illnesses. Hee, hee . . .
SSALLYE'S MOM: They say even a monk can't shave his head on his own, so I can't talk, but . . . (*Sigh.*) But who knows how a widow feels better than another widow? Ha, ha . . . (CHŎMNYE *and* SSALLYE'S MOM *laugh out loud and then turn to look at* SAWŎL, *who is sitting forlornly.*)
SAWŎL: You two are lucky you can laugh about it . . .
SSALLYE'S MOM: Well, there's no point crying, is there?
SAWŎL (*as if talking to herself*): Maybe marriage is the answer?
CHŎMNYE: Marriage?
SSALLYE'S MOM: Who should get married?
SAWŎL: What do you mean, who? Me, of course.
SSALLYE'S MOM (*looking dumbfounded*): What?
SAWŎL: Why shouldn't I get married? (*She glares at the two of them, who also look dumbfounded.*)
SSALLYE'S MOM: Well, nothing says you can't, but . . .
SAWŎL: Huh! So you mean who would marry a widow like me, eh? With a child, on top of everything else . . . (*A crazed look appears in her eyes.*)

CHŎMNYE (*trying hard to feign composure*): Ha, ha . . . Have you gone mad? What do you mean, get married? Married . . . ha, ha.

SAWŎL: Hey, is my getting married that funny? Huh! It would be funnier if I rotted away as a widow in this mountain valley.

CHŎMNYE: What else can we do? What use is blaming anyone now? It's like keeping track of a dead child's age. Or like a broken bowl . . . (*Sigh.*)

SSALLYE'S MOM (*speaking in a ballad-like tone as she mends a sock*): Oh, this fate of mine! A sandal has a partner, and a sock has a partner, too. Why am I fated to—

SAWŎL: Shut up!

SSALLYE'S MOM (*startled*): Oh, that made me jump! It's a good thing I'm not pregnant!

CHŎMNYE: Ha, ha . . . You're really jumpy! (*The two of them look at each other and laugh.*)

SAWŎL (*testily*): You mean you two don't mind having to live the rest of your life as a widow? Huh! (*Glaring at them sharply.*) Don't lie! You think I don't know?

CHŎMNYE: Oh, what are you talking about?

SAWŎL (*in a low voice*): It hasn't bothered you, living without a husband for two years? (*To* **SSALLYE'S MOM**.) Tell the truth. Go on, tell me!

SSALLYE'S MOM: Ha, ha . . . That . . . Well, who . . . Ha, ha . . .

SAWŎL: Chŏmnye! Why don't you tell me?

CHŎMNYE (*blushing*): I, I don't know! How could I . . .

SAWŎL: Is there anything we can't say to each other? Really, I just don't think I can live like this. Forget my child and my parents; I need a life.

CHŎMNYE: But living on your own isn't easy, is it? Even if you can't eat well and have to dress in rags, a family should live together, don't you think? Just like you and your family . . .

SAWŎL (*getting excited again*): Just like me! So you mean at my age I have to stop meeting people and live the rest of my life like a tossed-out acorn shell? We'll be thirty soon! Don't you see?

SSALLYE'S MOM: Who doesn't know how old they are? (*She picks up the thread and threads a needle.*)

SAWŎL: There's a saying, isn't there? A radish after New Year, and a woman after thirty . . .

CHŎMNYE (*calmly*): Well, soon the world will change. (*She chews noisily on the burned rice.*)

(*The sound of dogs barking in the distance makes the scene seem even more desolate. The sound of wind in the pine trees occasionally can be heard.*)

SAWŎL: Do you think so? Will we really start to live again?

SSALLYE'S MOM: Of course, we're bound to. Like you said, what crime have we committed to make us rot away like this?

SAWŏL: But as things are now, it's hard to imagine anything changing. It would be like lying down and waiting for rice cakes to drop out of the sky and turning into an old woman while you wait! And on top of that, we can't walk around like we want to because the roads are blocked, and at the drop of a hat they come down from the mountains and rob us.

SSALLYE'S MOM: Ssssh! Watch what you say! (*The wind blows even more strongly.*)

SAWŏL: Our only crime is to be poor. My husband dying and your husband disappearing: wasn't that because we can't feed ourselves and haven't been to school? Isn't that true? Chŏmnye!

CHŏMNYE (*with a deep sigh*): Who says it isn't? If you're poor, you can't do anything.

SSALLYE'S MOM (*lowering her voice*): Well, since we're talking about this, perhaps the world will change again sometime.

CHŏMNYE (*looking frightened*): Why?

SSALLYE'S MOM: According to what those mountain thieves said earlier, they're going to make it possible for us to live in comfort, but how do you think they're going to do that when they're dug down in the mountains like moles? And on top of that, when they take from us even the little food we have left?

CHŏMNYE: And there's no one we can stop and talk to about this.

SSALLYE'S MOM: So, they're just lying to us, aren't they? They tell us to trust no one else, but isn't that like waiting for the boy next door and becoming a virgin ghost?

SAWŏL: Not a virgin ghost but the ghost of a young widow!

SSALLYE'S MOM: Ha, ha . . . that's right. The ghost of a widow . . . ha, ha . . . (*At this point,* KKŭTSUNI *appears on the path. Her face is completely wrapped up in a piece of cloth so she is unrecognizable. She's holding a bamboo spear in her hand. She goes into the yard, breathing into her clasped hands.*)

KKŭTSUNI: Kwidŏk!

CHŏMNYE (*to the other two*): Did someone just call?

SSALLYE'S MOM (*cautiously*): Who is it? Oh, I'm frightened. (*She covers herself with her quilt.*) I'm not going out.

CHŏMNYE: Go out and see.

KKŭTSUNI: Is any one at home? (*Coming closer.*) It looks like there's someone in the room . . .

CHŏMNYE (*opening the door carefully*): Who is it?

KKŭTSUNI: Oh! Why didn't you answer before? It's Kkŭtsuni.

CHŎMNYE (*clasping her hand to her chest with relief*): Oh, Kkŭtsuni! Come in! What's going on?

KKŬTSUNI: Is Ssallye's Mom here?

SSALLYE'S MOM: What is it? (*She removes the quilt and comes out.*)

KKŬTSUNI: They said you're next on the night watch, and you should come quickly.

SSALLYE'S MOM: Shit! Time flies at times like this. Is it that time already?

KKŬTSUNI: Yes, they said the next person can't go home until you turn up.

CHŎMNYE: Don't stand there, come inside.

KKŬTSUNI: Is that all right?

CHŎMNYE: Of course, come in. (KKŬTSUNI *puts her spear down on the edge of the floor, takes the cloth off her head, brushes off her clothes, and goes inside.*)

SSALLYE'S MOM (*wrapping a cotton scarf around her head*): What's the point of night watch on a night as cold as this? It's just to torment us.

CHŎMNYE: There's more to come tonight, since I have to go out when Mother gets back.

SSALLYE'S MOM (*coming out onto the wood floor*): Oh, it's cold! (*Putting on her shoes.*) OK, I'll be off now!

CHŎMNYE: OK!

SAWŎL (*picking up her patched socks and coming out*): I'd better be off, too.

CHŎMNYE: Why? Stay a little longer.

SAWŎL: I have to go to bed early, clutching my pillow . . . given that a widow's only pleasure is sleep. (*She puts on her shoes. Meanwhile* KKŬTSUNI *warms herself around the broken fireplace in the middle of the room. She grabs the burned rice next to her and crunches on it.*)

CHŎMNYE (*to the two leaving*): Be careful.

SSALLYE'S MOM: See you in a bit. (SSALLYE'S MOM *goes out onto the path and turns to the left and* SAWŎL *goes home. The gusting wind blows even more strongly.*)

CHŎMNYE (*coming back into the room*): It's cold, isn't it?

KKŬTSUNI (*trying to swallow the burned rice, but when it catches in her throat, she starts to cough, like someone trying to swallow a radish*).

CHŎMNYE: What's wrong? Eh?

KKŬTSUNI (*swallowing the rice with difficulty*): The, the rice . . . (*Coughing as it goes down the wrong way.*)

CHŎMNYE: Ha, ha . . . You should eat more slowly . . . (*She sits down and resumes her work.*)

KKŬTSUNI: Has Kwidŏk gone to bed?

CHŎMNYE: Mm, she's in her grandfather's room.

KKŬTSUNI: Oh! With her grandfather? Ha, ha . . . A grown-up woman sleeping with her grandfather? Ha, ha . . . She really is strange, isn't she?

CHŎMNYE: Don't talk about her like that. She's a poor thing . . .

KKŬTSUNI: Mm . . . (*She rubs her red cheeks.*)

CHŎMNYE: I heard your mother is sick again?

KKŬTSUNI (*expressionless*): It looks like she'll die soon.

CHŎMNYE: How can you talk like that? You'll be punished.

KKŬTSUNI: How could I be punished any more than I have been already?

(CHŎMNYE *cannot think of a reply and lets out a long sigh.*)

CHŎMNYE: Did you eat dinner?

KKŬTSUNI: They just had a memorial service for their ancestors at Sŏun's house and brought me some squash and fish pancakes.

CHŎMNYE: So your mother didn't eat anything?

KKŬTSUNI: There's nothing to eat, but she said she'd lost her appetite anyway. That means she'll die soon, you see.

CHŎMNYE: Everything you say ends with her dying.

KKŬTSUNI: Really, it would be better to die.

CHŎMNYE: Who should die?

KKŬTSUNI: My mother.

CHŎMNYE: Oh, you shouldn't talk like that. (*A dog barks again.*)

KKŬTSUNI: Sister! I . . . I . . .[11] (*She pokes around with the fire tongs.*)

CHŎMNYE: Come out with it.

KKŬTSUNI: When Mother dies, I want to go to Seoul or Pusan.

CHŎMNYE (*surprised*): You?

KKŬTSUNI: Well, who else is there at home besides me?

CHŎMNYE: How are you going to do that?

KKŬTSUNI (*smiling*): There are ways. No one else must know but you.

CHŎMNYE: All right, tell me.

KKŬTSUNI: You won't tell Mother, will you?

CHŎMNYE: You said only I would know . . . Did someone say they would take you?

KKŬTSUNI: Mm . . . (*Moving closer.*) You know the lady from Pyŏngyŏng, who comes to our village now and then?

CHŎMNYE: The lady from Pyŏngyŏng? Oh! The peddler who goes around selling fabric? I've heard about her.

KKŬTSUNI: Mm. Last Harvest Festival she said that if you go to the city and work as a kitchen maid, you get plenty to eat and get paid each month.

CHŎMNYE (*as if to herself*): As a kitchen maid?

KKŬTSUNI: I can't live here. Maybe if Father hadn't died like that . . . And since Mother hasn't moved for almost a year since Father died, who can I rely on?

CHŎMNYE: How old are you now?

KKŬTSUNI: I'll be seventeen in the New Year.

CHŎMNYE: Seventeen . . . already?

KKŬTSUNI: So, I have to make some plans, don't I? If I make some money as a kitchen maid, I'm going to start a business. (*Hope flickers in* KKŬTSUNI*'s eyes.*)

CHŎMNYE: Where?

KKŬTSUNI: As long as it's not here, anywhere will do.

CHŎMNYE (*sighing*): You're lucky you can do anything you like.

KKŬTSUNI: You could, too, if you really wanted to.

CHŎMNYE: Of course I can't. There's all these ties . . . (*With a sigh of despair.*)

KKŬTSUNI (*smiling scornfully*): What use are wedding presents like that?

CHŎMNYE: Oh, you really . . . ha, ha . . . Is there anything you won't say?

KKŬTSUNI: We have to put ourselves first, don't we? Do you want to die before you've even enjoyed life?

CHŎMNYE: No, of course not. You don't understand the way I feel.

KKŬTSUNI: I don't? Hee, hee . . .

CHŎMNYE: What's so funny?

KKŬTSUNI (*in a low voice*): You mean that Kwidŏk's older brother might still be alive and could come back sometime, don't you? (*She smiles sweetly.*)

CHŎMNYE (*calmly*): It's true. It feels like he's still alive. I'm sure of it.

KKŬTSUNI (*decisively*): He's dead.

CHŎMNYE: No. I'm sure he's still alive.

KKŬTSUNI (*observes* CHŎMNYE*'s reaction before speaking*): Even if you found out that he was still alive, what good would it do?

CHŎMNYE (*looking suspicious*): What do you mean?

KKŬTSUNI: Even if he survives, he'll never be treated like a human being again. Just try living in this village for a while . . . Why don't you come with me?

CHŎMNYE (*looks at her in silence*).

KKŬTSUNI: Since you're pretty and you've been to school, you'll be able to get a better job than I can. What do you think? Shall I ask the lady from Pyŏngyŏng when she comes next time? She said we could even marry.

CHŎMNYE (*looking confused*): Marry? Ha, ha . . . (*She laughs despondently.*)

KKŬTSUNI: It's true.

(KYUBOK *appears on the mountain path. He's wearing tattered clothes and looks hungry. In addition, he's limping as if he has hurt his leg. He looks around for somewhere to hide. After looking down the path, he rushes down and hurriedly hides in the hut belonging to* CHŎMNYE'*s house, with stones rolling noisily down the hill behind him.*)

CHŎMNYE: Who is it? (*She looks outside.* KKŬTSUNI *clings to* CHŎMNYE'*s back, trembling. Outside, snowflakes begin to fall one by one. The only sound to be heard is a dog barking in the distance.*)

KKŬTSUNI: Isn't someone out there?

(*The sound of an empty tin can used to summon everyone in emergencies can be heard rattling in the distance.*)

KKŬTSUNI (*eyes open wide*): Oh no! Something's happened!

CHŎMNYE: Mm . . . Do you think they've come down from the mountain again?

KKŬTSUNI: Why would they come back when they just took our food this evening?

CHŎMNYE: I'll go and see. Do you want to stay here?

KKŬTSUNI: No. I'm too frightened to stay here on my own.

(*The tin rattles again. After a while,* MRS. CH'OE *appears on the path, her body wrapped up like a jug of country wine. She also is carrying a bamboo spear. From the opposite direction, two women come rushing along and bump into each other on the path.*)

WOMAN A: What's going on?

MRS. CH'OE: Hamdŏk's mother was on night watch duty and said she saw something rustling in the woods.

WOMAN B: Was it a thief?

MRS. CH'OE: Whatever it was, they said we all have to come out. Go and see what's going on.

WOMAN A: What are you going to do?

MRS. CH'OE: I just have to feed my grandchild and then I'll come. (*She hurries down the path and into her house.* WOMAN A *and* WOMAN B *leave the stage to the left, looking anxious.*)

KKŬTSUNI (*wrapping the cloth around her head*): I'd better go now.

CHŎMNYE: All right, you go ahead. I'll be there soon.

KKŬTSUNI (*going outside*): All right . . . Don't tell anyone what I just told you!

(*Women appear here and there on the path and anxiously whisper to one another.*)

GROUP A: Come quickly! (*At this, the commotion increases and they exit to the left.* MRS. CH'OE *comes out of her house and walks up onto the path.* CHŎMNYE *stands on the wood floor trying to see what is going on.*)

CHŎMNYE: Something seems to have happened. (*She goes back into the room, wraps her scarf around her head, turns off the lamp, and comes back out onto the wood floor. For a while there is silence on the stage, so that only the sound of the wind and the snowflakes can be heard. While* CHŎMNYE *goes into the shed to look for her spear,* KYUBOK, *who has been hiding in the hut, comes out into the yard and enters the kitchen.*)

CHŎMNYE (*coming out of the shed*): That's funny, my spear used to be there . . . maybe I put it in the kitchen . . . (*She goes into the kitchen and immediately bumps into* KYUBOK, *who threatens her with a knife.*)

CHŎMNYE: Who, who are you? (*Her voice is trembling, her words hardly audible.*)

KYUBOK (*in a low voice*): You know what happens if you scream, don't you? Do what I tell you. (CHŎMNYE *takes a step back, shaking.*)

KYUBOK (*moving closer to* CHŎMNYE): First, give me something to eat. And water . . .

CHŎMNYE (*just nods in silence*).

KYUBOK: You have some gasoline, don't you?

CHŎMNYE: Gasoline? Oh! Don't do that. Don't set fire to . . .

KYUBOK: Fire? No! I have to disinfect this wound in my leg.

CHŎMNYE: Your leg?

KYUBOK: Quickly! (*He holds his leg with both hands and groans, as if the pain is unbearable.*)

CHŎMNYE (*gradually relaxing a little*): All right! How did you hurt yourself?

KYUBOK: On the cliff . . . Aah . . . (*He struggles to endure the pain.*)

(*Someone can be heard in the distance.*)

KYUBOK (*flustered*): What, what is that noise? Is it coming this way? (*He looks toward the path.*)

CHŎMNYE: Yes.

KYUBOK (*pleading with her*): Please save me. I'll never forget it if you do. I'm not a Red. I don't know anything.

CHŎMNYE: So, you came . . . from Ch'ŏnwang Peak? (*She looks at him again.*)

KYUBOK: What? Yes. But, please save me. Where can I hide?

(CHŎMNYE *thinks for a while, and then she pulls him up.*)

CHŎMNYE: Hold onto my shoulders.

KYUBOK (*as if he hasn't understood fully*): What?

CHŎMNYE: Hurry up! Someone's coming, come on!

(CHŎMNYE *hurriedly leads* KYUBOK *away toward a large field at the right. For a moment, no one is on stage, but then* MRS. YANG *appears, panting.*)

MRS. YANG: Chŏmnye, Chŏmnye! Have you gone to bed?

(*She puts down her spear on the wood floor and shakes off her clothes. Snow is falling heavily now.*)

MRS. YANG (*opening the door and seeing that no one is inside*): That's strange! It's not her turn on night watch duty yet.

(CHŎMNYE *appears from the right and is flustered when she sees* MRS. YANG.)

CHŎMNYE: Mother, you're back already?
MRS. YANG: What are you doing in the field in the middle of the night?
CHŎMNYE: Oh . . . I've lost my spear, so I thought I could break off a bamboo stalk or something . . .
MRS. YANG: Didn't I say I was taking the spear? Here it is.
CHŎMNYE (*trying hard to hide her agitation*): Ha, ha . . . so that's where it is! I don't know what's wrong with me.
MRS. YANG: Nothing's happened, has it?
CHŎMNYE: What? Oh . . . no. Wasn't that the tin rattling earlier?
MRS. YANG: Yes, Hamdŏk's mother's making a fuss. She said she definitely saw something coming down from the mountain and running away, but who can believe her?
CHŎMNYE: She's always been very nervous, hasn't she?
MRS. YANG: That's what I mean. When we asked her if she had gotten a good look, she just kept saying we could poke her eyes out if we didn't believe her, ha, ha . . .
CHŎMNYE: Mother, go inside and rest.
MRS. YANG: Oh . . . go and see what's going on. They're waiting for everyone. (*She goes into her room. Left alone on the stage,* CHŎMNYE *walks on, staring ahead of her into space.*)
CHŎMNYE: He definitely said he wasn't a Red . . . I wonder where he came from? (*She closes her eyes and lifts her head up in the emptiness if troubled by something. Snow falls down on her face. Far off a dog can be heard barking.*)

Curtain

ACT 3

Scene 1

(*Same as in act 1. About three weeks later. It is morning. Warm sunlight brighten the wood floor and the hut, but the wind is still cold. As the curtain rises,* MRS. YANG *is sitting on the wood floor, wrapping eggs in straw. At her side,* KWIDŎK *is watching, a dull look on her face.* CHŎMNYE *comes out of the kitchen carrying dirty dishwater and pours it into the fertilizer bucket next to the privy. Her face looks brighter than it did earlier.*)

KWIDŎK (*behaving like a spoiled child*): I'm going, too, Mom, heh . . .

MRS. YANG (*still wrapping up the eggs*): I told you, you can't. You look after the house with your sister-in-law.

KWIDŎK: No. I want to see the market.

MRS. YANG: Look, girl, how do you think you're going to walk the sixty *li* there and back? Why don't you just be good and do as your mother says?

KWIDŎK: I can walk a hundred *li* . . .

CHŎMNYE (*stopping before she goes back into the kitchen*): Mother, take her with you. It's the first market day in a while, and you can show her around, and . . .

MRS. YANG: Are you crazy? Today's the end-of-year market, so it'll be packed.

KWIDŎK: So it'll be fun.

MRS. YANG: No. Who'll have to do all the worrying when you get lost again? Stay at home. (*She counts the eggs.*) Oh, two more have disappeared! (*She glares at* **KWIDŎK**.) You brat! You stole them again, didn't you?

KWIDŎK (*jumping up suddenly*): No . . . I don't know anything about it.

MRS. YANG (*hitting* **KWIDŎK** *on the back with her fist*): You idiot! Why did you take them when I told you not to?

KWIDŎK (*tearfully rubbing her back*): Really, I didn't eat them.

MRS. YANG: Who in this house would eat them except for you? Eh? Do you mean to say a snake swallowed them or a mouse stole them? Damn kid! (**CHŎMNYE** *hurries into the kitchen, looking embarrassed.*)

MRS. YANG: This never used to happen. Why have you suddenly become so greedy? (*Continuing her work.*) If these eggs disappear too, then we'll all starve. Until the new barley comes up, we have to exchange these eggs for food, don't you understand?[12] You brat, you're going to be eighteen, come the New Year. In the old days at your age, you'd already have a child who'd be calling you Mom.

KWIDŎK: I didn't eat them. Ask sister. When did I go to the chicken coop?

MRS. YANG: It was you last time, wasn't it?

KWIDŎK: Last time I ate one that sister gave me, but this time . . .

MRS. YANG: I don't want to hear any more. Oh, you damn child! If I'd known you were going to turn into an idiot and upset your mother, I'd have left you to die back then . . . To think I even used money I didn't have to buy you medicine!

CHŎMNYE (*washing her hands and coming out of the kitchen*): Oh, Mother. We should be grateful she's still with us . . . Don't say those things.

MRS. YANG: Even the gods are heartless. They took the son I leaned on as a pillar of strength and left me an idiot daughter.

CHŎMNYE: She wasn't born an idiot, was she? When I came to live here, she was sweet and full of energy . . . (*She strokes* KWIDŎK's *hair.*)

MRS. YANG (*to* KWIDŎK): You can't go! Go to the mountains and bring back some firewood!

KWIDŎK (*stepping back*): No! I'm going, too. If you don't take me, I'll go on my own . . .

MRS. YANG: Oh, that child can talk . . .

CHŎMNYE: Take her with you. She wants to go so badly . . .

MRS. YANG: How can I leave the house empty?

CHŎMNYE: I'll be here, won't I?

MRS. YANG: Leave you alone? When the world's turned upside down . . . won't you be scared all alone?

CHŎMNYE (*smiling*): Mother . . . Anyway, tigers don't come out in the daytime, do they? Ha, ha . . . I'll be all right.

KWIDŎK: They say there are visitors from the mountain, hee, hee . . .

MRS. YANG: Oh, damn child. You listen to everything everyone says, don't you? Tsk, tsk . . .

CHŎMNYE: Actually, when Kwidŏk's at home, it's harder to relax. Please take her with you.

MRS. YANG (*after thinking for a while*): All right, then wash your face and comb your hair.

KWIDŎK: Hee, hee . . . I've already washed. Look. (*She shows them her open hands and smiles.*)

CHŎMNYE: Ha, ha . . . That's a change. You've actually washed.

MRS. YANG: Miracles do happen . . . well. (*She brushes off her clothes, puts the wrapped eggs into a mesh bag, and goes inside.*)

CHŎMNYE (*to* KWIDŎK): Come here. Let's tidy up your hair.

KWIDŎK: Um. (*She sits down willingly on the edge of the wood floor.* CHŎMNYE *unbraids her hair and turns toward the room.*)

CHŎMNYE: Mother! Can you hand me the comb, please? (*To* KWIDŎK.) When you get back, wash your hair. (*She picks out a louse.*) Now you're going to be a year older, you've got to be a good girl, all right?

KWIDŎK (*laughing*): Mm . . .

MRS. YANG: Here it is! (MRS. YANG *tosses out the comb from the room.* CHŎMNYE *picks it up and begins to comb* KWIDŎK's *hair.*)

KWIDŎK: Sister!

CHŎMNYE: Mm?

KWIDŎK (*smiling to herself*): Will I . . . will I get married?

CHŎMNYE (*surprised*): Married?

KWIDŎK: Mm . . . They said I had to get married.

CHŎMNYE (*getting interested*): Who did? When?

KWIDŎK: In my dream.

CHŎMNYE: In your dream? Ha, ha . . . really.

KWIDŎK: Really.

CHŎMNYE: But dreams are just dreams . . .

KWIDŎK: There'll be lots of men at the market, won't there?

CHŎMNYE: Well, I suppose so . . .

KWIDŎK: There aren't any men here, so I can't get married can I? Hee, hee . . . There'll be lots at the market.

(**MRS. YANG** *reappears, looking tidy in a starched cotton skirt and jacket. She ties her jacket.*)

MRS. YANG: If you've finished combing her hair, let's get going.

CHŎMNYE (*pressing down the hair she has just braided*): She's all ready. (**KWIDŎK** *jumps up like a little child and steps down into the yard.*)

MRS. YANG (*putting on her shoes*): Put this scarf on.

KWIDŎK: I'm not cold. You put it on.

CHŎMNYE: All right. (*Holding the eggs.*) You'd better take this, hadn't you?

KWIDŎK: Mm! (*As she puts out her hands,* **MRS. YANG** *pushes her away and snatches the eggs.*)

MRS. YANG (*looking at* **CHŎMNYE**): Oh, that won't do! That's like telling a mouse to watch the grain. I'll take them. (**CHŎMNYE** *blushes with shame.*) Well, look after the house while we're gone. Oh, and when grandfather gets up, heat up some porridge for him.

CHŎMNYE: All right, be careful.

MRS. YANG: Don't leave the house empty . . . They say thieves have even been to houses where there's nothing to eat.

(**KWIDŎK** *jumps onto the path and is gone in no time. Once* **MRS. YANG** *has left, excited about the day to come,* **CHŎMNYE** *breathes a sigh of relief. She goes into the kitchen as if she's suddenly remembered something. Soon she hurries back out with two eggs and a rice bowl wrapped in her skirt. A crow flies by cawing.* **CHŎMNYE** *stops in front of the hut to have a good look around, and then she hurries into the big field to the right. At this point, the* **LADY FROM PYŎNGYŎNG**, *a peddler, appears from the left. She is carrying a large bundle and has a ruler under her arm. She looks around the house as she steps into the yard.*)

LADY FROM PYŎNGYŎNG (*talking to herself*): Isn't anyone here . . . I'll have a little rest before I go on. (*With a deep sigh, she puts down her bundle on the wood floor, then pulls up her skirt, takes an expensive cigarette out of a cigarette pouch, and begins to smoke. Looking around the house.*) There's no reason to go to the village in the morning . . . maybe they've gone somewhere else. (*She steps down into the yard and looks in the kitchen.*) Is anybody there? (*She goes in. The door to the inner room opens, and* **OLD KIM** *sticks his head out. Just awakened, his white hair looks like a lion's.*)

LADY (*frightened*): Oh, my god! He . . . help! (*She falls on her backside.*)

OLD KIM (*like a fool*): Baby . . . where've you gone? (*Rubbing his eyes.*) Oh, these damn eyes . . .

LADY (*standing up*): Why didn't you answer if you were here all the time?

OLD KIM (*unable to hear*): Where's the chamber pot?

LADY: What, the chamber pot? (*Shaking her hands.*) Phew . . . I thought it was a goblin. (*Going closer.*) Grandfather, are you alone?

OLD KIM (*rambling on senselessly*): I wonder if my head's itching because it's going to rain . . . (*He scratches his head.*) Where's everyone gone?

LADY (*confused*): Well, isn't that what I should say? Really . . .

OLD KIM: Well, they could have fed me before they went . . . tut, tut . . .

LADY: It's a deaf devil! Huh! (*Raising her voice.*) Grandfather! Where has everybody gone?

OLD KIM (*blocking the sunlight from his eyes*): Let's see . . . Young people these days have no manners. They don't know even how to treat their elders. Baby . . . Kwidŏk! (*He spits.*)

LADY: Trying to talk to him is like trying to straighten out your clothes by beating them with a cotton stick!

(*Just then,* **CHŎMNYE** *comes back, sees what is going on, and doesn't know what to do with the empty bowl she is carrying. She quickly throws it into the shed and feigns innocence.*)

CHŎMNYE: What's wrong, Grandfather?

OLD KIM (*turning around*): Oh, where've you been?

CHŎMNYE: Uh . . . I just went out for a while.

LADY: You wouldn't have known if daytime robbers had turned the house upside down. Grandfather's looking for the chamber pot. Go take care of him.

CHŎMNYE (*going inside*): Grandfather, go inside. The chamber pot's out back, isn't it?

OLD KIM: Bring me my breakfast! (*He disappears into the room.* **CHŎMNYE** *goes into the room, then comes back out, closing the door.*)

LADY (*putting on her working smile*): Why don't you take a look?

CHŎMNYE (*returning to her senses*): What? What is it?

LADY: Fabric. I have new fabric for jackets and skirts.

CHŎMNYE (*returning to the wood floor*): How can we worry about clothes in our situation? We're lucky if we can just cover our naked bodies and survive.

LADY (*artfully*): Oh, listen to the young wife. Really, how can you be young and not want new clothes? Come and take a look.

CHŎMNYE: Who said I don't want clothes? It's that devil money that I don't have.

LADY: If you don't have any money, then rice or grain will do. Anyway, why don't you take a look first . . . (*She spreads out the neatly folded fabrics one by one. The different colors of the artificial silks are all the more dazzling in the sunlight.*)

CHŎMNYE (*unintentionally reaching out her hand*): Oh! They're pretty, too!

LADY (*smiling cunningly*): You see . . . only a eunuch could see a girl and not salivate, and only a mortar stone could see silk and not want it, ha, ha . . .

CHŎMNYE (*laughing along with her*): You've got the gift of gab! I would change clothes twelve times a day if I could have my way.

LADY (*jumping in*): But you can always find money. Don't worry about that, just close your eyes hard and buy it! (*Spreading out a sky-colored piece of silk.*) Well, how about this piece? I'll let you have it cheap . . . eh? They say "clothes maketh the woman"; well, try dressing up in this. You'll look as fresh as paint . . . ha, ha . . . When you go out in this, all the men in this village and the next will come running around like spring maggots in a fertilizer bucket . . . hee, hee . . .[13]

CHŎMNYE: No! Not after someone like me.

LADY: Oh, what are you talking about . . . You're too pretty to rot away in a mountain valley like this. (*In a low voice.*) Are you still on your own?

CHŎMNYE (*with a bitter smile*): How could I be otherwise?

LADY (*pretending to be very sympathetic*): Really . . . when will there be a time when we can live in peace . . . (*Scratching her chin with the end of her ruler.*) By the way, on the way here I heard that there still are visitors from the mountains in this area?

CHŎMNYE (*surprised*): Well . . . well, it looks that way.

LADY: That's why there were so many inspections when I was coming here on the bus. At every stop there were the military police, the patrolmen, the local Self-Defense units, so you have to have your identity card in your hand the whole time . . . Look at this. This is more like a piece of tissue than an identity card, isn't it? (*She takes her crumpled identity card out of her cigarette pouch and shows it to* CHŎMNYE.)

CHŎMNYE (*looking at it curiously*): We still don't have anything like this.

LADY: Well, why would you have an identity card, unless you're like me, wandering around twelve months of the year? Lately if you don't have one of these, you can't go more than five *li*. 'Cause they won't even sell you a bus ticket . . .

CHŎMNYE (*deep in thought*): You must know the outside world pretty well, traveling here and there all the time.

LADY: Well, I don't know much, but . . . even in small towns people are doing all right, but if you cross just one river, it's a different world. And when you come into a mountain valley like this, there's a cold wind blowing. Yes, you don't see so much as a puppy in the ditches and fields . . .[14]

CHŎMNYE: Really . . . Even the police have only been around once or twice since the Reds fled to the mountains.

LADY: So even now they sometimes come down and steal? Really, it's as if I've traveled a thousand *li*, the world is so different on each side of the river. And I walked about one hundred *li*.

CHŎMNYE: But it must be interesting, to earn money and see the world.

LADY: I have no choice if I want to eat and live . . . as they say, hunger makes a criminal of any man. Now, even if I go into decent-looking villages, no one will buy my fabric. That's why I have no choice but to come to an isolated village like this.

CHŎMNYE: Really, you are quite something.

LADY: Well, if I don't do this, then the five of us would starve, and my son would have to give up school, so . . .

CHŎMNYE: So, you've lost your husband too.

LADY (*tears welling up in her eyes*): Yes, when the Reds came, he just . . .

CHŎMNYE (*looking sympathetic*): Oh . . . is that what happened?

LADY: He was a primary school teacher, and, well, they called him a reactionary, and . . .

CHŎMNYE (*very surprised*): A primary school teacher?

LADY: He was a good man, and his only crime was that he taught children to write . . . (*Tearfully.*) Is it any cheaper to live with one less person? We don't even have a house. All I have is five children. The oldest one, my son, goes to middle school . . . (*Wiping her nose on her petticoat.*) And so I started selling this, as I had to do something. Oh, I've just lived on, thinking I must have done something bad to have to suffer like this in this evil world, and it's not just once or twice that I've thought about drinking caustic soda . . .

CHŎMNYE: You must have. (*Pause.*) By the way, may I ask you something?

LADY: What?

CHŎMNYE: Do they kill everyone who has been in the mountains?

LADY: Of course! Those Reds have to be killed, don't they?

CHŎMNYE: What about people who've been tricked into following them and then escaped?

LADY (*looking puzzled at the unexpected question*): Well . . . well. But, why would they bother to let them live?

CHŎMNYE (*despondent*): So they would kill them . . . after all, a crime is a crime, I suppose.

LADY: But why are you asking that now?

CHŎMNYE: I was just asking. There's someone I know, but I suppose he'll either be killed if he surrenders or starve to death on the mountain, so whatever happens, I might as well consider him dead . . .

LADY (*comforting her*): But you never know, do you? Because dead people can survive, too. There was a case of that, you know. He was a distant relative of ours. Last autumn, as the Reds were retreating, they were tying up anyone who was even slightly important, just like you tie up dried fish, and then dragging them away. So he was pushed into a big basket, stabbed all over with spears, and left to die, but—you know what?—he survived, even though he had a dozen or more wounds all over his body. He thinks it was because his ancestors were watching over him, so now he's always busy fixing and tidying up his burial grounds. He never used to do that before. Ha, ha . . .

CHŎMNYE: Something like that happened in our village too. (*As if retracing the painful past.*) One day, when the People's army first came here, they made all the men from each house gather under Rabbit Rock.

LADY: Why? To kill them?

CHŎMNYE: Why would they have gone there if they'd known that from the beginning? They said that there was to be some lecture on how things were going or something and that everyone should be there. So the men from every house went. It was sunset and all the women were busy preparing dinner and rushing around . . . after a while there was a terrible sound of gunfire.

LADY: Really . . . they shouldn't have gone.

CHŎMNYE: But who on earth could have guessed that they would be killed so brutally? (*She seems to be recalling the past.*)

LADY: So, why did they say they killed them?

CHŎMNYE: It's unbelievable. They gathered under Rabbit Rock, and none other than the Southern army were pointing their guns at them. They said, "Everyone who opposes Communism, get out of line." They all were so frightened that they held up their hands and stepped out of line. Then all the guns fired.

LADY: My word. So it wasn't the Southern army, but a trick the Reds dreamed up to test them. Oh, my . . .

CHŏMNYE (*tearfully*): No one could bear to look at the scene. But one of them survived, even though he had been hit at least twice. Kkŭtsuni's father was a very kind, older man, but finally even he died of his wounds a few months later . . .

LADY (*sighing*): Oh, what an unlucky people we are! If we go up, we'll be killed, if we come down, we'll be destroyed . . . Are we nothing but drums to be beaten at will? Whenever they think of us, they hit us and kill us . . .

CHŏMNYE: I'm afraid there's going to be more unrest. My husband managed to escape before it all started, but there's no news whether he's dead or alive . . . (*She holds her jacket tie to her eyes.*)

LADY: It's always cloudy lately, isn't it? (*Changing the topic.*) Won't you buy just one piece?

CHŏMNYE: I can't just now. Maybe when the harvest festival comes around . . .

LADY (*a displeased expression momentarily crossing her face*): Better wait for your grandson's sixtieth birthday. (*She begins to wrap up her bundle.*)[15]

(*At this point,* KKŬTSUNI *and* CHŏNG-IM *appear on the path.*)

CHŏNG-IM: Here she is.

CHŏMNYE: Come in, Chŏng-im.

CHŏNG-IM (*turning to look at* KKŬTSUNI): The fabric seller's here . . . what did you buy?

CHŏMNYE: Where's the money? Your family's rich, Chŏng-im, so you can buy something, but . . .

LADY (*in good humor*): Come and take a look. It doesn't matter if you buy or don't buy, just take a look at everything first. Because peddling is about making people happy, too . . . How about this one?

CHŏNG-IM: Do you have any material for petticoats?

LADY: Of course. Mm . . . (*Laying out the fabric.*) How about this new diamond pattern?

KKŬTSUNI: If you're buying something, you'd just as well buy for a skirt and jacket.

CHŏMNYE: Skirt and jacket?

KKŬTSUNI (*pointing at* CHŏNG-IM): Chŏng-im says she's getting married.

CHŏMNYE: What? Really?

CHŏNG-IM: Kkŭtsuni! (*She glares at her.*)

KKŬTSUNI: So what? They'll all find out sooner or later . . . Hee, hee . . .

LADY: Well, this is a happy event! How about this piece? As you're very pale, this should suit you. Eh? How about it! (*She lays the fabric over* CHŎNG-IM's *shoulders.*)

KKŬTSUNI: Ooh, it is pretty!

(*In no time,* CHŎMNYE *is sitting alone staring blankly into space as if she has been pushed out of the group. The three of them fuss over this and that piece. Then the inner room door opens, and* OLD KIM *shouts out.*)

OLD KIM: What are you all up to?

(*The three of them step back in surprise, and th*e LADY FROM PYŎNGYŎNG *stands up, clutching her fabric.*)

KKŬTSUNI: Oh, that made me jump!

OLD KIM: Why haven't you brought me my breakfast? Eh? You good-for-nothings! Who gets anything by not feeding his elders?

CHŎMNYE: Please wait just a bit; I'll get it ready now. (*She goes into the kitchen.*)

LADY (*wrapping up her bundle*): Girls! Let's not do this in someone else's house; why don't we go to your house and choose more leisurely?

KKŬTSUNI: Let's do that. And we have things to talk about as well . . .

LADY (*wrapping the bundle*): Eh? Oh . . . ha, ha . . . That's right, I have things to say to the young single girls, too.

CHŎNG-IM: Let's all go together.

(*The three of them leave together, excited. As* CHŎMNYE *comes out of the kitchen and goes into the room carrying a miserable-looking breakfast tray,* OLD KIM *can be heard shouting. At this point,* KYUBOK *cautiously appears from behind the shed opposite. His face looks better, possibly because he's shaved, and he is walking more freely now that his wounds are healing. Far away is the droning of an airplane. When he sees* CHŎMNYE *coming out of the room, he calls to her in a low voice.*)

KYUBOK: Hey! Chŏmnye, Chŏmnye . . .

CHŎMNYE (*surprised and flustered, she goes over to him*): You can't do this! You mustn't come down here . . . Ah, go over there. (*She pushes him into the hut. The two of them fall over onto the straw on the ground, still clutching each other.*) Aah!

KYUBOK (*holding her firmly*): Chŏmnye!

CHŎMNYE: Not now! Grandfather's still here. Once he's gone out to the village, I'll come and see you. Please go and wait in the field.

KYUBOK: When I sit in the field, I can't stop thinking of everything that happened in the mountains, and I just can't stand it. (*Looking troubled.*) Chŏmnye, what should I do? (*He tries to hold* CHŎMNYE's *hand, but she pushes him away, looking around.*)

CHŎMNYE: We can't do this! Please go back. I'll be there soon, I promise.
KYUBOK (*earnestly*): Please stay with me! Chŏmnye! Please stay with me! (*He holds her wrist.*)
CHŎMNYE (*leading him away*): All right . . . I'll be there. I'll be there. What will we do if someone sees us? Let me go, and go wait for me. I'll be there soon.
OLD KIM (*from inside the room*): Bring me my burned-rice tea![16]
CHŎMNYE: He's calling me. I have to go.
KYUBOK: I have something to tell you, so be sure to come!
CHŎMNYE: All right . . . just go now.
   (KYUBOK *reluctantly disappears in the direction of the field once more.* CHŎMNYE *breathes a sigh of relief. The stage slowly rotates*[17] *and the lights fade. The scene changes during the blackout.*)

Scene 2

(*A mud hole, large enough to seat one person, has been dug out in a bamboo grove and covered with straw and sacks. With all the fallen leaves heaped up around, it's not immediately noticeable. The thick bamboo stalks are so tightly packed together that the outside world is not visible. A large stone has been placed in front of the hole. The bamboo leaves block out the sunlight, and it is dark even in the daytime. As the stage lights come up, two people sit side by side in the hole. They aren't speaking but are leaning against each other as if in love. From time to time, the sound of the wind shaking the bamboo adds a chill to the scene.* KYUBOK's *arm is wrapped around* CHŎMNYE's *waist, and he looks at her passionately.*)

KYUBOK (*holding her closer*): Chŏmnye, please don't leave me.
CHŎMNYE: You sound like a child.
KYUBOK: I feel like, for the first time, I know what it means to live. Because that's all I've thought about since you hid me in this bamboo grove.
CHŎMNYE: I'm so out of it I don't understand what you're talking about.
KYUBOK: That doesn't matter! As long as we can sit close together, like this . . . (*He tightens his grip around her waist.*)
CHŎMNYE (*closing her eyes as she tries to control her feelings*): Ah, please stop. If you . . . I'll . . . (*But she lets* KYUBOK *do what he likes with her body.*)
KYUBOK: That's right, it's just as you said; I'm a criminal. But I can't lie about the fact that I like you. You've saved my life, you've brought me love that I thought was gone forever, and you've . . . (*He is struggling to control his feelings.*)

CHŎMNYE: Stop . . . please stop. (*She throws herself around* KYUBOK*'s neck. In the distance a magpie cries.*)

CHŎMNYE: Kyubok . . .

KYUBOK: Mm? (*As if he is dreaming.*)

CHŎMNYE: You really must go down.

KYUBOK (*returning to his senses*): Go down . . . are you telling me to give myself up?

CHŎMNYE: You can't go on hiding like this forever, can you? Don't think of anything else; just give yourself up, please.

KYUBOK (*looking more and more troubled*): But I . . .

CHŎMNYE (*confidently*): What do you think? You haven't killed anyone; you were just dragged away . . . Surely you can just be punished for that, can't you?

KYUBOK: Just for that? No. I don't want to die. I can't go down!

CHŎMNYE: But what will you do if you stay here? Mm?

KYUBOK: If I give myself up, they'll shoot me. And my parents and my friends . . . even the children I taught will see me and . . . That's why there's nowhere to go! Chŏmnye! If it means I can live, then it doesn't matter if it's in a bamboo grove or a pigsty.

CHŎMNYE: Then go back up the mountain!

KYUBOK: What? (*Getting angry.*) How can you say that? Telling me to go back when I left the mountain because I hated it . . . They'll kill me. Chŏmnye, if that's . . .

CHŎMNYE (*struggling to suppress her own unhappiness*): So, what are you telling me to do? Do I have any money, or education? (*Tearfully.*) What are you telling me to do, when I live as though I'm already dead and don't understand what's happening to me . . . I have nothing. All I have are these wounds I carry. (*Crying.*)

KYUBOK (*coldly, and after looking at* CHŎMNYE *for a while*): Now I understand. You're scared to be with me. It must be difficult. You must hate it. (*He clutches some fallen leaves.*)

CHŎMNYE (*raising her tearful face*): What? Don't say that. (*Sobbing.*) What woman gives her body to a man she hates? Eh? To a man who's not even her husband?

KYUBOK (*deeply moved, he takes her wrist in his hand*): So save me. If you want to, we can go somewhere where no one will know us, just the two of us. I want to live like a human being, even now.

CHŎMNYE (*she looks at him with tear-filled eyes, not saying anything*).

KYUBOK: It's all right if I starve to death. Who knows how long I'll live, but as long as I'm alive, I want to live. Chŏmnye! What about it, will you come with me?

CHŎMNYE: Where to?

KYUBOK: Anywhere . . .

CHŎMNYE: But how are we going to leave when we don't have identity cards?

KYUBOK: Identity cards?

CHŎMNYE: They say that even if you're only going five *li*, they won't sell you a bus ticket if you don't have an identity card.

KYUBOK: Really . . . (*Looking disappointed.*) I have a friend who lives just two hundred *li* from here . . .

CHŎMNYE: And you think he'll be pleased to see you?

KYUBOK: We were at Teacher's College together; we were very close.

CHŎMNYE: But that was then, wasn't it?

KYUBOK: What?

CHŎMNYE: If only you hadn't been in the mountains, that friend probably would have greeted you with open arms. But, now . . .

KYUBOK: He won't? He'll think I'm a Red and hate me?

CHŎMNYE (*looking him straight in the eye*): Please give yourself up. If you think it's too difficult to go by yourself, I'll go and explain.

KYUBOK: To the police?

CHŎMNYE: Yes. And I'll go with you and share your punishment for having hidden you for twenty days.

KYUBOK: Chŏmnye!

CHŎMNYE: Once we've received our punishment according to the law, no one can curse or threaten us, can they?

KYUBOK: But the police won't let me live.

CHŎMNYE: They will. They say there were a lot of people who turned themselves in and were pardoned.

KYUBOK: But . . .

CHŎMNYE: Whatever happens, I'll go with you. I can't go on living on my own like this.

KYUBOK: Chŏmnye! Thank you. I'll think about it for a few days, all right?

CHŎMNYE: All right. But the sooner the better. They say if you beg for forgiveness, your head can't be cut off . . . there's no law saying that you can kill someone for no reason.

KYUBOK: That's right . . . You're right. (*Alternating between hope and anguish.*) Oh, when will we be able to scream and shout in the bright sun? I'm tired of living like this, hiding my breath in the shadows. If only I could shout as loud as I like.

CHŎMNYE: Ssssh, don't speak so loudly.

KYUBOK (*tenses for a moment, and then*): Ha, ha . . . Don't worry, there's no one can hear me but you. (*He embraces her. Just then there is the sound of rolling stones and a rustling noise.* CHŎMNYE *is taken aback and looks around nervously.*)

CHŎMNYE: What's that noise? (*She stands up and looks in the direction of the noise.*)

KYUBOK: What's wrong?

CHŎMNYE: That sounded like footsteps.

KYUBOK: Footsteps? No, who would . . .

CHŎMNYE: Mmm. There's no one who'd come into this grove . . . not before the shoots appear . . .

KYUBOK: It was probably a squirrel or a field mouse.

CHŎMNYE (*letting out an uneasy sigh*): I'd better go now.

KYUBOK: Stay and talk to me a little longer.

CHŎMNYE: I've left the house empty too long. Shall I bring another sack if it's too damp?

KYUBOK: It's OK . . . This is paradise compared with when I was in the mountains. (*Smiling.*) You could never understand how happy I am now.

CHŎMNYE: Well, I'd better go now.

KYUBOK: You'll come back at night, won't you? (*He holds her wrist and then lets it go.*)

CHŎMNYE: I'll try. But don't expect me. I don't know what's happening about night watch yet. (*She walks away as* KYUBOK *looks anxiously after her. The wind blows through the bamboo grove. Fade to black. Scene change.*)

Scene 3

(*Same as act 3, scene 1.* MRS. CH'OE *roughly pushes the door open and comes out of the room shouting.* SAWŎL *sits on the edge of the wood floor, staring straight ahead without seeing but with a kind of wild look in her eyes.*)

MRS. CH'OE: Crazy woman. Do whatever you like! (*Spitting.*) You're a mother; how could you want a new husband? Eh? What kind of a whore would do that?[18]

SAWŎL (*with a despairing look but also a sneer*): So what if I'm a whore? What's that got to do with you? I can do what I like.

MRS. CH'OE: Go ahead! Go to Pusan or Kapsan[19] and be a whore or a kitchen maid or whatever. Just do as you like.

SAWŎL: Don't worry about it. What . . . do you think I'm going to ask you to pay my fare or something?

MRS. CH'OE: You've got some nerve! Do you think someone's waiting somewhere to feed you?
SAWŎL: Huh! As long as I'm alive, I'll get by.
MRS. CH'OE: Go, go! So, it doesn't matter if I'm fed to the crows as long as you're doing OK, right?
SAWŎL (*hysterically*): What do you want me to do? Do you want me to wait forever for a corpse to come back to life? I can't, I just can't!
MRS. CH'OE: But don't you have a child?
SAWŎL: Huh! What use is a child? Will that make my life any better?
MRS. CH'OE: Have you really gone out of your mind? Why are you like this all of a sudden? Eh? What's gotten into you?
SAWŎL (*sighing deeply*): I'm sick of everything. If this is life, then I'd rather be dead.
MRS. CH'OE: Do as you like! It's your life! (*She storms outside.* SAWŎL *gets up and walks toward the bamboo grove as if suddenly overwhelmed by a feeling of emptiness. She meets* CHŎMNYE *coming down from the grove.*)
SAWŎL (*moving closer*): Chŏmnye!
CHŎMNYE (*startled*): Uh? Uh . . . Are you feeling better? (*She forces a smile.*)
SAWŎL (*deliberately*): Are you having fun?
CHŎMNYE: Fun? Ha, ha . . . What kind of fun is there in this valley? I suppose there's night watch duty and being robbed . . .
SAWŎL (*with a sharp look in her eyes*): You can't fool me.
CHŎMNYE: What do you mean, Sawŏl?
SAWŎL (*moving closer*): Who is he then? Eh?
CHŎMNYE (*flustered*): Ah, ah . . . What do you mean, who?
SAWŎL: That's what I'm asking you! (*Coaxingly.*) I won't tell anyone, so come out with it.
CHŎMNYE: What on earth are you talking about?
SAWŎL: Are you really going to beat around the bush like that? Then I'd better . . . I'd better go and see for myself. (*She walks toward the bamboo grove.* CHŎMNYE *turns white as she watches* SAWŎL *go several steps.*)
CHŎMNYE (*following* SAWŎL): Where are you going?
SAWŎL: I'm going to look for him.
CHŎMNYE: Who?
SAWŎL: The young man! (*Turning around.*) Who is he?
CHŎMNYE: No, no, Sawŏl . . .
SAWŎL: You know what I'm talking about, don't you? Ha, ha . . . (*Whispering.*) Where's he from? He's not your husband, is he? Come on, out with it.

CHŎMNYE (*not knowing what to say*): Oh, so that noise earlier, that was . . .
SAWŎL: Is he a relative? Now, I can't recall if you had any relatives like that . . .
CHŎMNYE: No . . .
SAWŎL (*probing*): Why are you being so vague? Eh? Who is it?
CHŎMNYE (*as if making a big decision*): If you promise, then I'll tell you.
SAWŎL: Promise what?
CHŎMNYE: Not to tell anyone . . .
SAWŎL: Ha, ha . . . Do you think I'm a child or something?
CHŎMNYE: You won't tell, will you? If you do, we'll all die.
SAWŎL (*surprised*): Die?
CHŎMNYE: That's why only you must know . . . OK?
SAWŎL: All right. So tell me.
   (CHŎMNYE *looks all around and then whispers something in* SAWŎL'*s ear. As* SAWŎL *listens, her face hardens like stone.*)
SAWŎL: He's a Red?
CHŎMNYE: Shhh!
SAWŎL (*deep in thought*): So, on that evening when it was snowing . . . the one who came down from Ch'ŏnwang Peak . . .
CHŎMNYE (*nods*).
SAWŎL (*as if solving a difficult puzzle*): Well, you never know. Why did you save him?
CHŎMNYE: Why? Well . . . Mm . . . (*She avoids eye contact with* SAWŎL, *as she can think of nothing to say.*)
SAWŎL (*changing her expression*): Why did you save him? Don't you hate him?
CHŎMNYE: Who's there to love or hate? I just felt somehow sorry for him.
SAWŎL: Sorry for him?
CHŎMNYE: He says he was a primary school teacher . . . But he fell in with the wrong crowd, was tricked, and dragged from this mountain to that mountain . . .
SAWŎL (*trying to guess* CHŎMNYE'*s true thoughts*): But he's still a Red, isn't he? Maybe it was him who killed your husband . . . You should have left him, no matter whether he was going to live or die. Why did you bring him here and hide him? Without anyone knowing, too.
CHŎMNYE: How could I do that? When I heard about his situation, I just felt sorry . . .
SAWŎL (*hinting at something else*): Your situation isn't any better, is it? Mm . . .
CHŎMNYE: My situation?

SAWŎL (*decisively*): And mine too! (*Sighs.*) Who has a harder life than us? Just like living corpses.

CHŎMNYE (*not understanding*): What?

SAWŎL: What do you mean, what? Do I have to tell you? (*With a sneer.*) But now you must have forgotten all about such problems.

CHŎMNYE: Such problems?

SAWŎL (*looking at* CHŎMNYE *with eyes full of passion*): That's right! You know nothing about the suffering of a woman who has to live alone in the prime of her life. You're lucky.

CHŎMNYE: Me?

SAWŎL: Because you've got a good man now. Isn't that right? (*She laughs vulgarly.*)

CHŎMNYE (*blushing madly*): Oh . . . (*She turns away.*)

SAWŎL (*moving closer*): Chŏmnye!

CHŎMNYE (*stands silently and looks wary*).

SAWŎL: I want to help him too.

CHŎMNYE (*enthusiastically*): Really?

SAWŎL: I understand your wanting to help that man.

CHŎMNYE (*grasping her hand*): Thank you. Then, you won't tell anyone?

SAWŎL: Of course not! But you have to promise me one thing.

CHŎMNYE: Promise you?

SAWŎL: Let's take turns looking after him each day.

CHŎMNYE (*suspiciously*): Take turns?

SAWŎL: That's right. I'll feed him, too. He must have starved in the mountains! It's too much of a burden for you on your own.

CHŎMNYE (*moved*): Oh, it would be so good if you did that! He's really a good person. He keeps saying how sorry he is that he was deceived by the Reds.

SAWŎL: In return, you mustn't interfere with anything I do.

CHŎMNYE: Interfere?

SAWŎL: When I meet him, you must pretend you know nothing. Do you understand?

CHŎMNYE: But . . .

SAWŎL: If you won't promise that, then I won't keep my promise either. How about it?

CHŎMNYE (*annoyed*): I know what you're thinking. But really he's not a bad person, so please don't bother him. Eh?

SAWŎL (*looking disgusted*): You're telling me not to go near him, right? What gives you the right to be the only one to feed and save him?

CHŎMNYE: It's not that, but he . . .

SAWŎL: I don't want to hear about it! You just do what you like. I have my own ideas, too. (*She tries to push* CHŎMNYE *aside, but* CHŎMNYE *blocks her way.*)

CHŎMNYE: Sawŏl! That's not what I meant . . .

SAWŎL: What are you doing? I told you to do what you like.

CHŎMNYE (*beginning to cry*): Please, I'm begging you. I don't mind whatever you do, as long as you help him to live! I feel so sorry for him.

SAWŎL (*smiling*): You promise?

CHŎMNYE: Just don't let anyone else know. He says he's going to give himself up as soon as his wounds heal. So . . .

SAWŎL: Don't worry. If that man's important to you, then he is to me, too. (*Controlling her rising desire.*) I'll look after him very carefully. Don't you worry.

(**CHŎMNYE** *falls on the wood floor and collapses in tears, clasping her pounding heart.* **SAWŎL** *slowly walks toward the bamboo grove.*)

Curtain

ACT 4

(*Same as the previous scene. Approximately three months have passed, and it is an early spring afternoon. Nothing has changed except that the path is sunny, and in one corner of the yard some green grass has sprouted and the forsythia are in bloom. The whirring engines of waves of reconnaissance planes pass in and out of earshot. From time to time, a distant gunshot can be heard, as it echoes through the valley. Then it is silent again. On the wood floor of* **MRS. YANG**'s *house,* **MRS. YANG**, **NEIGHBOR KAP'S WIFE**, **NEIGHBOR ŬL'S WIFE**, *and* **SSALLYE'S MOM** *trim mugwort and other mountain roots they have gathered.* **MRS. CH'OE** *sits on the wood floor of her house, staring blankly.*)

SSALLYE'S MOM (*looking up at the sky as if to follow the sound of a plane*): Why don't they just get it over with instead of going round and round the sky like that? Oh, it's driving me crazy . . .

NEIGHBOR ŬL'S WIFE: Aren't you scared? I'm tired of listening to those guns. What will we do if it starts all over again? . . .

SSALLYE'S MOM: Starts again? Now the National army has come in . . . (*Pointing to the mountain.*) They're like rats caught in a jar.

NEIGHBOR KAP'S WIFE: If only they'd come sooner, we would have suffered a lot less. When I think of what the Reds have stolen from us and how hard they've made it for us, it makes my blood boil.

MRS. YANG: Didn't you hear what the man from the police said last time? The mountains are so rugged that they couldn't fight in winter. But now that it's thawing, they're going to pop off the Reds like roasted beans. (*Gunfire sounds in the background.*)

NEIGHBOR ŬL'S WIFE: Well, there's one less worry now the National army is here, but we've still got to survive until the barley's ready. We haven't had a chance to grow anything properly.

MRS. YANG: We won't starve as long as we're still alive. And as long as there's some arrowroot around, we'll be all right.

NEIGHBOR ŬL'S WIFE: But it's not that easy to collect arrowroot, is it? For a start, someone has to go and get it. You've got your daughter and daughter-in-law so that's not a problem, but for us . . . Oh! I don't know how we'll survive.

SSALLYE'S MOM (*stepping down into the yard and talking to* MRS. CH'OE, *who is still sitting, looking preoccupied*): Why are you sitting there like a dug-up barley stalk? Come over here and talk to us. (MRS. CH'OE *slowly walks over to them.*)

NEIGHBOR KAP'S WIFE: How is Sawŏl now?

MRS. CH'OE (*sighing*): Still the same. They say that if it's your fate to be unlucky, you'll break your nose even if you fall over backward. When will my worries ever end?

NEIGHBOR ŬL'S WIFE: I wonder what's wrong. At that age, even pine needles should taste sweet.

MRS. CH'OE: Well, she throws up everything she eats, so I don't know how she's going to survive. I even scraped together enough money to buy rice gruel but—blaaa! (*She holds her hand to her mouth and pretends to be vomiting.*) If she eats soup then, blaaa! You have to see it to imagine it.

SSALLYE'S MOM: If you didn't know any better, you'd think she's pregnant. Ha, ha . . .

NEIGHBOR KAP'S WIFE: Wretched thing. How can she be pregnant without a husband?

MRS. CH'OE: She can't keep anything down . . . she's all skin and bones, and her eyes have really sunken in . . . If I speak to her, she doesn't answer but just sits in the corner . . . I can't bear to look at her, so I stay outside all the time.

MRS. YANG: Well, there are all kinds of strange illnesses. It's a shame there's not a doctor nearby to take a look at her.

SSALLYE'S MOM: Maybe it's her nerves, worrying because she can't get married?

NEIGHBOR KAP'S WIFE: Don't be absurd! Get married?

SSALLYE'S MOM: Wasn't she fussing about getting married just last winter?

MRS. CH'OE: Well she doesn't talk like that anymore. Really, if someone wanted to take her now, I'd let her go. I can't put up with this in my old age.

NEIGHBOR KAP'S WIFE (*standing up*): Well, it's all up to fate, so there's nothing we can do . . . But if times changed, then things would be better, I'm sure. (*To the others.*) I'll be off now.

NEIGHBOR ŬL'S WIFE (*following her*): You're right . . . we've been here a long time.

MRS. CH'OE (*standing up*): I'd better go see if she's eaten anything . . . (*She goes to her house.*)

MRS. YANG: Yes, go take a look. (*She continues to trim the mugwort. The other three go out to the path and leave the stage after saying good-bye.*)

SSALLYE'S MOM: Where's Chŏmnye?

MRS. YANG: She's gone to get some arrowroot.

SSALLYE'S MOM (*after a pause*): Mrs. Yang.

MRS. YANG: Mm?

SSALLYE'S MOM: I heard a strange rumor.

(*Just then,* **MRS. CH'OE** *opens the door to her house and calls out loudly.*)[20]

MRS. CH'OE: Oh! You're getting sick again? What are we going to do? Just hold on. I'll come in and rub your back. (*She quickly disappears into the room.*)

MRS. YANG: A strange rumor?

SSALLYE'S MOM (*looking all around her*): No one else must know.

MRS. CH'OE: Tell me. (*She picks up another piece of mugwort.*)

SSALLYE'S MOM: They say there's a strange man in the village . . .

MRS. YANG: A strange man?

SSALLYE'S MOM: Yes. And he comes to Rabbit Rock at night.

MRS. YANG (*surprised*): No, why on earth would he come to that haunted rock? Even the dogs won't go there.

SSALLYE'S MOM: But isn't it strange that he goes there and not alone, but with a woman?

MRS. YANG: Are you sure it's not a ghost?

SSALLYE'S MOM: Positive. Someone even saw them there.

MRS. YANG: Who?

SSALLYE'S MOM (*in a low but confident voice*): I did.

MRS. YANG: Uh? You did? When?

SSALLYE'S MOM: On the night of the last winter offering. I couldn't stop thinking about Ssallye's father and just started walking, and where did I end up? . . . at Rabbit Rock.

MRS. YANG: And then?

SSALLYE'S MOM: And then, I clearly saw a man and a woman rush into the woods to hide. I covered my face and turned back, I suppose because I was so surprised.

MRS. YANG: That's strange. Where could a man be staying in our village?

SSALLYE'S MOM: And then Yongshik's Mom said she saw him once too.

MRS. YANG: At Rabbit Rock?

SSALLYE'S MOM: Yes.

MRS. YANG (*deep in thought*): Why on earth would he go to that dreadful place? It's so haunted no one will even go there in broad daylight...

SSALLYE'S MOM: Well, that's how he can avoid being seen, isn't it?

MRS. YANG: Of course, you're right. So who was the woman?

SSALLYE'S MOM: That's the point... um...

MRS. YANG: Eh? Who? Oh, hurry up and just tell me.

SSALLYE'S MOM (*pointing toward* MRS. CH'OE*'s house*): Rumor is that it's Sawŏl.

MRS. YANG (*very surprised*): Sawŏl? No, how...

SSALLYE'S MOM: But it's suspicious, isn't it? Always throwing up and not being able to eat anything...

MRS. YANG (*as if she has just understood*): That's right! So Sawŏl is...

SSALLYE'S MOM: That's the only possibility, isn't it? It's clearly a woman's sickness.

MRS. YANG: But we need to know who the man is.

SSALLYE'S MOM: Really, it's unbelievable. But we can't ask her directly.

MRS. YANG: Sawŏl's pregnant. A pregnant widow? Ha, ha...

SSALLYE'S MOM: Oh, why are you laughing?

MRS. YANG: It's too absurd to be true. (*She asks insistently.*) Are you sure you're not mistaken? Did you really see her?

SSALLYE'S MOM (*stepping back*): Even though it was night and I couldn't see that clearly, it's still obvious from Sawŏl's symptoms and the timing. We've all had babies, haven't we?

MRS. YANG (*in a low voice*): You must be careful what you say. If you go talking about this just anywhere, you could be in big trouble.

SSALLYE'S MOM: That's why I said I was going to tell only you, isn't it?

MRS. YANG: That's right... Let's not talk about this anymore. Heedless gossip can get people killed.

SSALLYE'S MOM: All right, I understand.

(SSALLYE'S MOM *leaves.* MRS. YANG *sits thinking for a while and then goes to* MRS. CH'OE*'s house, her face full of curiosity.*)

MRS. YANG: Sawŏl's Mom, are you there? (*An answer comes from inside the room.*) It's me. How is she doing?

MRS. CH'OE (*opening the door and poking her head out*): Well, it's the same, day and night. Now she's even throwing up bile. (*She scratches her head.*) Come in.

MRS. YANG (*feigning innocence*): She should be getting better, how can this be . . .

(*She goes into the room and closes the door. At this moment* **KYUBOK** *hesitantly appears from the direction of the bamboo grove to the right. He looks paler than before, but he's put on weight. He's carrying a bowl, and after looking all around he goes into* **MRS. YANG**'s *kitchen. Just then* **OLD KIM** *comes out of his room stretching and sits down on the wood floor.* **KYUBOK**, *coming back out with a bowl full of water, meets* **OLD KIM** *face to face.* **KYUBOK** *freezes as if struck by lightning.*)

OLD KIM: When did you come here as a farmhand?

KYUBOK (*grasping for words*): Uh . . . I, uh . . .

OLD KIM: Damn women. Now they've even got a farmhand 'cause they don't want to work . . . Um, damn lazy women.

(**KYUBOK** *is so confused he doesn't know where to go. Then* **KWIDŎK** *appears on the path. She is carrying a leaf whistle in one hand and a basket full of roots in the other. When* **KYUBOK** *realizes that someone is coming, he flees quickly to the right. The old man takes off his jacket and starts trying to catch lice. But he cannot see very well and just rubs his eyes. He has no idea that* **KWIDŎK** *has returned, even though she's blowing on the leaf whistle.*)

KWIDŎK: Granddad! Where's Mom?

OLD KIM (*rambling on about other things*): Well, I suppose because it's spring. That's why it's itching so much . . . (*He scratches his body.*)

KWIDŎK: Ha, ha . . . Granddad's a deaf idiot!

OLD KIM: Come here and catch this louse.

KWIDŎK: No! (*Putting her basket down on the ground.*) Mom, Mom!

(**MRS. YANG** *comes out of* **MRS. CH'OE**'s *house.*)

MRS. YANG: Take good care of her. If only it was closer, you could get the shaman to do an exorcism. I'll be going! (*She closes the door behind her. A crooked smile appears on her face.*) Um! Thinks she can pretend everything's all right. (*She goes into her yard.*)

KWIDŎK: Mom, give me something to eat.

MRS. YANG: What? Eat? Has a beggar got into your stomach? The sun hasn't gone down yet, and you want to eat? Damn thing. (*Even* **OLD KIM** *can hear her shouts.*)

OLD KIM: I'm starving, too! Bring me my dinner.

MRS. YANG: Oh no! Now we have grandfather and granddaughter in time with each other. (*Clucking her tongue and going closer.*) Where's dinner going to come from? You should be grateful you can eat twice a day.

OLD KIM (*getting angry*): That's right, so you think you can starve the old ones and feed a farmhand instead, eh?

MRS. YANG: Why on earth are you talking about a farmhand? Since when have we been able to afford a farmhand?

OLD KIM: No one ever got rich by neglecting their elders. If you can feed a farmhand, then you can bring me my dinner. Go and get it, I'm telling you!

MRS. YANG: Have you really gone senile now? Going on and on about farmhands and . . .

KWIDŎK: Granddad's an idiot. Hee, hee . . .

MRS. YANG (*spitefully*): Oh? And what about you, then? If you've nothing to do, go up the mountain and bring back some arrowroot. Your sister-in-law's already gone.

KWIDŎK: No. I've already picked these roots. (*She holds out the basket.*)

MRS. YANG (*taking the basket and looking inside*): Oh, no . . . You think these are roots?

KWIDŎK: What do you mean they're not roots?

MRS. YANG: Oh, you brat! Are these roots? Eh? It's just grass that no one can eat. Oh, I wish you'd drop dead! Go on! (*She grabs hold of* **KWIDŎK**'s *hair.*)

KWIDŎK: Aagh! Aagh!

(**CHŎNG-IM** *comes down the path dressed up prettily. She's holding a worn-out suitcase in one hand as if she is going on a journey. Her sky blue silk skirt and pink jacket only make her look more like a country bumpkin.*)

CHŎNG-IM: Mrs. Yang.

MRS. YANG: Chŏng-im, what's going on? You're all dressed up . . . Eh? Are you going somewhere?

CHŎNG-IM (*shyly*): Yes. I just wanted to say good-bye before I leave . . .

MRS. YANG: Really? So you really are going, then? Well, is your bridegroom a rich man?

CHŎNG-IM: As long as we have enough to live on . . .

MRS. YANG: You're doing the right thing. You're all alone now, so it'll be easy for you to remarry, but . . .

KWIDŎK (*looking over* **CHŎNG-IM**'s *clothes with envy*): You're getting married? Um . . .

CHŎNG-IM: You take care, Kwidŏk. (*To* **MRS. YANG**.) When Chŏmnye gets back, tell her I had to leave before I could say good-bye to her.

MRS. YANG: All right, you'd better be going now.

CHŎNG-IM (*going outside*): Now that it's time to leave, I feel sad.

MRS. YANG: Wherever you go, look after your husband. Whatever anyone says, a woman's OK if she marries the right man. (KWIDŎK *goes out after her.*)

CHŎNG-IM: Oh, I should see Sawŏl, too, before I leave. (*She goes to* MRS. CH'OE's *house.*)

CHŎNG-IM (*in front of the door*): Is anyone there?

MRS. CH'OE (*from inside the room*): Is that Chŏng-im? Oh, I don't know whether to be happy or sad, eh?

CHŎNG-IM: How's Sawŏl? (SAWŎL *comes out. With her hair undone, she looks thinner and more nervous than ever.*)

CHŎNG-IM: Sawŏl!

SAWŎL (*holding her hand*): Well, you kept saying you'd get married, and now it's finally happening.

CHŎNG-IM: Mm. What else could I do? Even if people criticize me . . .

SAWŎL: Who's criticizing you?

CHŎNG-IM (*lowering her eyes*): They're blaming me for finding a new husband. (*At these words,* MRS. CH'OE *and* MRS. YANG *both turn away awkwardly.*)

SAWŎL: If they criticize you, it's just because they're jealous. You can't go on living alone forever. You're doing the right thing.

CHŎNG-IM (*almost in a whisper*): Why don't you, too, Sawŏl?

SAWŎL (*looking uneasy*): Oh no . . . I . . . (*Pause.*) You'd better be going.

CHŎNG-IM: Mm! Take care then.

(*She walks toward the path.* MRS. YANG, MRS. CH'OE, *and* KWIDŎK *follow her off the stage.* SAWŎL *is left leaning vacantly against the door, and tears start to fall from her eyes. A mountain bird cries.*)

SAWŎL: If only I were a bird, I would fly away. Every day I just feel worse and heavier and heavier . . . (*She rubs her stomach.*)

(CHŎMNYE *comes down from the mountain carrying a mesh bag full of arrowroot. She starts to go in her house but sees* SAWŎL *leaning against the door and goes up to her.*)

CHŎMNYE (*in a businesslike tone*): How are you feeling?

SAWŎL: Oh, just the same. Have you been picking arrowroot?

CHŎMNYE: Do you want to chew some to kill time? (*She gives her a small piece.*)

SAWŎL: I don't feel like eating anything.

(*A heavy silence falls between them. A low-flying military plane can be heard.*)

CHŎMNYE: What are you going to do?

SAWŎL: What do you mean?

CHŎMNYE: You can't fool me. (*She looks at* SAWŎL'*s stomach.*) With the baby, I mean.
SAWŎL: ... (*She hides her stomach as if it bothers her.*)
CHŎMNYE: People are going to find out ... (*Pause.*)
SAWŎL: I suppose this is my punishment. What use is a baby to me? (*Trying to control her distress.*) Ah, I just wish I were dead.
CHŎMNYE: You think everything would be fine if you were dead?
SAWŎL: Well, what do you suggest I do?
CHŎMNYE: You've got to run away with him somewhere or do something. If you leave everything like this, we'll all be found out.
SAWŎL: Why do I have to run away with him? What about you, Chŏmnye?
CHŎMNYE: I can't live with him.
SAWŎL: What on earth are you talking about?
CHŎMNYE: I've finally realized the truth. I always thought it was my husband's fault that I never got pregnant. But now I've realized that I just can't have a baby. (*Sighing.*) ... That's why it has to be you, who ...
SAWŎL: What use is that? I hate babies. Just thinking about them makes me shiver.
CHŎMNYE: Don't talk like that. Women who can't have babies are defects. So that makes me the same as Kwidŏk. (*She begins to cry.*)
SAWŎL: Ah ... What's wrong with God? Gives none to those who want one and too many to those who hate them!
CHŎMNYE: Don't say that; you'll be punished.
SAWŎL: Punished? Ha, ha ... (*Laughing hysterically.*)
CHŎMNYE: What's so funny?
SAWŎL: Well, isn't this enough of a punishment yet? (*Tearfully.*) Do I have to be punished anymore? Eh?
CHŎMNYE: What can we do about it? It was wrong what we did.
SAWŎL (*her eyes flashing*): Is it wrong for two women to like the same man?
CHŎMNYE (*looking worried*): It's not a small mistake, is it? We've also been harboring a criminal. Ah ... I, I just have no idea what to do ... (*Crying.*)
SAWŎL (*glaring at her fiercely*): If you don't know, who does?
CHŎMNYE: Well, it won't be long before the National army surrounds this mountain, and then he's bound to be caught, isn't he?
SAWŎL: Really? No, do you really think so?
CHŎMNYE: Rumor has it they're going to set fire to the mountain to make sure to get every single Red hiding on Ch'ŏnwang Peak ...

SAWŏL: Fire?
(*The sound of airplanes approaching again.*)
CHŏMNYE: They say that when airplanes suddenly appear like that, it's because they're looking for people in the mountains. If only he had given himself up right away, like I told him to.
SAWŏL (*fiercely*): You mean that it's all because of me that he didn't, right?
CHŏMNYE: You're not completely blameless.
SAWŏL: So now you're saying it's my fault? Um, so it's my fault if he dies, eh?
CHŏMNYE: That's right. If you had just ignored what I was doing that time, then maybe both of us would have given ourselves up and already gone somewhere far away. But you had to have your way . . .
SAWŏL: Shut up! So you're trying to put the blame on me now that everything's finished, eh? I liked him just as much as you did. I'm a widow just like you. We're both just widows who've lived two years without a man around. Who's to say one of us is right and the other wrong?
CHŏMNYE: But if we don't do something, we'll all die.
SAWŏL: So what should we do?
CHŏMNYE (*as if she's suddenly had an idea*): Sawŏl! Why don't the three of us try to escape together?
SAWŏL: And then after we've escaped?
CHŏMNYE (*at a loss for words*).
SAWŏL: The three of us aren't going to live together for the rest of our lives, are we?
CHŏMNYE (*confused*): Well . . . well . . . Of course, how could the three . . .
SAWŏL (*distressed*): So what should we do? My stomach's already beginning to bulge . . . (*She hits her head against the wall, crying.* CHŏMNYE *watches her in silence and then gets up and leaves.*)
SAWŏL (*hysterically*): Chŏmnye . . . What . . . what can we do?
(CHŏMNYE *walks slowly away, saying nothing. She walks toward the privy, and then leans against the privy wall and closes her eyes as if she is dizzy.* SAWŏL *goes inside her house, distressed.* KYUBOK *slowly appears. When he sees* CHŏMNYE, *he walks up to her.*)
KYUBOK: Chŏmnye! Chŏmnye!
CHŏMNYE (*opening her eyes with a start*): What are you doing down here?
KYUBOK: I have to talk to you . . . (*He pulls her toward the privy.*)
CHŏMNYE: No. Let go of my hand! What will we do if someone comes . . . please!
KYUBOK (*his expression hardening*): So what if they come?
CHŏMNYE: Please leave me alone.
KYUBOK: But I can't go on forever living like a cow or a pig, can I?

CHŏMNYE: What are you talking about?

KYUBOK (*cursing his fate*): Like a pig shut in a sty, eating what is brought to him and being forced to mate with any sow. It's not human; I've become an animal. A pig!

CHŏMNYE: Kyubok!

KYUBOK: I can't stand it anymore. I've made a decision.

CHŏMNYE: What?

KYUBOK: The army has begun its mopping-up operation, hasn't it? I have to do something before . . .

CHŏMNYE: You mean you're going to give yourself up?

KYUBOK: What else can I do?

CHŏMNYE: But what will happen to me and Sawŏl? You've depended on us . . .

KYUBOK: Depended on you? Liar! Don't lie to me!

CHŏMNYE (*begging him*): Don't go. You can't.

KYUBOK: You weren't helping me. You used me! You were starved for two years, and so you kept me like a beast so I could satisfy your needs!

CHŏMNYE: But didn't I beg you to give yourself up in the beginning?

KYUBOK: So, why are you telling me not to now? Eh? (*Pause.*) Why don't you say something?

CHŏMNYE: Oh! I don't know! I just don't know.

KYUBOK: That's great! So now I'm no use to you anymore, am I? (*He goes to leave, but* CHŏMNYE *stops him.*)

CHŏMNYE: No! You can't go now. (*Clinging to him.*)

KYUBOK: Let go. I've resigned to die. Sawŏl used me too and now she hasn't showed up for several days . . . She looks down on me as a criminal.

CHŏMNYE: That's not true. Sawŏl's expecting your . . .

KYUBOK: My what?

CHŏMNYE (*in a cold and distinct voice*): Sawŏl is expecting your child.

KYUBOK: Child . . . (*Pause.*) No, how could that be?

(*The sound of gun and machine-gun fire from the airplane flares up much closer than before. Crowds begin to gather noisily on the path, looking up at Ch'ŏnwang Peak.*)

KYUBOK: What's that noise?

CHŏMNYE: People are coming! Go back and hide. We'll talk about this later. Go! Go!

(KYUBOK *hesitates for a moment but then quickly disappears toward the bamboo grove to the right. Amid the merciless sound of machine-gun fire,* CHŏMNYE *collapses on the ground as if she has passed out.*)

Curtain

ACT 5

(*Same as the previous scene. Two days later. It is evening. The curtain rises amid the sound of heavy shells and machine-gun fire. In the middle of the yard* **MRS. YANG** *and* **MRS. CH'OE** *have rolled up their sleeves and are fighting.* **NEIGHBOR KAP'S WIFE**, **NEIGHBOR ŬL'S WIFE**, **KWIDŎK**, *and several others stand around watching them.*)

MRS. CH'OE (*pointing at* **MRS. YANG**): I said, just tell me who's spreading that rumor!

MRS. YANG: Who do you think you're pointing your finger at?

MRS. CH'OE: So what if I point my finger? All you have to do is tell me who said my daughter's pregnant . . . all right?

MRS. YANG (*haughtily*): I said I can't tell you, so there's nothing I can do about it. How many times do I have to tell you?

MRS. CH'OE (*threateningly*): So you're really not going to tell me?

MRS. YANG (*unyielding*): That's right. I can't tell you, so what are you going to do about it? Eh? Are you going to go up the mountain and tell on me? It's a different world now, so just you try getting me into trouble! Huh! (*She sneers.*)

MRS. CH'OE: All right! You can talk. So you're going to get your revenge now the National army has arrived. All right, just do as you like! (*Furious.*) But there's not one of us here who hasn't suffered. If there's anyone here who didn't cooperate with them in the mountains, let her step forward. If I've got to go down, then I'll take everyone with me. (*As the people around her begin to move uneasily, she becomes even more excited.*) Is there anyone here who hasn't given them food? Is there anyone here who hasn't done night watch duty? Eh? And who was our best village leader then?

MRS. YANG: You're out of your mind.

MRS. CH'OE: They say that if the lucky goblin can't bring luck, he brings curses. So why don't you just tell me her name?

NEIGHBOR KAP'S WIFE (*stepping between them*): What are you two doing? What's the use of digging up the past? Tsk, tsk. Is there anyone today who you can shake without dust coming off? Since when have we been able to live as we wanted to? Eh? (*Everyone appears to agree.*) It was like that under Japanese rule, and it's been the same since liberation . . . There's no point in digging up other people's mistakes. You only reap what you sow. So why don't you two just stop it!

MRS. CH'OE: It was enough to make my hair turn gray when my daughter was widowed so young, but to say—with no proof!—that she's pregnant, that's just attacking an innocent person, isn't it?

NEIGHBOR ŬL'S WIFE: If you have a daughter, you always have to face these worries. Clearly someone's made up this whole story. Who on earth could believe she's pregnant in this village full of widows? Ha, ha.

MRS. CH'OE: That's why I keep asking her to tell me who said so, but she just keeps not answering.

MRS. YANG: Why are you asking me?! You can ask your daughter, can't you? Um!

MRS. CH'OE: What?

MRS. YANG (*unable to restrain her anger any longer*): If your daughter is so sweet and pretty, why don't you go and ask her yourself! You live under the same roof as she does; can't you see what's happening to her body? Eh? Haven't you ever been pregnant?

(**MRS. CH'OE** *is dazed and momentarily lost for words, as if* **MRS. YANG**'*s words are just too confident and full of reason.*)

NEIGHBOR KAP'S WIFE: Oh, please just stop this! How can you fight like this over meaningless rumors when you're both old enough to be grandmothers?

MRS. CH'OE (*going for* **MRS. YANG** *again*): If I ask my daughter and this turns out to be a lie, what are you going to do?

MRS. YANG: I'll pull out my hair and make a shoe with it.

MRS. CH'OE (*accepting her promise*): Really? Just wait there a minute. (*As she goes to leave,* **NEIGHBOR ŬL'S WIFE** *blocks her way.*)

NEIGHBOR ŬL'S WIFE: You're like little children. If you've got so much time, go and gather roots or something. When widows live together, there will always be rumors floating around!

MRS. CH'OE: Let's settle this once and for all! Why should I be treated like this and have to take it? Oh, it's just awful!

(*Two fully armed* **SOLDIERS** *appear from the left. Everyone trembles uneasily and gathers to one side, watching carefully.*)

SOLDIER A: Is this the village leader's house?

(*The villagers look at one another and say nothing.*)

SOLDIER B: Who is the village leader?

(*They are so frightened they cannot answer.*)

SOLDIER A (*to* **MRS. CH'OE**): Is it you?

MRS. CH'OE: No. (*Pause, she looks around and then points at* **MRS. YANG**.) It's her.

SOLDIER B: Why didn't you answer?

MRS. YANG (*bowing*): Oh . . . I . . . I'm just the village leader in name; it's my daughter-in-law who does all the work. No one knows anything except my daughter-in-law . . .

SOLDIER A: Where is she?

MRS. YANG: Oh . . . She's . . .

(*The two* **SOLDIERS** *look at each other.*)

SOLDIER A: Well, you'll do; why don't you come with us?

MRS. YANG (*as if she's just received an electric shock*): Uh? I, I . . .

(*The others are so surprised they look as if they might scream at any moment.*)

MRS. YANG: I've done nothing wrong. I've . . .

SOLDIER B: Why don't you just come with us, and we'll sort this out. Let's go!

(**MRS. YANG** *sits down on the floor and kicks her feet.*)

MRS. YANG: Why do you want me to go? I won't! I won't!

SOLDIER B: Who said we were going to kill you? The commander wants to see you, so come with us.

MRS. YANG: No, I said I won't go.

NEIGHBOR KAP'S WIFE: What on earth has happened?

SOLDIER B: We were just ordered to bring her back . . . All right, get up now.

NEIGHBOR ŬL'S WIFE: Why don't you just go, Mrs. Yang? Why on earth would they kill an innocent person?

MRS. YANG (*glaring at* **MRS. CH'OE** *as if she has suddenly thought of something*): I understand. You told on me, didn't you?

MRS. CH'OE (*not knowing what is going on*): I told on you?

MRS. YANG: You did, didn't you? All right! I'll go! If you can't bear to let me live, then I'll go and tell them everything. Do you really think I won't talk or something? Huh, all right! (*She gets up, shakes down her clothes, and then speaks to the* **SOLDIERS**.) Let's go. I have something to tell you. (*She leads them away.* **SOLDIERS** *A and B follow, looking at each other with troubled expressions.*)

KWIDŎK: Mommy, where are you going? I'm going with you.

NEIGHBOR ŬL'S WIFE: Kwidŏk!

MRS. YANG (*turning around*): Kwidŏk! When your sister-in-law gets back, tell her to come down.

KWIDŎK: Mommy, I'm going too. (*She starts to follow, but the others stop her. When* **MRS. YANG** *has left, they all wring their hands and look helpless.* **MRS. CH'OE** *stands alone deep in thought.*)

NEIGHBOR KAP'S WIFE: I wonder what's going on?

NEIGHBOR ŬL'S WIFE: Someone's probably said something again, don't you think?

NEIGHBOR KAP'S WIFE: But last time the National army came, didn't they say that we shouldn't worry because they wouldn't hold us responsible for past mistakes?

NEIGHBOR ŬL'S WIFE: But still. (*In the distance, machine-gun fire can be heard again.*)

NEIGHBOR ŬL'S WIFE: Kwidŏk! Don't just stand there doing nothing. Go and get your sister-in-law! Where did she say she was going?

KWIDŎK: She went to do the washing down at the well.

NEIGHBOR KAP'S WIFE: Then go and get her. Tell her your mother's been taken away by the National army. Go on!

KWIDŎK: No. Mommy didn't take me with her, so why should I do what she says?

NEIGHBOR ŬL'S WIFE: Oh, what an idiot! She doesn't understand anything. Go and fetch her, and then if you come to our house, I'll give you some colored rags.

KWIDŎK: Really? Then, I'll go. You have to give me a lot of rags. Hee, hee . . . (*She bounces away like a rabbit.*)

NEIGHBOR KAP'S WIFE (*with a sigh*): Yet more problems!

NEIGHBOR ŬL'S WIFE: What?

NEIGHBOR KAP'S WIFE: If they start calling people up one by one, then someone's bound to get hurt. When the police start telling people to come and go, something always happens.

NEIGHBOR ŬL'S WIFE: Well.

(**MRS. CH'OE** *walks slowly over to her house. As the sound of gunfire increases, smoke rises from below. A crowd runs up the hill shouting "Fire!" . . . "It's on fire!"*)

NEIGHBOR KAP'S WIFE: There's a fire?

NEIGHBOR ŬL'S WIFE: I don't know. If they keep shooting like that, then there's bound to be one, I suppose.

(**SSALLYE'S MOM** *comes rushing up from the river, panting.*)

NEIGHBOR ŬL'S WIFE: What's happened?

SSALLYE'S MOM: Now those Reds are going to get it for sure. (*She smiles as if she is pleased, and the crowd gathers around her.*)

NEIGHBOR ŬL'S WIFE: What's going on?

SSALLYE'S MOM: I don't know, but if they set fire to what's left of the woods, then there won't be anywhere to hide, will there? On the way here, I watched them pour on gasoline and then fire some shots . . . the whole lot went up in flames. It felt good, I tell you. (*As if boasting.*)

NEIGHBOR KAP'S WIFE: Felt good? Are you mad? Everything goes up in flames, and you feel good?

SSALLYE'S MOM: But this fire's different, isn't it? If I had my way, they'd burn down the whole mountain.

NEIGHBOR ŬL'S WIFE: What?

SSALLYE'S MOM: I can't live here anymore. We've got to leave, just like Kkŭt-suni and Chŏng-im did. We could live here a hundred years, and all we'd know is pain and suffering. Ah . . .

NEIGHBOR ŬL'S WIFE: Did you see Kwidŏk's Mom on the way up?

SSALLYE'S MOM: No. (*A commotion breaks out among the women.*) Why?

NEIGHBOR KAP'S WIFE: Well, she was taken away by the National army.

SSALLYE'S MOM: Eh? What has she done to . . .

NEIGHBOR ŬL'S WIFE: If you think about it, she's not completely innocent. She was the village leader.

SSALLYE'S MOM: What, you think so, too? She also was the village leader when the Republic of Korea was in power . . .

NEIGHBOR ŬL'S WIFE: But she stayed on when the Reds came here, didn't she?

SSALLYE'S MOM: They wouldn't take her away just because of that.

(*The fire gradually begins to spread.* CHŎMNYE *comes rushing down from the right, carrying her washing in a basket.*)

CHŎMNYE (*struggling to catch her breath*): Did they really take Mother away?

NEIGHBOR KAP'S WIFE: Yes, they did. You'd better go quickly. They said the commander had asked for her. That must be the one who was here the day before yesterday.

CHŎMNYE (*putting down her washing basket on the wood floor and tidying her hair with her hands*): What could have happened? I can't think straight, what with those flames coming closer and those planes overhead.

SSALLYE'S MOM: Do you want me to go with you?

CHŎMNYE: It's all right. Take care of the washing. (*Taking off her apron and throwing it down.*) Did they go down there?

NEIGHBOR ŬL'S WIFE: Mm. Go quickly. Be sure to apologize, whatever you do! No one's killed who begs for mercy, OK?

CHŎMNYE: Yes. Then I'd better be going. (*As she rushes up the hill,* KWIDŎK *calls her.*)

KWIDŎK: Where are you going? I want to go, too.

CHŎMNYE: Stay at home.

KWIDŎK: No. I'm going with you.

(CHŎMNYE *has no choice but to take* KWIDŎK *with her and disappears. Everyone watching clucks her tongue in disbelief.*)

NEIGHBOR ŬL'S WIFE: Poor thing, she probably thinks it's some kind of festival.

NEIGHBOR KAP'S WIFE: They say that for bamboo to be of any use, its skin needs to be good but that a person's of use only if he's all right *inside*.

SSALLYE'S MOM: Oh, look at that fire! (*Her face is full of wonder.*)

(*Mother and daughter can be heard arguing in* **MRS. CH'OE**'s *house until finally* **MRS. CH'OE** *opens the door and comes out. Her eyes are full of anger.* **SAWŎL** *leans against the door.*)

MRS. CH'OE: So, you'd even mislead the only mother you have in this world? Eh? Damn you! How could you lie to me, of all people?

SAWŎL: Mother, whatever I say now is not going to help anything.

MRS. CH'OE: Who the hell is the father? Tell me his name! Who's the bastard who put you in this condition?

(*The people gathered to the right mutter with curiosity.*)

SAWŎL (*calmly*): I told you I can't tell you.

MRS. CH'OE: Can't tell me? Is he the son of a rich man? Or an official?

(**MRS. CH'OE** *cannot control her anger and leaps at* **SAWŎL**, *grabbing her hair and shouting.*)

MRS. CH'OE: Tell me, quickly! Now that you're in this state, it's over for both of us.

SAWŎL (*she endures the pain in silence*).

SSALLYE'S MOM (*jumping up to stop* **MRS. CH'OE**): Oh, let go of her! Even though you won't give a sick person medicine, you shouldn't hit her, should you? Come on now, leave her alone.

MRS. CH'OE: Get out of my way. She's no daughter of mine, she's my enemy.

SSALLYE'S MOM: Please control yourself. She's sick; you shouldn't . . .

(**MRS. CH'OE** *is pushed to the side when* **SSALLYE'S MOM** *proves to be too strong for her.*)

MRS. CH'OE: You whore! Who told you to have a baby? Eh? Who's done this to you, aaargh . . . (*Sitting down on the floor unable to control her anger.*) Aaargh . . . you idiot, oh! (*She begins to cry.* **SAWŎL** *just sits still, not shedding a tear.*)

SSALLYE'S MOM: Sawŏl! Go inside quickly. Lie down! Go on!

SAWŎL: I'm all right.

SSALLYE'S MOM: Go inside quickly. (*She helps her into the room and closes the door.*)

MRS. CH'OE (*in a tearful voice*): They say the most unexpected thing . . . they must have been talking about me. Made my daughter into a whore . . .

Oh, how could my fate be so . . . (*She pounds the floor. The villagers help up* MRS. CH'OE *and take her to* MRS. YANG's *house.*)

NEIGHBOR KAP'S WIFE: You'll have to cope with this. There's nothing else to do. We've managed to survive up until now, just try to forget . . .

MRS. CH'OE: Oh, how can I forget this? Give me some water . . . some water . . .

(MRS. CH'OE *sounds like she's alternately singing and crying as she speaks.* SSAL-LYE'S MOM *quickly brings some water from the kitchen. After a drink,* MRS. CH'OE *starts to wail plaintively. Just then* MRS. YANG, CHŎMNYE, SOLDIERS A *and* B, *and* KWIDŎK *appear from the left. One of the soldiers is holding a gasoline can.*)

NEIGHBOR ŬL'S WIFE: Oh, Kwidŏk's Mom is back.

(*Everyone is pleased to see them back and gathers round. But* MRS. YANG *and* CHŎMNYE *both look very worried.*)

NEIGHBOR KAP'S WIFE: What's going on?

MRS. YANG (*looking dispirited*): How can you do that? Do you think that's just any kind of bamboo grove?

NEIGHBOR ŬL'S WIFE: Uh, what about the bamboo grove?

MRS. YANG: They told me that they're going to set fire to our bamboo grove.

SSALLYE'S MOM: Why would they do that?

SOLDIER A: As you all know, we have to destroy any possible hiding places in our slow fight to clear out all the Communist guerrillas. And we have to be able to see everything clearly when we look down from the air . . .

(*They all nod in approval as if they have understood what is going on.*)

MRS. YANG: But you have to leave that bamboo grove alone! How can I stand by and watch you burn the grove that has been passed down by my ancestors from generation to generation? You'll have to kill me first.

SOLDIER B (*as if he sympathizes*): How many times do we have to explain? (*To* SOLDIER A.) OK, go ahead. (*When the two of them start to move toward the bamboo grove to the right,* CHŎMNYE *blocks their way.*)

CHŎMNYE: You can't go near there.

SOLDIER A: What's wrong with you now?

CHŎMNYE (*begging them*): Please, just spare that bamboo grove. If we lose that, we'll all die. If you want to save our family, then please save our bamboo grove. Please! (*Everyone becomes tense because of* CHŎMNYE's *desperate attitude.*)

SOLDIER A: The army has to follow orders. We can't change the whole army's plans because of one person's circumstances. Please move out of the way!

CHŎMNYE: Please, I beg you! (*She clings to him, and* MRS. YANG *clings to* SOLDIER B.)

MRS. YANG: Please! Don't you take care of your ancestors and rites in your families? Please, can't you understand our situation? I protected that grove, even when my son wanted to sell it and start a business. And now you want to . . .

SOLDIER B (*pushing her aside*): Please get out of the way . . . (*He quickly jumps past her, and* SOLDIER A *follows.*)

CHŎMNYE (*as if she is crazy*): No! You can't go in there!

MRS. YANG: Oh! Our family is ruined. Our family . . . (*As she moves forward, the others stop her. A short time passes, and then several gunshots are heard; smoke spreads along with the sound of the bamboo burning.* CHŎMNYE *and* MRS. YANG *step back silently as if they've lost their senses. More than despair, emptiness prevails.*)

SSALLYE'S MOM: Oh, what a waste of such a bamboo grove . . .

NEIGHBOR ŬL'S WIFE: And it wouldn't have been long before the bamboo shoots would have appeared . . . Oh, what a waste . . .

NEIGHBOR KAP'S WIFE: Aah . . . Everything we live on disappears bit by bit, and only our age increases . . .

(*Flames rise up into the sky, now dyed a red more beautiful than that of a peony. Here and there people are gathered. Their faces are despondent in the face of the roaring flames.*)

CHŎMNYE (*suddenly getting up*): Kyubok! Kyubok! No! (*Several people pull her back as she tries to jump in.*)

SSALLYE'S MOM: Come on! Chŏmnye! Pull yourself together.

CHŎMNYE: I want to die in the fire, too. Let me go.

MRS. YANG (*exhausted*): Oh, my son. If I'd known this would happen, I'd have sold it like you wanted.

(*Suddenly there are shouts from the* SOLDIERS *of "Get the bastard!" and "Who is that?" Then there are several gunshots. Everyone is frightened and moves to the right.* CHŎMNYE *just stands still.*)

SSALLYE'S MOM: What's that noise?

NEIGHBOR ŬL'S WIFE: It looks like someone was in there. (OLD KIM *comes out of his room.*)

OLD KIM: Oh my ears are hearing everything wonderfully today. What are they hunting? I do like wild boar with some rice wine . . .

(SOLDIERS A *and* B *appear dragging* KYUBOK, *who has been shot dead. A new commotion arises in the crowd. After laying* KYUBOK *down in the yard, the* SOLDIERS *look around the crowd.*)

SOLDIER A: Who is this?

(*No one answers.*)

SOLDIER B: Isn't he from the village?

NEIGHBOR KAP'S WIFE: It's been at least two years since there was any trace of a man in our village.

(*The* **SOLDIERS** *whisper something to each other as if this were very strange.*)

NEIGHBOR ŬL'S WIFE: Well, this is a shock . . . To think there was a man hiding in the bamboo grove.

NEIGHBOR KAP'S WIFE: Maybe he came down from the mountain?

(**SOLDIER A** *hurries away along the path.*)

SOLDIER B: No one knows anything about him, even though it looks like he'd dug a hole and hidden in the grove for a while? (*They all shake their heads.* **CHŎMNYE** *just looks down at him with a vacant look.*)

MRS. YANG: A man in our grove? (*To* **CHŎMNYE**.) You hadn't seen him either, had you?

CHŎMNYE (*just shakes her head without answering*).

SSALLYE'S MOM: That's very strange . . . (*She looks at* **MRS. YANG**, *and her look seems to spread until everyone is looking at* **MRS. CH'OE**. *When* **MRS. CH'OE**, *who has been looking on in disbelief, realizes that they all are looking at her, she becomes angry.*)

MRS. CH'OE: Why are you all looking at me? (*Pause.*) I know. You think it was this man my daughter slept with? All right. I'll bring her out here so we all know for sure. (*She goes into her house calling out* **SAWŎL**'s *name.* **OLD KIM** *goes up and looks at the corpse and shouts out, slapping his knee.*)

OLD KIM: That's that new farmhand.

EVERYONE (*as if by arrangement*): Farmhand?

MRS. YANG (*in a loud voice*): Do you know who he is?

OLD KIM: Mm . . . Isn't that our farmhand?

MRS. YANG: Oh, you've gone senile, senile! Do you think we can afford a farmhand?

(*Everyone laughs loudly. Then there is a scream from* **MRS. CH'OE**, *and she looks out from her house.*)

MRS. CH'OE: Help! My daughter . . . oh, my daughter . . .

SSALLYE'S MOM: Sawŏl?

(*The crowd rushes over.* **MRS. CH'OE**'s *wails grow louder, and a baby can also be heard crying.*)

NEIGHBOR KAP'S WIFE: She's swallowed caustic soda? Oh . . .

(**CHŎMNYE** *goes quietly up to* **KYUBOK**'s *body and properly straightens out his arms and legs.*)

SOLDIER: Don't touch him.

CHŎMNYE (*with almost no expression*): A dead man won't come back to life and talk just because I've touched him. Everything's just ashes . . .

(*She stands up slowly. As the sky burns a deep blood red, it is reflected on* **KYUBOK**'s *face, and he looks even more gruesome. In the distance a magpie is crying.* **OLD KIM** *sits on the floor and asks for food again.*)

OLD KIM: Isn't it dinnertime yet? Oh, my ears seem to be hearing really well today.

(**MRS. CH'OE**'s *wailing increases.*)

Curtain

NOTES

1. The Sobaek mountain range runs elliptically through south-central South Korea, from Chiri Mountain in the south to Sobaek Mountain in present-day North Korea at the northern end of the range.
2. A *hop* is a unit of measure equal to 0.18 liter, or about 0.16 of a dry quart measure.
3. As made clear in other plays in this volume, Koreans are keenly aware of social relationships based on age, education, social status, and the like. Even in "P" Village, where people have known one another for years and nearly everyone is dirt poor, advanced age entitles a status clearly reflected in the characters' choice of words. That is, Mrs. Ch'oe refers not only to *what* Mrs. Yang says but also to the lowered status Mrs. Yang creates for her through word choice and grammar. Mrs. Yang justifies her treatment of Mrs. Ch'oe on her being ten years older than she.
4. Koreans often use indirect means to refer to others, so the Korean equivalent of "you" is seldom used. Here, there is a gendered significance: once the first child is born, women are referred to as the "mother of [child's name]." Even if Mrs. Ch'oe knew the first names of the women to whom she is speaking, it is unlikely that she would use them. Thus titles such as "Ssally e's mom" are used, with "mom" signaling a sense of familiarity among the women, but in a more socially formal way than the usual American "mom" suggests.
5. Korean homes traditionally were heated by flues under the floor that conveyed heat from a small "furnace" at one end of the house. But "P" village is so poor that there is little charcoal or wood to burn for heat, thus Ŭl's wife's discomfort. These days, even high-rise apartments use floor heat, the warmth coming from water running through pipes in the concrete floor.
6. Another wording of the saying is "When the hen crows, the household collapses," meaning that order collapses when women are in charge of men's affairs.
7. A *mal* is a unit of measure equal to about eighteen liters. A *toe* (*twe*) is a little more than three pints.
8. Here, 150 *li* is equivalent to 0.5 kilometer, or 0.3 mile.

9. Mrs. Ch'oe suggests that those locals who had aligned themselves with Rhee Syngman and were in power after 1948 should not be treated well now that the village is in territory controlled by North Korean (and Chinese) forces.
10. Although he probably has not read any of the Confucian classics, Old Kim likely is referring to aspects of Confucian and Neo-Confucian principles embedded in daily life and comprising the "Way of Heaven." The relevant principles here are loyalty to one's father, respect for the aged, and display of proper etiquette toward the head of the household (Old Kim).
11. Although Kkŭtsuni is not related to Chŏmnye, she uses a term for an older female that suggests familiarity or closeness to her.
12. Until only recently, life for Korean farmers was what Americans call "hardscrabble," a day-in-day-out struggle with weather, insects, worn-out land, and taxes. The late winter could be a time of immense suffering and even famine as the foodstuffs saved from the fall dwindled. When reduced to a diet of turnip soup (if there were any turnips), roots, tree bark, and other foods provided by nature, children's tongues could turn black, illness was common, and famine became a familiar guest. Surviving until the spring growth was known as "climbing the hill of barley." If one could survive the "climb," the barley would be on the other side of the hill.
13. The analogy is earthy. The fertilizer would be a collection of human night soil, garbage, and other disposables that created an inviting environment for flies to lay eggs.
14. Varied inferences may be attached to this line, with two quickly coming to mind. First, food is so scarce that even dogs can't survive, and second, all the dogs have been eaten by hungry peasants or guerrilla forces.
15. One's sixtieth birthday is a special one in Korea, but the Lady from Pyŏngyŏng is being sarcastic here. The subtext is close to "You'll buy some fabric when pigs fly."
16. Many Koreans look forward to a meal-ending "tea" made by pouring hot water or weak tea on the crunchy, burned rice remaining at the bottom of the pot after the soft rice has been removed and eaten.
17. The playwright envisioned a revolving stage as the solution to the many scenes requiring quick changes. This solution is interesting because no theater in Korea at the time this play was written had a built-in revolving stage.
18. In traditional Korean society, widows were expected to remain unmarried and loyal to the dead husband and his family line. Accordingly, the high death rate among men during the Korean War placed a special strain on women in rural villages, and many widows were caught in a triangle of survival, need for male companionship, and rigid traditional ways.
19. Pusan (now South Korea's second-largest city) is hundreds of miles from the mountain valley in which the play takes place. Kapsan (Gapsan on some maps) is a

remote town in the northeastern mountains of North Korea, once a place of exile for those who displeased ancient kings.

20. The stage direction can be confusing. Because there is no need for Mrs. Ch'oe to go into her house and then open the door to yell at her daughter, this line seems to be a remnant of old staging practices. The reader (or a director) thus can omit Mrs. Ch'oe's lines, with no damage to the scene's development.

O CHANG-GUN'S TOENAIL
(O CHANG-GUN ŬI PALT'OP)

PAK CHOYŎL

Pak Choyŏl was born in 1930 in what is now North Korea. Along with countless others, he fled to the south during the Korean War, leaving behind his family. After serving in the Republic of Korea army for some twelve years, he left in 1963 to enter the Theater Academy at the Drama Center in Seoul, driven, Pak notes, by a need to fill an intellectual void in his life. He is a major figure in the Korean theater, often mentioned along with O T'aesŏk and Ch'oe Inhun, as one whose work marked a departure from the previously dominant realism in the 1960s and 1970s. In Pak's case, this meant innovatively blending farce, allegory, and elements of the theater of the absurd. He wrote ten plays, as well as dramas for both radio and television. The majority of his plays touch in some way on the division between north and south, the suffering of the Korean people, and the absurdities evident in government intransigence on both sides. Pak's desire for the unification of north and south is evident throughout his works.

His first play, *Sightseeing Zone*, also known as *The P'anmunjŏm Eviction Suit* (*Kwan-gwang chidae*, 1963), questions the motives of the governments of both North and South Korea, as well as those of the United States and the United Nations. But because government censors were skeptical of this work, Pak was investigated and the play was never produced. His second play, *The Rabbit and the Hunter* (*T'okki wa p'osu*, 1964), deals with a love–hate relationship between two lovers, but the analogy to north–south relations is evident. It was a commercial hit and received an award for best play of the year.

Pak soon began writing a play nearly every year, but it was his eighth play, *O Chang-gun's Toenail* (*O Chang-gun ŭi palt'op*, 1974), that made Pak a cause célèbre when the government censorship committee refused to grant a license to perform the play, citing its antimilitary aspects and reading Pak's longing for his mother and home in the north as pro-Communist sentiment. Pak wrote only two more plays after 1974, both dealing with the division between north and south. His struggle with censors, some of whom were fellow playwrights, finally took an emotional and artistic toll, and Pak left the theater to protest government censorship. It was not until 1988 and the softening of theater-licensing regulations under the No Taeu (Roh Tae Woo) government that the play was staged by the Mich'u Drama Group in Seoul.

O Chang-gun's Toenail is the only play in this collection without notes, as its universal characters seem to need no supporting information. The translation here is of Pak Choyŏl's 1994 revision of his 1974 work.

Pak Choyŏl is now a member of the Korean National Academy of Arts and an adjunct professor of playwriting in the School of Drama at Korean National University of the Arts, in Seoul.

O CHANG-GUN'S TOENAIL
(O CHANG-GUN ŬI PALT'OP)

TRANSLATED BY BRUCE FULTON AND JU-CHAN FULTON

PLAYWRIGHT'S PRODUCTION NOTES

1. The players must above all else imagine themselves in a fairy tale. In this play, the sun smiles, trees walk about, and cows have affection for humans.
2. The "Chang-gun" in the title is not the Korean word *changgun*, which means "military general," but is instead a given name. The inspiration for this name comes from the tendency of some Korean parents to name a son Chang-gun in the hopes that he will grow up brave, healthy, and famous.
3. O Chang-gun is the only son of the destitute widow of a tenant farmer. Until he is drafted into the army, he has never ventured more than a few miles from home and knows little more of life than "going out to the fields by starlight and returning home by moonlight." Not surprisingly, his vocabulary is extremely limited.
4. O Chang-gun's conduct in the army brings tragedy on himself but is a continual farce to others. We might suppose that he was the first soldier to be nicknamed Counselor and referred to as "an accident waiting to happen."
5. O Chang-gun goes to war in the late 1920s, when twin-engine bombers were first used. If you were to look at a photograph of him just before he entered battle, his headgear would remind you of a Prussian soldier's iron helmet, and his uniform, that of a soldier in the Japanese Imperial army.
6. I would suggest that each actor or actress play several of the dozens of characters in this play. The actor who plays O Chang-gun, though, should limit himself to that role.

7. All the characters except O Chang-gun, his mother, and his fiancée should wear an expression of perpetual displeasure. All the props, and of course the costumes, should be simple and exaggerated, as in a fairy tale, and should express the bygone time and setting of the 1920s.

Characters

O CHANG-GUN
HIS MOTHER
KKOTBUN, his fiancée
MŎKSOE, a cow
POSTMAN A
POSTMAN B
People from the country of Easterly:
> **TRAINING CAMP DRILL INSTRUCTOR**
> **ASSISTANT DRILL INSTRUCTOR A**
> **ASSISTANT DRILL INSTRUCTOR B**
> **MACHINE GUNNER**
> **MEDICAL OFFICER**
> **INTERN**
> **NURSE** (commissioned officer)
> **PERSONNEL OFFICER**
> **RECRUITS A, B, C, D**, and several others
> **BUREAUCRAT A**
> **BUREAUCRAT B**
> **BUREAUCRAT C**
> **DRIVER**
> **FIELD ARMY COMMANDER**
> **AIDE-DE-CAMP**
> **INTELLIGENCE OFFICER**
> **OPERATIONS OFFICER**
> Various other staff officers
> **CAPTAIN**, reconnaissance unit
> **MASTER SERGEANT**, reconnaissance unit

People from the country of Westerly:
> **FIELD ARMY COMMANDER**
> **CAPTAIN**, information unit (camouflage A)
> **SERGEANT FIRST CLASS** (camouflage B)
> **STAFF SERGEANT** (camouflage C)

LANCE CORPORAL (camouflage D)
CORPORAL (camouflage E)
OFFICER, artillery observation unit
SOLDIER, artillery observation unit
MP OFFICER
Various MPs
Various high-ranking officers
Trees walking about in O Chang-gun's hometown

SCENE 1 (PROLOGUE): A POTATO FIELD

(*Pitch darkness, a somber melody played by a clarinet. A shaft of light appears and advances across the stage, seeking the melody. The* **CLARINET PLAYER** *and a* **WOMAN**, *both dressed in dark gray and carrying a chair on their back, enter from the right and follow the light. They stop center stage and gaze to the rear at the horizon. A murmur can be heard offstage rear. Listen carefully and you realize it's someone sobbing. The* **WOMAN** *and the* **CLARINETIST** *listen for a moment. The* **WOMAN** *begins humming, as if to soothe the person who is weeping. The clarinet follows along with the humming. The* **WOMAN** *and the* **CLARINETIST** *turn from the horizon toward the audience, as if to ask sympathy for the person weeping offstage. Then they walk stage left, where they sit down in their chairs, taking pains to sit with the correct posture. The* **CLARINETIST** *turns toward the horizon and plays a short, enchanting melody in a higher key than before. As if kindled by the sound, the sun rises. It is five times normal viewing size. The stage lights brighten as the sun appears. The* **CLARINETIST** *and the humming* **WOMAN** *are narrators, magicians, players, and audience, all in one. Until the final curtain, they will stay where they are, unseen by the other characters.*

As the magical melody of the clarinet continues, three meager-looking **TREES** *glide onstage and take their places.* **FLOWERS** *quickly toddle onstage behind the* **TREES** *and settle all about them. Two* **DOGS**—*a male and a female*—*come onstage, pestering each other, and begin to lick each other. An old* **CAT** *appears, alternately flinching and watching the* **DOGS**, *then ignoring them as it crosses the stage. Finally, it meows in peevish disgust. The startled* **DOGS** *jump, then flee offstage. The sound of a man singing out of tune approaches. Enter* **O CHANG-GUN**, *wearing an A-frame on his back and carrying a plow over his shoulder.*)

CHANG-GUN (*sings*):
   Mommy, Mommy, my mommy,
   Why did you give birth to me?

Am I the best you could do?
I was a mistake, unplanned, and I've suffered for it since.
The day breaks and I'm off to do the chores;
Am I the son of a bull?
Da-da-da, da-da-da.
(He takes the plow from his shoulder and is about to hurl it to the ground in anger. But he checks himself, sets it down gently, and looks offstage.)
Damn thing's trailing behind again. Hey! Mŏksoe! Get a move on!
(From offstage, the sound of a bell. Enter **MŎKSOE**, *the cow. She looks quite realistic except that she walks on her hind legs. Around her neck is a bell and a yoke which is attached to the plow. She holds a switch, which she respectfully offers with both hooves to her master.* **CHANG-GUN** *takes the switch and threatens* **MŎKSOE** *with it.)*
You're turning into a lump! What's the matter, you got spring fever, too?
*(***MŎKSOE** *looks toward the audience if to say, "What do you expect?")*
Well, all right—I guess there's no law that says only people get spring fever. *(Connecting the plow to* **MŎKSOE**'s *yoke.)* Mother told me that once upon time animals could talk, like people do . . . Don't you have to go, you? *I do. (Urinating against a tree.)* She said trees could talk, too. And she said this tree was planted by our thirteenth-generation ancestor. Maybe back then this one could talk. It'd be nice if you could talk, like the animals did in the old days.

MŎKSOE: Moo. *(Beats her breast, as if in frustration.)*

CHANG-GUN *(moving to another tree)*: Thank goodness for you that you can understand, anyway. You know, the blacksmith can't even hear. *(Looks down at his groin.)* Hey! What's going on here? *(***MŎKSOE** *runs over to* **CHANG-GUN**.) Look here! See where it's all red and swollen? *(***MŎKSOE** *cranes her neck to get a better look, then nods.)* Aha, don't see too well, do you? Now I remember—a bedbug bit me there last night. *(***MŎKSOE** *glares at* **CHANG-GUN**, *then stomps back to where she was, angry at his indelicate behavior.)*
Of all the parts that a bedbug could have bitten . . . *(Abruptly chuckling.)*
*(***MŎKSOE** *looks puzzled.)* Wondering why I'm laughing, aren't you? I was just thinking of Kkotbun—what kind of look she'd give me if I showed her this. *(Chuckles again.)* What do you say, Mŏksoe? Funny, huh? *(***MŎKSOE** *pushes him in the chest, as if to scold him.)*
(With a grunt of pain) Hey! Easy with those hooves—they're like cast iron. How many times do I have to tell you? Even your love taps leave bruises. I've told you till the cows come home. And bulls don't like rough

cows any more than men like rough women—remember that. What if word gets out about those hooves? If those young bachelors get wind of that, you'll never find a mate. (MŎKSOE's *head droops.*) Hey now, no need to get depressed. I'm the only one who knows about those hooves. (*Pats her on the shoulders.*) Come on. Let's get going on that potato field. (*The two of them briefly stretch and loosen up.*)

(*In a sing-song voice*) Come on, let's go, Mŏksoe—uh-uh—this way—that's it, that's it—a little faster now—that's too fast—OK, that's better. (*The sound of a lark;* CHANG-GUN *gazes up at the sky and resumes his normal tone of voice.*)

Skylark, skylark, when I hear your voice I think of Kkotbun. (*Drawing out the words ever so long.*)

Your voice resembles hers.

It always tickles my ears.

Skylark, skylark.

Kkot-bun, Kkotbun.

(*The distant bellowing of a bull;* MŎKSOE *stands tall and pricks up her ears.*)

Who told you to stop?

(*Again the bellowing of the bull.*)

(*Startled*) Yes, indeed, you hear him. (*Puts down the plow, examines* MŎKSOE *from various angles.*) Yessir—time to fix you up with a bull. Wow, what a butt!

(MŎKSOE *shows off her hindquarters and chest.*)

All right, I get the message. And I thought you weren't fully grown yet. Well, I guess we've got to fix you up. There's just one thing. (*A brief, pensive gaze at the field.*) It's going to take five days to plant this potato field. Then we'll take a day off, and the day after that—OK, then, seven days from now. (*Struck by a thought.*) Wait a minute, that's no good—that's the day Father died. Wouldn't be proper doing it then.

(MŎKSOE *moos repeatedly, the rhythm sounding like that of "What's so improper about it?"*)

"What's so improper about it?" Well! Spoken just like an animal.

(*More mooing from* MŎKSOE: *"None of your insults."*)

On the other hand, those customs don't apply to you. All right, then, even though it's the anniversary of Father's death, we'll fix you up with a bull.

(MŎKSOE *jumps for joy and moos.*)

But in return, you'll have to work hard for me.

(MŎKSOE *moos, then, without waiting for her master's command, begins plowing the field animatedly.* CHANG-GUN *chases after her. Offstage,* KKOTBUN's *bull bellows in response to* **MŎKSOE**. *The two animals repeat the exchange. The clarinet sounds, stirring up* **CHANG-GUN**, *who begins to guide the plow. The* **CLARINETIST**'s *companion begins humming.* **CHANG-GUN** *resumes his singsong voice.*)

> Come on, Mŏksoe, let's go.
> Quick now, quick, let's turn around.
> Keep your eyes on the road, or you'll be an old squinty . . .
> The sun's up high, halfway 'cross the sky . . .
> Hurry on up, it's time for lunch . . .

(**CHANG-GUN**'s *singing is out of tune with the clarinet and the humming. From a distance comes the dull roar of bombers flying in formation. The humming dies out and the clarinet stops.* **CHANG-GUN** *and* **MŎKSOE** *stop and look apprehensively toward the sky. The sound of the airplanes slowly begins to fade; everything on earth seems cruelly suffocated by it. Man and beast stand stock still gazing toward the sky until the sound fades into the distance.*)

Shitheads! Have to fly right over our village! One of these days they'll bomb us by mistake, and then what? (*Pause.*) Bang! Zing! (*Pause; then, turns in every direction with grand flourishes.*) Heads up, you sons of bitches!

(**MŎKSOE** *moos spiritedly:* "Heads up, sons of bitches!")

(*Enter Chang-gun's* **MOTHER** *carrying a wooden tub atop her head; she stops.*)

MOTHER: Now don't you be cussing at the sky.

CHANG-GUN: It wasn't the sky—it was airplanes. If they bomb us by mistake, we're dead. And all the fields'll be ruined.

MOTHER: Seems you haven't heard the news from the town over the mountain.

CHANG-GUN: What news?

MOTHER: An old fellow who lives over there saw a plane and cursed it right and left, just like you did. The pilot heard him, came down on a rope, beat the old man silly, and went back up.

CHANG-GUN (*startles, then regains his composure and looks toward the sky*): Where'd you hear that?

MOTHER: The old salt peddler told me.

CHANG-GUN: Mother, I don't believe it.

MOTHER: It's true. The old man's an in-law of the salt peddler—why would he want to lie to him? He said the pilot was some young rascal, still wet behind the ears. He was covered all over with armor that shone like white gold. Didn't say a word—just beat the man silly. (*Once again,* **CHANG-GUN** *is filled with fear; he gazes toward the sky again.*) Now don't you fret. It flew on by, so they couldn't have heard you cussing them. But from now on, when a plane goes overhead, just pretend you don't see it or hear it.

CHANG-GUN (*nods*): You do the same, Mother.

MOTHER: For sure. (*Tying a cloth wrapper around the wooden tub.*) Why don't you sit down.

CHANG-GUN: Mŏksoe—you can go back to the cowshed and have your lunch.

(**MŎKSOE** *moos and sticks out a hoof, asking for the whip.*)

After you're finished, you can take a short nap—until I count to five hundred—well, a thousand—all right, fifteen hundred. Take a rest; you've worked harder than normal today. But then back you come!

(**MŎKSOE** *moos.*)

MOTHER: We put a lot of boiled beans in your feed today.

(**MŎKSOE** *moos with excitement, then exits, doing some tricks with the whip.*)

CHANG-GUN (*pantomimes eating, then sprawls on his back*): Could you count to fifteen hundred and then wake me up?

MOTHER: All right. (**CHANG-GUN** *begins to snore.*) Sleep as long as you want. (*As if singing a lullaby.*) One . . . two . . . three . . . (*The sound of airplanes flying overhead; as if to protect her son,* **MOTHER** *raises her voice as she continues to count.*)

(*Enter* **POSTMAN A**. *Hobnails about a foot long protrude from his boots, giving him a lanky appearance.*)

POSTMAN A: Good day. I've come from the post office. (**MOTHER** *nods while continuing to count.*) I have a letter for Mr. Chang-gun. (**MOTHER** *nods again and gestures toward her son. As the* **POSTMAN** *is about to wake him,* **MOTHER** *stops him with a frown and motions for him to produce the letter. The* **POSTMAN** *takes a large, thick document from his pouch.* **MOTHER** *takes it and looks it over. Because she is illiterate, she hands it back to the postman and motions for him to read it aloud.*)

(*Scowling at her*) "Notice of conscription! O Chang-gun, Esquire, citizen of Easterly: In accordance with Article so-and-so of the Military Service Act, you are hereby conscripted into active duty. Report to the District 5 Conscript Holding Area by so many hours on such-and-such a date. In accordance with Article such- and-such of the Military Service Act, failure to comply will result in life imprisonment. The District 5 Holding Area is located at such-and-such a place. Signed on such-and-such a date, Commander in Chief of Conscription, District 5." (*With a self-important air.*) Is that clear? (*Although she doesn't understand,* **MOTHER** *nods, still counting.*) He's being ordered to report tomorrow. Do you understand? (**MOTHER** *thinks for a moment, then shakes her head.*) No?

CHANG-GUN (*waking up and stretching*): Mother!

MOTHER: Why are you awake so soon? I've only just . . . Go back to sleep.

CHANG-GUN: What a dream! (*Notices the* POSTMAN.) Mother, who's that?
MOTHER: He says he's from the post office.
CHANG-GUN: Post office? (*Paying no further attention to the* POSTMAN.) Mother, I dreamed I was a soldier and went off to war—what do you think of that?
MOTHER: Like I say, you always have the silliest dreams when you're nodding off. Now go back to sleep.
CHANG-GUN: God, it was scary! Shells this big, whizzing like lightning, right into my mouth.
MOTHER: That's enough, son. You think instead about what the gentleman brought here. I don't have the slightest notion what it's about . . .
POSTMAN A: O Chang-gun, it's true—you're going in the army. These are your orders.
CHANG-GUN: Huh? What do you mean? (*Reads the notice.*)
MOTHER: Is it true, Son?
CHANG-GUN: Looks that way.
MOTHER: Heavens! What am I going to do? If I had known, I never would have accepted the letter.
POSTMAN A: In any village there's always a couple of obstinate mothers who do the same thing. (*To* CHANG-GUN.) I need your thumbprint here. (CHANG-GUN *stamps the document with his thumb.*) (*Aside.*) It's as big as my big toe! (*To* CHANG-GUN *and his* MOTHER.) Twenty years ago, I saw action when we went to war with Westerly. Because I'm so short, I was chosen for company liaison work. By the time the war was over I had shuttled between the company command post and the battalion command post 3,365 times. I was really lucky. (*Gesturing to various parts of his body.*) A bullet whizzed by here, another one there, and another one there. I've never told any of this to my mother. Can you imagine the shock it would give her? (*As if recalling a time he wants to relive.*) Whenever I think back to that time, it seems like a dream. (*Gestures again to various parts of his body where he narrowly escaped being wounded and then, oblivious to* CHANG-GUN *and his* MOTHER, *swaggers offstage.*)
CHANG-GUN: Mother! I'm going to tell Kkotbun.
MOTHER (*vacantly*): If I'd known this, I would have helped him marry Kkotbun a long time ago.
CHANG-GUN: Would you tell Mŏksoe that she can sleep for another fifteen hundred? (*Exiting.*) Kkotbun! (*Continues to call her from backstage, his voice becoming distant.*)
MOTHER (*listens dully for a time to his voice, then suddenly*): My son.
(*Clarinet and humming. Exit* MOTHER. *Exit* TREES *from the potato field.*)

SCENE 2: BESIDE A WELL

(*Clarinet and humming; the sun is in the same place as in the previous scene. A luxuriant* TREE *glides onstage. Enter* KKOTBUN *carrying a water jar on her head and toting a huge wooden crate. She sets down the crate center stage, where it serves as a well. Pantomimes filling her water jar and sings.*)

KKOTBUN:
    Drip drop, plink plunk, spring water
    Dripping like milk from my mother's breast
    Dripping like wee-wee from a bed-wetting boy
    Night and day
    Drip drop, plink plunk, drip drop, plink plunk
(*"Kkotbun!" from offstage. Enter* CHANG-GUN. *He walks up to* KKOTBUN.)
CHANG-GUN (*calls one last time, longer and louder*): Kkotbun!
KKOTBUN: Whenever I hear your voice, it makes me happy.
CHANG-GUN: Kkotbun! (*Again, the name is drawn out; pause.*) Take a look.
KKOTBUN: What's that? (*Pause. Reads; her face takes on a vacant expression.*)
CHANG-GUN: I might get killed by a shell.
KKOTBUN (*pause*): Not everyone who goes in the army gets killed!
CHANG-GUN: Well, what about Soedol, Puksoe, and Ch'ilbo? Didn't they all get killed? Ch'ilwŏl and Tolsoe, too . . .
(*A bull and a cow call each other in the distance.*)
KKOTBUN: Chang-gun, let's get married—right here. (CHANG-GUN *looks puzzled.*) We'll go behind that tree and get married. We'll make a baby before you go in the army.
CHANG-GUN: Are you, crazy?!
(KKOTBUN *takes* CHANG-GUN *by the hand and leads him behind the* TREE. *The call of magpies, then skylarks. The sun turns its face away. The* TREE *bends to conceal the couple. The* CLARINETIST *and the* HUMMING WOMAN *approach the* TREE *and produce romantic music, then return to their seats. Eventually the couple reappears and strolls toward the audience. The* TREE *straightens.* CHANG-GUN *begins to scratch his back ferociously.*)
KKOTBUN: What's the matter?
CHANG-GUN: I think I got ants crawling all over me. (*Finds some and tosses them aside.*) Get out of here, you!
KKOTBUN: You bad ants! You shameless insects!
CHANG-GUN: I'd better get going. Got to plow that potato field. Make things easier for Mother while I'm gone.
KKOTBUN (*stops*): Do you think it'll be a boy or a girl?

CHANG-GUN: I hope it's twins—one of each . . . (*Exits*.)
KKOTBUN (*a dull expression on her face; then, abruptly*): My husband.
   (*Clarinet and humming. Exit* **KKOTBUN**. *Exit* **TREE**. *Lights out*.)

SCENE 3: TRAINING CAMP A

(*Darkness, the clomp of combat boots of marching soldiers. A noncom reprimands the soldiers in the strident squawk of a heron: "Worthless son of a bitch." "Piece of shit." "Forward march!" "To the rear, march!" Atten-shun!" "Open your eyes!" And so on. Then, a notch louder: "Count off!" "One"—"two"— "three"—"five." "Again!" "One"—"two"—"three"—"five." "Again!" The stage brightens to reveal barbed wire strung slantwise across the stage. Upstage of the barbed wire, Private* **O CHANG-GUN** *and the other members of his infantry squad are standing in line counting off. It is* **CHANG-GUN** *who has been calling out "five" instead of "four"; he does so again.*)

ASSISTANT DRILL INSTRUCTOR: You! Step out! . . . Don't you know how to count?
CHANG-GUN: I do, sir!
ASSISTANT DRILL INSTRUCTOR: Then do it.
CHANG-GUN: One, two, three, four, five, six—
ASSISTANT DRILL INSTRUCTOR: That's enough—back in line.
CHANG-GUN: Yes sir!
ASSISTANT DRILL INSTRUCTOR: Good-for-nothing idiot!
CHANG-GUN (*rejoining the ranks*): Yes sir!
   (*Laughter from the other recruits.*)
ASSISTANT DRILL INSTRUCTOR: Can the laughter! Count off!
   (*Blissfully unaware,* **CHANG-GUN** *again mistakenly shouts "Five!" The lights fade to the sound of the clarinet.*)

SCENE 4: TRAINING CAMP B

(*In the darkness, the voice of the* **DRILL INSTRUCTOR** *from just offstage.*)

DRILL INSTRUCTOR: I'll now conclude this lecture on the methods of nighttime infiltration.
   Assistant drill instructor! Lights!

(*Lights. Behind the barbed wire is a machine-gun nest.*)

Let's suppose that machine gun is the target of our attack. We should anticipate three obstacles between us and the target. Number one, mines. Let's assume for the moment that we're lucky enough to avoid them. Number two, barbed wire. As a rule, it's equipped with a warning signal. But let's assume once again that we're lucky enough to be able to climb over it. Number three, the enemies' eyes. And if we're fortunate, we'll avoid them. If things work out this way, then the infiltration will be perfect. But the fact of the matter is, there's no such luck. Most infiltration attempts sooner or later are detected by the enemy and meet resistance in the form of heavy fire, exploding mines, and barbed wire, so you have to force your way through. So we'll have infiltration training, starting with Squad 1. During the infiltration one of the land mines will explode, and you'll be exposed to live machine-gun fire. But the bullets will travel five feet above the ground. Assistant drill instructors, see to it that the firing is kept at that height!

(**ASSISTANT DRILL INSTRUCTORS A** *and* **B** *lay themselves prone in front of the machine-gun nest; each raises a plank straight up in the air.*)

Machine gun, fire!

(*The machine-gun barrel spits fire, splintering the two planks at a height of about five feet.*)

Lights out! (*As soon as the lights dim.*) Starting with First Squad, forward!

(*The darkness is punctuated by the sound of the machine-gun fire and the explosion of a land mine.*) For-ward! Move! . . . Hey! What the hell are you doing?! You! What are you doing?! . . . Lights!

(*The stage brightens to reveal* **CHANG-GUN** *huddled on the ground, trembling.*)

Assistant drill instructors, who is this idiot? What? P'o Chang-gun? O Chang-gun. O Chang-gun, what do you think you're doing there? . . . Stop the firing! Assistant drill instructors, get over there!

(*The two* **ASSISTANT DRILL INSTRUCTORS** *run to where* **CHANG-GUN** *is huddled and look down at him.*)

ASSISTANT DRILL INSTRUCTOR A: Fuckup!
ASSISTANT DRILL INSTRUCTOR B: Asshole!
DRILL INSTRUCTOR: Kick him.

(**ASSISTANT A** *kicks* **CHANG-GUN**, *then* **ASSISTANT B**. *No reaction from* **CHANG-GUN**. *The two* **ASSISTANT DRILL INSTRUCTORS** *look in the direction from which the* **DRILL INSTRUCTOR**'s *voice is coming, awaiting further orders.*) Another one!

(*The two* ASSISTANTS *each give* CHANG-GUN *another kick. Again, no reaction. They await further orders.*) Is he dead?
ASSISTANT DRILL INSTRUCTORS A and B (*together*): Alive, sir!
DRILL INSTRUCTOR: Worthless piece of shit! Bring him here!
   (CHANG-GUN *is dragged offstage, eyes gaping, body trembling. He cannot stand, as if the lower half of his body is paralyzed.*) Lights out! Resume the exercise! Machine gun, fire! Second Squad, forward!
   (*Darkness. The sound of gunfire continues for a time. Then, the clarinet.*)

SCENE 5: INFIRMARY OFFICE

(*Lights up to reveal the* MEDICAL OFFICER, *stethoscope around his neck; an inexperienced* INTERN, *who still has the look of a student; a* NURSE, *who resembles* KKOTBUN.)

MEDICAL OFFICER: How long have you been an intern?
INTERN: This is my first week.
MEDICAL OFFICER: You'll need to learn how to distinguish the soldiers who are faking illness.
INTERN: Yes sir.
   (*Enter* CHANG-GUN, *supported by* ASSISTANT DRILL INSTRUCTORS A *and* B.)
MEDICAL OFFICER (*with a knowing glance at the* INTERN): Sit him down there.
ASSISTANT DRILL INSTRUCTOR A: He can't sit up by himself.
MEDICAL OFFICER: Was he wounded in the butt?
ASSISTANT DRILL INSTRUCTOR A: No, sir.
MEDICAL OFFICER: Well?
ASSISTANT DRILL INSTRUCTOR A: During an exercise, he suddenly . . .
MEDICAL OFFICER: Turned into a jellyfish, is that it?
ASSISTANT DRILL INSTRUCTOR A: Yes, sir.
MEDICAL OFFICER: I'll take care of him. (*Swaggers over to* CHANG-GUN *and speaks in a menacing tone.*) You—sit up right now, or you can kiss your ass goodbye! (*To the two* ASSISTANT DRILL INSTRUCTORS.) Sit him down!
   (*The two* DRILL INSTRUCTORS *do so.* CHANG-GUN *remains standing up. The* DRILL INSTRUCTORS *are astonished.*)
   (*To the* INTERN) Note that! (*Roughly examines* CHANG-GUN's *neck, then pulls out his military identification tag.*) Military ID number—O 24378596. Name—O Chang-gun. Rank—private second class. Occupation—farmer. Education—three years of winter vacation reading and writing instruction from the high school literacy volunteers.

INTERN: How could you know without asking him!?
MEDICAL OFFICER: "Experience is your best teacher"—Carlisle. Note that! We'll start the clinical examination now. You two, explain the circumstances.
ASSISTANT DRILL INSTRUCTOR A: An infiltration exercise had begun.
ASSISTANT DRILL INSTRUCTOR B: First Squad charged.
ASSISTANT DRILL INSTRUCTOR A: They were detected by the enemy.
ASSISTANT DRILL INSTRUCTOR B. Machine-gun fire at five feet.
ASSISTANT DRILL INSTRUCTOR A: Simulated explosion of a land mine.
ASSISTANT DRILL INSTRUCTOR B: First Squad continued their charge.
MEDICAL OFFICER: All right. And this soldier wouldn't move?
ASSISTANT DRILL INSTRUCTORS A and **B:** Yes, sir.
MEDICAL OFFICER: Note the following! Diagnosis—nervous breakdown and a state of helplessness caused by mine explosion and machine-gun fire. (*Gestures to indicate that the examination is over; takes out a cigarette.*)
  Treatment: (*Lights the cigarette.*) Continue training, exposing him often to frightening situations until he is no longer frightened . . . (*To the* **NURSE**.) Two cc's of epidrine! (*The* **NURSE** *injects* **CHANG-GUN**.)
CHANG-GUN (*stares intently at the* **NURSE**): Kkotbun! (*Nods off.*)
MEDICAL OFFICER: Lay him down! (*The two* **DRILL INSTRUCTORS** *lay* **CHANG-GUN** *on the floor.*)
INTERN: "Kkotbun"? Is that what he said?
MEDICAL OFFICER: Sister complex. Probably the name of an older sister.
  (*The* **INTERN** *nods, satisfied with this explanation. All look down at the snoring* **CHANG-GUN**.) Definitely a farmer.
  (*The* **INTERN** *nods. Again, all look down at* **CHANG-GUN**. *The lights dim; all except* **CHANG-GUN** *exit. The mooing of* **MŎKSOE** *in the distance.*)
CHANG-GUN (*in his sleep*): Kkotbun! Kkotbun!
  (*Suddenly* **KKOTBUN** *appears at his side.*)
KKOTBUN: My goodness, you're quite the soldier now.
CHANG-GUN (*eyes closed*): Do I look scary like the other soldiers?
KKOTBUN: Uh-huh. And you're using a gun?
CHANG-GUN: Sure. Today I almost killed myself—the rifle went off by mistake.
KKOTBUN: Oh, my goodness.
CHANG-GUN: How many letters have you got from me?
KKOTBUN: Eleven.
CHANG-GUN: The twelfth's right here. (*Indicates his head.*) Want to hear it?
KKOTBUN: No—I like getting it in the mail.
CHANG-GUN: Every night I dream about you.

KKOTBUN: A dream where we're sleeping together?
CHANG-GUN: What about you?
KKOTBUN: Me, too.
CHANG-GUN: Last night I dreamed we were near the spring where you do the wash.

    We were side by side, pissing—you squatting, me standing. A couple of tree frogs were watching us. (**KKOTBUN** *laughs.* **CHANG-GUN** *also laughs, shifting from side to side in his sleep, then suddenly is quiet. He slips into a deep short sleep.*) So, any sign of our baby yet?

KKOTBUN: A few days ago something strange started happening.
CHANG-GUN: Yeah? What was that?
KKOTBUN: It feels like something's growing down low in my belly.
CHANG-GUN: Has to be our baby. I'll bet it's twins. Take good care of 'em. Make sure your quilt's tucked nice and snug around your belly at night.
KKOTBUN: All right, I'll be careful. (*Gathers the folds of her skirt and holds them against her abdomen.*) I'm off. (*Exits.*)
CHANG-GUN (*getting to his feet as a sleepwalker would*): Take care. (*Pause; then abruptly.*) My wife! (*Collapses and sinks into a deep sleep, breathing heavily.*) (*Humming; pause; clarinet.*)

SCENE 6: TRAINING CAMP C

(*Darkness; then a spotlight on the* **PERSONNEL OFFICER**.)

PERSONNEL OFFICER (*in an effeminate tone*): Allow me to introduce myself; I'm the personnel officer at training camp headquarters. Private O Chang-gun's regiment finished the prescribed course of training this morning. During this time, O Chang-gun's training record was as follows: (*Displaying a chart.*) Marksmanship—zero; disassembling firearms—zero; squad tactics—zero; conduct off the field— two points. Awards and punishment: he received no awards and was disciplined twice. The first time, he was sentenced to two days' hard labor for using the generals' toilet. The commandant of the training camp was forced to wait thirty minutes outside the toilet while someone sang inside; the man was discovered to be Private O Chang-gun. The second time, he was confined to the guardhouse for three days for being absent without leave from a nighttime search exercise. On the night in question, Private O Chang-gun's regiment suspended their exercise in order to discover his whereabouts. Three hours later he was found asleep next to a cow on a farm bordering the training field... Tomorrow at 0830 hours, Private O Chang-gun's regiment is to be transferred to a unit under the command of the Fifth Field Army. Before these recruits are sent to the front line, samples of their fingernails and hair must be collected in case they become casualties and their remains cannot otherwise be identified. (*Lights. Behind the* **PERSONNEL OFFICER**, *all the* **RECRUITS** *are trimming their fingernails with huge scissors, except for* **CHANG-GUN**, *who is trimming his toenails.*)

Hurry it up, men.

SOLDIERS (*in unison*): Yes sir.

SOLDIER A: If I'd known about this, I would've kept them long.

SOLDIER B: I'd hate to think of my wife and little boy bowing down in from of my dirty fingernails.

SOLDIER C: Then get rid of the dirt, like me.

SOLDIER B: Hey, that's a swell idea. Well, here goes. (*Spits on his fingernail clippings. then rubs them clean.*)

PERSONNEL OFFICER: Private O Chang-gun! I ordered you to cut your fingernails—I didn't say anything about toenails.

CHANG-GUN: I already cut my fingernails, sir.

SOLDIER B: So, you figure on having your family bow in front of your toenails, too.

SOLDIER A: I guess I might as well cut my toenails, too.

SOLDIER C: And me.

SOLDIER B: Me too.

(*All the recruits bend over and trim their toenails. They fall silent, thinking about death. Clarinet and humming.*)

PERSONNEL OFFICER (*suddenly vehement*): Stop it right there! Atten-shun! I know what you men are thinking. You're thinking about death. Let me tell you something: the more you think about death, the more it works its way inside you and pretty soon you feel awful. To help you men get rid of your awful thoughts, we're going to have ourselves a little singsong. I'll go first.

(*The* **PERSONNEL OFFICER** *sings. The* **SOLDIERS** *look on, their faces blank. The clarinet joins in but is silenced by the* **WOMAN**. *Her humming begins to disrupt the* **PERSONNEL OFFICER**'s *song. Clarinet and humming.*)

SCENE 7: CHANG-GUN'S POTATO FIELD

(*Clarinet and humming; the* **TREES** *have taken their former places onstage; Chang-gun's* **MOTHER** *and* **MŎKSOE** *are plowing the field. The sun wears a sullen expression.*)

MOTHER: Mŏksoe, not so fast. I'm not Chang-gun, you know . . . (**MŎKSOE** *moos:* "Got it—not so fast, not so fast." *Pause. The plowing continues. Sighing, Chang-gun's* **MOTHER** *plaintively but mechanically hums a work song in time with her steps. Then, ever so dolefully, she sings.*)

    Chang-gun, my Chang-gun

    Son, my son . . .

(**MŎKSOE** *moos sorrowfully in time with the song. The humming* **WOMAN** *joins in. Looking at* **MOTHER** *and the cow, you would think they were bearing a coffin. With the same melody,* **MOTHER** *says, "Oh, my aching back," then squats.*)

(**MŎKSOE** *moos once, following the same melody, and settles on the ground. The sound of airplanes flying in formation overhead. Enter* **KKOTBUN**.)

KKOTBUN: Mother!

MOTHER: Well, hello. I see you've got another letter.

KKOTBUN: Yes, indeed. I'll read it for you: "Letter number twelve. How is everyone?"

MOTHER: The poor boy—I keep telling him not to fret over us.

KKOTBUN: Yes, I wish he wouldn't. "I dreamed of home again last night."

MOTHER: With all those dreams, when does he find time to sleep? . . .

KKOTBUN: Yes, really. "I dreamed Mother is still plowing the field."

MOTHER: Well, you're right. If you were here, though, we'd be done by now . . .

KKOTBUN: "And Kkotbun said she was pregnant, and her belly's sticking way out." Will you listen to that!

MOTHER: Crazy boy! I thought they'd cure him of those wild dreams once he went in the army . . . What next?

KKOTBUN: "And I have a hunch that she really is pregnant with our baby."

MOTHER: That boy—he must be out of his mind! (*Pause.*) Kkotbun, you know how women get pregnant. You do, don't you?

KKOTBUN: Oh, Mother!

MOTHER: Sure you do. There's a way to make a baby, and unless you do it like that, you don't get pregnant. It's been that way since long, long ago . . . Tell me what he says next.

KKOTBUN: "Here in the infirmary there's a nurse who looks just like you."

MOTHER: A one-track mind.

KKOTBUN (*laughs*): "I've heard we're leaving for the front line in a few days. Well, time for me to stop now—I have to stand the night watch."

MOTHER: Is that it?

KKOTBUN: Yes.

MOTHER: Kkotbun, how about giving me that letter?

KKOTBUN: All right. But . . .

MOTHER: I'll keep it in my waistband and then give it to you tomorrow. All right?
KKOTBUN: Sure.
(*Pause.*)
MOTHER: He said he'd be going to the front line in a few days?
KKOTBUN: Yes.
MOTHER: The front line—that's where they all get killed. But I hope it doesn't turn out that way.
KKOTBUN: Me too.
MOTHER: I know a lot of people get killed there. (*Pause.*) Did he ever say when the war's going to end?
KKOTBUN: I don't believe so.
MOTHER: Well, it has to end sometime.
KKOTBUN: I would think so.
(*Pause.*)
MOTHER: Wouldn't it be wonderful if it was today?
KKOTBUN: What would be wonderful?
MOTHER: If the war ended today. (*Pause; the sound of airplanes flying in formation.*)
   Seems like the planes are coming by more often these days.
KKOTBUN: Yes.

(*The sound of the airplanes seems to blanket the sky. The two women look up at the sky, Chang-gun's* MOTHER *caressing the letter,* KKOTBUN *rubbing her stomach. Pause.* MOTHER *covers her eyes with her hand to hide her tears.* KKOTBUN, *doing likewise, slowly exits.* MŎKSOE *approaches* MOTHER *and holds out the whip.* MOTHER *takes the whip, listlessly rises, and begins plowing. Exhausted, she gradually begins to nod off while plowing. Finally, she sinks softly to the ground,* MŎKSOE'S *reins in her hands.* MŎKSOE *continues forward a moment, and the reins are pulled from* MOTHER'S *hand.* MOTHER *falls asleep where she is. It is a few moments before* MŎKSOE *realizes that* MOTHER *is sleeping. She quietly approaches, looks down at her for a moment, then turns to the audience and moos ever so plaintively . . .* MOTHER *is startled awake by the mooing; she bolts up to a sitting position . . .* MŎKSOE *stops mooing, has* MOTHER *lie down, and pats her until she goes back to sleep. But she can't make her patting gentle enough, and* MOTHER *awakens.* MŎKSOE *pats* MOTHER *very carefully and helps her back to sleep, then turns to the audience and purses her mouth in a silent moo . . .* MŎKSOE *resumes plowing, this time by herself, mooing very softly to the tune of a field song.* MOTHER *takes long, wheezing breaths as she sleeps. In the space of two or three breaths, the stage darkens, with only a spotlight remaining on* MOTHER. *Enter* CHANG-GUN. *He looks down at his* MOTHER *for a while.*)

CHANG-GUN: Mother . . . Mother . . .

MOTHER (*slowly rising*): I see you only in my dreams.

CHANG-GUN: And you come to me only in my dreams . . .

MOTHER: You'd think I could visit you at least once while I'm awake.

CHANG-GUN: How many times do I have to tell you? I can't move an inch off the base without leave. Dreams are the only place I can walk free without a pass.

MOTHER: Now don't get cross . . . Have you eaten dinner yet?

CHANG-GUN: Mother, it's daytime now. It's daytime and you're dreaming.

MOTHER: Goodness, you're right.

CHANG-GUN (*looking attentively at her*): Mother, you look so much older.

MOTHER: Since you left, a day seems like a year.

CHANG-GUN: Mother. I want you to have a long life.

MOTHER: Well, I ought to be able to hang on until you come home, at any rate . . . But there's something I'm thinking about more than that—I'm thinking how wonderful if I could trade a few years of my life to make yours a few years longer.

CHANG-GUN: Where'd you come up with a damn-fool idea like that?

MOTHER: Father in heaven, I'd die on the spot if only I could.

CHANG-GUN: You think God's going to bother himself with stuff like that? (MŎKSOE *bellows*.) Uh-oh, another assembly. Mother, take care.

MOTHER: Wait a minute—what's the hurry?

CHANG-GUN: Didn't you hear that shout? It means there's an assembly.

MOTHER: You simpleton—that's Mŏksoe! (MŎKSOE *bellows again*.) Does that sound like a shout to you?

CHANG-GUN: OK, OK. It's just that whenever I hear a loud noise it sounds like the call for assembly. (*Chuckles*.) I'd better get back anyway. Mother, take care.

MOTHER: Hold on, Son, why the hurry? This is a dream. Take your time.

CHANG-GUN: I'm sorry, Mom, but like I said, in the army they don't give you any time to chitchat.

MOTHER: For goodness sake. Son—Son . . . (*Eyes closed, she reaches out toward the vanishing figure of her son. Shortly, she slumps easily to the round and sleeps, sobbing*.)

(*Lights. Enter* POSTMAN B. *Like* POSTMAN A, *he is lanky*.)

POSTMAN B: Ma'am. Say, ma'am. (MOTHER *awakens and looks up at the* POSTMAN. *Indifferent to his arrival, she continues sobbing*.) Ma'am . . . Ma'am.

(MOTHER *regains her composure and looks up again at the* POSTMAN.)

You're the mother of Mr. O Chang-gun, are you not? I have some mail.

MOTHER: Goodness gracious, a letter from my son.

POSTMAN B: I'm afraid not. It's a letter for your son.

MOTHER: It is? Who could it be from? I can't read—would you tell me what it says?

POSTMAN B: By all means. "Notice of conscription. O Chang-gun, Esquire. In accordance with Article so-and-so of the Military Service Act, you are hereby conscripted into active service. Report to the District 5 Conscript Holding Area by so many hours on such-and-such a date. In accordance with Article so-and-so of the Military Service Act, failure to comply will result in life imprisonment. Signed on such-and-such a date, Commander in Chief of Conscription, District 5."

MOTHER: Haven't I heard that somewhere before?

POSTMAN B: Simply put, they're telling your son he's been drafted.

MOTHER: Well, I knew it sounded familiar. I'm afraid you just missed him, Mister.

POSTMAN B: Missed him?

MOTHER: A letter like that came for him a couple of weeks ago from another gentleman.

POSTMAN B: What?!

MOTHER: Maybe they don't know he arrived at training camp? I suppose . . . But it's two weeks since he left.

POSTMAN B: It's impossible. Are you serious?

MOTHER (*producing the letter from her waistband*): Take a look at this if you don't believe me.

POSTMAN B (*quickly reads*): "Letter number twelve." (*Reads on, occasionally aloud.*) "How is everyone doing? . . . had another dream of home again last night . . . Mother still plowing the field? . . . really is pregnant with our child . . . belly sticking way out . . . have to stand the night watch." (*Looks back and forth from the letter to* **MOTHER**, *then returns the letter.*)

(*Clarinet. Exit* **POSTMAN B** *and* **TREES**. *Exit* **MŎKSOE**, *leading* **MOTHER**, *who is holding the reins.*)

SCENE 8: THE BUREAUCRATIC REALM

(*Positioned on the stage in the form of a triangle are* **BUREAUCRATS A, B,** *and* **C**. **BUREAUCRAT A** *represents the postal service.* **BUREAUCRAT B** *represents District 5 Conscription Headquarters.* **BUREAUCRAT C** *represents army headquarters. All three wear an expressionless air of officialdom. Chang-gun's* **MOTHER** *and* **KKOTBUN** *stand before* **BUREAUCRAT A**.)

BUREAUCRAT A: The cause of this error is that there are two young men by the name of O Chang-gun in the same neighborhood.

MOTHER: But aren't their faces completely different?

KKOTBUN: And my fiancé is big as an ox, but the son of that wealthy O family is slender like a deer.

OFFICIAL A: We immediately dismissed the postman who delivered the conscription notice by mistake. At the same time, we have notified District 5 Conscription Headquarters about it. Still, O Chang-gun must also bear responsibility.

KKOTBUN: How so?

OFFICIAL A: Did he not accept a conscription notice?

MOTHER: All he did was take what was given him.

BUREAUCRAT A: At the end of every conscription notice is the date of birth of the recipient—year, month, day. The birthdate on this notice is that of Mr. O's son and not your son, Madam.

MOTHER: I thought maybe you gentlemen had gotten it wrong.

BUREAUCRAT A: But the notice also has an address. Mr. O's family is number 124, yours is 125.

MOTHER: Since when?

BUREAUCRAT A (*pause*): Miss, why don't you go with Grandmother here and see the commander in chief of conscription. I'll write you an introduction. (*Takes out a notepad, jots down a few words, puts the message in an envelope, and hands it to* **KKOTBUN**. **MOTHER** *and* **KKOTBUN** *move to* **BUREAUCRAT B**.)

(*Aside*) Who the hell would have thought there'd be two fellows named O Chang-gun? What's so special about that name?

BUREAUCRAT B: These two conscription notices were in perfect order. Didn't they tell you that at the post office?

KKOTBUN: They told us to come here, and you would take care of it.

BUREAUCRAT B (*to the* **MOTHER**): Madam, we have just issued a request that the conscription notice whereby your son mistakenly entered the army be returned, said notice then to be delivered to the other O Chang-gun.

MOTHER: So, if that notice gets returned, then my son gets returned, too?

BUREAUCRAT B: I'm not so sure about that. But I'll write you a letter of introduction to the army authorities. (*Aside, while the* **MOTHER** *and* **KKOTBUN** *are approaching* **BUREAUCRAT C**.) It wouldn't matter to us if there were three people named O Chang-gun. The important thing is to fill in the date of birth and the address correctly.

BUREAUCRAT C: In order to prevent this kind of mistake, the army authorities try to verify these particulars at the conscript holding area. According to our investigation, at the time Private O Chang-gun's date of birth and address were being checked at the holding area, he didn't say a word about any mistake.

MOTHER (*nervously*): My son has a bad habit of saying yes to whatever anyone asks him. He's just a babe in the woods.

BUREAUCRAT C: You, acknowledge, then, that the army authorities did no wrong?

KKOTBUN: All we want is to have him back.

BUREAUCRAT C: I realize that. At the same time, please understand that his joining the army in place of another, and his having been assigned an identification number as a private in the army, are two entirely separate matters. If he really did join the army as a result of someone else's draft notice, then by all rights he should be discharged. But standard army regulations don't outline a procedure for discharging someone on the grounds that he joined the army in place of another. I'm afraid we need to enact a new set of army regulations straightaway. To enact those regulations requires time. But because it's wartime, everyone's busy. And it's difficult to assemble all the members of the army regulations committee in one place. Madam, you're familiar with General Ch'oe, I presume? You aren't?! Why, he's the greatest military strategist in our country. Last night his daughter-in-law gave birth to twins, but he was so involved in his duties that he read only half of the telegram. I had to read him the rest. (*Chuckles, then abruptly stops.*) At any rate, we'll do our best to resolve this matter concerning your son.

KKOTBUN: A few days ago we received a letter from him saying he would soon be posted at the front.

MOTHER: He's been at the training camp only a couple of weeks, you know.

BUREAUCRAT C: There's been an unexpected increase in the number of casualties at the front, and so we've been compelled to shorten the training period for the recruits.

KKOTBUN: Could you do something before he leaves for the front?

BUREAUCRAT C: I'll do my best.

MOTHER: Oh, Chang-gun, my unfortunate Chang-gun, my boy.

(**KKOTBUN** *puts an arm around* **MOTHER** *and places her other hand on her own stomach. They exit slowly,* **KKOTBUN** *supporting* **MOTHER**.)

BUREAUCRAT C: O Chang-gun—five generals—a five-star general! (*Touches his own insignia.*)

(*Clarinet.*)

SCENE 9: ON THE ROAD TO THE FRONT

(*Some* **SOLDIERS** *are sitting in the back of a camouflaged armored truck. The road is bumpy, and the* **SOLDIERS** *are being shaken about. The road goes up a hill and down, is crossed by a ditch, and then turns to gravel. The shaking is squashing the* **SOLDIERS** *together.*)

SOLDIER A: Driver! Driver!
DRIVER: "Military driver" is the correct form of address.
SOLDIER A: Military driver!
DRIVER: "Military driver, sir"! I'm a private first class, you know.
SOLDIER A: Military driver, sir!
DRIVER: Yes?
SOLDIER A: Could you go a bit slower?
  (*The* **DRIVER** *drives more roughly. Pause.*)
SOLDIER A: My insides feel like they're upside down.
SOLDIER B: My butt feels like it's been rubbed ragged.
SOLDIER C: I feel like my head's full of gravel.
  (*Pause.*)
CHANG-GUN (*nodding off*): Nothing's more comfortable than riding on the back of a cow.
  (*Pause.*)
DRIVER (*abruptly stopping the truck and getting out*): Everybody out and take a leak!
  (*The* **SOLDIERS** *get out.*)
SOLDIER A: How much farther do we have to go?
DRIVER: Twelve miles.
SOLDIER B: God, look how yellow it is!
SOLDIER C: Mine too!
  (*The other* **SOLDIERS** *look their way, then urinate in turn.*)
DRIVER: Get it all out—every last drop. The front line's going to scare the piss out of you . . .
  (*The distant sound of artillery.*)
SOLDIERS: Do you hear those guns?
  (*The* **SOLDIERS** *strain to listen. The boom of the artillery gradually grows louder. Clarinet.*)

SCENE 10: THE OFFICE OF THE EASTERLY FIELD ARMY COMMANDER

(*The* INTELLIGENCE OFFICER *is conducting a briefing in front of a huge map showing the current progress of the war.*)

INTELLIGENCE OFFICER: In addition, our air reconnaissance confirms not only that the enemy's artillery has moved en masse more than six miles forward but also that the enemy has suspended its defense-works operation and is continuing on a daily basis only with its infiltration training. Apart from that, various pieces of information, considered all together, lead us to three certain conclusions: first, the enemy knows that our forces lack the capability to take the offensive; second, the enemy will attack us within a week; and, third, the main thrust of the attack will certainly be against the vanguard of our Fourth Army Corps.

FIELD ARMY COMMANDER: Hmmm, so the enemy knows that the territory held by our Fourth Army Corps is precisely our weakest area. (*Pause.*) Intelligence officer, your report fails to mention that the commander of the enemy forces has at his disposal a much more capable intelligence officer than I do. (*Pause.*) Operations officer—

OPERATIONS OFFICER: Yes sir.

(*The* COMMANDER *gestures with his chin for the* OPERATIONS OFFICER *to go up to the map and present his briefing. The* OFFICER *does so.*)

OPERATIONS OFFICER: If it's true, as the intelligence officer reports, that the enemy is venturing a counterattack, then I propose withdrawing our forces to line B. I've concluded that the advantages offered by line B's location would likely offset the enemy's superior strength.

FIELD ARMY COMMANDER: If we initiate a defensive operation at our present line of advance, we'd have to expect our forces to sustain some losses, wouldn't we?

OPERATIONS OFFICER: Such an operation would probably require two divisions.

FIELD ARMY COMMANDER: Advancing from line B to our present position required one division. If we withdraw to line B and then advance to our present position again, we'll use up another division. And to make a stand at line B would also require a division. I'd rather use those two divisions here.

OPERATIONS OFFICER: But don't forget that if we settle in at line B, we could maximize the enemy's losses; those losses would be considerably less at our present line of advance.

FIELD ARMY COMMANDER: I've never retreated from a forward line. I take that back—it happened once, when I was wounded in the shoulder. (*Maneuvering his shoulder and wincing.*) Goddamned injury's like the tail of a bitch in heat. Come sniffing around, and it perks right up. (*Resolutely.*) We'll maintain our present position at the front. Effective immediately, the authority of the various commanders shall be expanded so that they can summarily punish any officers or men who attempt to retreat. One week from now, there will be two new infantry divisions and a cavalry division under the command of the field army, to be supplemented by a heavy artillery brigade. Until then, we shall withstand the enemy's attacks at our present position and then launch a counterattack. (*To the* **INTELLIGENCE OFFICER**.) I'll see you now. (*To the other* **OFFICERS**.) Gentlemen—dis-missed (*Exit remaining* **OFFICERS**. *Long pause.*) If the enemy carries through its plan of attack, we'll be completely cut off from the rear, won't we? (*Pause.*) Accordingly, my determination is quite reckless, wouldn't you say? (*Pause.*) War is a high-stakes game. And I'm going to take a gamble. In gambling you don't always win with a good hand. A fellow with a worthless hand can bluff a fellow with a full house. (*Assumes an all-knowing expression.*)

INTELLIGENCE OFFICER: Sir, are you suggesting a counterintelligence operation?

FIELD ARMY COMMANDER: Exactly. If we can get the enemy to overestimate our capabilities, they might abandon their plans to attack. Under the assumption that this counterintelligence operation will succeed, I've determined to maintain our present position.

INTELLIGENCE OFFICER: But what are the odds that such an operation will succeed?

FIELD ARMY COMMANDER: Doesn't matter. Gamblers always bet that they'll win. Besides, in this particular game, there's nothing to lose. (*Pause.*) Choose your most capable intelligence officer and have him get captured in a natural way and devise a means to slip the enemy this misinformation under interrogation.

INTELLIGENCE OFFICER: Yes sir. I understand.

(*While massaging his shoulders, the* **FIELD ARMY COMMANDER** *gestures with his chin for the other to leave. Exit* **INTELLIGENCE OFFICER**.)

FIELD ARMY COMMANDER: Aide-de-camp! (*Enter* **AIDE-DE-CAMP**.)
Have you found a soldier to massage my shoulders?

AIDE-DE-CAMP: Yes sir. Among the troops who arrived today there's a fellow who's strong as a gorilla.

FIELD ARMY COMMANDER: Oh? Well, bring him in.
AIDE-DE-CAMP: Yes sir. (*Exit.*)
(FIELD ARMY COMMANDER *sits down in a chair, massaging his shoulder. Enter* CHANG-GUN, *making an awkward attempt to goose-step because he is full of tension. He comes to an abrupt halt at a distance from the* COMMANDER *and salutes in a flash.*)
CHANG-GUN (*screaming, his voice cracking so that it's almost impossible to understand him*): Private O Chang-gun reporting to massage your shoulders, sir!
FIELD ARMY COMMANDER: I see. Now what did you say your name was?
CHANG-GUN: O Chang-gun, sir!
FIELD ARMY COMMANDER: O Chang-gun?
CHANG-GUN: Yes sir!
FIELD ARMY COMMANDER: I see. (*To himself.*) O Chang-gun, eh?
CHANG-GUN (*mistakenly thinking he's being addressed*): Yes sir!
FIELD ARMY COMMANDER (*with a forbearing smile*): You don't have to scream. (*Gesturing toward his shoulders.*) If you would?
CHANG-GUN: Yes sir! (*Goose-steps behind the* COMMANDER *and begins massaging, but he does so too forcefully at first.*)
FIELD ARMY COMMANDER (*groans in pain; pause*): Where are you from, soldier?
CHANG-GUN: Magpie Village, sir.
FIELD ARMY COMMANDER: Tell me about your family.
CHANG-GUN: There's just my mother, sir.
FIELD ARMY COMMANDER: I'll bet you miss her.
CHANG-GUN: Yes sir, I do. (*Sniffles, overcome by thoughts of his mother.*)
FIELD ARMY COMMANDER: When did your father pass away?
CHANG-GUN: One year and five days after I was born, sir. (*Sniffles again.*)
FIELD ARMY COMMANDER: And how old is your mother?
CHANG-GUN: Sixty-two, sir. (*Voice begins to quaver.*)
FIELD ARMY COMMANDER: The last thing you look like is a soldier.
CHANG-GUN: Yes sir.
FIELD ARMY COMMANDER (*astonished silence; then*): When did you start training, anyway?
CHANG-GUN: Two and a half weeks ago, sir.
FIELD ARMY COMMANDER: What's it been like so far? (*Waits for an answer.*) When a superior asks you a question, soldier, you'd better answer, loud and clear.
CHANG-GUN: I'm—I'm scared, sir.
FIELD ARMY COMMANDER: Of what?

CHANG-GUN: Everything, sir. There's not a thing that doesn't scare me.
FIELD ARMY COMMANDER: Good lord—a coward.
CHANG-GUN: Yes sir.
FIELD ARMY COMMANDER (*astonished silence; then*): I've never seen a soldier like you. All right, that's enough. Come here.
CHANG-GUN: Yes sir.
   (CHANG-GUN *comes around in front of the* COMMANDER, *who observes him silently for a short time.* CHANG-GUN *stands at attention, full of anxiety. His fingers twitch. Enter* INTELLIGENCE OFFICER.)
FIELD ARMY COMMANDER (*to* CHANG-GUN): Report to my aide-de-camp.
CHANG-GUN: Yes sir. (*Shouts.*) Assignment completed, sir! (*Salutes in a flash, then turns too quickly, almost losing his balance. Exit tottering.*)
INTELLIGENCE OFFICER (*offering the* COMMANDER *some papers*): Allow me to brief you on the officer we're sending behind enemy lines for the counterintelligence operation, sir.
FIELD ARMY COMMANDER (*pushing away the papers*): Don't bother, I've chosen a man myself—that soldier who just left. Why didn't you think of him?
INTELLIGENCE OFFICER: Him?!
FIELD ARMY COMMANDER: His face inspired me. While I was watching it, I thought of another way to play this game. Actually, I shouldn't call it a game. No matter how capable and solid an intelligence officer we send behind enemy lines, there's too much danger involved. The enemy's intelligence officers aren't idiots . . . I'll arrange it so that that soldier is interrogated by the enemy without realizing he's being used in a counterintelligence operation. First, we'll give him the wrong impression about the situation with our forces here. Every time we have a staff meeting, I'll have him massage my shoulders, and that way, he'll hear the same briefing I do. Of course, the briefing will be all misinformation. So when he's captured and interrogated by the enemy, they'll receive the entire line. (*Looks at the other with his all-knowing expression.*)
(*Clarinet.*)

SCENE 11: THE SAME

(*The* CAPTAIN *of a reconnaissance unit stands before the* FIELD ARMY COMMANDER *and the* INTELLIGENCE OFFICER.)

INTELLIGENCE OFFICER: Before the enemy can attack, they'll be desperate to capture one of our men in order to collect some reliable, extensive intelligence about our forces. All the captain will have to do is dump this cowardly soldier of ours somewhere within sight of the enemy's observation post.

CAPTAIN: Won't he try to run away if he's left there by himself?

FIELD ARMY COMMANDER: He doesn't even have the courage to do that. Any more questions?

CAPTAIN: No sir.

FIELD ARMY COMMANDER: All right, then, let's call in the soldier and put together a good scenario. Aide-de-camp, send in Private O Chang-gun!

AIDE-DE-CAMP (*from offstage left*): Yes sir!

FIELD ARMY COMMANDER: Intelligence officer, it would be better if you were out of sight.

INTELLIGENCE OFFICER: Yes sir. (*Exit stage right.*)

(*Enter* **CHANG-GUN**.)

CHANG-GUN: Private O Chang-gun reporting to massage the shoulders of His Excellency, the field army commander. (*Goose-steps over to the* **COMMANDER** *as before, alternately spreading and clenching his fingers as a kind of warm-up.*)

(*The* **CAPTAIN** *gazes at* **CHANG-GUN** *with mixed feelings.*)

FIELD ARMY COMMANDER: I won't need a lot today. And don't put too much into it.

CHANG-GUN: Yes sir. (*Long pause.*)

FIELD ARMY COMMANDER: Did you get enough to eat this morning?

CHANG-GUN: Yes sir. I had three rations, sir. (*Long pause.*)

FIELD ARMY COMMANDER: And did you dream about home last night?

CHANG-GUN: No sir, I didn't have any dreams at all. But this morning, sir, a letter arrived from home.

FIELD ARMY COMMANDER: Mm-hmm. That must have brightened your day.

CHANG-GUN (*a long sigh; momentarily stops massaging*): The letter said that I joined the army by mistake in place of another O Chang-gun, who is the son of a rich man in my hometown—is that possible, Excellency?

FIELD ARMY COMMANDER: I don't understand.

CHANG-GUN (*naively nodding in agreement*): I have no idea what it means either, Excellency. (*Long pause.*)

FIELD ARMY COMMANDER: By the way, Captain, how many men did you lose yesterday during your reconnaissance?

CAPTAIN: Five killed and eleven wounded, sir.

FIELD ARMY COMMANDER: Hmm. (*Pause.*) Private O Chang-gun.

CHANG-GUN: Yes sir.

FIELD ARMY COMMANDER: Don't you feel ashamed of yourself massaging my shoulders every day while the other men are getting killed and wounded at the front?

CHANG-GUN: Yes, Excellency. But since I don't know how to use a rifle, I'm better off massaging your shoulders. Just the thought of firing a rifle makes my heart jump. So whenever we had rifle practice at the training camp, the drill instructors would say, "You stupid idiot, you're wasting bullets!"

(*Long pause.*)

FIELD ARMY COMMANDER: Captain, take this man to the reconnaissance unit and mold him into a soldier. (**CHANG-GUN** *flinches.*)

CAPTAIN: Excellency, what the reconnaissance unit needs is crack soldiers who have enough courage to pull their share. A coward like this will just get in the way—

FIELD ARMY COMMANDER (*cutting him off*): You don't understand. I'm not transferring him to the reconnaissance unit— just for the time being, take him under your wing and see if you can put some spunk into him. Besides, I'm not happy having a soldier massage me who's never experienced hardships at the front.

CAPTAIN: I understand, sir.

FIELD ARMY COMMANDER: I guess you've heard what I said, Private O Chang-gun?

CHANG-GUN (*with a tearful expression, his voice trailing off*): Yes sir, Excellency.

FIELD ARMY COMMANDER (*to the* **CAPTAIN**): You can return to your unit now.

CAPTAIN: Yes sir. When will you send me that coward, sir?

FIELD ARMY COMMANDER: Take him with you.

CAPTAIN: All right, sir. I'll be leaving, then. (*Salutes; to* **CHANG-GUN**.) Follow me.

(**CHANG-GUN** *looks intently at the* **CAPTAIN** *and violently massages the* **FIELD ARMY COMMANDER**'s *shoulders, expecting him to change his mind.*)

FIELD ARMY COMMANDER (*turning for the first time to face* **CHANG-GUN**): Don't you want to go?

CHANG-GUN (*with a tearful expression*): No sir, Excellency.

FIELD ARMY COMMANDER: Don't be afraid—just follow along. Perhaps the Captain will save the dangerous assignments for someone else. After all, I'll need you to come back and massage my shoulders.

(**CHANG-GUN** *continues massaging. Pause.*)

FIELD ARMY COMMANDER (*in the low, icy tone of one who will brook no opposition*): That's enough. (**CHANG-GUN** *stops massaging.*)

Follow him. (**CHANG-GUN**, *a wretched look on his face, walks over to the waiting* **CAPTAIN**.)

(*Gently.*) I'll be calling for you again. So long, Private O Chang-gun.

CHANG-GUN (*stifling tears*): Good-bye, Excellency. (*Turns to go.*)

FIELD ARMY COMMANDER: You forgot to salute.

(**CHANG-GUN** *hurriedly turns back and snaps off a salute. The* **FIELD ARMY COMMANDER** *nods in response. Exit* **CHANG-GUN** *and the* **CAPTAIN**. *The* **FIELD ARMY COMMANDER** *sends a sympathetic look after* **CHANG-GUN**. *Enter* **INTELLIGENCE OFFICER**. *He stands deferentially behind the* **COMMANDER** *and joins him in looking in the direction where* **CHANG-GUN** *has disappeared.*)

He's the only soldier who's ever made me feel sentimental. Me—who's gotten tens of thousands of soldiers killed or wounded . . . I should have kept him around longer. (*Pause; without expression, speaking in a monotone as if reading from a book.*) Call him back. (*Turns to the* **INTELLIGENCE OFFICER**.) Don't move!

(*Clarinet.*)

SCENE 12: A GROVE

(*The stage is dark.*)

VOICE OF THE RECONNAISSANCE UNIT CAPTAIN (*shouting*): Master sergeant, take that coward up to the front and dump him there! Maybe a night out will put a little pluck into him!

VOICE OF THE MASTER SERGEANT (*shouting*): Yes sir! Let's go, idiot!

(*The stage brightens just enough to reveal a grove of peculiar-looking trees. The* **MASTER SERGEANT** *and* **CHANG-GUN** *are lying on their stomachs facing the audience.*)

MASTER SERGEANT: I'll be back at daybreak. But before I leave, here's your assignment and some things to watch out for. Number one, if you see or hear anything out there in front of you, give the password immediately; if there's no answer, shoot. Remember—the enemy's in front of you; we're behind you. Got it, idiot?

CHANG-GUN: Yes sir.

MASTER SERGEANT: Number two—no smoking under any circumstances. A lighted cigarette can be seen from two and a half miles away. The enemy has advanced to within a mile and a quarter. Got it, idiot?

CHANG-GUN: Yes sir.

MASTER SERGEANT: And that's it. (*Patting* **CHANG-GUN** *on the shoulders.*) All right, then, see you tomorrow morning. (*Gets to his knees and turns to leave.*) Oh, almost forgot to give you the password for tonight. It's "lady's . . . butt." "Lady's . . . butt." Say it, idiot.
CHANG-GUN: "Lady's . . . butt."
MASTER SERGEANT: Again.
CHANG-GUN: "Lady's . . . butt."
MASTER SERGEANT: Listen to this friggin' idiot. All right, I'm off. (*Gets to his knees, turns to leave, and suddenly thrusts his bottom up.*) Oooh! Damn password's given me blue balls! (*Exit.*)
(*For some time,* **CHANG-GUN** *sits silently, trembling. Suddenly a long, high-pitched sound like the call of a loon. Silence. The cry of a fox. Silence. The hoot of an owl. Silence. The roar of a lion. Silence. The gentle warble of a goldfinch. Long silence.* **CHANG-GUN** *stirs and takes out a cigarette.*)
CHANG-GUN: Hmmm, could have sworn the master sergeant said something about cigarettes . . .
(*A momentary pause as he attempts to remember, and then he lights the cigarette. The moment he does so, lights appear upstage, illuminating a Westerly artillery observation tower.*)
LOOKOUT: Enemy sighted. Map C, coordinates 2445–1256—
OFFICER, ARTILLERY OBSERVATION UNIT: Hold it. We have orders to report any sighting to the intelligence office at once. (*Picks up the mouthpiece to a radio set and gestures as if making a report.*)
(*The instant the Westerly officer picks up the mouthpiece, a spotlight appears on the Easterly* **FIELD ARMY COMMANDER, INTELLIGENCE OFFICER, RECONNAISSANCE UNIT CAPTAIN,** *and* **MASTER SERGEANT.**)
MASTER SERGEANT: I must have told that stupid son of a bitch half a dozen times not to smoke.
FIELD ARMY COMMANDER (*abruptly turning away from the others with a crestfallen look*): If he gets killed by a shell because of that cigarette . . . (*Aims at the other three, as if with a rifle.*) the rest of you are going to die, too.
ARTILLERY OBSERVATION OFFICER (*replacing the mouthpiece*): The intelligence office will take it from here.
(**CHANG-GUN** *puffs on his cigarette, trembling as before. A long pause.*)
FIELD ARMY COMMANDER (*still talking to himself*): Why haven't they shot him yet? Are they asleep? (*In a loud voice, turning back to the others.*) Goddamned lookouts . . . (*Takes out a cigarette; the* **INTELLIGENCE OFFICER** *hurriedly lights it for him.*)
(*Long pause. Five* **TREES** *advance stealthily toward* **CHANG-GUN.** *At first unaware,* **CHANG-GUN** *eventually senses something and stiffens. The* **TREES** *halt. Pause.*)

CHANG-GUN (*in a low, trembling voice*): Lady's . . .
TREE A (*in a soft whisper*): Butt!
CHANG-GUN (*flinches, then looks around nervously*): Could have sworn I heard someone answer.
(*Pause.* CHANG-GUN *is about to resume smoking when the* TREES *move again.* CHANG-GUN *senses the motion and stiffens again. The* TREES *halt. Pause.*)
CHANG-GUN: Lady's . . .
TREE A: Butt.
(CHANG-GUN *flinches and looks around nervously. He begins to tremble more violently and sucks on his cigarette. Suddenly* TREE B *is stepping on* CHANG-GUN's *rifle, and the remaining trees have surrounded him. Too startled to utter a sound,* CHANG-GUN *can only look up at them, slack jawed. A hand quickly appears from behind the trunk of* TREE B *and snatches* CHANG-GUN's *cigarette. As* CHANG-GUN *gazes vacantly up at* TREE B, *a hand appears from* TREE C *and slaps him across the right cheek.* CHANG-GUN *shifts his gaze toward* TREE C, *and a foot appears from* TREE E *and is poised to kick him but is restrained by* TREE A.)
All right, that's enough.
(TREE A *casts off his camouflage, revealing himself as the* CAPTAIN *of a Westerly intelligence unit. The remaining* TREES *do likewise, revealing themselves as a* SERGEANT FIRST CLASS, *a* STAFF SERGEANT, *a* LANCE CORPORAL, *and a* CORPORAL.)
CHANG-GUN: Wh—who are you gentlemen?
SERGEANT FIRST CLASS: We're butts! (*The others laugh.*)
CAPTAIN: Search him!
SERGEANT FIRST CLASS: Yes, sir. (*To* CHANG-GUN.) Get up!
CORPORAL: You heard him, asshole—get up!
(*The* CORPORAL *kicks him, and* CHANG-GUN *springs to his feet. The* FOUR MEN *under the* CAPTAIN *begin frisking him. They are very fast, adept, and thorough at their work. Finally, they turn him upside down and shake him as if he were a large bag. Then, having completed their inspection, they await further orders. The* CAPTAIN *motions to the men to take* CHANG-GUN *away. The* CORPORAL *kicks* CHANG-GUN *again.*) Let's go.
(*Exit* CHANG-GUN, *prodded by the muzzle of the* CORPORAL's *rifle.*)
FIELD ARMY COMMANDER (*observing everything through a telescope*): Cruel, vicious bastards! (*In a lifeless tone.*) He wouldn't hurt a fly—how can they treat him like that!
(*Enter* AIDE-DE-CAMP, *accompanied by an* MP.)
AIDE-DE-CAMP (*rushing onstage*): Excellency! That fellow's a fake. (*The* FIELD ARMY COMMANDER *lowers his telescope in amazement.*) Private O Chang-gun—he's a fake. (*To the* MP.) Read the arrest warrant.

MP *(reads)*: Warrant of arrest. Rank—private second class. Army identification number—024378596. Name—O Chang-gun. The above-named person is hereby arrested for assuming the name of another and fraudulently entering the army. Effective immediately the commanding officer is to relieve the above-named recruit of his duties and surrender him to the bearer of this warrant. By order of the prosecutor for courts-martial, on behalf of the Commander in Chief of the Army, such-and-such a date.
(Pause; looks in turn from the **FIELD ARMY COMMANDER** *to the others.)*

AIDE-DE-CAMP: I thought something was fishy about that fellow. He was too foolish, too naive, too honest, too much of a coward.

INTELLIGENCE OFFICER: On the contrary. Now that I think about it, he must be fearless, judging from the nonchalant way he lit up that cigarette ... You know, he has to be an infiltrator from the other side—no doubt about it.

MP: Excellency, would you kindly relieve the suspect of his duties and surrender him?

FIELD ARMY COMMANDER *(explodes in laughter)*: Now I know what Private O Chang-gun was talking about this morning. *(Laughs.)*
(Clarinet.)

SCENE 13: WESTERLY POW INTERROGATION ROOM

*(***CHANG-GUN** *and the* **CAPTAIN** *of the intelligence unit sit across from each other with a small table between them. The* **FOUR ENLISTED MEN** *under the* **CAPTAIN** *stand guard behind* **CHANG-GUN***.)*

CAPTAIN: Before we begin the interrogation, there's something I'd like to show you. If you lie to me, this is what will happen to you. *(Gestures with his eyes to the* **SOLDIERS***.)*
(The **SERGEANT FIRST CLASS** *pulls on a rope, and a puppet rises from the floor and hangs in the air upside down. The* **STAFF SERGEANT** *flails the puppet with a club. With every blow, the two* **CORPORALS** *scream in feigned agony and a bell jingles inside the puppet.)*
   Enough. *(Coldly, to* **CHANG-GUN***.)* Got it? *(Paralyzed with fright,* **CHANG-GUN** *gulps nervously instead of answering.)* Fine. Let's start, then. ID number?

CHANG-GUN (*stuttering in his haste to answer*): 024—024 (*Embarrassed at having forgotten, steals glances at the puppet, which remains suspended in the air.*)
    024 . . . 378576.
CAPTAIN: Name?
CHANG-GUN: O—O Chang-gun, sir.
CAPTAIN: I take it that's O Chang-gun, right?
CHANG-GUN: Yes, sir.
CAPTAIN: Occupation before entering the army?
CHANG-GUN: Growing po-potatoes, sir.
CAPTAIN: What the . . . ?
SERGEANT: You piece of shit—
CAPTAIN (*restrains the* SERGEANT; *in a soft voice*): I'll ask you again—occupation before entering the army?
CHANG-GUN: Growing potatoes, sir.
CAPTAIN: Now I get it—you're a farmer.
CHANG-GUN: Yes sir.
CAPTAIN: Current unit?
CHANG-GUN: First Squad, First Platoon, of the reconnaissance company attached to the Fifth Infantry headquarters, sir.
CAPTAIN: Date of assignment to this unit?
CHANG-GUN: Today, sir.
CAPTAIN: Today? Your previous unit, then?
CHANG-GUN: Office of the commander, Fifth Infantry headquarters, sir.
CAPTAIN (*in surprise*): Repeat that.
CHANG-GUN: Office of the commander, Fifth Infantry headquarters, sir.
    (*The* CAPTAIN *bolts to his feet.* CHANG-GUN *involuntarily does likewise. The* CAPTAIN *withdraws to a corner and beckons the* SERGEANT FIRST CLASS.)
CAPTAIN (*in a low voice*): I'd better report this to the intelligence officer. (*Rushes offstage.*)
    (*The* SERGEANT FIRST CLASS *pushes* CHANG-GUN *back to his seat;* CHANG-GUN *gazes up at him in fright. Lights out. A shout of "Attention!" and then lights. The* ENLISTED MEN *under the* CAPTAIN *stand at attention facing offstage. Enter Westerly* COMMANDER IN CHIEF *flanked by his staff. The* ENLISTED MEN *position chairs behind the* COMMANDER IN CHIEF *and his staff. Exit* ENLISTED MEN. *Pause.*)
COMMANDER IN CHIEF: Brief me on your conclusions.
CAPTAIN: Yes sir! The interrogation has revealed that we have completely underestimated the strength of the enemy. (*Indicating a chart.*) Here

you see a comparison of the enemy's strength based on our intelligence, and the enemy's strength based on the results of the interrogation. As you can see, we thought we were facing three infantry divisions and one field artillery brigade. But it is now confirmed that there are four infantry divisions, one cavalry division, and two field artillery brigades.

(*Murmuring among the* COMMANDER IN CHIEF *and his staff. The* CAPTAIN *flips over the chart to reveal another chart.*)

This additional information, which you see here, confirms for us the distribution of the enemy's strength. (*Pause.*) Questions, gentlemen?

OFFICER A: How credible are the captive's statements?

CAPTAIN: The captive is an ignorant farmer who has no military understanding whatsoever. He's incapable of exaggerating what he overheard. On the contrary, his poor memory makes it quite likely that he's left out much of what he's heard and seen.

COMMANDER IN CHIEF: I'm in full agreement, Captain. This is an idiotic, porcine specimen. Captain, let's give my staff a look at this soldier.

CAPTAIN: Yes sir!

(*Exit* CAPTAIN, *watched closely by the staff. Enter* CAPTAIN, *followed by* CHANG-GUN, *who is under guard.* CHANG-GUN, *consumed with fear, now looks like a shell of himself. He stares at the staff with hollow, unfocused eyes. The* COMMANDER IN CHIEF *gestures for him to be taken away. As soon as he and his guard have disappeared, the* COMMANDER IN CHIEF *rises.*)

COMMANDER IN CHIEF: We almost fell for the enemy's tricks. They've done a pretty clever job of fooling us into underestimating their strength. They thought that underestimating their strength would dupe us into building an insufficiency of defensive positions. They planned to lure us into attacking them and depleting our strength and then at an appropriate time launching a full-scale counteroffensive . . . I'm canceling our plan to attack and ordering every unit to immediately assume a defensive posture at its present location and devote itself exclusively to building defensive positions.

(*The staff members stand. Exit* COMMANDER IN CHIEF *followed by his staff.*)
(*Clarinet. Lights out.*)

SCENE 14: WESTERLY INTERROGATION ROOM AND EXECUTION GROUND

(CHANG-GUN's *shrieks and the sound of him being beaten. Lights.* CHANG-GUN, *hanging upside down, is being tortured by the* CAPTAIN *of the intelligence unit and his men. Enter* COMMANDER IN CHIEF, *followed by* OFFICER A.)

COMMANDER IN CHIEF: Halt! (*The* CAPTAIN *and his men come to attention.*)
    Let him down!
(CHANG-GUN *is swiftly lowered, unconscious, to the floor, where he lies limply. The* COMMANDER IN CHIEF *approaches and lashes* CHANG-GUN *mercilessly with his riding crop.*)
    Dung heap! You're a worthless piece of shit compared with this officer. Help him into a chair!
(*The* CAPTAIN *and the* SERGEANT FIRST CLASS *quickly lift* CHANG-GUN *and, after placing him in a chair, support him on each side. Long pause.* CHANG-GUN *regains consciousness. The* COMMANDER IN CHIEF *pours some water from a pitcher and offers it to him.* CHANG-GUN *docilely accepts it, drinks, then suddenly begins sobbing.*)
    You can stop your acting now. You've carried out your assignment. Thanks to you, the enemy has gained time and we've let slip an opportunity to attack. We didn't find out until today that you were lying to us . . . For heaven's sake, stop your acting . . . What is your real name and rank?
(CHANG-GUN's *sobs grow louder. This question has been put to him so often that he can only sob in response. The* COMMANDER IN CHIEF *observes him for a time, marveling at what he assumes to be* CHANG-GUN's *performance, then motions* OFFICER A *to a corner and speaks to him.*)
    No matter what we try to get from him, it's all nonsense. Arrange for his execution by firing squad at 1800 hours sharp.
OFFICER A: Yes sir.
COMMANDER IN CHIEF: One more thing—at 1800 hours have all the men at headquarters pay their respects to the condemned man.
OFFICER A: Yes sir. (*Exit.*)
(*The props are removed, and a* FIRING SQUAD *enters in formation. The* CAPTAIN *and* SERGEANT FIRST CLASS *escort* CHANG-GUN, *still weeping, to a wooden post and tie him to it. An* MP OFFICER *ties a black bandana over* CHANG-GUN's *eyes.*)
MP OFFICER: Does the condemned have any last words?
CHANG-GUN (*looking up toward the sky, calls out with all his heart and soul*): Mother! . . . Kkotbun! . . .

(*Long pause. The* MP OFFICER *looks to the* COMMANDER IN CHIEF, *who motions to him to proceed.*)

MP OFFICER: Ready!

CHANG-GUN (*cries out again with all his heart and soul*): Mother! . . . Kkotbun! . . . Mŏksoe! . . .

MP OFFICER: Fire!

(*The sound of firing in unison.* CHANG-GUN's *head drops.*)

COMMANDER IN CHIEF (*turning to* OFFICER A): He kept it up right to the end. (*Mimicking* CHANG-GUN.) "Mother . . . Kkotbun." . . .

The most ignorant hick couldn't have acted more like a hick than he did.

(*The* COMMANDER IN CHIEF *salutes* CHANG-GUN. *The others do likewise.*)
(*Humming.*)

SCENE 15: THE YARD OF O CHANG-GUN'S HOUSE

(*A* STAFF SERGEANT *stands holding* CHANG-GUN's *funerary urn. Opposite him are Chang-gun's* MOTHER, KKOTBUN, *and* MŎKSOE.)

STAFF SERGEANT (*reading* CHANG-GUN's *death notice*): I, the Commander of the Easterly Fifth Field Army, hereby notify you with utmost sadness of the glorious death in action of infantry private O Chang-gun. Private O Chang-gun was second to none in his patriotism and martial spirit. He had only these last words: "Long live Easterly!" Signed, Commander, Easterly Fifth Field Army, such-and-such a date.

MOTHER: I can't believe that my son Chang-gun is inside this.

STAFF SERGEANT: It was impossible to bring his remains because his body is in enemy territory. So I've brought the hair and fingernails he trimmed before going to the front line.

MOTHER (*opens the urn and looks inside, motionless*): Oh, Chang-gun, my son . . .

KKOTBUN (*standing stiff as a board while rubbing her stomach*): Chang-gun, my baby's father . . .

(MŎKSOE *lows until out of breath. The* TREES *in the potato field and beside the well enter the yard in the manner of a military guard bearing a casket. While repeating a long wail,* MŎKSOE *meets the advancing* TREES *as a head mourner would and gestures toward* MOTHER *and* KKOTBUN *as if to console them. Humming; a moment later the clarinet sounds in a much higher pitch than in previous scenes. At the sound of the clarinet, all movement stops. The procession then resumes, in time with the humming and the clarinet, and slowly exits. The stage darkens and the humming and the clarinet continue to issue forth. The* **CLARINETIST** *and the* **HUMMING WOMAN** *begin to cross the stage with their chairs on their backs. In the middle of the stage, they stop and look into the darkness, then look toward the audience, as if asking for sympathy, before resuming their slow journey across the stage.)*

Curtain

PLEASE TURN OFF THE LIGHTS
(PUL CHOM KKŎ CHUSEYO)

YI MANHŬI

Yi Manhŭi is viewed by some scholars as the most influential dramatist of the 1990s. His creative dramaturgy and moving language have earned him many awards, leading one critic to describe him as the "alchemist of the Korean language." Born in Taech'ŏn City in 1954, Yi graduated from Dongguk University in 1978 with a degree in Indian philosophy. He subsequently spent two years at the Kumsan Buddhist Temple, a religious experience reflected, in Yi's words, "in the fusion of my ardor for religion and literature."

Maiden Flight (*Chŏnyŏ pihaeng*, 1982) was the first of his works produced, followed by *Lepers* (*Mundi*, 1989), a commercial success, the first of many to follow.

Among Yi's fourteen plays are *It Was a Small Darkness Inside the Hole of a Buddhist Woodblock* (*Kŭgosŭn mokth'ak kumŏng sok ŭi chagŭn ŏdumiŏssumnida*, 1990), a work exploring the reverberations of a monk's attachment to the past; *The Pig and the Motorbike* (*Twaeji wa otobai*, 1993), depicting a man torn by the murder of his malformed child and lust for a former pupil; *Blooming and Fading, Blooming and Fading* (*P'igojigo p'igojigo*, 1996), a poetic work written, as the director Kang Yŏnggŏl noted, for the old and those growing old; and *A Betting Couple*, also known as *A Dog on Top of a Dragon* (*Yongddi kaeddi*, 1997), a comedy featuring the mayhem created by a mismatched newly wed couple who cannot live without each other. Yi's most recent stage work is *Let's Go over the Hill* (*Ŏndŏk ŭl nŏmŏsŏ kaja*, 2007), a play about a couple in their sixties who have known each other since grade school and now are finding the truth of their past feelings. Yi also has had success as a screenwriter, most notably for the screenplay *When I Turned Nine* (*Ahopsal insaeng*, 2004), winner of the best film script award at the twelfth Ch'unsa (Korea) Film Festival.

Although not without controversy, *Please Turn Off the Lights* (*Pul chom kkŏ chuseyo*, 1992) was a critical and unprecedented financial success, running for more than four years, with subsequent revivals. As in some of Yi's other works, the protagonist struggles with personal desires and guilt connected with his past. Kim Chinhŭi notes that the protagonist is a metaphor of contemporary South Koreans, endeavoring to attain socioeconomic transformation through strength yet unable to be free of the "victim consciousness" linked to Korea's history. Yi uses flashbacks to bring the intrusive, inescapable past to life in the present and challenges the reader/audience by intertwining the "real-time" thoughts and dialogue of each character's public persona with each character's private persona, represented as an alter ego.

Yi Manhŭi is a professor in Dongguk University's Graduate School of Culture and Contents Technology.

PLEASE TURN OFF THE LIGHTS (PUL CHOM KKŎ CHUSEYO)

TRANSLATED BY KIM CHINHŬI

CHARACTERS

KANG CH'ANG-YŎNG
PAK CHŎNGSUK
CH'ANG-YŎNG'S ALTER-EGO (A-E)
CHŎNGSUK'S ALTER-EGO (A-E)
MAN, to play multiple roles (M-R)
WOMAN, to play multiple roles (M-R)

(*The overall color of the stage is quite dark. The floor, walls, chairs, bed, and other props are either made out of or adorned with dark-colored marble. The two* **ALTER-EGOS** *are sitting on chairs side by side in the center of the stage, showing no particular expression on their faces.* **CH'ANG-YŎNG** *and* **CHŎNGSUK** *are standing at the right corner of the stage, their bodies entwined, leaning slightly against the wall.* **CHŎNGSUK**'s *back is against the wall, and* **CH'ANG-YŎNG** *is pressing his palm against the wall. Their legs are intertwined. At first glance, their posture gives the impression of a passionate embrace. Yet, somehow they both look awkward and rigid. They gaze blankly at each other. From time to time,* **CH'ANG-YŎNG** *puts his free hand up* **CHŎNGSUK**'s *skirt, rubs his cheeks against hers, or presses his mouth to hers.* **CHŎNGSUK** *does not seem to mind* **CH'ANG-YŎNG**'s *touches, yet she doesn't appear to welcome them, either, which is a telltale sign that she is not entirely a willing partner. But she has not completely rejected him. Their touches and kisses, which appear to be sensual and stimulating, unfold slowly and smoothly, as if in a scene from a motion picture. The* **MALE MULTIROLE** *and the* **FEMALE MULTIROLE** *walk onto the stage.*)[1]

MALE M-R: History is made when an ordinary event turns into a scandal. If an ordinary event winds up just staying ordinary, then it is ordinary. But if an ordinary event blows up into a scandal, then it becomes history. If you get caught cheating, then it's history. If you don't get caught, it'll pass as ordinary. If a teacher smacks his student in the head and the whole thing passes without incident, then it's ordinary. But if the student's eyes turn white, and his mouth fills with white froth, then it makes history. If you are hit by a brick falling from the sky and die with your head cracked open, then it's history. If the brick doesn't hit you, then it's ordinary. If the egg you tossed into the air lands in a tree, it's ordinary. If it lands on the head of your boss, then it's history. If you rape the woman next door and it goes without a hitch, then it's ordinary. If she reports you to the police or her belly swells up with a child, then it makes history. As they always say, the sky's the limit when it comes to fantasies. If you can manage to suppress your fantasies, it's ordinary. If you act on your fantasies, then you make history. History happens when, by some accident, ordinary events turn into a scandal.

FEMALE M-R: Words can't always fully explain our behavior. Human behavior can be very complicated at times—more complicated than we can possibly imagine. We use the word *destiny* whenever we're at a loss and can't find a way to explain our behavior. "It's our destiny," we say. "Destiny is unavoidable, so what could we have done to change it?" How scientific is the word *destiny*? Actually, it's brimming with nonscientific elements. Here's a hypothesis: a man who was crossing the Eighty-eighth Bridge on August 8 in 1988 was killed after being hit by a car with the license plate number, 8-8888. The time of his death was 8 seconds and 8 minutes after 8 o'clock. For that particular car to cross that particular site required superhuman precision. For that man to cross that particular point in his travel also required superhuman precision. For this rendezvous to have happened, everything—the manner and speed of his walk, the way he blew his nose, wiped his eyes, looked around, tripped, pulled up his socks, scratched his balls—required extraordinarily precise coordination. Let's trace his movements from just one hour before the accident. If he had said "good-bye" just one more time, or skipped it, as he was leaving his family home, if he had looked at a woman's legs one more time or ignored them, or if he'd spat the words "son of a bitch" one more time at the cab driver whose car splashed water all over him (poor guy!), then he might have avoided the accident. Life defies science. Life is full of nonscientific, unexplainable elements. If destiny was a pure product of science, then those nonscientific elements would have to be part of science. But no: If we add nonscience to science, the lump sum is not just science.

MALE M-R: It's called destiny.

FEMALE M-R: Which is neither a scientific necessity nor a nonscientific accident.

MALE M-R: Meaning that we can choose a new destiny at will.

FEMALE M-R: Who am I then?

MALE M-R: I'm made of two parts: body and soul, the soul having two opposing parts.

FEMALE M-R: That means we all have a duality within us. Here, take a look. (*To the* **MALE** *and* **FEMALE ALTER-EGO**.) Come on out. We're one.

MALE M-R: We're one, too. I am the appearance of myself.

CH'ANG-YŎNG'S ALTER-EGO: And I represent the other side of my soul.

FEMALE M-R: I am the appearance of myself.

CHŎNGSUK'S ALTER-EGO: And I represent the other side of my soul.

MALE M-R: Hey, honey, it's so nice out. Come for a drive with me?

CH'ANG-YŎNG'S A-E: I want to have sex with her.

FEMALE M-R: You mean, just the two of us?

CHŎNGSUK'S A-E: This son of bitch makes me sick.

FEMALE M-R: Now, this is the play you've come to see tonight.

MALE M-R: Repeat after me. Son of a bitch.

FEMALE M-R: Repeat after me. Son of a bitch.

MALE M-R: Sooooon of a bitch.

FEMALE M-R: Stress the vowels. Sooooon of a bitch.

MALE M-R: Son of a bitch.

FEMALE M-R: This time, don't stress the vowels. Son of a bitch.

MALE M-R: Why are we doing all this? (*Laughs.*) We're just doing it for the sake of doing it.

FEMALE M-R: That's right. Don't try to find any meaning in what we're doing. When you look for meaning, the search ends up overwhelming you. Then you lose the truth altogether. Want to see an example?

(**MALE M-R** *and* **FEMALE M-R** *stand face to face at center stage.*)

MALE M-R (*affectionately*): I love you. (*Turns and walks away.*)

FEMALE M-R (*following him*): What did you say? Did you say you love me? What do you mean by that? What do you think I am? A slut? What's the meaning of all this? Are you telling me you want to see me later? Want to date me? Want a one-night stand? What's it all about? What do you mean, you "love" me?

MALE M-R (*exiting*): I just love you.

FEMALE M-R (*exiting*): I said, what do you mean when you say that you love me?

(*A little bit later.*)

CHŎNGSUK (*trying to break away from* **CH'ANG-YŎNG**'s *arms*): It's not working. Tonight, it's so . . .

CH'ANG-YŎNG: Don't run away from me. (*Puts his arms around* **CHŎNGSUK**.)

CHŎNGSUK: What do you want from me?

CH'ANG-YŎNG: I don't want anything from you. (*Puts his mouth over* **CHŎNGSUK**'s.)

CHŎNGSUK (*after kissing her a few times*): That's enough.

CHŎNGSUK'S A-E: I don't like this. He'll think I'm easy.

CH'ANG-YŎNG'S A-E: It's strange. They're both women, but her breath's not bad like my wife's.

CH'ANG-YŎNG: Do you know what comes to mind as soon as I walk into this place?

CHŎNGSUK'S A-E: A medal for a chaste woman?

CH'ANG-YŎNG: It's repotting.

CHŎNGSUK: Repotting?

CH'ANG-YŎNG: I have an orchid at home whose roots have outgrown the pot. It breaks my heart whenever I see it.

CH'ANG-YŎNG'S A-E: Whenever I look at the orchid, I want to change the pot . . .

CHŎNGSUK: So, you think I'm like that orchid, do you?

CHŎNGSUK'S A-E: I saw one like that, too. Its roots looked like millions of earthworms coiled together.

CH'ANG-YŎNG: That's what you need, too: change the pot.

CHŎNGSUK'S A-E: Change the pot?

CH'ANG-YŎNG'S A-E: That's right.

CHŎNGSUK'S A-E: Just as we go through stuff like death, transformation, and rebirth?

CHŎNGSUK: It'd be easier to destroy me than change me.

CH'ANG-YŎNG: Don't worry. Even the bird in a cage can soar into the sky, given freedom and enough time to adjust.

CH'ANG-YŎNG'S A-E: Bird in a cage? That's such a cliché. Can't you think of something more original?

CHŎNGSUK'S A-E: He's making trouble. He wants me to change my life. After all this time? Because of you, my life has been . . .

CHŎNGSUK: So, your resignation from Congress is also part of this repotting project, is it?

CHŎNGSUK'S A-E: I'm not asking for anything in return. I'm doing it because of the pain inside.
CH'ANG-YŎNG: How did you hear about it already?
CHŎNGSUK: It made the headlines last night.
CH'ANG-YŎNG: I thought you didn't watch television.
CHŎNGSUK'S A-E: Right. Did you also think I was an angel who doesn't poop or pee?
CHŎNGSUK: It created quite a stir. Congressman Kang Ch'ang-yŏng resigns because of an ethics violation.
CH'ANG-YŎNG'S A-E: She looks tired. What's the matter with her tonight?
CHŎNGSUK'S A-E: Why do I keep saying the wrong things? His heart must be breaking.
CH'ANG-YŎNG: I guess a seat in Congress wasn't meant for me after all.
CHŎNGSUK'S A-E: Should I apologize?
CHŎNGSUK: So, you've made up your mind?
CH'ANG-YŎNG: I have. You don't think I'm just being impulsive, do you?
CHŎNGSUK'S A-E: Why does he say things that he doesn't mean? Impulsive? When have I scorned or mocked him before?
CH'ANG-YŎNG: All right. Let's forget about it. I'm being oversensitive.
CH'ANG-YŎNG'S A-E: I'm actually a screwball. During a press conference, my mouth can be spitting out words like *citizen* and *social welfare*, but my eyes are fixed on the sexy legs of a female reporter in the first row. I get nervous. I'm afraid someone will see what I'm really like.
CH'ANG-YŎNG: I was just playing the victim. Please understand.
CHŎNGSUK: It's all right.
CHŎNGSUK'S A-E: This is working out just fine. Feels like he's back to his old self.
CH'ANG-YŎNG (*lays* **CHŎNGSUK** *on the bed*).
CHŎNGSUK: Will you tell me the truth?
CH'ANG-YŎNG: About what?
CHŎNGSUK'S A-E: I don't feel any excitement down there.
CHŎNGSUK: What is it that you want? I know you don't want me.
CH'ANG-YŎNG: You're right.
CH'ANG-YŎNG'S A-E: We've been friends for such a long time, so it's hard to become lovers. But I haven't given up. Have sex with me tonight, then you will be rid of your chastity belt and finally liberated.
CHŎNGSUK'S A-E: Women are different from men.
CHŎNGSUK: Women don't want sex without love.
CH'ANG-YŎNG (*smiles*).

(*Flashbacks.* **CHŎNGSUK'S A-E** *is sitting face to face with the* **MALE M-R** *playing* **TEACHER HONG. CH'ANG-YŎNG'S A-E** *sits face to face with the* **FEMALE M-R** *playing* **CH'ANG-YŎNG'S WIFE.*)

HONG (*intentionally groping for words once in a while to give the impression of an amorous poet*): My eyes fill with crystal tears of joy, when I gaze at the beautiful river on a rainy day like today. The thick clouds clustering around the green mountains look as lovely as beauty queens, especially when you look at them through those diamond drops of rain. Aren't they splendid?

CHŎNGSUK'S A-E: You said you had something to discuss with me.

TEACHER HONG: I heard that you're single.

CHŎNGSUK'S A-E: What about it?

TEACHER HONG: How'd you like to go for a drive to Ch'unch'ŏn?

CHŎNGSUK'S A-E: And then what?

CH'ANG-YŎNG'S WIFE: I love Chaeung all the more because of his innocence. I can't find that in you. You always try to hide things from me, but he isn't like that. He's different from you.

CH'ANG-YŎNG'S A-E: Honey!

CH'ANG-YŎNG'S WIFE: I'm not interested in you any more. I should've left you a street gang—

CH'ANG-YŎNG'S A-E: Watch it . . .

CH'ANG-YŎNG'S WIFE: I didn't mean to hurt your feelings.

HONG: From the moment I laid my eyes on you, I wished I wasn't married to another woman.

CHŎNGSUK'S A-E: Mr. Hong.

HONG: I've seen you through the windows, teaching your classes. Whenever I catch sight of you, something trembles at the bottom of my heart. I try to calm down. But . . .

CHŎNGSUK'S A-E (*rising*): If you have time to kill, why don't you work on your lesson plans? You've been misinformed. My husband is in America on a business trip. (*Grabbing the tab.*) I'll pay for your coffee. (*Sitting again.*) Please leave.

CH'ANG-YŎNG'S A-E: Let's not talk about Chaeung any more.

CH'ANG-YŎNG'S WIFE: Why stop here? What's wrong with discussing Chaeung? Because he's handicapped? What's a handicap? His heart knows no hatred. Is his heart handicapped? Is his smile handicapped? He's a better person than you are. Don't measure him with your eyes. Your eyes don't have any principles. (*Exits.*)

HONG: Miss Pak . . .

CHŎNGSUK'S A-E: What? You have something else to say?

HONG: Sorry. Well . . . I guess you'd better pay for the coffee. (*Exits.*)
(*Actors return to their seats.*)

CH'ANG-YŎNG: Words may facilitate communication within a system, but they also bind us to that same system. Here's a case in point: barking dogs don't bite.

CHŎNGSUK'S A-E: What are you getting at?

CH'ANG-YŎNG: People of many words often fail to act.

CHŎNGSUK'S A-E: I can relate to that.

CH'ANG-YŎNG: Picture a wide green pasture where animals range peacefully. Then, picture this city we're living in, where billions of creatures are crammed together. Do you see the difference?

CHŎNGSUK: I believe I do.

CHŎNGSUK'S A-E: Once there lived a tribe of monkeys, peaceful and happy on a large piece of land. But then the monkeys were relocated to a smaller, gated piece of land. Lazy bums, tramps, dictators, sycophants, and conniving backstabbers started to show up, just like in the human world. The tribe's chief slept on higher ground, and his skin started to take on a glowing color that set him apart from all the other monkeys.

CH'ANG-YŎNG'S A-E: In confinement, creatures lose their primal innocence.

CH'ANG-YŎNG: We need to recover our primal innocence.

CHŎNGSUK: Even if we have to break the law to recover it?

CH'ANG-YŎNG: That won't be necessary.

CH'ANG-YŎNG'S A-E: Every living creature is born with the energy of renewal—the energy that allows us to change our destiny.

(CH'ANG-YŎNG *throws himself to on top of* CHŎNGSUK, *embracing her tightly.*)

CHŎNGSUK'S A-E: Uh-oh. He's coming on hard. What am I going to do?

CH'ANG-YŎNG'S A-E: Should I sell the building in Hannam to pay for Chaeung's medical treatment?

CHŎNGSUK'S A-E: I think I'll move that painting over there. That'd look better.

CH'ANG-YŎNG'S A-E: What was she like with Talho in bed? Is she a moaner? What did it sound like? Like this? (*Moans.*)

CHŎNGSUK'S A-E: That's right! I should have decreased the stitch at the twenty-seventh row. Damn it! Does this mean I should start all over again?!

CH'ANG-YŎNG'S A-E: Do I really have to rush it so much with her? I should sort this out first. I wonder what Yŏngshil's doing right now? Yŏngshil with her snowy white skin. Just one glimpse of her inner thigh drives me crazy. A girl who's gone overseas to study,[2] but she's really sexy.

CHŎNGSUK'S A-E: It's not sex that he wants. What on earth does he want from me? Maybe someone's hiding in here and filming us? What for?

CHʻANG-YŎNG'S A-E: The thought of Yŏngshil makes me feel better already. (*Romantic music is playing.* **FEMALE M-R** *plays* **YŎNGSHIL**, *who has just come out of the shower.*)

YŎNGSHIL: You dirty old man. Don't look at me like that. What part of my body do you like best?

CHʻANG-YŎNG'S A-E: Your ankles.

YŎNGSHIL: Oh . . . really?

CHʻANG-YŎNG'S A-E: Most women have fat ankles, but not you.

YŎNGSHIL: Any other parts?

CHʻANG-YŎNG'S A-E: I also admire your intelligence.

YŎNGSHIL: Does your wife know about us?

CHʻANG-YŎNG'S A-E: She knows . . .

YŎNGSHIL: She does?

CHʻANG-YŎNG'S A-E: She thinks you're just a reporter trying to interview a famous politician.

YŎNGSHIL: She must have been a beauty when she was younger.

CHʻANG-YŎNG'S A-E: Who?

YŎNGSHIL: Your wife.

CHʻANG-YŎNG'S A-E: She's still young enough.

YŎNGSHIL: But you'll still help advance my career . . . ?

CHʻANG-YŎNG'S A-E: Come here. (*Exit together.*)

CHŎNGSUK: What's on your mind? Why are you staring at me like that?

CHʻANG-YŎNG: People might mistake us for lovers.

CHŎNGSUK: I guess so. (*With a sarcastic laugh.*) Hooh, hooh, hooh.

CHŎNGSUK'S A-E: That's a lie.

CHʻANG-YŎNG: You don't think so?

CHŎNGSUK: Is that what you really wanted to say?

CHʻANG-YŎNG: I was distracted, actually . . . Lately, when I hear a song in the morning, it stays with me until bedtime.

CHŎNGSUK: Same with me. I hum the same song all day. Shall I put some music on?

CHʻANG-YŎNG: Not now.

CHŎNGSUK: You look tired. Glass of wine?

CHʻANG-YŎNG: No thanks. I'd rather lie down here.

CHŎNGSUK: You should go home.

CHŎNGSUK'S A-E: Don't go. Let's talk some more.

CHʻANG-YŎNG (*looks at his wristwatch*).

CHʻANG-YŎNG'S A-E: I still have time. It's twenty to eleven.

CHʻANG-YŎNG: Sometimes I take a walk at this hour in the park near my house. I see all sorts of things out there. Groups of young people meet there for a sing-along. They must have a lot of fun, I guess. Or maybe not? Maybe they get tired of singing one song after the other? I wonder if some of them just lip-synch, and their minds are really preoccupied with something else.

CH'ANG-YŎNG'S A-E (*singing*): Tuman River, its blue waves . . . What's so great about that song, anyway? Oh well . . .

CHŎNGSUK'S A-E: What did he say?

CHŎNGSUK: I didn't hear him, either.

CHŎNGSUK'S A-E: Hey, where's your mind wandering off to?

CHŎNGSUK: Here, there, and everywhere. Well, honestly, my mind just went blank.

CHŎNGSUK'S A-E: Ask him to help you start a small business. Tell him you want a small noodle shop in a place with lots of foot traffic. Tell him that you're lonely.

CHŎNGSUK: I don't want to.

CHŎNGSUK'S A-E: Why not?

CHŎNGSUK: I don't want him to think I'm lonely. I'll seem like an idiot.

CHŎNGSUK'S A-E: How about a flower shop?

CH'ANG-YŎNG: Young couples look really sweet walking along with their arms around each other, but sometimes I have dark thoughts about them, too.

CHŎNGSUK'S A-E: Not interested in the flower shop either?

CHŎNGSUK (*nods; not interested.*)

CHŎNGSUK'S A-E: Same for an art gallery?

CHŎNGSUK (*nods in agreement*).

CHŎNGSUK'S A-E: Damn it, you're so stubborn!

CH'ANG-YŎNG: Really, I don't think those couples are always happy together. Holding each other like that probably ends up feeling sweaty and slimy after a while. But they probably can't take their arms away, afraid they may give their partners the wrong idea.

CHŎNGSUK'S A-E: That's exactly how I feel. You and me, two frigid human beings, what are we doing now? Trying to do the impossible? (*To* CHŎNG-SUK.) It feels awkward. It's driving me crazy. Say something, anything!

CHŎNGSUK: That sounds like a totally bizarre interpretation of a very common sight.

CH'ANG-YŎNG: Meaning?

CHŎNGSUK'S A-E: Isn't he rather vulgar?

CHŎNGSUK: Oh, nothing I guess.

CH'ANG-YŎNG: Sometimes I wonder about An Chunggŭn, the great patriot.[3]

CHŎNGSUK'S A-E: When I was young, I used to think he was a doctor . . .

CH'ANG-YŎNG: Did he grow into being a patriot, or was he a born patriot? If he was born that way, then I . . .

CH'ANG-YŎNG'S A-E: I seem petty, don't I?

CHŎNGSUK'S A-E: It's so frustrating.

CH'ANG-YŎNG: The word *pravda* in Russian means "truth," but the newspaper with that name printed lies everyday for decades.

CH'ANG-YŎNG'S A-E: What's that got to do with us?

CH'ANG-YŎNG (*to* CH'ANG-YŎNG'S A-E): Good question.

CH'ANG-YŎNG'S A-E: Are you by any chance thinking of Talho?

CH'ANG-YŎNG: Who?

CH'ANG-YŎNG'S A-E: Well, you mentioned lies and *pravda*.

CHŎNGSUK'S A-E: How can I get out of this mess? Tell him I have to make a phone call? Tell him it's time to water my plants or I need to run to the restroom. The restroom! Not very original. And then he might picture me sitting on the toilet.

(*Flashback.* MALE M-R *plays* KIM TALHO, *who is trimming his toenails. He is on the phone with* CH'ANG-YŎNG'S A-E.)

TALHO: Hello, what's up?

CH'ANG-YŎNG'S A-E: Hello, who's this?

TALHO: Who is it?? It's *me*, Talho! I see your picture in the newspaper everyday. Your auditing gig in Congress looks great. I'm really proud of you. With a friend as successful as you are, I feel like I'll make it big, too. As a matter of fact, I've sent one of my guys to Seoul. He's going to call you. I need your help. If things work out this time, I'll pay back every cent. Hello . . . you there?

CH'ANG-YŎNG'S A-E: Go on.

TALHO: I need a hundred grand.

CH'ANG-YŎNG'S A-E: Are you blackmailing me?

TALHO: Blackmailing you!? We're friends! I'm just asking you to help me out. Ah, one more thing. Please take good care of my wife. Don't you feel sorry for her? But don't use her all up, OK? Who knows? I might return to Seoul. Hah, hah, hah. (*Hangs up.*)

CH'ANG-YŎNG: He's a son of a bitch, that husband of yours!

CHŎNGSUK: Sounds like the pot calling the kettle black.

CHŎNGSUK'S A-E: Why'd he mention Talho?

CHŎNGSUK: I heard rote practice is the worst learning strategy.

CH'ANG-YŎNG: It might be the only way for kids like Chaeung to ever learn.

CHŎNGSUK: I hardly even think of him as my husband.

CH'ANG-YŎNG: Chŏngsuk, you need to be more assertive. Everything you say is couched with probably, maybe, perhaps . . .

CHŎNGSUK'S A-E: I know there's a lot to learn.

CH'ANG-YŎNG: Even in my wildest dreams it never occurred to me that you'd marry Talho.

CHŎNGSUK'S A-E: Who betrayed who first?

CH'ANG-YŎNG: Did you know you're like that, so mousey?

CHŎNGSUK'S A-E: I'm not interested.

CH'ANG-YŎNG: Men are strange.

CHŎNGSUK: Women are too.

CHŎNGSUK'S A-E: That's a lie! That's an incredibly insensitive remark. People say men are this way and women are that way. They say women prefer to stay home, and men prefer to stay *away* from home. It's all just stereotypes.

CH'ANG-YŎNG: People say men defy destiny and women accept it.

CHŎNGSUK'S A-E: There are plenty of female bosses and male gofers. Like in the movies. (*Impersonating a gangster.*) Bang, bang, bang. Yo! Come here! (*A timid-looking young man with a set of earphones over his ears enters, dancing to the music.*)

MALE M-R: Did you call me?

CHŎNGSUK'S A-E: You're the only one here. Who else would I be calling? Listen up! If you keep making a move on that chick at the beauty parlor, I'll put a hole in your head. Understand?

MALE M-R: I didn't do anything.

CHŎNGSUK'S A-E: Did you hear what I said?

MALE M-R: Yes. Yes, I understand.

CHŎNGSUK'S A-E: Get down on your knees and crawl.

(**MALE M-R** *exits on knees.*)

CH'ANG-YŎNG: Do you know how that bastard Talho is doing in America?

CHŎNGSUK'S A-E: If he dares to show himself around here, I'll put a muzzle on his big ugly mouth.

CHŎNGSUK: I heard he's living the good life with an American woman.

CHŎNGSUK'S A-E: A Yankee girl!?

CH'ANG-YŎNG: I heard he's having a fine old time. By day he's sipping cocktails by the swimming pool, at night rolling dice in the casino.

CH'ANG-YŎNG'S A-E: He's gambling with my money!

CH'ANG-YŎNG: Sometimes, when he's tired of blonde girls, he might think of you. But don't be fooled. It doesn't mean he still loves you.

CHŎNGSUK: I know that.

CH'ANG-YŎNG'S A-E: Hey, you, Korean broad!!

CH'ANG-YŎNG: You are a Korean woman. You see obedience and dependency as virtues. You patiently wait for your husband to come home even if he's the lowest cheating creeps on the planet. You say, it's all my fault, it's my destiny.

CHŎNGSUK'S A-E: Now's the time. On your feet! It's your chance.

CHŎNGSUK (*on her feet*): I can imagine myself having a fling with someone. A swimming coach, maybe. I'm capable of thinking all kinds of things, you know.

CHŎNGSUK'S A-E: You and I have been mulling over our relationship for more than ten years. Sometimes I get jealous picturing you making love to your wife. But I still can't relate to you sexually. To me, you're like a father, a priest, a brother.

CH'ANG-YŎNG (*puts his arms around* **CHŎNGSUK** *from behind her*).

CHŎNGSUK: What is it with you today?! Do you really want me? That's not really what you want, is it?

CHŎNGSUK'S A-E: Do I look easy? Do I look like a shriveled-up, sex-starved widow?

CH'ANG-YŎNG: Let's just try to be cool about it. I know it's not easy.

CHŎNGSUK: We both know it's impossible.

CH'ANG-YŎNG: You're waiting for a man who doesn't deserve you.

CH'ANG-YŎNG'S A-E: Talho's having the time of his life. He must enjoy the fact that you're waiting for him. Doesn't that make you mad? The other day on the phone, he told me not to "use you up."

CHŎNGSUK'S A-E: Do you really want to know what annoys me? What's wrong with me? I'm not a gift or a sympathy offering. So don't treat me like one.

CHŎNGSUK: Are you saying you feel responsible for me? When I'm with you, I can't stop seeing the faces of my mother, brother, priest, even my husband.

CH'ANG-YŎNG: I know what you mean. It's the same with me. All sorts of things racing through my head.

MALE M-R (*as* **CH'OE BYŎNGCH'ŎL**, *a fishmonger*): Live squid, fresh today, straight from the ocean! Live squid, fresh today, straight from the ocean! (*To* **CH'ANG-YŎNG**.) That's enough, Ch'ang-yŏng. Live squid, fresh today, straight from the ocean! (*Exits*.)

CH'ANG-YŎNG: Even my poor dead friend, Byŏngch'ŏl, keeps telling me to stop. You remember Byŏngch'ŏl, don't you?

CHŎNGSUK: I do. You used to tell me about him all the time.

CH'ANG-YŎNG: Did Talho talk about Byŏngch'ŏl, too?

CHŎNGSUK: No, he didn't. He's not the kind of man who opens up. At home, he used only two sentences to talk to me: "Where are the papers?" and "Make the bed!"

CHŎNGSUK'S A-E: Do you feel good now that you've resigned?
CH'ANG-YŎNG: Byŏngch'ŏl is like a god to me.
CHŎNGSUK: I heard you owed him quite a bit.
CH'ANG-YŎNG: That's right. I owe him my life.
CHŎNGSUK'S A-E: You're a fool. Why can't you just forget about the past?
CH'ANG-YŎNG: I think I'll go visit his grave tomorrow.
CHŎNGSUK'S A-E: Take me with you.
CHŎNGSUK: It's on an island down south, isn't it?
CH'ANG-YŎNG: Mm . . . Kangsan Island, a two-hour boat ride from Mokp'o.
CHŎNGSUK'S A-E: Take me with you, please.
CHŎNGSUK: Are you going alone?
CH'ANG-YŎNG: I am.

(*Flashback. Three men are out of breath as if they have been running to escape danger, faces covered with large dark glasses and baseball caps pulled down to their noses.* **CH'ANG-YŎNG'S A-E** *plays* **BYŎNGCH'ŎL**, *and* **MALE M-R** *plays* **TALHO**.)

BYŎNGCH'ŎL: Ch'ang-yŏng!
CH'ANG-YŎNG: What?
BYŎNGCH'ŎL: Talho!
TALHO: What?
BYŎNGCH'ŎL: Let's split here. I'll take care of the rest. Alone.
CH'ANG-YŎNG: No, this thing'll . . .
BYŎNGCH'ŎL (*throws a punch at* **CH'ANG-YŎNG**): You talk too much. Go back home now. Sit tight and act as if nothing's happened. Don't go anywhere, even if you're scared, or they'll end up busting all of us.
CH'ANG-YŎNG: What about you?
BYŎNGCH'ŎL: I'm going to lie low for a while.
TALHO: Where are you going? We should live and die together. Nobody saw us. Your old lady won't say a word about it, either.
BYŎNGCH'ŎL: You never know. It's best we play it safe. If the police suspect any one of us, both of you should point the finger at me. If push comes to shove, I can take off on a smuggler's boat.
CH'ANG-YŎNG: I can't let you do that. I'm the one who did it. Why should you take all the blame?
BYŎNGCH'ŎL: It's my problem! You got caught in it, that's all.
CH'ANG-YŎNG: I did it, and I'll take the blame.
BYŎNGCH'ŎL: Listen to me, snot nose!
CH'ANG-YŎNG: No, I won't.
TALHO: Ch'ang-yŏng, do what Byŏngch'ŏl tells you, man. You know how mad he gets when anyone argues with him. Nothing's gonna happen to any of

us. Even if we're found out, people will side with us. They'll applaud us. That son of a bitch, Dog Meat, is better off dead.

CH'ANG-YŎNG: That's enough.

BYŎNGCH'ŎL (*to* **CH'ANG-YŎNG**): All right. You want to square it with me? (*Gets down on his knees; handing* **CH'ANG-YŎNG** *a brick.*) Here. Hit me! Hit! What's the matter? (*Rising; takes the brick back.*) It's your turn. Get down on your knees. (*Screaming.*) You son of a bitch! I'll smash your skull to bits.

CH'ANG-YŎNG (*trembles; tears dropping*).

BYŎNGCH'ŎL: If your tears are made of water, then mine are made of blood. You son of a bitch! (*Drops the brick.*) I'll be in touch with you two when things settle down. See you later. (*Exiting.*) Thanks, guys.

(**MALE M-R** *and* **CH'ANG-YŎNG'S A-E** *exit.* **CH'ANG-YŎNG** *puts the brick back where it was. He walks toward* **CHŎNGSUK**.)

CHŎNGSUK'S A-E: Tell him that you want to go see the ocean with him. You can talk to him about your art gallery on the boat. He won't reject your ideas. Go on.

CHŎNGSUK (*changing the subject*): It looks like it's going to rain. It feels humid, too, doesn't it?

CHŎNGSUK'S A-E: You're pathetic! (*Clucks her tongue sarcastically.*)

CH'ANG-YŎNG: Do you have an atlas?

CHŎNGSUK: I think so. (*Walks to her desk.*) I thought I put it here. When I was young, I really enjoyed studying maps. Even now, it's hard to believe how many other countries there are out there. Still, I guess all those people live lives pretty much like ours.

CH'ANG-YŎNG: I'm sure they do.

CHŎNGSUK (*looks for the atlas*).

(*Flashback.* **CHŎNGSUK**'s *back reminds* **CH'ANG-YŎNG** *of his secretary.* **FEMALE M-R** *as* **CH'ANG-YŎNG'S SECRETARY**. *She is looking for something.* **CH'ANG-YŎNG**'s *eyes move back and forth between the* **SECRETARY** *and* **CHŎNGSUK**.)

SECRETARY: Excuse me, sir; did you remove the files that I left here?

CH'ANG-YŎNG: No, I didn't.

CH'ANG-YŎNG'S A-E (*harassing her sexually*): Nice outfit. The color really suits you. And you sure look good in a miniskirt. Do you have time later?

SECRETARY: The files aren't here. Should I look for them in the cabinet?

CH'ANG-YŎNG: No, that's all right. You can go back to your desk.

CH'ANG-YŎNG'S A-E (*politely, yet in a very flirtatious manner*): Is there anything I can do for you? Just tell me. I'll do anything you ask.

CH'ANG-YŎNG: Miss Kim. (*In a businesslike manner, yet with an overtly sexual tone.*) Is there anything I can help you with?

SECRETARY (*surprised*): I beg your pardon?

CH'ANG-YŎNG: Oh, never mind. (*Hanging his head.*)
CH'ANG-YŎNG'S A-E (*walking toward* CH'ANG-YŎNG): What is your problem, man?
CH'ANG-YŎNG: I hate myself.
CH'ANG-YŎNG'S A-E: Because you want to come on to a girl even at a time like this?
CH'ANG-YŎNG (*nods*).
CH'ANG-YŎNG'S A-E: Other men aren't so different from you. Even during a funeral service, men get a hard-on when they see a pretty girl. Their mind is on the stock market when they pick up newspapers, enter a sauna, or drink coffee. Their head is crammed with duels between good and evil.
CHŎNGSUK: No, I can't find the atlas. Haven't you been to Kangsan Island before?
CH'ANG-YŎNG: I just wanted to have a look at it.
CHŎNGSUK: I see. It's strange.
CH'ANG-YŎNG: What is?
CHŎNGSUK: You.
CH'ANG-YŎNG: Me? How?
CHŎNGSUK'S A-E: You look drained today, as if you've been bewitched. (*To* CHŎNGSUK.) He's been a gentleman all these years. He's never touched me before the way he did tonight. Why doesn't he tell me why he resigned from Congress? I'm sure he came here to talk about it. Maybe I should ask him first?
CH'ANG-YŎNG: Do you think I'm acting strange?
CHŎNGSUK: Yes.
CH'ANG-YŎNG: Really?
(*The doorbell rings.*)
CHŎNGSUK'S A-E: Who could it be at this hour?
CH'ANG-YŎNG'S A-E: Have the reporters traced me here?
CHŎNGSUK: Who is it?
VOICE OF BAKER: It's me, the baker, from next door.
CHŎNGSUK'S A-E: Oh great! It's the guy from next door. What's got into him—calling on me so late?
CHŎNGSUK (*opens the door*): How are you? What brings you here at this late hour?
BAKER (*played by* MALE M-R, *dressed in shorts and slippers*): It's late, isn't it? You haven't turned in yet?
CHŎNGSUK: Not yet.
BAKER: My kids literally pushed me out of house and told me to bring you this fresh-baked pumpkin pie. I tried to resist by wedging myself in the doorframe, but those kids of mine outmuscled me. They got me out of

the house . . . They must take after me. Strong like me, after all these years of kneading and baking . . . Have a bite. My kids think the world of you. Thanks for taking such good care of them. I know they can be a nuisance . . . They grew up without their mother around.

CHŎNGSUK: Don't mention it. Come in.

BAKER: Really? But, my feet are dirty.

CHŎNGSUK: You don't have to take off your slippers.

CHŎNGSUK'S A-E: His feet are damn ugly.

BAKER: It looks so modern in here. (*Looks around from the entryway.*) Wow . . .

CHŎNGSUK'S A-E: What if he really comes in?

BAKER: Everything's so fancy and high-class in here. Your place sure looks different from mine.

CHŎNGSUK: Probably because I live by myself.

BAKER: This house just oozes with a woman's touch.

CHŎNGSUK: How's your business at the bakery?

CHŎNGSUK'S A-E: You're an idiot. Don't ask him questions. He'll babble on for ever.

BAKER: Today was really something. A rookie policeman walked into my store and told me he needed to use the phone. I thought he should pay for it, but he said he needed it for his job. Out of loyalty to my country, I told him to go ahead. How much would one phone call cost me anyway? Even if I am poor, I still have my dignity and self-respect. But then this rookie upstart just called his home "Honey, it looks like rain. You'd better put the lids on the kimchi pots in the backyard. Are the kids home yet? Soup made with rice water tastes better." By golly, he was on the phone for more than an hour! I didn't say a word to him, though. I can be really patient in a situation like that.

CHŎNGSUK'S A-E (*referring to the* **BAKER**): He's too much, isn't he? Hey, Mr. Baker. Your mouth is as big as your biceps; your tongue must come with an electric motor.

BAKER: You know what a walkie-talkie is, don't you? Well, that rookie upstart pulled one out of his back pocket and got the volume all the way up and said, "Hey, I'm on patrol. Over." And his partner said, "Blah blah. Over." Click, click, click. It was so noisy and irritating that I couldn't concentrate on my sales. I had to shout at the top of my lungs: "What did you want? The sticky buns? The plain ones? The ones with red bean or green tea?" But that damn fool didn't show any sign of leaving. He just sat down and kept on eating my pastries. He even ordered a glass of water. Damn it! I reached the point where I just had to say something, even if it landed me in trouble. I stood up. (*With a sheepish grin on his face.*) Oh, am I talking too much? Anyhow, I stood up and told him: "What's there to investigate in a bakery? Is that green tea bun a spy? Is the wheat bread a thief? Is the rice cake a burglar?" You know, a second cousin of mine is a lieutenant in the Kuro Precinct. But I tried not to make a scene. I was very patient with him. I just gritted my teeth and tried to get through the whole thing. But that little jerk treated me like I was a piece of gum on the sole of his shoe. I asked him to explain why he . . . When I was younger, I used to . . .

CHŎNGSUK: If you're finished . . .

BAKER: Yes?

CHŎNGSUK: I have a guest.

BAKER: Ah, is that right? (*Finally seeing* CH'ANG-YŎNG.) How are you?

CH'ANG-YŎNG: Well, thank you. And you?

BAKER: What, he's a man. (*To* CH'ANG-YŎNG.) Huh! (*At the sight of the well-known congressman* KANG.) Huh! That's him! Uh? Maybe not.

CHŎNGSUK: Thank you for the pie.

BAKER: Don't mention it. He's a dead ringer for Congressman Kang.

CHŎNGSUK: Is that so?

BAKER (*looking at his wristwatch*): Huh. It's eleven o'clock. It's very late. Is it really eleven o'clock already? (*To* CH'ANG-YŎNG.) Do you have the time? (*Not getting any response.*) Is he asleep? Ah, it's already eleven o'clock. Quite late, isn't it? (*Exits.*)

(CHŎNGSUK *bolts the door. She is about to tell* CH'ANG-YŎNG *that she wasn't able to stop the* BAKER *from intruding, but* CH'ANG-YŎNG *is deep in thought.* CHŎNGSUK *sits next to him quietly. Flashback.* FEMALE M-R *plays* CH'ANG-YŎNG'S WIFE.)

CH'ANG-YŎNG'S WIFE: I can't do that. I know what you're up to. In your way of thinking you'd be better off with your wife and child out of the way, wouldn't you?

CH'ANG-YŎNG'S A-E: Why are you always playing at being the perfect mother and wife type? Give yourself a break, why don't you?

CH'ANG-YŎNG'S WIFE: What are we to you? Is medical treatment the real reason you want to send Chaeung to America? Do you really think they can find a cure for him? What will they do? Slit open his head and pour vinegar in it? Well, I guess American vinegar must be different from the stuff we have here. You know perfectly well that he's just different from other kids. And it eats at you, doesn't it? He embarrasses you. To a big shot like you, he's nothing but an eyesore that you want to get rid of. Blame me. Go on, lay the blame on me all you want. I'll take it all, and I'll wait as long as it takes.

CHʼANG-YŎNG'S A-E (*gets to his feet*).

CHʼANG-YŎNG'S WIFE: Don't pretend you're angry with me. If you want to walk out on me, go ahead. Have you *ever* felt hurt because of anything I've done? If you at least show me that much emotion, I might feel alive again. I know how you are with those young girls at work! That's who you'd like to run off to now, isn't it? I don't know why you even bothered to come home tonight! Why do you point the finger at me?

CHʼANG-YŎNG'S A-E (*sits down*).

CHʼANG-YŎNG'S WIFE (*sobbing*): What have you done to me?! Why do I have to suffer like this for your mistakes?

CHAEUNG (*a youngster, barely able to walk and talk;* **MALE M-R** *as* **CHAEUNG**): Hee, hee, hee. (*The laugh of a mentally deficient child.*) Momma! Daddy! Don't fight!

CHʼANG-YŎNG'S A-E: Chaeung, go back to your room.

CHAEUNG: Daddy. (*Giggles.*) Hee, hee, hee . . .

CHʼANG-YŎNG'S WIFE (*drawing* **CHAEUNG** *into her arms*): Oh, my poor baby. (*Exits with* **CHAEUNG**.)

CHʼANG-YŎNG: Chŏngsuk.

CHŎNGSUK: Yes?

CHʼANG-YŎNG: We're all free agents.

CHŎNGSUK'S A-E: His conversation jumps around from one topic to another. Sometimes his sentences don't even have a subject. Is that because he thinks too much? Am I like that too?

CHʼANG-YŎNG: We condemn churchgoers who turn out to be crooks. How could a Christian do that? What did he say in his prayers? If a woman cheats on her husband, we think she's the worst kind of woman there is. A whore who deserted her family; the lowest of the low. But I believe each problem has its own circumstances.

CHŎNGSUK: I don't understand.

CHʼANG-YŎNG: Well, even a whore might have a story to tell. Even if she cheated on her husband, perhaps she never stopped loving her children. And perhaps the crook is a true Christian when he's in the church . . . They say it's not possible to love two women at the same time, so one of the women must be just a good time. But I believe it's possible to love both at the same time. There's more than one path to our lives. Each road is distinct and independent from the others.

CHŎNGSUK'S A-E: That sounds about right.

CHŎNGSUK: Well . . .

CHʼANG-YŎNG: I learned that from my wife.

CHŎNGSUK: What? Are you still not getting along with her?

CH'ANG-YŎNG: When you dislike someone, how does it start? Just as the baker said (*The* BAKER *can come back onto the stage, gesturing as in previous scenes.*), life is hard. It may be easier to deal with difficult situations.

CH'ANG-YŎNG'S A-E: I hate my wife's body odor. I don't like her snoring or the way she breathes. Even the way she chews her food disgusts me. She stuffs food in her mouth with one purpose only: survival.

CHŎNGSUK: Why don't you try to sort things out with her?

CH'ANG-YŎNG: Of course I will. I will love her with all my heart. Sometimes she's actually quite lovely.

CH'ANG-YŎNG'S A-E: Especially when she's with Chaeung. As long as my wife loves Chaeung, I won't be able to leave her.

CH'ANG-YŎNG: How can love and hatred be so mixed together?

(*Flashback.* CH'ANG-YŎNG'S A-E *and* FEMALE M-R *as the* WIFE *are in a hospital.*)

CH'ANG-YŎNG'S A-E: Hospital corridors are always dim, even with dozens of lights on the ceiling.

CH'ANG-YŎNG'S WIFE: . . .

CH'ANG-YŎNG'S A-E: Don't you hate the smell of disinfectant?

CH'ANG-YŎNG'S WIFE: Chaeung might be awake now. Why don't you go back to your office?

CH'ANG-YŎNG'S A-E: The doctor said he'll live.

CH'ANG-YŎNG'S WIFE: The night air must be cold. I'm sure you have a lot of work to do.

CH'ANG-YŎNG'S A-E: Honey, I'm sorry.

CH'ANG-YŎNG'S WIFE: It's getting late.

CH'ANG-YŎNG'S A-E: Let's start over!

CH'ANG-YŎNG'S WIFE: You must be busy with speeches to prepare as usual.

CH'ANG-YŎNG'S A-E: I'm done with all that.

CH'ANG-YŎNG'S WIFE: What do you mean?

CH'ANG-YŎNG'S A-E: First, I'm going give up my seat in Congress. I'll call a press conference.

CH'ANG-YŎNG'S WIFE: You've made a difficult decision.

CH'ANG-YŎNG'S A-E: You know I'm an old hand at dealing with difficulties. The answers are often found in the problems.

CH'ANG-YŎNG'S WIFE: Won't you regret it? It's your life's work.

CH'ANG-YŎNG'S A-E: What more is left for me to do at my age?

CH'ANG-YŎNG'S WIFE: You should think it through, though.

CH'ANG-YŎNG'S A-E: It's my destiny. Well . . . (*About to exit, turns back to her.*) I love you.

CH'ANG-YŎNG'S WIFE: Obligatory love—that's what it is.

CH'ANG-YŎNG'S A-E: It's instinctual, too.

CH'ANG-YŎNG'S WIFE: True love. You can't make it happen, no matter how hard you try. Love is destiny.

CH'ANG-YŎNG'S A-E (*stares at his wife*).

(*The telephone rings.* **MALE M-R**, *as* **BAKER**, *is calling. He is darning a sock. The telephone receiver is cradled on his shoulder.*)

BAKER: Hello, it's me again. The baker. You haven't turned in yet?

CHŎNGSUK: Not yet.

BAKER: How was the pumpkin pie? Delicious, wasn't it?

CHŎNGSUK: Ah, yes, it was.

BAKER: Miss Pak, what are you doing now? I'm reading a book. It's such a good book that I lost track of the time. All of a sudden, it occurred to me . . . (*Lowering his voice.*) Just listen. Is the man still there?

CHŎNGSUK: He is.

BAKER: Are you in any danger? Just answer me yes or no.

CHŎNGSUK: No.

BAKER: Do you know him well?

CHŎNGSUK: Yes.

BAKER: Huh, what a relief. I've already changed into my taekwondo gear and was debating which weapon to take with me: a baseball bat or an iron stick. I was ready to take him down. The world's gone mad, these days. So many weirdos are around.

CHŎNGSUK: Well then . . .

BAKER: What a relief to know you're safe. By the way, my clock says its eleven fifteen; what time do you make it . . . ?

CHŎNGSUK (*hangs up*).

BAKER: Hello! Hello! She hung up. It's very late. (*The needle pricks his finger.*) Ouch! That hurt. It's very late.

CHŎNGSUK (*laughing*).

CH'ANG-YŎNG: Who was that?

CHŎNGSUK: It was the baker. (*Laughing.*) Hooh, hooh, hooh . . . He said he was reading a book . . . Mr. Kang![4]

CH'ANG-YŎNG: Yes?

CHŎNGSUK: Shall I tell you what you were thinking about just now?

CH'ANG-YŎNG: What?

CHŎNGSUK: You were thinking of hooking me up with the baker.

CH'ANG-YŎNG'S A-E: What? How did she . . . ?

CHŎNGSUK'S A-E: Look at him. He's odious.

CHŎNGSUK: That's something I don't like about you.

CHŎNGSUK'S A-E: He's sorry for me. Blind sympathy—that's what it is.

CH'ANG-YŎNG: We'd be healthier if we let ourselves be more like animals.
CHŎNGSUK'S A-E: Wild beasts would be more like it.
CH'ANG-YŎNG'S A-E: Wild beasts. She just likes the way that sounds.
CHŎNGSUK (*suppressing her growing anger*): Is a husband a pet?!
CHŎNGSUK'S A-E: Hold on. He was only joking.
CHŎNGSUK (*rather embarrassed by her emotions*): Health isn't everything.
CH'ANG-YŎNG: I imagine raising kids under those circumstances hasn't exactly been a picnic for the baker.
CHŎNGSUK'S A-E (*to* CHŎNGSUK): Hey, why don't you let him win this round?
CHŎNGSUK: That's for sure.
CH'ANG-YŎNG: He seems like a good guy, that's all. I didn't mean anything else.
CHŎNGSUK: I know.
CHŎNGSUK'S A-E: I know what he's thinking: "A man with the baker's personality would be a good match for her." Every time he comes across a decent man at work or an attentive cab driver on the street, he immediately starts thinking about setting them up with me.
CHŎNGSUK: Do you know any widowers or divorced men? I look pitiful, don't I? I'll be turning forty soon, and here I am acting like a helpless little chick waiting for her mother to bring home the food.
CH'ANG-YŎNG: I'm sorry if I upset you.
CHŎNGSUK: I was just talking to myself.
CH'ANG-YŎNG'S A-E: I just want to see you happy.
CHŎNGSUK'S A-E: Am I the main character in your "happy" scenario?
CH'ANG-YŎNG'S A-E: The reason that I can't be with you is not because of my friendship with Talho. It's because you're a heartbreaker.
CH'ANG-YŎNG: How are your knees?
CHŎNGSUK: They're much better now, as you can see.
CH'ANG-YŎNG: Are you planning to teach again?
CHŎNGSUK: I'm not sure yet.
CHŎNGSUK'S A-E: The school was like a stagnant pond, and I was like a dead fish in it. Trees are supposed to grow upward, but we were busy cutting them down.
CH'ANG-YŎNG: If I had teaching credentials, I'd take up teaching in a heartbeat. Right now.
CHŎNGSUK (*smiles doubtfully*).
  (*Flashback. In the* PRINCIPAL'*s office.* MALE M-R, *wearing a wig, as the* PRINCIPAL.)
PRINCIPAL: I told you I can't do it.

CHŎNGSUK: Won't you reconsider?

PRINCIPAL (*sitting*): Look, here. Teaching is not the only thing we do here. As teachers, we also have to be role models for our young students. I can't keep a woman on my payroll who gave birth to a child only seven months after her wedding. (*To himself.*) She'll ruin our reputation.

CHŎNGSUK'S A-E: He acts like he's a saint. We all know he's a regular at the cabaret club.

CHŎNGSUK: I see what you mean, but . . .

PRINCIPAL (*interrupting*): I can tell you've come here on behalf of the female teachers to protest my decision. Go back to your desk. The decision won't change as long as I'm the principal. Such disgraceful conduct has no business in my school. I won't tolerate it.

CHŎNGSUK'S A-E: Unbutton your blouse. And spread your legs a bit.

CHŎNGSUK (*does as she's told*): It's not that I don't understand your point of view. But does she really have to resign? Isn't there something else we can do?

PRINCIPAL: No, there is not.

CHŎNGSUK'S A-E: It's working. The tone of his voice is changing.

CHŎNGSUK (*angling her torso forward*): I'd like to . . .

CHŎNGSUK'S A-E: That angle gives him a perfect view of your breasts.

CHŎNGSUK: I apologize on Miss Kim's behalf.

PRINCIPAL: I told you, I won't change my mind. (*Stealing a look at* CHŎNGSUK'*s breasts.*) I told you, I won't change my mind. Go back to work.

CHŎNGSUK: So, it's really final, then?

PRINCIPAL: That's right.

CHŎNGSUK'S A-E (*to* CHŎNGSUK): Step aside. I'll take care of this. (*To* PRINCIPAL.) Isn't it hot in here? Please . . . Will you help me with this zipper? Oh, please don't peek. (*Turns around and hugs the* PRINCIPAL. *To* CHŎNGSUK.) Oh, I feel so ashamed. Don't look.

CHŎNGSUK: I'm looking at myself! What's wrong with that?

CHŎNGSUK'S A-E: Don't you get embarrassed when you see yourself naked in front of the mirror, even if you're alone?

CHŎNGSUK: All right. (*Turns away.*)

PRINCIPAL: Miss Pak. You can't do this. This is a sacred place. It's the principal's office. What if someone comes in . . .

CHŎNGSUK'S A-E: Let them come in. Having sex is more fun when there's a risk of getting caught.

PRINCIPAL: Huh . . . Huh.

CHŎNGSUK'S A-E: Why don't you like me?

PRINCIPAL: It's not that I don't like you.

CHŎNGSUK'S A-E: We live in a very complicated world. (*Stroking the bald spots on the* PRINCIPAL's *head.*) How can you have fun if you've always got your nose to the grindstone? (*Undoes his necktie.*) You need to escape from all this.

PRINCIPAL: I know what you mean, but . . .

CHŎNGSUK'S A-E: You look just like the man I'm in love with.

PRINCIPAL: Really?

CHŎNGSUK'S A-E: Of course there's a big age difference.

PRINCIPAL: I'm young at heart!

CHŎNGSUK'S A-E: Will you be at the cabaret club tonight?

PRINCIPAL: Well . . . Hum-hum.

CHŎNGSUK'S A-E: I might be there tonight.

PRINCIPAL: Is that so? Well then, let's get together later and have some fun.

CHŎNGSUK'S A-E: I'd like that. So, should Miss Kim turn in her resignation?

PRINCIPAL: Uh, no.

CHŎNGSUK'S A-E: She doesn't have to?

PRINCIPAL: No. It'll be OK.

CHŎNGSUK'S A-E (*slapping the* PRINCIPAL's *face*): You son of a bitch.

CHŎNGSUK: Good. I'll go back to my desk, then. (CHŎNGSUK *and* CHŎNGSUK'S A-E *exit.*) I should have used your strategy from the beginning.

CHŎNGSUK'S A-E: You can't do it.

CHŎNGSUK: I can't?

CHŎNGSUK'S A-E: Would you really sacrifice your body to save Miss Kim's job?

CHŎNGSUK (*sitting next to* CH'ANG-YŎNG; *laughing*).

CH'ANG-YŎNG: What is it?

CHŎNGSUK: A funny thought just crossed my mind. The Bible says that adultery is a sin even if it's locked in your heart.

CH'ANG-YŎNG: That's right.

CHŎNGSUK: If that's the case, then a person like me . . .

CH'ANG-YŎNG: Well, a person like me is far worse . . .

CHŎNGSUK: You know, I'm kind of bored since I stopped teaching. It's been several years now.

CH'ANG-YŎNG: What would you like to do?

CHŎNGSUK'S A-E: I want to run an art gallery.

CHŎNGSUK: I'm thinking about it.

CH'ANG-YŎNG'S A-E: Teaching's a great job for a woman.

CHŎNGSUK: Standing long hours in class could put strain on my knees.

CH'ANG-YŎNG: True.

CHŎNGSUK: I'd like to start something new soon.

CHŎNGSUK'S A-E: I feel bad that he's paying my bills.

CHŎNGSUK: Perhaps I can adopt a child.
CH'ANG-YŎNG: Don't!
CH'ANG-YŎNG'S A-E: Children break your heart. They rip out your heart and break it.
CHŎNGSUK: I haven't made up my mind yet.
  (CHŎNGSUK *and* CH'ANG-YŎNG *have run out of things to say to each other.* CH'ANG-YŎNG'S A-E *and* CHŎNGSUK'S A-E *also are lost for words.* CH'ANG-YŎNG *is about to say something about the painting on the wall.* CHŎNGSUK *looks like she is about to chime in, but* CH'ANG-YŎNG *stops short of speaking.* CHŎNGSUK *remains silent, too.* CH'ANG-YŎNG *fixes his gaze at a vase on the table, and* CHŎNGSUK *does the same. A large bouquet of baby's breath is sitting in the vase. A single-stem white lily stands tall above the baby's breath.* CH'ANG-YŎNG *and* CHŎNGSUK *exchange meaningful smiles.*)
CH'ANG-YŎNG: About the flowers.
CHŎNGSUK: I bought them at the wholesale market.
CHŎNGSUK'S A-E: I wonder why he did it. If there's an ethics violation, am I connected somehow? He was so confident. What made him resign? I haven't been able to do anything all day. I've been sad. As if something inside had been destroyed.
CHŎNGSUK: Actually, your notoriety has always been very comforting to me. Whenever a screwball teacher bothered me, I'd say, "Hey you! Did I ever mention that I'm very closely connected with Congressman Kang?"
CH'ANG-YŎNG: The flowers don't go together. The lily is just like me, but that's a bit far-fetched, isn't it?
CHŎNGSUK: I don't know.
CHŎNGSUK'S A-E: To me you're like the lily, and I'm the baby's breath, always trying to protect you.
CH'ANG-YŎNG'S A-E: I'm sorry about that.
CHŎNGSUK'S A-E: All I get to see is your back. Except for once in a blue moon, when you turn around to look at me.
  (*Flashback.* CHŎNGSUK'S A-E *walks into the house of* CH'ANG-YŎNG'S A-E *carrying a bouquet of flowers.*)
CHŎNGSUK'S A-E: Mr. Kang.
CH'ANG-YŎNG'S A-E (*flustered at the sight of* CHŎNGSUK'S A-E, *trying to tidy up the place*): Well . . . Miss Pak! What brings you here . . . ?
CH'ANG-YŎNG: Back then, it felt strange when you called me Mr. Kang.
CHŎNGSUK: I didn't know how else to address you.
CH'ANG-YŎNG: It didn't make much sense. You were a teacher, and I was a farm worker. Whenever you called me mister, I wouldn't even realize it was for me.

CHŎNGSUK'S A-E: Mr. Kang.
CH'ANG-YŎNG'S A-E (*cautiously*): Why the flowers?
CH'ANG-YŎNG: No one had ever given me a bunch of flowers before then.
CHŎNGSUK'S A-E: I bought them for you. I couldn't find a vase, so I emptied out a bean-paste container . . .
CHŎNGSUK: Back then, almost every night I stayed up writing poems, painting, or listening to music. During the day, I used to be half asleep. My audio system was probably the best one in that whole little town.
CH'ANG-YŎNG: Probably the best in the whole county.
CHŎNGSUK: I saved up for months to buy that sound system.
CH'ANG-YŎNG: Whenever I passed through the campus, I heard music coming from your place.
CHŎNGSUK'S A-E: Mr. Kang. I brought these for you.
CH'ANG-YŎNG'S A-E: Ah, yes . . . what shall I do with them?
CHŎNGSUK'S A-E: How about putting them over there?
CH'ANG-YŎNG'S A-E: Oh, sure. This is really a first for me. (*Takes the flowers.*)
CHŎNGSUK'S A-E: What were you doing?
CH'ANG-YŎNG'S A-E: I was about to do my laundry. (*Takes out a piece of clothing from underneath the bed but pushes it back right away when he realizes it's his underwear.*)
CHŎNGSUK'S A-E (*laughs*): Don't mind me. I won't be in your way.
CH'ANG-YŎNG'S A-E: No, no, I'll do it later.
CHŎNGSUK'S A-E: Is Chaeung in bed?
CH'ANG-YŎNG'S A-E: Yes.
CHŎNGSUK'S A-E: He must be exhausted, following his dad around all day.
CH'ANG-YŎNG'S A-E: I've got nothing to offer you, not even tea or coffee.
CHŎNGSUK'S A-E: Should I just stand here?
CH'ANG-YŎNG'S A-E: Oh, please come in and have a seat.
CHŎNGSUK'S A-E: I'm fine. But don't you have something for me . . . ?
CH'ANG-YŎNG'S A-E: How about a glass of water?
CHŎNGSUK'S A-E: No, not that . . .
CH'ANG-YŎNG'S A-E: Then what can I . . . ?
CHŎNGSUK (*laughing*): Back then, I ran to your house every night in bare feet. In my dreams, that is.
CHŎNGSUK'S A-E: I meant, do you have something for me to sew or clean?
CH'ANG-YŎNG'S A-E: I beg your par . . . ?
CHŎNGSUK'S A-E: Well, I'll see you later.
CH'ANG-YŎNG'S A-E: What about the flowers . . .
CHŎNGSUK'S A-E: They're from my heart, and my heart's here all the time.

(CH'ANG-YŎNG'S A-E *and* CHŎNGSUK'S A-E *gaze at each as if they have just been struck by lightning. Both of them return to their seats.*)

CH'ANG-YŎNG: I couldn't understand why you . . .

CHŎNGSUK: If there was a reason, I wanted to find it, too. I loved watching you walking to and from the orchard, with Chaeung always lagging a few steps behind you. Those were good times.

CHŎNGSUK'S A-E: You were intense. Your head was like your paintings and poems—filled with thoughts of Ch'ang-yŏng.

CH'ANG-YŎNG: That was a beautiful place to live.

CHŎNGSUK'S A-E: The school was like a tiny brown creature, nestled under the big leafy trees. After class, we used to roam around the hills and mountains like a shepherd and flock.

CH'ANG-YŎNG: Don't you want to go back there?

CHŎNGSUK: Sure I do. I'd like to go there and live as a shepherd.

CHŎNGSUK'S A-E: I don't like that place. It's too lonely there. The only voice I heard was my own, and only in echoes. These days I'm too cynical to live surrounded by rabbits and squirrels.

CHŎNGSUK: Why did you leave?

CH'ANG-YŎNG: Because I wanted you to go on living there peacefully.

CHŎNGSUK (*laughing*): Is that right? So did I end up living peacefully in that place?

CHŎNGSUK'S A-E: No. I don't think about it any more, but at the time I felt abandoned in that strange, backcountry place.

CH'ANG-YŎNG'S A-E: Please forgive me.

CHŎNGSUK'S A-E: That's all right. I shouldn't have burdened you with all that.

CH'ANG-YŎNG: You know what a nincompoop is? It's a person who's stupid and dense.

CHŎNGSUK: And?

CH'ANG-YŎNG: I was a nincompoop then, and I'm a nincompoop now. Nothing's changed.

CHŎNGSUK (*puts her hair up, feeling hot*).

CHŎNGSUK'S A-E: Should I keep my hair in a ponytail or cut it short? Did he see the hair under my armpits? Ah, it's getting hot in here. How about you?

CHŎNGSUK: I'm OK.

CHŎNGSUK'S A-E: I feel light-headed. What's wrong with me?

CHŎNGSUK (*to her* A-E): Well . . . (*To* CH'ANG-YŎNG.) Warm? Would you like a glass of ice water?

CH'ANG-YŎNG: Do you have any liquor? Any *soju*?

CHŎNGSUK: I might have some left over from the other day. (*Looks for* soju.) I've got half a bottle.
CH'ANG-YŎNG: Do you drink by yourself?
CHŎNGSUK: Sure, why not?
CHŎNGSUK'S A-E: Some days I pour the *soju* into a big soup bowl and drink it bottoms up.
CH'ANG-YŎNG: When you're lonely?
CHŎNGSUK: Am I ever *not* lonely?
CH'ANG-YŎNG: How do you cope with it? The loneliness.
CHŎNGSUK (*laughs*).
CHŎNGSUK'S A-E: Don't tell him. You'll regret it.
CHŎNGSUK: I pull down all the blinds, take off my clothes, and walk around the apartment. And I talk.
CH'ANG-YŎNG: With whom?
CHŎNGSUK: With my alter-ego.
CHŎNGSUK'S A-E: That's me.
CHŎNGSUK: My a-e is very different from me. She likes to wear miniskirts. She has short hair. She's smart, cheerful, and witty.
CHŎNGSUK'S A-E (*lifting her chin*): I'm shrewd and seductive. And vibrant.
CHŎNGSUK: She always tells me to be honest with myself.
CHŎNGSUK'S A-E: Hey, Kang Ch'ang-yŏng! Get a divorce and marry me!
CHŎNGSUK: She hassles me too, sometimes.
CHŎNGSUK'S A-E: You're the kind of girl who just can't open up, not even once in your life.
CH'ANG-YŎNG'S A-E: Well, he's just the same. (*To* CH'ANG-YŎNG.) You're a weakling. No nerve.
CH'ANG-YŎNG: I want to split people open, get inside, and find out what it's like in there.
CH'ANG-YŎNG'S A-E: Quite a sight, I imagine!
CHŎNGSUK'S A-E: All sorts of germs must be wiggling around inside.
CH'ANG-YŎNG'S A-E: A Christian who embezzles his banks. A Buddhist monk who practices shamanism.
CHŎNGSUK'S A-E: A husband who spends money like water on booze and women while his wife is trying to make ends meet by selling sandwiches out of a cart. A woman who haggles loudly in the open market but acts like an empress in department stores.
CH'ANG-YŎNG'S A-E (*to* CH'ANG-YŎNG): How about you?
CHŎNGSUK'S A-E (*to* CHŎNGSUK): How about you?
CHŎNGSUK: When I said I wanted to become a nun, my alter-ego told me to become a painter. I ended up being neither.

CH'ANG-YŎNG'S A-E: No . . . it looks to me like you've become both.

CHŎNGSUK: When I was young, I always dreamed of being a nun.

CH'ANG-YŎNG: Your days must have been filled with loneliness and innocence.

CHŎNGSUK: That's probably the image I want to project.

CH'ANG-YŎNG'S A-E: Perhaps. But even if you are set on keeping yourself chaste, your alter-ego must be running wild.

CHŎNGSUK'S A-E: You're right. Sometimes when I'm drunk, I get the urge to throw myself into a stranger's arms. (*As if drunk.*) Hey, want to have a drink with me? I'm not a virgin, you know. I know how to have fun. I feel it all down here—sweet, salty, spicy, sour, and achy—I know all about it. (*Screaming out of desperation.*) Ah! Like trees soaring to the sky, like trees soaring to the sky!

CHŎNGSUK: Go home. It's late. Your wife will be waiting for you.

CHŎNGSUK'S A-E: Stay with me tonight. We can drink all night . . .

CH'ANG-YŎNG'S A-E: My wife is at the hospital, with Chaeung.

CH'ANG-YŎNG: One day, in high school, I got on a bus. It was during rush hour, so the bus was packed like a sardine can. Back then, my mother worked as a kitchen maid at a Buddhist temple. I saw my mother squatting on the floor of the bus. A large aluminum basin was sitting in front of her. The basin was full of something but I couldn't tell what was in there because it was covered with a cloth. Passengers kept tripping over the basin, but my mother didn't take any notice of them. She was just watching out for her basin. The bus driver's assistant yelled at her, "I told you not to get on my bus!" My mother didn't respond. She was dressed in worn-out clothes, and her face looked wrinkled and gray with age. When the bus reached our stop, my mother exited from the front door, and I went out the back. People on the street helped her hoist the bowl on top of her head. I followed my mother all the way to our house, staying about ten yards behind her, trailing along the winding road of the shantytown where we lived. When I arrived home, my mother uncovered the bowl . . . The white rice that she earned as her wages was spilling out of it.

(*Flashback.* FEMALE M-R *as the* MOTHER.)

MOTHER: Ch'ang-yŏng, it's me.

CH'ANG-YŎNG'S A-E: Mother!

MOTHER: You must be hungry.

CH'ANG-YŎNG'S A-E: Not really.

MOTHER: A monk told me your name doesn't serve you well. I'm sorry.

CH'ANG-YŎNG (*to himself*): Kang Ch'ang-yŏng.[5]

CH'ANG-YŎNG'S A-E: Can't blame the name.
MOTHER: It's all my fault.
CH'ANG-YŎNG'S A-E: That's what I meant.
MOTHER: I've always wanted to be like a big tree for you. To shade you from the heat and shelter you from the rain.
CH'ANG-YŎNG (*to* **CHŎNGSUK**): My mother wanted me to live a normal, happy life.
MOTHER: Even when I'm dead, I'll still be a disgrace to you. I'm not even fit to look at you. It'd be better if I just disappeared.
CH'ANG-YŎNG'S A-E: Mother, I didn't mean that. I know it's impossible to escape from destiny, and your life was your destiny. Please come and see me as often as you can. Even if I live to be an old man, my life will be too short to cleanse myself of the sins I committed against you.
MOTHER: You're a good son, Ch'ang-yŏng.
CH'ANG-YŎNG'S A-E: What?
MOTHER: Forget about Chaeung. Take him to an orphanage. His blood is tainted, and his flesh smells of sin.
CH'ANG-YŎNG'S A-E: Don't say that, mother. It's my duty to care for Chaeung. I have to.
MOTHER: Your heart is too soft.
CH'ANG-YŎNG'S A-E: He's started talking, and he's not sick any more.
MOTHER: But the evil inside him can never be washed out.
CH'ANG-YŎNG'S A-E: My wife loves him, too.
MOTHER: Take him to an orphanage!
CH'ANG-YŎNG'S A-E: Mother!
MOTHER: Don't call me Mother!
CH'ANG-YŎNG'S A-E: Mother.
MOTHER: If you're hungry for love, then open your heart to your wife.
CH'ANG-YŎNG'S A-E: Mother.
MOTHER: I know, I know. (*Exits.*)
CHŎNGSUK (*reads a poem*):
> Each time you said "good-bye" on your way to work,
> Each time you turned to go farther away from home,
> The sight of your back filled my eyes with tears.
> Every morning we shared our farewells, in poverty.
> The bag on your back was heavy then with manuscripts;
> Now a lunchbox weighs on your shoulders.
> Look at the bright faces of your children;
> I hoist our little ones up to meet your eyes.
> At home I find the keys,

Keys that can kindle fires in your body and soul,
Keys that can unlock the chest of eternal energy.

CH'ANG-YŎNG: That's a good poem. Did you write it?

CHŎNGSUK: I did.

CHŎNGSUK'S A-E: I wrote it down while I was imagining our married life together.

CH'ANG-YŎNG: People who can't imagine the possibility of change will never succeed.

CHŎNGSUK'S A-E: What now?

CH'ANG-YŎNG'S A-E: All these years, I've rushed to finish that old race called success. I've worked night and day, just hoping to cross the finish line one day sooner. I was so afraid of getting old, without having done anything. But it dawned on me recently. Life is just a practice run until we turn sixty. The real game starts when we turn sixty. What we're doing now is just practice for the real game later.

CH'ANG-YŎNG: Chŏngsuk . . . Why don't you give yourself a fresh start? Your past can't have been all for nothing.

CHŎNGSUK: Meaning what?

CH'ANG-YŎNG: You can be a poet.

CH'ANG-YŎNG'S A-E: You can be a poet, a nun, a painter, a teacher. So many things. Don't you want to get engrossed in something? I don't want you to waste your talents. But don't go spreading yourself too thin, either.

CH'ANG-YŎNG: Your true talent is the one that outshines all the others.

CHŎNGSUK: How can I become a poet at this late stage in my life?

CH'ANG-YŎNG: Are you afraid of failure?

CHŎNGSUK (*laughs*).

CH'ANG-YŎNG: I don't . . .

CHŎNGSUK: Go on.

CH'ANG-YŎNG: I don't care for amateurs.

CHŎNGSUK: Meaning . . . ?

CH'ANG-YŎNG: I mean, poetry should be more than just a hobby. If not poetry, then pursue your painting—professionally, I mean.

CH'ANG-YŎNG'S A-E: Don't settle for life as an art teacher. You can be someone who deals in life's mysteries.

CHŎNGSUK: Without formal training, it's impossible to become a professional painter.

CH'ANG-YŎNG (*impersonating* **CHŎNGSUK**): It's impossible.

CHŎNGSUK'S A-E: That's why I never get very far with anything. Isn't it strange? I see you as a born poet, even though you haven't written a single poem yet.

CH'ANG-YŎNG: Why don't you take your poetry more seriously? Your indifference is very frustrating.

CHŎNGSUK'S A-E: Wives of poets must be happy.

CH'ANG-YŎNG: Happiness is only an illusion. Nobody can really be happy in this world.

CHŎNGSUK'S A-E: I agree. Happiness is only the flip side of vanity.

CH'ANG-YŎNG (*hands a cigarette to* CHŎNGSUK *and lights up his own. Stares at the smoke coming out of his mouth and nose*): Two days ago, Chaeung attempted suicide. He took poison.

CHŎNGSUK: What? How did that happen?

CH'ANG-YŎNG: Things happen suddenly. We're all blind to our destiny, but sooner or later it catches up with us.

CHŎNGSUK: What *happened*?

CHŎNGSUK'S A-E: Is he dead?

CH'ANG-YŎNG: He's fine now. Life is more tenacious than it looks. He'll live a long life, a long and plodding life.

CHŎNGSUK'S A-E: He must have been really traumatized.

CH'ANG-YŎNG: His stomach had to be pumped. It must still hurt, but he's recovering well in the hospital.

CHŎNGSUK: Why did he attempt suicide?

CH'ANG-YŎNG: He wouldn't tell me.

CH'ANG-YŎNG'S A-E: You *know* why.

CHŎNGSUK'S A-E: I thought something was odd about him tonight.

CH'ANG-YŎNG: I was going to send him to America for physical therapy.

CH'ANG-YŎNG'S A-E: Son of a bitch. That's a lie!

CH'ANG-YŎNG: To be honest, I wanted to send him away because I couldn't bear the sight of him any more. My wife and I argued about it all the time, even right in front of him. I thought he couldn't understand our fights, but it turns out he got it all. He probably thought that my wife and I could be happy together if he was dead.

MALE M-R (*as* CHAEUNG): Hee, hee, hee. Daddy! Dad! Do I look cute? Hee, hee, hee. (*Exits.*)

CHŎNGSUK'S A-E: I can't believe that Chaeung would do that.

CH'ANG-YŎNG'S A-E: My political ambition blinded me.

CHŎNGSUK'S A-E: Chaeung must have been as much use to an ambitious father as a lame leg.

CHŎNGSUK: Mr. Kang . . .

CH'ANG-YŎNG (*cuts off* CHŎNGSUK *with a gesture*): Please don't.

CH'ANG-YŎNG'S A-E: Nothing you say can comfort me now. It's something I have to deal with on my own.

CHŎNGSUK'S A-E: I pity him, though.

(*The telephone rings.*)[6]

CHŎNGSUK'S A-E (*walks to the phone*): It must be him—the baker. I'd better make it clear that it's time for him to cut it out. (*Picking up the phone.*) Hey, you. Stop pestering me. Don't you ever sleep? Don't you have to get up at the crack of dawn to knead dough? (*Hangs up the phone.*)

CHŎNGSUK (*picks up the phone*): Hello. No, you have a wrong number. (*Hangs up the phone.*) He thought he called a Chinese restaurant.

(*The telephone rings.*)

CH'ANG-YŎNG: I'll get it this time. (*Picks up the phone.*) Hello.

MALE M-R (*as a teenage prankster*): You're not meant to answer, dumb ass. I want to talk to your wife, get it? (*Hangs up the phone.*)

CH'ANG-YŎNG (*hanging up the phone*): He didn't even give me a chance to say anything.

CHŎNGSUK: Must be that junior high kid. He was a little early today. He usually phones just before midnight.

(*The telephone rings again.*)

CHŎNGSUK'S A-E: I'd better get a new number.

CHŎNGSUK (*picks up the phone*).

TALHO (*played by* MALE M-R. FEMALE M-R *plays a white woman.* TALHO *is resting his head on the woman's lap, his legs crossed*): Hello, hello.

CHŎNGSUK: Hello?

TALHO: Chŏngsuk, It's me.

CHŎNGSUK: Who's calling?

TALHO: It's *me*, your husband, Talho! Have you forgotten your husband's voice already?

CHŎNGSUK: What do you want?

CHŎNGSUK'S A-E: What's got into that son of a bitch? He hasn't called for years.

TALHO: It's been a while. How've you been? How's everything with you? I've been really busy with work. Still, I might be able to visit you next year, or maybe the year after.

CHŎNGSUK: What do you want?

TALHO: Watch your manners. So, we haven't talked to each other for a while. No need to be so cold.

CHŎNGSUK'S A-E: Son of a bitch. He's probably lying back with his legs crossed and some Yankee girl beside him.

TALHO: How's your work at school?

CHŎNGSUK'S A-E: I haven't taught for some time now, you son of a bitch.

TALHO: Are you still in touch with Ch'ang-yŏng? You know you can call him up if you need any help. He'll take good care of you for me. So, any news?

CHŎNGSUK: What kind of news?

TALHO: Never mind. I wired you some money. Buy yourself a new outfit. A pretty one, OK?

CHŎNGSUK'S A-E: I wouldn't mind rotting in jail if I could just smother him to death first.

TALHO: I've got to go. By the way, what's going on with Ch'ang-yŏng?

CHŎNGSUK'S A-E: Finally he's getting to the point.

TALHO: I heard he left Congress. Quite a shock, huh? Koreans here in America are talking about it, too. I called him, but his secretary told me he'd gone somewhere. I was wondering if you know why he resigned.

CHŎNGSUK: Me?

TALHO: You don't know *anything*? What the hell is a violation of ethics? If you find out where he is, call me any time, OK? My number here is . . . Well, I'll call you again tomorrow.

CHŎNGSUK'S A-E: That crazy son of a bitch. He's afraid I might show up at the door of his apartment.

TALHO: Hey!! If you have time, why don't you go visit Ch'ang-yŏng? He's been playing the gentleman all these years, but now he's gone and blown it all. I wonder if he'll work things out. (*Hangs up.*)

(*Daydream sequence.* CHŎNGSUK'S A-E *runs to the sleeping* TALHO *with a shotgun in her hands. She pokes* TALHO *with the gun to wake him.*)

TALHO: Chŏngsuk, when did you arrive in America?

CHŎNGSUK'S A-E: Get up!

TALHO: What's going on?

CHŎNGSUK'S A-E: Stand over there and keep your mouth shut!

TALHO: Chŏngsuk . . .

CHŎNGSUK'S A-E (*to the* AMERICAN WOMAN): You, too.

AMERICAN WOMAN: Me too?

CHŎNGSUK'S A-E: Hurry up.

AMERICAN WOMAN: I don't speak Korean.[7]

CHŎNGSUK'S A-E: Hurry up.

AMERICAN WOMAN: What's all this?

CHŎNGSUK'S A-E: Sit down. Stand up! Sit! Stand!

(TALHO *and* AMERICAN WOMAN *do as they are told.*)

CHŎNGSUK'S A-E: Talho, you disgraceful bastard, come here!

(CHŎNGSUK'S A-E *thrusts the gun at* TALHO's *chest.* TALHO *falls down.* CHŎNG-SUK'S A-E *steps on* TALHO's *head.*)

CHŎNGSUK'S A-E: Don't you ever dare to telephone me again. I don't want to see your ugly face either. Understand?

AMERICAN WOMAN: Answer her! Quickly!!

TALHO: I understand! I understand!

CHŎNGSUK'S A-E (*fires several shots into the air*): Rotten son of a bitch.

(TALHO *and* AMERICAN WOMAN *exit.*)

CH'ANG-YŎNG: Was that Talho?

CHŎNGSUK: It was. He was looking for you. Has he asked for money again?

CH'ANG-YŎNG: He did.

CHŎNGSUK: How much did he want this time?

CH'ANG-YŎNG: Not a lot.

CHŎNGSUK: Don't do it.

CH'ANG-YŎNG: I don't intend to.

CHŎNGSUK: I don't understand how you two became friends.

CH'ANG-YŎNG: He's changed.

CHŎNGSUK'S A-E: Do you think so? Did Talho really love me once? Did he leave for America because he knew that I was in love with Ch'ang-yŏng? Is that why he keeps disrupting our lives, out of revenge?

CHŎNGSUK: He's been the same person all the time I've known him.

CH'ANG-YŎNG: I don't know . . .

BYŎNGCH'ŎL (*played by* MALE M-R): Fresh today! Live squid from the East Coast! Ch'ang-yŏng, you're a good man to think of Talho like that.

CH'ANG-YŎNG'S A-E: Byŏngch'ŏl, it's you!

BYŎNGCH'ŎL: People are all pretty much the same in the end. When we fall in love, don't we all fear betrayal?

CH'ANG-YŎNG'S A-E: Yeah . . . I was going to visit you at your grave tomorrow. Sorry I couldn't do it earlier.

BYŎNGCH'ŎL: That's all right. See you tomorrow.

CH'ANG-YŎNG'S A-E: Byŏngch'ŏl, what should I do about Chŏngsuk?

BYŎNGCH'ŎL: You're doing fine, man.

CH'ANG-YŎNG'S A-E: Thanks.

BYŎNGCH'ŎL: No problem. (*Exits.*)

CHŎNGSUK: Talho's not asking for money just as a favor from a friend, is he?

CH'ANG-YŎNG: Probably not.

CHŎNGSUK: Is it because of what happened?

CH'ANG-YŎNG: Yeah, I think so.

CHŎNGSUK: How did you guys end up in that mess?

(*Flashback.* **CH'ANG-YŎNG** *sits on the ground, wearing dark sunglasses and a baseball cap pulled down to cover his face. Birds are singing.* **BYŎNGCH'ŎL** *and* **TALHO** *enter, each carrying a shovel.*)

TALHO: Whew! That good-for-nothing bastard was damned heavy. Probably with the weight of all his sins. (*To* **BYŎNGCH'ŎL**.) You must be beat. Man, I'm thirsty. I sure could use a tall cold beer right now. (*To* **CH'ANG-YŎNG**.) Don't worry. Nothing happened.

CH'ANG-YŎNG: Did you finish burying him?

TALHO: Yeah, it doesn't take long to knock someone off. (*To* **CH'ANG-YŎNG**.) I mean, that son of a bitch Dog Meat deserved it. All over Pongch'on, the name Dog Meat meant bad news. Everyone was scared of him, even little kids. Don't you worry. If he were still alive, dozens of other innocent lives would be in danger.

BYŎNGCH'ŎL: What's on your mind?

CH'ANG-YŎNG: My mother.

TALHO: Your mother?

CH'ANG-YŎNG: That's right.

TALHO: Why?

CH'ANG-YŎNG: Don't know. It just came to me. What should we do now?

TALHO (*takes off his gloves*).

BYŎNGCH'ŎL (*wiping the fingerprints off his shovel; laying the shovel on the ground*): Be careful. Watch out what you say, especially when you're drunk. Give me your gloves. (*Puts* **TALHO**'s *gloves in his pockets.*)

TALHO: I get it! I get it! That's common sense.

BYŎNGCH'ŎL (*sitting next to* **CH'ANG-YŎNG**): Ch'ang-yŏng.

CH'ANG-YŎNG: What?

BYŎNGCH'ŎL: I know what's on your mind. You did what I was supposed to do. That's what happened. *I* killed him, really.

CH'ANG-YŎNG: What do we do now?

BYŎNGCH'ŎL: Let's stick to the plan we made before. We all go home for now. I go to my mother's house in the country. We all act normal. Whenever that son of bitch crosses your mind, have a drink, have sex. If that doesn't work, well, take a trip.

TALHO: Right! Time heals everything. Let some time go by, and all this'll be forgotten. Shit happens. Like when the pitcher hits the batter and he drops dead. An accident, and you're not alone, man. The world's full of crooks pretending to be saints. Anyway, you only did it out of friendship and loyalty.

CH'ANG-YŎNG: I didn't mean to kill him.

BYŎNGCH'ŎL: I know.
TALHO: Dog Meat was the worst of the lot.
CH'ANG-YŎNG: Someday it'll be found out.
TALHO: Nobody saw it but us and Byŏngch'ŏl's mother. Who'll squeal? Quit worrying!
BYŎNGCH'ŎL: Quiet! Someone's coming. (*Exits.*)
(CH'ANG-YŎNG *walks toward* CHŎNGSUK.)
CHŎNGSUK: Do you still think of Talho as your friend?
CH'ANG-YŎNG: Not any more. I've put him out of my mind.
CHŎNGSUK'S A-E: Ch'ang-yŏng's such an idiot. He should have cut off Talho when he first started blackmailing him. What took him so long to refuse to pay? Did Ch'ang-yŏng go along with it because of me?
CH'ANG-YŎNG: We were childhood friends. We grew up together in Bongch'on's shantytown. Byŏngch'ŏl's mother ran a whore house there. Dog Meat was a local punk. He acted like he owned that brothel and like Byŏngch'ŏl's mother was his wife. He used to wreck the place, breaking the furniture and trashing the joint. But nobody ever had the guts to stand up to him. Byŏngch'ŏl was always waiting for his chance to get even. Well, it was a day just like any other. We all were nervous, scared of the trouble that Dog Meat was going to stir up. Dog Meat walked in, drunk. He started to beat up Byŏngch'ŏl's mother. Byŏngch'ŏl jumped up and . . .
CHŎNGSUK and CHŎNGSUK'S A-E: And?
CH'ANG-YŎNG: All I could see was my mother's face right there in front of me.
CHŎNGSUK: *Your* mother?
CH'ANG-YŎNG: I must have been out of my mind. I went and thumped Dog Meat over the head with an iron bar.
CHŎNGSUK: *You* did?
CH'ANG-YŎNG: That changed everything.

Intermission

CHŎNGSUK: You won't regret giving up your political career?
CH'ANG-YŎNG: My father-in-law would be disappointed, if he was still alive. He's the one who got me started. I got to where I am because of his connections.
CHŎNGSUK: Won't you miss it? Men are fascinated by power, right?
CH'ANG-YŎNG: Every ordinary moment of my life turned into history. I've always been nervous about that—watching my step. What if a historian

decides to investigate my life? I've come to a conclusion now: no matter how hard we try, the past can never be erased.

CH'ANG-YŎNG'S A-E: Politics is like the game of rock, scissors, and paper. If I show a rock twice in a row, my opponent will show a rock because he thinks I'll show the scissors next time. I know he'll show a rock, so I show the paper. That's how it goes in the game called politics. A stupid balancing act, like walking a tightrope. And once a scandal catches up with us, we're all ruined.

CHŎNGSUK: Just as well you gave it up, then.

CH'ANG-YŎNG: That's for sure.

CH'ANG-YŎNG'S A-E: Reporters leap at the first sign of a scandal. Once they know your secrets, they'll never leave you alone.

CH'ANG-YŎNG: It was a split-second decision . . . but now my career is just one more part of my twisted history.

CHŎNGSUK: Try to forget it. Talho's not worth it. He's an extortionist!

CH'ANG-YŎNG: The saddest thing is that I'm not so different from Talho. You, too. Why do you wait for him?

CHŎNGSUK'S A-E: I don't.

CH'ANG-YŎNG: Words don't matter.

CH'ANG-YŎNG'S A-E: Actions matter.

CHŎNGSUK'S A-E: But some actions don't require much of you.

CH'ANG-YŎNG'S A-E: Those kinds of actions don't have the power to change history.

CHŎNGSUK'S A-E: I don't want change.

CH'ANG-YŎNG'S A-E: I think you do.

CHŎNGSUK'S A-E: Leave me alone.

CHŎNGSUK: Do I look like I'm waiting for Talho?

CH'ANG-YŎNG: Well, it certainly doesn't look like you're through with him.

CHŎNGSUK: Changing who I am and cutting ties with Talho are two *very* different things!

CH'ANG-YŎNG: Show me some action.

CHŎNGSUK: Like what?

CH'ANG-YŎNG: Anything.

CHŎNGSUK'S A-E: Even if we sleep together, nothing will change. Men are strange. They think sex is the answer to every problem. If their wives complain, their response is: "OK, OK. Let's sort it out in bed tonight. Then you'll be happy tomorrow."

CH'ANG-YŎNG: Once there was a man who lived together with his son and the son's wife. They were dirt poor. The son and his wife were actually living together without being married because they were too poor to afford a wedding. The daughter-in-law worked at a factory, supporting her husband while he prepared for his bar exam. A few years later, the husband finally passed the bar exam, but then he shacked up with a new woman. He cut off all ties with his father as well. The father had a stroke from the shock. The daughter-in-law took care of the sick old man for years, with the meager wages she made at the factory. Her father-in-law told her to give up on his son, but she kept on waiting for him and never complained. The old man said that if heaven didn't forbid it, he would have comforted and pleasured her as if he was his own son.

(*Flashback.* MALE M-R *as* TALHO, *who is working at a sign shop.* CHŎNGSUK'S A-E *arrives at the shop.*)

CHŎNGSUK'S A-E: Excuse me, is this Talho's Signs?
TALHO (*doesn't lift his head but answers*): That's what the sign says, isn't it?
CHŎNGSUK'S A-E: I'm looking for Mr. Kim Talho.
TALHO (*lifting his face*): That's me.
CHŎNGSUK'S A-E: Do you know Kang Ch'ang-yŏng?
TALHO: Who are you?
CHŎNGSUK'S A-E: Do you know where he is?
TALHO: I heard he's in Yanggu in Kangwŏn Province.
CHŎNGSUK'S A-E: We worked together at the same elementary school once.
TALHO: So, you're a teacher, are you?
CHŎNGSUK'S A-E: Yes. Mr. Kang left Yanggu without saying good-bye. Do you know where he is now?
TALHO: You lend him money? He take off with your things?
CHŎNGSUK'S A-E: Not at all. I just wanted to see him again.
TALHO: How did you find this place?
CHŎNGSUK'S A-E: Ah . . . I traced the address on the envelope . . .
TALHO: Is that right? (*Small laugh.*) That son-of-a-bitch never could stay in one place for long. His gypsy karma must have kicked in again.
CHŎNGSUK'S A-E: Do you know where he is?
TALHO: Maybe. Huh, huh, but . . . (*To himself.*) Might be dead for all I know.
CHŎNGSUK'S A-E: What!?
TALHO: He used to say that he wished he could just drop dead.
CHŎNGSUK'S A-E (*collapses on the floor*).
TALHO: Are you all right? (*Exits.*)
CHŎNGSUK: Go! You'd better go see Chaeung in the hospital.
CH'ANG-YŎNG: I guess I should . . . I don't have the courage.
CHŎNGSUK (*to her* A-E): Courage?
CHŎNGSUK'S A-E: Just like the sick old man in his story.

CHŎNGSUK: I see. (*To* CH'ANG-YŎNG.) Well, if courage won't get you there, how about your sense of duty?

CH'ANG-YŎNG: You're a strange woman.

CH'ANG-YŎNG'S A-E: I keep feeling like I'm just about to fall in love with her, but then it seems to freeze. Then, just when the feeling's about to die completely, it flares up, and I want to devour her but . . .

CH'ANG-YŎNG: What keeps me alienated from my wife?

CHŎNGSUK: You mean even before you were married?

CH'ANG-YŎNG: I mean after we got married.

CHŎNGSUK: I don't know.

CH'ANG-YŎNG: Well, as my wife would say, "Maybe it's just the institution."

CH'ANG-YŎNG'S A-E: That's the thing that's always in our way. If it were just two of us without the whole marriage thing going on in the background, then I'm sure we could've worked it out.

CH'ANG-YŎNG: Whenever I look at you, I see a whole string of faces: Talho, Byŏngch'ŏl, my wife, my mother. One after the other.

CHŎNGSUK: You can truly love your wife—not out of obligation—if you really want to; if you follow your gut feelings.

CH'ANG-YŎNG: But my gut feelings are already part of "the institution." I can't escape from social pressure. (*Walks toward the desk with a vase.*)

CHŎNGSUK: Erase me from your memory.

CH'ANG-YŎNG: I couldn't do that even if I wanted to.

CHŎNGSUK: Can you help me open a small art gallery?

CH'ANG-YŎNG: A gallery?

CHŎNGSUK: This is so humiliating.

CHŎNGSUK'S A-E: I feel like a parasite. I've been in your way all these years. Since you can't erase me from your memory, I'm trying to give you the next best option.

CHŎNGSUK: Cut me off. Don't come back here any more.

CH'ANG-YŎNG: How are your knees?

CHŎNGSUK: They're fine.

CH'ANG-YŎNG: I own a three-story building downtown. You can move in next month. I'll transfer the ownership to you.

CHŎNGSUK: Mr. Kang.

CH'ANG-YŎNG: Will you read me that poem again?[8]

(CH'ANG-YŎNG *and* CHŎNGSUK *feel excruciating pain for their ill-fated love.* CHŎNGSUK *recollects her encounters with* TALHO, *and* CH'ANG-YŎNG *remembers his encounters with his* WIFE. CH'ANG-YŎNG *keeps flicking his lighter, which does not work.* CHŎNGSUK *recites her poem.*)

(1) CHŎNGSUK:

Each time you waved "good-bye" on your way to work,

(2) **TALHO** (*played by the* **MALE M-R**, *putting on his clothes*): Chŏngsuk, get dressed. I'm sorry about what happened.

CHŎNGSUK'S A-E (*naked; with a blank face*): Please leave me alone. I'm not listening.

TALHO: Ch'ang-yŏng isn't here. He's not a fisherman. That was a lie.

CHŎNGSUK'S A-E: I know . . . Please leave me alone.

TALHO: Get dressed.

CHŎNGSUK'S A-E: Go ahead and look if that's what you want.

(3) **CH'ANG-YŎNG'S A-E** (*smoking a cigarette on the sofa; then, getting up*): You're an idiot. Don't even think about it. I'm nothing but a useless bum.

CH'ANG-YŎNG'S WIFE (*played by the* **FEMALE M-R**; *in lingerie; sobbing sitting next to* **CH'ANG-YŎNG**): I told you. I still love you. I don't care if you're a bum.

CH'ANG-YŎNG'S A-E: I feel sorry for you.

WIFE: Then marry me.

CH'ANG-YŎNG'S A-E: Are you nuts!? I'm a construction worker on minimum wage. I don't have any money. Don't have anything except my two balls.

WIFE: I don't want anything from you. I just want to be with you. I'd follow you all the way to the end of the world.

CH'ANG-YŎNG'S A-E: I don't care what you want. Stupid girl. I don't even like you.

WIFE: I'm going to make you love me.

CH'ANG-YŎNG'S A-E: For God's sake! You are so stupid! I've dated dozens of stupid girls, but you're the worst of the lot.

(1) **CHŎNGSUK**:
    The sight of your back filled my eyes with tears.
    Every morning we shared our farewells, in poverty.
    The bag on your back was heavy then with manuscripts;

(2) **TALHO**: I'll do the right thing, I swear. I'll marry you.

CHŎNGSUK'S A-E: Did you think I'd stay with you just because of what you've done to me?

TALHO: I wasn't sure. I'm a loser, that's me. A lowlife jerk.

CHŎNGSUK'S A-E (*cries*): I wish you'd just crawl away and die.

(3) **CH'ANG-YŎNG'S A-E**: Say! You met Chaeung, didn't you? He's my son. A child from a girl I used to date.

WIFE: Yes, I met him.

CH'ANG-YŎNG'S A-E: And you still like me?

WIFE: I like you. I like Chaeung , too.

CH'ANG-YŎNG'S A-E: He's deformed.

WIFE: If we get married, I won't have a child of my own. I'll raise Chaeung as my only child.

CH'ANG-YŏNG'S A-E: You're driving me nuts! For a girl with a college education, you're unbelievably dumb. Did you know I'm a murderer, too?

WIFE: You told me that already, at least twice.

(1) **CHŏNGSUK**:
>Now a lunchbox weighs on your shoulders.
>Look at the bright faces of your children

(2) **TALHO**: I'm sorry. I, Talho Kim, am not very bright. I can't cope with complications.

CHŏNGSUK'S A-E: What's your point?

TALHO: Please try to see it my way. I like you the same way you like Ch'ang-yŏng. I've never felt this way about a woman before.

CHŏNGSUK'S A-E: Do you still consider yourself Ch'ang-yŏng's friend?

TALHO: Forget about him. He doesn't love you. If he did, he would've called you already. He could've called you at the school if he'd wanted to. But he never called. Didn't I try to look for him every chance I had? "My name is Talho and Chŏngsuk is looking for you, Ch'ang-yŏng" and "We want to hear from you." I told everyone wherever I went.

(3) **CH'ANG-YŏNG'S A-E**: I've never done anything to give you the idea that I liked you. Have I?

WIFE: I know, I know. Honey, I'm rich, and you're . . .

CH'ANG-YŏNG'S A-E: Don't call me Honey.

WIFE (*shouting*): You're just a useless bum, working on a construction site. Why don't you like me?

CH'ANG-YŏNG'S A-E: No reason. It's just not meant to be.

WIFE (*getting angrier*): Have you even tried to like me? Why are you being so difficult? I'm offering to marry you—a useless bum!

CH'ANG-YŏNG'S A-E: All right. There's more. I have tuberculosis. I'm going to die soon.

WIFE (*with pity*): I saw the blood in your mouth, on the first day we met. My heart ached for you . . .

(1) **CHŏNGSUK**:
>I hoist our little ones up to meet your eyes.
>At home I find the keys.

(2) **CHŏNGSUK'S A-E**: Do you know where Ch'ang-yŏng is?

TALHO: No . . . well, actually I do. But he told me not to tell anyone.

CHŏNGSUK'S A-E: What a heartless man he is! Did he tell you to cut me off? Did he tell you to do this to me?

TALHO: No.

CHŎNGSUK'S A-E: Go away!

TALHO: Ch'ang-yŏng told me that you two weren't meant to be. You're like a pearl, and he's a piece of shit. I know that I'm beneath your station, too, but I love you. Is that a sin?

CHŎNGSUK'S A-E: You love who?

(3) **CH'ANG-YŎNG'S A-E**: Stupid bitch. (*Slaps the* **WIFE**.) Stay away from me!

WIFE: That won't work. (*Crying.*) How can you call me stupid? You're the one who's really stupid and pathetic, a menial worker with a handicapped five-year-old son to support, barely making a living. You've got one foot in the grave—throwing up blood night after night. Is there anything about you that's not pathetic?

CH'ANG-YŎNG'S A-E (*grabbing the* **WIFE**): Stop it! Stop. I don't want to hear it!

WIFE: You need me, Ch'ang-yŏng.

(1) **CHŎNGSUK**:
> Keys that can kindle fires in your body and soul.
> Keys that can unlock the chest of eternal energy.

(2) **TALHO**: Chŏngsuk. I haven't told you about this before because Ch'ang-yŏng's my friend. Part of me was aching to tell you, but I kept holding it back.

CHŎNGSUK'S A-E: What are you talking about?

TALHO: Forget about Ch'ang-yŏng. He's a married man now.

CHŎNGSUK'S A-E: What did you say?

TALHO: He married a rich girl last week. She's a college student. I heard she's tall and pretty, too.

CHŎNGSUK'S A-E: What?

TALHO: That's why I did that to you.

(3) **CH'ANG-YŎNG'S A-E**: We can't be lovey-dovey all the time.

WIFE: I know. But it's my destiny. Asking you to love me has been a doomed project from the beginning.

CH'ANG-YŎNG'S A-E: Love and sympathy are two different things.

WIFE: I love you.

CH'ANG-YŎNG'S A-E: Your feelings for me are temporary. And life is long. I can't love you. I just don't feel anything for you.

WIFE: Then just get married and go through the motions. Welcome to the institution of marriage.

CH'ANG-YŎNG'S A-E: What's that supposed to mean?

WIFE: Marriage isn't a big deal. People get married and live together all the time. It doesn't always mean they're madly in love with each other.

CH'ANG-YŎNG'S A-E: You really are a stupid bitch.

(*The above three scenes end.*)

CHŎNGSUK: Mr. Kang
CH'ANG-YŎNG: What is it?
(*A love song is playing.*)
CHŎNGSUK:
>I listen to music when I'm lonely,
>I drink when my heart is breaking,
>I take a walk when I'm feeling down,
>My smile lights up again when warmth touches my heart.
>Some days I live like a crazy woman.
>Some days I play about like a child.
>I'm no stranger to a life of solitude.
>They say I'm mature now because I've been through all these things.
>They say that experience makes us grow toward the light.
>But some experiences are too much to bear.
>There is something that I can't endure—
>It is missing you.
>Missing you for an eternity.

CH'ANG-YŎNG: I met her at the construction site.
CHŎNGSUK: You mean your wife?
CH'ANG-YŎNG: Yeah. I was about to leave for home, and a fancy car drove in. The director of the company got out of the car with his daughter. I was coughing up blood on the corner of the street. The girl saw me. She came to see me every day from then on.
CHŎNGSUK: She was your destiny.
CH'ANG-YŎNG: It's strange, isn't it?
CHŎNGSUK: What is?
CH'ANG-YŎNG: About my wife . . .
CHŎNGSUK (*silently questioning*).
CH'ANG-YŎNG: I told her everything about my past to scare her off. I even exaggerated how bad it was. But there's still one thing I haven't told her.
CHŎNGSUK: Don't hold it in.
CH'ANG-YŎNG: When I came home on leave once from military service, and my home looked like a disaster zone. My younger brother was on the run from the police. My mother was eight months pregnant and no husband in sight. My younger sister was crying day and night. I felt powerless to help. I drank my way through every day of that leave. After I returned to my post, no news came from home. I lay awake worrying night after night, and spent my days thinking about going AWOL. One day I received a telegram: "Mother dead." I got special leave to go home. When I got there, I learned that my mother had hanged herself after giving

birth to a child. My brother had been sentenced to life in prison, and my sister had gone to work in a brothel. The little baby is Chaeung.

CHŎNGSUK: So you mean Chaeung's actually your brother?

CH'ANG-YŎNG: That's right. Is that what you'd call destiny? After I was discharged, I joined a street gang for a time. After that, I worked hard to change my life. Some time later, I met my wife and went into politics. I wanted to fight my destiny, and I believed I could only do it by working like a dog. I used to say to myself, "Go on. Dig all you want. Dig it up. My past doesn't matter. People like me are the strongest of all. My past is not an ordinary past. I should wear it like a medal of honor on the suit of my present success." But despite all that bravado, I still wanted to hide the fact that I am a murderer and that Chaeung is my brother.

CHŎNGSUK: Tell your wife the truth.

CH'ANG-YŎNG: I will, but first I need to visit Byŏngch'ŏl's grave.

CH'ANG-YŎNG'S A-E: My political ambition has made me live the life of a weakling. I felt sick every time I saw my smiling mug in the newspaper.

CH'ANG-YŎNG: I'm going to call another press conference.

CHŎNGSUK: You have a new plan?

CH'ANG-YŎNG: I'm going to self-destruct in front of the reporters.

CH'ANG-YŎNG'S A-E: I'm a hoodlum, that's the truth. I'm going to tell the press everything that I've told you tonight.

CH'ANG-YŎNG: I'm telling them everything, even about Chaeung.

CH'ANG-YŎNG'S A-E: People will spit on me and treat me like a criminal.

CH'ANG-YŎNG: Just like a dirty dish. You have to get the dirt off before you can use it again.

CHŎNGSUK: Are you planning to return to politics?

CH'ANG-YŎNG'S A-E: In accordance with the course of destruction, transformation, and renewal?

CH'ANG-YŎNG: Maybe politics. Maybe something else. I want to free myself of all social obligations. I've kept the secret of Chaeung to myself, thinking it was a way of showing respect for my mother. He's a product of my mother's misfortune, but he's my responsibility. That's how I understood my loyalty and filial obligation to my poor mother. But there's more to it, actually. Chaeung's part of a carefully calculated situation, which I have taken advantage of to fulfill my ambitions as a politician. So you see, my present situation is even more abominable than my past.

CH'ANG-YŎNG'S A-E: I've been deceiving myself all these years.

CH'ANG-YŎNG: What is truth to us?

CHŎNGSUK: Truth?

CHŎNGSUK'S A-E: What is truth?

CH'ANG-YŎNG: Truth is the name of the destination we're supposed to reach.
CHŎNGSUK'S A-E: Writers write, scientists experiment in the lab, and Buddhist monks pray. But I don't do anything. I have no destination.
CH'ANG-YŎNG: Chŏngsuk, what's your destination?
CHŎNGSUK: I don't know.
CH'ANG-YŎNG: If you don't see a destination to reach, then you haven't found the truth yet. My destination is my mother. To me, my mother is the truth.
CHŎNGSUK: I didn't expect you to say that.
CH'ANG-YŎNG: It's true. My mother's the reason I've never gotten close to you.
CH'ANG-YŎNG'S A-E: No, I stopped myself from getting close to you. Mother kept telling me to unload Chaeung from my shoulders, but I held on tight. I used to scream at her that Chaeung was my own sin, my destiny. I used to be ashamed to call her my mother. I used to scream at her in my dreams. Now, when I come home, Chaeung runs to me, barely able to stand on his crippled legs.
CH'ANG-YŎNG: Whenever Chaeung calls me "Daddy," my wife's face flashes before my eyes. I keep taking the whole thing as my punishment, a fate that can't be avoided.
CH'ANG-YŎNG'S A-E: I was denied by God. I was denied by heaven. My mother could have been the fountain of truth for me, but I never saw it. And I've ended up living the life of a sinner on her behalf.
CHŎNGSUK'S A-E (*on her knees; praying*): Holy Father, please forgive him. Let me share his suffering . . .
CH'ANG-YŎNG: When the secret is revealed, my mother will be reduced to nothing. I'll be destroyed too. Then I'll finally be able to face my mother. She raised us despite humiliation and dishonor. She raised us with love.
CH'ANG-YŎNG'S A-E: That's the kind of love my mother always had for me.
CHŎNGSUK: It feels like you've had to do a lot of thinking to figure that out.
CH'ANG-YŎNG: You need to heal yourself too. You need to heal yourself with the energy of renewal.
CHŎNGSUK: Energy of renewal?
CH'ANG-YŎNG: Every living breathing creature has the energy of renewal. It lets us cleanse ourselves! It lets us be innocent and clean again, even if we're mired in layers of corruption. Like birds and fish returning to their birthplaces, we can go back, too. No other energy compares with this energy.
CHŎNGSUK'S A-E: Do I have the energy of renewal?

CH'ANG-YŎNG'S A-E: We're afraid to let go of ourselves. Afraid we'll be like wild beasts. But that only makes us weaker. Destiny is destiny. We have to accept it and then let it be renewed. When I accepted my destiny, I finally realized how lonely you must have been.

CHŎNGSUK'S A-E: But I don't want to love you out of obligation. When we're in a tough situation, I want us to be able to see the truth in each other's eyes. We can keep our stories in our hearts, for now. There'll be time for them to come out later—when our eyes have had a good rest. I want to be the place where your soul can find solace. I'll pray for you. I'll wait for you.

CHŎNGSUK: I used to tell myself that I should forget you because you can't be mine. The flowers on the hills are beautiful, but they don't have to belong to me. They are beautiful just because they exist . . .

(*A love song is playing.*)

CHŎNGSUK'S A-E: I won't wait for you forever.

CH'ANG-YŎNG'S A-E: Listen to what the sky tells you. Listen to the wind whispering.

CH'ANG-YŎNG'S A-E: I've been in constant motion—no dreams, no expectations, no direction.

CH'ANG-YŎNG'S A-E: We need to repot ourselves.

CHŎNGSUK'S A-E: Repot ourselves?

CH'ANG-YŎNG: Like in your poem, I'm trying to rekindle a fire.

CHŎNGSUK: Grass grows back stronger after it's been cut.

CH'ANG-YŎNG'S A-E: I have so many things to say to you, but they're locked in my heart. I can't find a way to say them now.

CHŎNGSUK'S A-E: You don't have to tell me anything any more. Poets speak with their hearts.

CH'ANG-YŎNG'S A-E: There must be a place for us to go.

CHŎNGSUK'S A-E: Just like there must be a way for every one of us to find the truth?

CH'ANG-YŎNG'S A-E: That's right. Whether it's to become a poet, a nun, a painter, or stay on as a teacher.

CHŎNGSUK: Please turn off the lights.

Curtain

NOTES

1. Kang Ch'ang-yŏng and Pak Chŏngsuk are presented in both their surface realities and their inner lives, as expressed by their respective alter-egos. On the surface,

the characters' dialogue and behavior generally are quite realistic, although the inner logic of a particular section may not be evident at first. In some sections, for example, the alter-ego belonging to one character interacts with the primary personality of the other, leaving one to wonder whether the action is taking place in the tangible world or in the character's inner thoughts. The reader—and actor—must absorb impressions and information as the play progresses, trusting that all the parts of the play, like a jigsaw puzzle or a pointillist painting, will make dramatic and theatrical sense at the play's conclusion.

2. For some Korean men, a girl who studies overseas is "damaged goods," somehow tainted.
3. An Chunggŭn (1878–1910) led a volunteer army opposed to the Japanese annexation of Korea. An assassinated the Japanese resident general, Itō Hirobumi, and was in turn captured and executed.
4. The formal "Mr." here reflects Korean reticence to address others on the casual first-name basis so common in the United States.
5. The Buddhist monk connects the last sounds in each of Ka*ng* Ch'a*ng*-yŏ*ng*'s names to "zero" or "nothing."
6. Chŏngsuk's alter-ego's actions present what Chŏngsuk really wants to say in response to the phone call but doesn't.
7. Obviously, in the original Korean text, the American woman could not understand what is being said in the scene, so any production of this translated version can omit this line without harm to the play.
8. Three scenes take place side by side. The characters are on the stage at the same time. A director must decide whether to overlap the scenes, intermix selected lines, or have the characters in two scenes "freeze" while the other scene plays.

BELLFLOWER (TORAJI)

O T'AESŎK

Perhaps the most influential Korean theater artist of the last quarter century, O T'aesŏk won a newspaper literary contest in 1969 on his way to a career leading to international stature as playwright, director, and theorist. Born in southern Ch'ungch'ŏng Province in 1940, he studied philosophy at Yonsei University. Following a period of study in New York City, during which he was exposed to a wide range of experimental theater, he returned to Seoul. In the early 1970s, along with Pak Choyŏl and Ch'oe Inhun, O emerged as a leading innovative playwright opposed to *shin-gŭk*'s realistic theater.

Several qualities can be discerned in O's oeuvre of some sixty plays. He has been a tireless experimenter, employing elements of Western absurdism, using media to advantage, and mining traditional Korean arts and shamanism for artistic inspiration and expression in the search for what O calls "Korean-ness." He views Korean history as essentially tragic, and it plays a central role in many of his works. O deconstructs Korean history to comment on contemporary Korean society. Often centering on a family or a group of people functioning much like a family, his plays are resistant to logical analysis because O values illogical jumps and cuts in the text and performance. His works reflect his directorial reliance on improvisation, physicality, and the energies derived from highly rhythmic language, often reflecting regional dialects. Whatever literary values O's scripts may have, it is in the viewing of a performance that a fuller sense of his theater is gained.

Kim A-jŏng's *The Metacultural Theater of Oh T'ae-Sŏk* (1999) presents five of his plays. *Lifecord* (*T'ae*, 1974) uses the dethronement of the mid-fifteenth-century King Tanjong to portray the necessity of a strong bond within a family or community. *Ch'unp'ung's Wife* (*Ch'unp'ung ŭi ch'ŏ*, 1976) relies on a traditional Korean mask dance play about an old man mistreated by a female entertainer, only to be saved by the wife he earlier disowned. *Intimacy Between Father and Son* (*Pujayujin*, 1987) is based on King Yŏngjo's condemnation of his only son to death in a rice box, a violation of fundamental Confucian values. *Bicycle* (*Chajŏngŏ*, 1983), based on an event during the Korean War in which inhabitants of O's home village were burned alive by People's Liberation Army troops, explores scars left on the Korean psyche by the Korean War. *Why Did Shim-Ch'ŏng Plunge into the Sea Twice?* (*Shim-ch'ŏnginŭn wae indangsue tubŏn mom ŭl tŏnjŏt nŭnga*, 1990) uses an old *p'ansori* story to critique the loss of human values in materialistic Korean society.

In *Bellflower* (*Toraji*, 1992), O uses the Chosŏn reformer Kim Okkyun to depict what happens to well-meaning men (and nations) when they are caught up in events they cannot control and traditional values are shunted aside, telling Kim's story through an epic collage of Brechtian-like techniques, historical persons and events, traditional mask dance, and absurdist elements. The play's language has a texture very different from that of other plays in this collection. Often formal, O's language variously reflects Korean's love of language, the drama's presentational epic structure, court decorum, Korean social structure, and O's deep interest in the sweep of Korean history.

BELLFLOWER (TORAJI)

TRANSLATED BY YI HYŏNGJIN AND RICHARD NICHOLS

Characters

KIM OKKYUN
KING KOJONG
QUEEN MINBI
CHAMBERLAIN
YI ŬNGSHIK
HONG CHONG-U
MR. KU
SHIMAMURA (島村)
MIN YŎNG-IK
SŎ JAEP'IL
YU CHAEHYŎN
YUN T'AEJUN
HAN KYUJIK
TAKEZOE (竹添) SHIN'ICHIRŌ
ISE (伊勢)
KATŌ (加藤)
ISHII (石井)
SAITŌ (在藤)
POLICEMAN
RESEARCHER
TŌYAMA (頭山)
ITŌ HIROBUMI (伊藤博文)
YI ILSHIK
WADA (和田)
O PO-IN
EXECUTIONER
COURIERS
KIM KYUHWA

TAKEMATSU (竹松)
JAPANESE FISHERMEN
YI TOJAE
YI MINSHIK
YI JUN
YI SANGSŎL
YI WAN-YONG

Time of the Play

Late 1884 to sometime after late 1907.

PRELUDE

(*A court maid peeps into* **KOJONG**'s *bedchamber, then the other maids look in. The* **CHAMBERLAIN** *appears and comes to* **QUEEN MINBI**'s *bedchamber.*)[1]

CHAMBERLAIN: Your Majesty.
(*A child exits the* **QUEEN**'s *bedchamber as he pulls up his pants. The* **QUEEN** *appears and crosses to* **KOJONG**'s *bedchamber. She hangs a maid who has shared* **KOJONG**'s *bed.*)

IN THE PRESENCE OF THE KING

(**KOJONG, QUEEN MINBI, KIM OKKYUN,** *and* **CHAMBERLAIN.**)

OKKYUN: Your Royal Highness, China and France finally are at war because of the incident in Vietnam.
MINBI: If China and France fight each other, which do you think will win?
KOJONG: If China and Japan fight each other, which will win?
OKKYUN: It would be difficult to predict the victor if China and Japan fight without allies, but if Japan and France unite against China, I'm sure Japan will be victorious.
MINBI: Then isn't the time right to gain our independence?
KOJONG: Isn't the time right to gain our independence?
OKKYUN: Your Highness's lesson is well taken, but a royal subject, one holding a place in your heart,[2] still is siding with China, and I fear that independence would not be feasible, even if Japan wanted us to have it.

MINBI: You seem to have some reservations about me, but since this is a life-or-death matter for our country, how could I, as a mere woman, stand in the way of the weighty affairs of state? Speak frankly.

OKKYUN: When I analyze the current world situation, the European countries' position toward the Orient seems to have drastically changed over the past decade, and powerful nations like England, France, and Russia now are competing for dominance in the Orient. Meanwhile, France, which has wanted to exploit the Orient since Napoleon I was in power, has already instigated a Sino-French war, and it is clear that outcome will be unfavorable to China. After the Chinese have been defeated and the French begin reaching toward Chosŏn, how can we protect ourselves with our beggared national forces? Also, since the Russians are about to advance into East Asia, with what tactics can we defend ourselves? Moreover, because the relationship between China and Japan has recently deteriorated and Japan is working day and night to strengthen its military capability, a Sino-Japanese war seems inevitable.[3] Then Chosŏn will turn into a battlefield for others. While domestically the surrounding situation deteriorates, our treacherous ministers are filling the royal court and questioning your royal wisdom. They spend their time fighting among themselves and abusing their power by fawning on China. It's pitiful to see what they are doing with state affairs. Thus our priority in domestic policies, using great care and sincere devotion to politics, must be to reform our systems; expel ignorant, stubborn, and incompetent aristocratic ministers; abolish clan-based political infighting, and empower ourselves. Our priority for the outside world must be to declare our independence to all nations, open our doors, and embrace new knowledge.

MINBI: Now that I know your thoughts, I will entrust these critical and urgent affairs of state to you and your discretion. Don't doubt me again.

OKKYUN (*addressing the* KING): Prompted by your gracious teaching tonight, I venture to ask for a secret, handwritten message that I might carry with me at all times. (KOJONG *writes a secret message, sets the stamp frame, and stamps his royal seal.*)

KOJONG (*to the* CHAMBERLAIN): Execute the order without delay. (KOJONG *exits.*)

OKKYUN (*to the* CHAMBERLAIN): Here is the list of new cabinet members. Please give it to His Royal Highness in the meeting tomorrow morning. Yi Chŏngwŏn: prime minister, Hong Yŏngshik: deputy prime minister, . . .

UN-NI DISTRICT

(HONG CHONG-U's *house.* HONG, HONG'S WIFE, YI ŬNGSHIK, *and* MR. KU. *An area in which to mourn* HONG's *late father is set up in the corner.*)

ŬNGSHIK: This family register looks perfect. Do you really mean to sell it?
CHONG-U: At my age, I don't want to serve as the royal cemetery grave keeper.
ŬNGSHIK: But isn't this a government post that your father handed down to you? If you sell the register, you won't be eligible to take the civil service exams.[4]
CHONG-U: State exams that only kids from Min's family pass? I have no desire for that. I'd rather try to become a special royal envoy.
ŬNGSHIK: Are you saying that you want to go abroad?
CHONG-U: Once I become a special envoy, I supposedly would serve His Royal Highness from a place of advantage, wouldn't I? Then I could wait while looking for a higher post.
ŬNGSHIK: Where do you want to go?
CHONG-U: Japan is close; I'll go there first.
ŬNGSHIK: But Taewŏn-gun[5] won't sit by quietly and watch. Why not be more patient, wait a little longer, and then . . .
CHONG-U: No hope for Taewŏn-gun, either. Kim Okkyun and Pak Yŏnghyo—I'm fed up with the quarrels between Taewŏn-gun and Queen Minbi.[6] The Progressive Party is a better choice than Taewŏn-gun. Isn't that obvious? Isn't it time that someone new came on the scene and did something different and exciting? I am sick to death of watching this country sink into misery when I have no chance or place to get involved! Ah! What a crazy world!
ŬNGSHIK: But selling your family register won't help anything. It wouldn't even cover your ferry ticket.
CHONG-U: I'm going to make a living selling water. I've already learned how to court customers. "Wa-ter, wa-ter!" (MR. KU *appears. He and* CHONG-U *bow deeply to each other.*)
MR. KU: I heard that you put your government post up for sale.[7] Why are you . . . instead of carrying on your inheritance?
CHONG-U (*he shows a family register book wrapped in a piece of cloth*): I don't know how much it's worth.
MR. KU (*he is illiterate*): What's the title of this government post?
CHONG-U: It's a managerial position at Hyoch'ang Park.[8] Here the register has an official stamp from Yŭk-wŏn Palace, which has jurisdiction over it.

MR. KU: So it has. But why are you selling it? What's the matter?

CHONG-U: With the money I get from selling this post, I'll be able to go to Japan. Once I've been there, another government post will open.

MR. KU: A government post in Japan? Would that one be better than the one you already have?

CHONG-U: It's not what I receive in Japan; it's a government post as a special royal envoy that will allow me to report directly to His Royal Highness what I see and hear in Japan.

MR. KU: That's what an express messenger does? Oh my, that job makes my legs hurt; I wouldn't want it. To me, this one looks better. A managerial position at the park . . . what does someone in this post do?

CHONG-U: It's the general manager position at the royal cemetery.

MR. KU: The general manager at the royal cemetery . . . the general manager at the royal cemetery . . . it really is a manager position, right? I'll pay thirty *nyang*. (*He takes out coins.*)[9]

CHONG-U: This family identification tag . . . I don't think you understand exactly what this really is. Please hold this in your hand. With this, your children will be eligible to take civil service exams. What did you say you do for a living in Chongno Street?

MR. KU: I sell linen and cotton.

CHONG-U: With this tag, your drapery stores will be given a tax exemption.

MR. KU: Tax, tax . . . three hundred *nyang*. (*He takes out more coins.*)

CHONG-U: You are quite a generous man.

MR. KU: Will this be enough for the ferry to Japan?

CHONG-U: I'll add to it by shouldering this rack and selling water. "Wa-ter! Wa-ter!"

(*As the two start laughing, in the corner is spotlighted a miniature building that looks like a single-story tile-roofed post office building, the Ujŏngguk. Clamoring voices are heard here and there.*)

SCENE OF THE DEDICATION CEREMONY AT THE UJŎNGGUK POST OFFICE

OKKYUN (*holding the* KING*'s handwritten secret message and speaking to the audience as though they were fellow conspirators*)[10]: December 4, 1884! Around 8:00 tonight, to create confusion, we will set fire to a royal villa in Angukdong. In the chaos at the dedication site, we will execute Min Yŏng-ik[11] and his conservative rabble. Then we will immediately escort His Royal

Highness from Ch'angdŏk Palace to Gyŏng'u Palace, where we can guard him easily and declare a national reform movement. Our secret code is "Do you know the Way of the universe?" The password is "Full moon." Then "Do you know the Way of the universe?"

VOICE 1: Someone from Hong Hyŏn's family came to see you.

VOICE 2: We made a mess of it! We failed to set the royal villa on fire.

OKKYUN: If not the royal villa, tell them to set fire to some nearby private homes instead!

(**SHIMAMURA**, *an official at the Japanese consulate, rushes in.*)

SHIMAMURA: What was the news?

OKKYUN: We failed to set the royal villa on fire.

SHIMAMURA: Now what are you going to do?

OKKYUN: We've come with another tactic. Don't worry.

VOICE: Everything's falling apart! The police are all over the place, guarding every street corner because we failed to set fire to the villa, and our attempts to burn two nearby thatched houses also failed. The situation is urgent, and we should attack the banquet hall immediately! Please give the order.

OKKYUN: Things could get worse if one of foreign diplomats in the hall is injured in the confusion. Instead, set this on fire. (*Referring to the miniature post office. He strikes a match and sets the miniature on fire. Cries of "Fire" are heard everywhere. At this moment, when* **MIN YŎNG-IK** *steps into the yard of the Ujŏngguk Post Office, an assassin slashes his chest with a single stroke of his sword.* **MIN** *cries out and collapses.*)

CH'ANGDŎK PALACE

(**YU CHAEHYŎN**, *a court eunuch, appears.*)

CHAEHYŎN: Who are you?

OKKYUN (*accompanied by* **SŎ JAEP'IL**): Inform his Royal Highness that we are here.

CHAEHYŎN: For what purpose?

OKKYUN: Who do you think you are talking to? His Royal Highness is in grave danger.

(**KOJONG** *appears.* **OKKYUN** *addresses him.*) The situation is deteriorating; fires are blazing all around the royal palace. Shots have been fired. It's chaotic! It would be best for Your Royal Highness to stay away from the royal palace for a while.

KOJONG: Now? In the middle of the night—
VOICE: The royal palanquin is ready.
OKKYUN: Please escort His Royal Highness to Gyŏng-u Palace.
(*In the corner,* YU CHAEHYŎN *intentionally drops the royal seal, breaking it, as if to keep it out of* OKKYUN*'s hands.*)
KOJONG: Why go there?
OKKYUN: Everything will be fine once we call on Japanese forces to guard the palace. (QUEEN MINBI *appears.*)
MINBI: If we call on the Japanese forces, do you think the Chinese will just sit by quietly and watch?
OKKYUN: I will call on the Chinese forces also. (YUN T'AEJUN *and* HAN KYUJIK *appear.*)
KYUJIK (*to* OKKYUN): Stop! (*Then.*) Your Majesty, what are all these comings and goings in the dead of night?
OKKYUN: Your duty is to bring your soldiers to guard the royal palanquin! How dare you, stop it! Prepare to die!
(SŎ JAEP'IL *draws a sword and slashes* YUN T'AEJUN, *who collapses.*)
T'AEJUN: Why? Why did you have to kill me?
(YU CHAEHYŎN *reappears in time to see* QUEEN MINBI*'s reaction to the situation.*)
CHAEHYŎN (*to* MINBI): Please calm yourself, Your Majesty. China's Yuan Shikai is proceeding to the royal palace with six hundred soldiers to be received by His Royal Highness.¹²
OKKYUN: We can't permit that! (*To* CHAEHYŎN.) Stop them outside the East and West gates. (*He cuts off* CHAEHYŎN*'s right arm.*) Go back to Yuan Shikai and tell him that this is what is waiting for him as soon as he passes through the gates.
MINBI: Why do you insult China, which has offered to protect us?
OKKYUN (*holding up the* KING*'s handwritten secret message, he shouts*): National reform! With this proclamation of the new platform for national reform, all court officials shall make sure that nothing interferes with its implementation. Meaningless tribute to China will be abolished. The privilege of family lineage will be abolished, and people's rights to equality will become law. Real estate law will be reformed. The Bureau of Eunuchs will be abolished. Corrupt, power-abusing officials will be punished severely. The Bureau of Commerce Development and its control of peddlers will be abolished. Criminal cases will be reviewed, and the innocent will be released. Ministers and deputy officials will attend the meetings at the National Assembly every day. All formerly established posts, except those of the National Assembly and the core

ministers, will be abolished. Here is the list of the new ministers. (*Hands the list to* **KOJONG**.)[13]

(**TAKEZOE**, *the chief Japanese envoy, appears*.)

TAKEZOE: The situation is no longer favorable for Japanese troops to remain. We will withdraw our forces.

OKKYUN: What? What are you talking about? You should wait at least until we've climbed the tree before you shake it! How can you even think of withdrawing your forces now? Once we figure out how to stand on our own feet, yes . . . but please hold on for three or four more days.

TAKEZOE: Chinese forces have already taken up positions with six hundred troops at both the West and East gates. We Japanese have only two hundred soldiers. The situation is out of our hands.

OKKYUN: You know that we also have eight hundred soldiers!

TAKEZOE: They don't look like soldiers to me. They don't even have a single decent weapon.

OKKYUN: If your forces withdraw, we are doomed to fail. Three days! Please stay with us! (*Sounds of cannons, followed by rifle fire are heard in close distance. Clamorous noises shake the air.* **OKKYUN** *directs the bearers*.) Take the palanquin to the North Gate!

KOJONG: Where are we going?

OKKYUN: We'd better go to the port of Inchŏn and then figure out what to do next.

KOJONG: I am not going to Inchŏn. Go to the North Royal Tomb where the king and queen are buried. If I must die, I will die there.

(*One of the soldiers holding the palanquin on his shoulder is struck by a stray bullet and collapses in a spray of blood*.)

OKKYUN: How dare they shoot at us! His Royal Highness is here!

TAKEZOE: It's because Japanese forces are guarding you.

OKKYUN: Then withdraw your troops!

TAKEZOE: We will pull back for a short time, but the Chinese have humiliated our forces, and we will respond in kind. (*As he leaves*.) Kim Okkyun, do you want to stay here or go to Inchŏn?

(**OKKYUN** *and* **SŎ** *kneel imploringly in front of* **KOJONG**.)

OKKYUN: Your Royal Highness, my proper duty is to stay and serve Your Majesty, but . . .

KOJONG: Deserting me at this hour of peril? Where are you going to go?

OKKYUN: Your Royal Highness, how could I dare to abandon Your Majesty under any conditions? This is only a brief farewell so that I can live to see another day, making myself ready for the sake of this country and Your Royal Highness.

MINBI (*incensed*): You, Kim Okkyun . . .
(*Battle cries of "Get the traitor! Get the Jap bastards!!" are heard nearby amid the sound of rifle shots.*)

ŌSAKA, JAPAN

(*A public bathhouse. A Japanese man wearing only a traditional Japanese loincloth sits on a wooden bench, legs spread out, reading a newspaper.* HONG CHONG-U *is scrubbing him.*)

A JAPANESE (*he shows* CHONG-U *the newspaper*): Kim Okkyun, of the coup d'état.
CHONG-U: We all had high hopes, but they were dashed. It was over in three days.
A JAPANESE: The Japanese prime minister also is reflecting on that. (*He reads the newspaper.*) "We should not necessarily blame Kim Okkyun or the Reform Party for the failure of the coup d'état, led by that party. Rather, the responsibility for its failure should lie with our government officials. Takezoe, our chief envoy, is a Confucian scholar, incapable of accomplishing such a critical mission. If we had assigned the mission to Maeda, the Japanese consul general in Wŏnsan, would the outcome have been the same?" The implication of the article is that the failure is not Kim's but our government's. Were many people hurt because of this incident?
CHONG-U: There was a cleansing of the Min clan. Min T'aeho, Min Yŏngjik—Min Yŏngjik, this guy survived—Cho Yŏngha, Han Kyujik, Yi Joyŏn, Yun T'aejun—Yun is head of the court eunuchs, managing the court maids. The man at this post is castrated to prevent any sex scandals in the court, but he has as much authority as the Japanese deputy prime minister. Who's the head of the Japanese government now?
A JAPANESE: Itō, an unfortunate mistake created by Inoue Kaoru's ill-advised policy. The deadly enemy is Itō. Here is his picture in the newspaper. (*He hands over the newspaper.* CHONG-U *takes a careful look.*)
CHONG-U: Please pretend you didn't see this. (*He spits on the picture of* ITŌ.) Itō, you look good that way!
A JAPANESE: Were you also a bathhouse scrubber when you were in Chosŏn?
CHONG-U: I was a water seller in Namsan.[14] "Wa-ter, Wa-ter!"
A JAPANESE: What brought you here . . . study?

CHONG-U: There is someplace I need to see. Which country most helped Japan modernize to such an extent?

A JAPANESE: Missionaries from France, maybe. That's what intellectuals in this country often say.

CHONG-U: Then I need to go there and learn.

A JAPANESE: You're a patriot. Anyone who spits on the face of Itō is a patriot. I don't think a bathhouse scrubber could make enough money to go to France. But these days you can make big money in Japan if you're shrewd. For instance, if a tailor shop does well, a shoe store will make money too. That's how it works now in Japan. Everyone is crazy about imitating Westerners. Don't you think they need thread to mend suits? I have a friend who is running a big cotton thread factory in Osaka. I'll give you my business card; please go see him.

CHONG-U: I shall never forget your favor.

YŪRAKUCHŌ RESTAURANT, TŌKYŌ

(*At a Japanese restaurant,* KIM OKKYUN *plays mahjong with the young Japanese men* ISHII *and* SAITŌ, *a drinking table at their side.*)

OKKYUN: Mr. Ise, Mr. Ise. (ISE SHIN, *the host, appears.*) I've run out of money for a stake. Please lend me two thousand wŏn.[15]

ISE: Unless it is for living expenses . . .

OKKYUN: I gambled away hundred thousand wŏn to learn this game when I was in Chosŏn. I'll pay you back double or triple.

ISE: Permit me to say that your way of life these days calls for serious reflection. A minister of the state idly gambling his life away does not look . . . You need to be aware of what others think of you.

OKKYUN: Don't worry. I'll win. I'll win big.

(KATŌ, *his family doctor, enters the room out of breath and flushes with anger at the scene.*)

KATŌ: What is this? You said you were in critical condition, but . . .

OKKYUN: Please lend me twenty thousand wŏn! I'm thinking of starting a rice-selling business. If I buy twenty thousand wŏns' worth of rice now, it will become worth two or three hundred thousand wŏn soon. I'm absolutely certain! You'll see.

KATŌ: We'll never see each other again.

(*He throws down a few paper bills and leaves.* ISE *follows him.*)

ISE: Mr. Katō, I'll pay his debts. Please don't get upset. He's already drunk too much . . .

OKKYUN: One thousand wŏn, two thousand, and . . . six hundred, seven hundred . . .

(ISHII *draws a sword placed nearby.* SAITŌ *holds* OKKYUN's *arms backward and crosses them.* ISHII *puts* OKKYUN's *face at the point of the sword and shouts.*)

ISHII: You hold forth about the state of East Asian affairs, but if you're truly concerned about Chosŏn's future, how is it that you live idly, wasting your life? You're shallow! What if your selfish hand-wringing about the current situation ends up implicating us more deeply? That would be regrettable and cause for a great deal of grief. Therefore, by killing you, I'm going prevent a dissolute coward like you from ruining the grand plan for East Asia. Show your neck and prepare to die!

OKKYUN (*freeing his arms, he snatches away the sword and puts it down*): As it happens, His Royal Highness already has lost the three major islands in Chŏlla Province. Kŏmun Island has been lost to the British.[16] His Royal Highness's anger must be beyond imagination. According to the Chinese Li Hongzhang,[17] the British navy anchored at Kŏmun only to observe Russian movements, so there was nothing to worry about. If that's true, isn't it obvious that Russia would also demand to have an island on the pretext of observing British movements? Ha, ha, ha, ha, . . . If our court ministers were asked where England is, nine out of ten would be blank, unable to answer—it's like when a bug comes to bite me, I can neither feel the pain from the bite nor identify what kind of bug is biting me. But I abandoned His Royal Highness and now am wandering in Japan shamelessly begging for my life, so I, a bastard, ought to die hundred times over, without question! (*Silence.*) Cut off my head, Mr. Ishii. Soon either Europe or America will invade and pillage China. If you are interested in shaping a new vision for East Asia, look closely at this situation and study it. Don't do anything stupid now!

(*A* POLICEMAN *enters. He hands over some documents.*)

POLICEMAN: Your destination is Yokohama. Pack up!

ISE: Yokohama. Why?

ISHII (*looking at the document*): He's supposed to go to Ogasawara. Who's behind this? Let me find out.

OKKYUN: Where's Ogasawara?

POLICEMAN: It's a forsaken island between here and Hawai'i.

OKKYUN: Let's go. I have no other baggage.

(ISE *covers his face with hands.*)

PARIS, FRANCE

(*An office at Gime Oriental Museum.* **HONG CHONG-U** *and a* **RESEARCHER**.)

RESEARCHER: Look, your picture is printed in the magazine *Figaro*. "This young man is the first adult student from Chosŏn to set foot in France. One of the active supporters of the Enlightenment movement in Chosŏn, he now is fighting against the old system. We should take an interest in this man of reformist spirit who is trying to achieve his goal by working his way through school without government assistance."

CHONG-U: Public interest in me is appreciated, but it's too late for that. Now I must go back to reform Chosŏn. Please congratulate me, for my country now will be as enlightened as Japan. What I mean by reform is—

RESEARCHER: Then, were you a government official of Chosŏn?

CHONG-U: Yes, a special royal envoy. Now I have become His Royal Highness's close aide. In the meantime, I have thoroughly studied your French system. As a token of my appreciation, let me give you a copy of this book. I hope my French translation makes sense.

RESEARCHER: What's is it?

CHONG-U: It's my preface to the translation of "The Story of Shimch'ŏng," an old Korean tale. "I am well aware that this preface is written for French citizens who are accustomed to the lifestyle of the Republic. I am convinced, however, that they would not criticize Chosŏn's adherence to the government system established by our ancestors. It is a matter of a people's temperament. The influence of weather on people's customs was proved long ago. No one would blame Indians for not dressing as Eskimos do. Likewise, it is natural that different states have different government systems. Although we are retaining our government system as it is, at this time we would like to benefit from some aspects of European civilization as well. Therefore, we are promising in advance to devote our respect and love to those who wish to aid us in this matter."

RESEARCHER: What has surprised you most since you came to France?

CHONG-U: When I arrived in Marseille, I saw a huge horse. It was really gigantic.

RESEARCHER: What do you like least?

CHONG-U: I am leaving . . . for the country on the other side of the continent, where the sun is rising. His Royal Highness is waiting there.
(*He places a picture of His Royal Highness on the floor and prostrates himself before it in a deep bow.*)

RESEARCHER: Who is this? Your father?
CHONG-U: His Royal Highness.

OGASAWARA ISLAND

(*On the seashore,* KIM OKKYUN, *thin and haggard, is crawling around on all fours like a dog. He is playing with an empty ten-gallon beer barrel, moving it to and fro with his forehead and face, rolling the wooden barrel while muttering something inaudible.* WADA, *a youth, who later will witness* OKKYUN*'s last moments in Shanghai, is watching him nearby.*)

OKKYUN: When I was locked up in a depressed mood in the ferry, Ise-san, the easterly wind was blowing so hard for the entire three days and nights I thought that aha, God was doing this to set me free, but he brought me here only to be dumped in Ogasawara. Oh my, the wind was beyond description. It blew me here across two hundred miles of ocean in half a day.
(*Bumping the wooden barrel with his forehead,* OKKYUN *rolls it.* WADA *takes away the barrel and hands a Korean melon to him. After looking at it in a daze,* OKKYUN *devours it ravenously. His appearance is not at all different from that of a beggar's. Suddenly his gaze fixes on the empty sky as if he were following a flying bird.* WOMEN *who before were digging shellfish now sit nearby and giggle as they watch* OKKYUN *at play. He decides to become their plaything and suddenly starts jumping up and down, more and more vigorously.*)
    Hey, stork! Hey, crane!
    Your father passed away, I heard.
    Why don't you scoop up water in a trumpet shell,
    Ay, ay, wail hard, ay, ay, wail hard,
    (*He picks up an imaginary turban shell.*)
    Ay, ay, ay, ay, ay, ay . . .
(*The* WOMEN *imitate the sound, almost as if they are keeping rhythm with it. For* OKKYUN, *exiled to this godforsaken island in another country, more than a year has already passed. He can no longer remember* KOJONG*'s face as it begins to flicker and fade from his memory, even though he promised* KOJONG *he would return to see him on some bright day. He starts singing "A Song of Longing for a Lover" by Songgang Chŏng Ch'ŏl (1537–1594), who himself had longed for King Sŏnjo while banished to Changpyŏng.*)
    "Meanwhile, for some reason I descended to this mundane world,

My hair, combed nicely when I came down, has been unkempt for three years.
Though I have rouge and powder, for whom do I make up my face?
My heart smolders with a grievous grudge, layer upon layer,
The only thing I do is sigh; the only thing I see is my streaming tears.
Life is limited, anxiety is boundless.
Heartless time flees like running water.
Seasonal change knows its time and returns soon after having passed me by.
While I watch and listen here and there, so many things I have thoughts about!
Suddenly a spring breeze stirs the piled-up snow,
Then an apricot tree outside the window sends forth a couple of blossoms.
While the weather is cold and unremarkable, what is the occasion for this subtle spreading scent?
The moon in the twilight follows me and throws a beam on the corner of the pillow.
It looks like she is sobbing or rejoicing to see me; perhaps it could be my lover—or what?
Now I long to pluck an apricot flower and send it to my lover,
But I wonder what my lover would think when he sees you?"

(*As if throwing a stone, he throws the turban shell. In* **OKKYUN**'s *eyes,* **WADA** *now looks like* **KOJONG**. **OKKYUN** *kneels and bows deeply, with his hands in front, banging his forehead on the ground.*)

Your Royal Highness, I beg to ask most humbly: please carefully map out a grand plan for the nation to prevent the decline and demise of the country so that Your Royal Highness can successfully emulate the great accomplishments of the Chosŏn dynasty over the last five hundred years. Today the world situation appears . . .

(*A woman playfully covers his head with a large bamboo basket. Now he looks like he's wearing a prisoner's mask.*[18] **KIM OKKYUN** *pretends that a dragonfly has landed on the top of his head. He tries to catch it with his index fingers but misses it. As he runs after the dragonfly, he tries to captivate it by singing.*)

Dragonfly flying around and around, fly flying around and around,
Please don't fly high and higher, you might get caught in a spiderweb.
Dragonfly flying around and around, fly, flying around and around,
Please don't fly over the fence, play with me, with me.
Dragonfly flying around and around . . .

IN THE PRESENCE OF THE KING

(*The* CHAMBERLAIN *and* HONG CHONG-U *are prostrated before* KOJONG *and* QUEEN MINBI, *giving a report.*)

CHAMBERLAIN: Your Royal Highness, this is Hong Chong-u, the first man from Chosŏn to study in France.
MINBI: Where did you say Kim Okkyun was these days?
CHAMBERLAIN: It is reported that he has been exiled to Ogasawara, an isolated island in the farthest seas.
KOJONG: Do you know the old story of Hyŏngga?[19]
CHAMBERLAIN: He was the assassin sent by Prince Dan of the Chinese Yan dynasty.
KOJONG: You be our Hyŏngga and go to Japan.
MINBI (*to* CHONG-U): Even though His Royal Highness put confidence in and entrusted him with a major role in the affairs of state, he, in return, killed six ministers and fled. He has deceived His Royal Highness. Go dispose of Kim Okkyun, and then return as the commissioner of trade and commerce.
(*The* CHAMBERLAIN *and* CHONG-U *rise.*)
CHONG-U: I will carry out the order as I am told.
CHAMBERLAIN (*opening and reading the secret message*): "Kim Okkyun, I would like to confer with you face to face and map out a grand scheme for East Asia in the next hundred years. Come to China. Li Hongzhang." Give this to Kim Okkyun. (*Hands the message to* CHONG-U.)

SENIOR MINISTERS' MEETING IN JAPAN

(HONG CHONG-U, ITŌ HIROBUMI, TAKEZOE, *and* TŌYAMA.)

TAKEZOE: This is last night's report from the Yokohama Port Authority. It states that Kim Okkyun has arrived by ship.
TŌYAMA: He already is in Tokyo, staying at the house of Gogure Yurakuzō.
ITŌ: Gogure . . . He's a member of the antigovernment faction, the Liberty Party. (TŌYAMA *nods in agreement.*) Are they planning to attack Chosŏn again, with Kim Okkyun leading?
TAKEZOE: I suppose it's possible.
ITŌ: Don't they know how fiercely Chosŏn will fight back? If they bungle it, Japan will have hell to pay. Get rid of Kim Okkyun.

TŌYAMA: If we lay hands on him, I am afraid that will attract the attention of the Japanese intelligentsia and surely incite the Liberty Party. In such circumstances, wouldn't it be best to let China deal with Kim Okkyun?

ITŌ: China . . .

(**CHONG-U** *appears.*)

TŌYAMA: Here's a secret messenger from Chosŏn, sent by Kojong.

(**CHONG-U** *hands over a large envelope to* **TŌYAMA**.)

CHONG-U: This is a secret message from Li Hongzhang of China.

(**TŌYAMA** *opens the envelope and reads.*)

DAIWA DISPENSARY OF CHINESE HERBAL MEDICINE, TŌKYŌ

(*Brown envelopes containing Chinese medicine are hanging from the ceiling like blocks of fermented Korean soybeans.* **KIM OKKYUN** *and* **WADA** *appear.*)

OKKYUN (*giving a password*): Do you have Cornelian cherry? (**YI ILSHIK** *enters.*)

ILSHIK: You are here, sir. I am Yi Ilshik. The reason I contacted you is this: I was wondering if I could be of help to you, since I have some extra business capital.

OKKYUN: Let me borrow ten thousand wŏn.

ILSHIK: The money isn't here; it's deposited in a bank in Shanghai. Because the account contains more than several ten thousand wŏn, you may use as much as you need. I'll send some of my shop staff with you; please go with them to withdraw . . .

(*A gunshot.* **YI** *clutches his thigh and collapses.* **CHONG-U** *appears.*)

CHONG-U: Let's get out of here.

OKKYUN: Who are you?

CHONG-U: I've brought you a secret message from Li Hongzhang. His son is looking for you, so I volunteered to come here. (*He hands over the secret message.*)

OKKYUN: Who are you?

CHONG-U: I'm Hong Chong-u.

OKKYUN: The first man from Chosŏn to go to France?

CHONG-U: It's dangerous here.

(**OKKYUN** *and* **WADA** *leave.* **ILSHIK** *and* **CHONG-U** *exchange knowing glances.*)

THE HOUSE OF TŌYAMA

(*The* **TŌYAMA** *family's treasured sword can be seen in the corner.* **KIM OKKYUN** *is sitting across from* **TŌYAMA**, *and* **HONG CHONG-U** *and* **WADA** *are sitting in the corner.* **KIM OKKYUN** *hands over the secret message.*)

OKKYUN: This is a secret message from Li Hongzhang.
TŌYAMA (*reading*): "I would like to confer with you face to face and map out a grand scheme for East Asia in the next hundred years. Come to China. Li Hongzhang." (**OKKYUN** *examines the blade of the* **TŌYAMA** *family's treasured sword.*)
OKKYUN: I have to take this sword. I need money, and this should provide enough. (**TŌYAMA** *turns pale.*[20] **OKKYUN** *puts the sword back on the sword stand.*) The word *money* was inappropriate. In truth, I need something impressive to present to Li Hongzhang.
TŌYAMA: An old saying has it that a flower in a splendid garden blossoms early only to wither early. Human life is so unpredictable, destined to be either long or short before its time. I hope you'll be especially careful.
OKKYUN: So far, Fukuzawa, Godō, and Ishii have worked hard in every way, taking the initiative to raise war funds for me. I tried to reopen a mountain mine in southeast Chosŏn; I gave it up because it already had been mined out. Because of bad luck, my plan to dispose of the Sadake family's forest in Japan to raise war funds also failed. Add to that my exile in Ogasawara and Hokkaidō for four or five years each, and ten years passed by all too soon.

ON THE DECK OF THE FERRY *SEKIMARU* IN KŌBE HARBOR

(*On the deck. A single light flashing around the pier appears hazy and dim as if wrapped in the fog. Appearing are* **KIM OKKYUN**, **HONG CHONG-U**, **WADA**, **O PO-IN**, *secretary of the Chosŏn legation, and* **ISHII** *and* **SAITŌ**, *who have come to see* **KIM OKKYUN** *off.*)

OKKYUN: Thank you for everything you have done for me. Permit me to ask one more favor. I have jotted down according to date what I could recall of events surrounding the dedication ceremony at the Ujŏngguk Post Office a decade ago. We could call it "A Daily Account of the Year 1888." Please edit it and publish it.

ISHII: Let us go with you.

OKKYUN: Wada is with me; don't be anxious. Let's not worry about my personal safety. If you have a chance to see Pak Yŏnghyo, please tell him to take extra precautions.[21] (*A boat whistle is heard.* ISHII *and* SAITŌ *nod to* OKKYUN *and disembark in haste.* CHONG-U *and* PO-IN *enter their cabin carrying trunks.* OKKYUN *and* WADA *remain on deck. The ship gets under way. Someone on deck begins to play the accordion.*) On the night when the Ujŏngguk Post Office was dedicated, there was a celebration party. Almost all the powerful court officials and ministers gathered, and the American legate was dancing. Around 9:00 P.M., a fire broke out at a private house on the north corner of the Ujŏngguk Post Office intersection. (*He strikes a match and demonstrates by setting the matchbox on fire.*) Min Yŏng-ik's back was slashed by a sword, and the next morning a new cabinet was announced. The deputy prime minister, chief of the national police, deputy minister of foreign affairs, minister of defense, minister of culture and education—they were young pillars of the state, but all were executed within three days. Yuan Shikai of China aimed his cannons at the royal palace. (*Attempting to lift the mood with humor.*) The Chinese certainly like cannons. Boom! Boom!

WADA: Takezoe, the Japanese envoy, betrayed your trust and faith. I heard that he refused to let you board the ferry, *Senseimaru*, in Inchŏn. Did he really do that?

OKKYUN: Why don't we talk about Chosŏn's future instead? The man accompanying Hong Chong-u is an assassin coming to kill me. Keep your eyes open!

WADA: Let me deal with him first.

OKKYUN: I've come this far by using him. I have to meet Li Hongzhang. So if we get rid of Hong, we no longer will have a way to meet Li. Remember that.

WADA: Was it Li who sent him?

OKKYUN: No, Hong's Korean.

WADA: Then isn't he even more dangerous?

OKKYUN: But there're two of us—let's wait and see. (*The sound of an accordion is heard.*) Why don't we try a Chosŏn lion dance? (WADA *bends forward behind* OKKYUN *to grasp the hem of his coat.* OKKYUN *repeatedly drills* WADA *in his dance steps. Though clumsy, their movement now resembles a lion dance.*)[22] Only if one keeps time with the other will it turn into a dance. Understand?

WADA: Right foot first, correct?

OKKYUN: Left, right, left . . .

(*The sound of the accordion now changes into the elegiac sound of a bamboo flute used in the Pukch'ŏng lion dance.* CHONG-U *and* PO-IN *appear.* OKKYUN *dances swaggeringly while holding in his hands one of the yellow life preservers from the ship, now resembling a lion dance mask. The dance by* OKKYUN *and* WADA *generates a kind of fantastic beauty.* PO-IN *and* CHONG-U *look on.*)

PO-IN (*referring to* OKKYUN): Was he originally a dancing master?

CHONG-U: Everyone in Chosŏn is a dancing master.

PO-IN: Then show me the steps. Let me learn some.

CHONG-U: A nobleman does not dance.

PO-IN: Then he's not a nobleman?

CHONG-U: He is a great nobleman. But, it doesn't matter if even a monk eats meat as long as he is enlightened.

(*A radiant neon sign reading "Shanghai" glides down to hang upstage. A crying seagull flaps its wings in the air. The yellow preserver that* OKKYUN *is holding around his face now is seen as a bull's-eye. A gun held in* CHONG-U's *right hand flashes with the sound of a gunshot. Three flashes.* OKKYUN *rises in the air, leans to one side, and the body slides down to the deck.* WADA *cradles him in his arms and sobs.*)

IN THE PRESENCE OF THE KING

(KOJONG, CHAMBERLAIN, *and* HONG CHONG-U.)

CHONG-U: Before he died, Kim Okkyun left a request for Your Royal Highness.

KOJONG (*his gesture signals* CHONG-U *to continue*).

CHONG-U: His request: "Please do not take sides between China and Russia. Instead, our pressing need is to hold Japan in check by using them appropriately. Always keep a watchful eye on Japan."

CHAMBERLAIN (*following the signal from* KOJONG, *he reads on behalf of the* KING): "I am afraid that your appointment as commissioner of trade and commerce now would attract unnecessary public attention. Therefore, I'm appointing you governor of Cheju Island; go there and see how things fare."

YANGHWAJIN SAND HILL

(*Around dusk. At Yanghwajin sand hill, where a blazing bonfire to one side scatters its dismal flames.* **KIM OKKYUN** *lies in a coffin. A head-cutting* **EXECUTIONER** *brandishes a sword to the tune of a primitive flute as if he is catching a fly. Because he is about to slash an already dead body, the point of his sword does not carry much enthusiasm. It looks as if he is moving around unwillingly and sluggishly while drunk or as if he is crying for* **OKKYUN**'s *death.* **HONG CHONG-U** *appears off to one side. Suddenly, the point of the* **EXECUTIONER**'s *sword comes alive as it jumps around crazily. It weaves in and out around* **CHONG-U**, *and it now is about to brush him as it passes close by. At the moment the* **EXECUTIONER** *is poised as if to bring down the sword on* **CHONG-U**'s *head,* **COURIERS** *from eight provinces appear. The* **COURIERS** *begin to dance like the* **EXECUTIONER**. *Now they start a group dance, led by the* **EXECUTIONER**. *Finally, the* **EXECUTIONER** *jumps on the coffin and cuts* **OKKYUN** *into eight pieces. He shouts as he throws away each piece.*)[23]

EXECUTIONER: Send both arms to P'yŏngan Province and Hamgyŏng Province, the ribs to Kyŏnggi Province, the gut to Ch'ungch'ŏng Province, two thighs to Hwanghae Province and Kangwŏn Province, two legs to Chŏlla Province and Kyŏngsang Province, and leave the enemy's head here in Hanyang. (*As the* **EXECUTIONER** *shouts orders, the* **COURIERS** *accordingly take* **OKKYUN**'s *body parts assigned to them and leave the scene, each repeating his destination. The* **EXECUTIONER** *places* **OKKYUN**'s *head on a tripod and sets a streamer over it. The streamer reads, "A criminal of high treason, an immoral criminal,* **KIM OKKYUN**, *whose body was hacked into pieces!" The* **EXECUTIONER** *shouts at the backs of the* **COURIERS**.) Be sure you do it right!! If you happen to lose it, you'd better cut off your own leg to offer up instead. He, he, he . . . ! (*The* **EXECUTIONER** *lies down inside the coffin as if he himself wishes to replace* **OKKYUN**'s *dismembered body.* **WADA**, *wearing a soldier's headpiece, enters and looks around carefully. He deftly takes down* **OKKYUN**'s *head and wraps it in his own clothing while silently shedding tears. Then he gathers* **OKKYUN**'s *remaining clothes and leaves the scene in haste.* **HONG CHONG-U** *watches all this.*)

REGICIDE OF QUEEN MINBI

(*At Okhoru Pavilion, site of* **QUEEN MINBI**'s *bedchamber. In the moonlit courtyard, a group of mercenary Japanese samurai brandishing swords are seen in flickering silhouette, and then the silhouette itself appears to be drawn into the pavilion.*

Women's screams rise up soon after, and a group of court maids in blood-soaked underclothes rush out of the building, collapsing in the courtyard with painful groans. Suddenly, QUEEN MINBI *is seen, struck on the forehead by a sword. Even though she struggles to hold herself upright, she collapses on her side and breathes her last. Court maids, whose blood-soaked underclothes seem to be ablaze, rise in spectral figures surrounding* QUEEN MINBI *as they dance.* QUEEN MINBI *herself appears to be going up in flames. Surrounded by the flaming specters,* QUEEN MINBI *now becomes part of a pillar of fire and disappears from view.)*

CHEJU ISLAND

(KIM KYUHWA, HONG CHONG-U*'s concubine, is singing, neatly dressed in a white skirt and a traditional indigo blue jacket. She is a superb singer of traditional songs.* TAKEMATSU, *the Japanese consul in Mokp'o City,*[24] *addresses* CHONG-U *in a most courteous manner, as representative* JAPANESE FISHERMEN *stand by.)*

TAKEMATSU: Sir, it is quite natural that you and people on the island are angry. I will be sure to teach all Japanese residents on the island a good lesson and take strong measures to prevent any further infringement of the vested rights of Cheju Island's fishermen. If anyone violates the order, he will be sent to Japan immediately and severely prosecuted. Now, I pray you, rescind the order to evacuate Japanese residents.

CHONG-U: Did you come here on the order of Ambassador Hayashi?

TAKEMATSU: According to our 1883 agreement, Japanese residents are legally permitted to remain in Chosŏn, and because these residents are entitled to exercise extraterritoriality, they . . .

CHONG-U: Where do you think you are? You came here only to suck up to the Chosŏn people! How dare you Japanese beat up Cheju Island fishermen and claim extraterritoriality! All seventy-three Japanese households on this island must leave immediately!

JAPANESE FISHERMEN (*words overlapping*): I'm the one who started it! Please punish me. I will submit to your punishment completely, no matter what it is.

TAKEMATSU: The start of the incident was that . . . a Chosŏn fisherman captured a Japanese fishing boat and sold the catch to Mokp'o fish markets . . .

JAPANESE FISHERMEN: That's what really happened.

CHONG-U: I will give you three days to prepare to leave.

TAKEMATSU: An expulsion order is not a simple matter. Once escalated to a diplomatic issue, it will . . .

CHONG-U: Hong Chong-u, governor of Cheju, does not recognize the extraterritoriality of foreign residents. Report that to the ambassador. Ask him to send navy destroyers. I shall oppose you. I have wasted three years as governor of Cheju, and I'm deeply ashamed every time I see the island residents. But this will now be a grand opportunity for me. Go ahead! Bring on your forces without delay!

TAKEMATSU: I have come without the knowledge of my superiors . . . I myself, on my own . . . in order to bring the situation under control . . .

(*A courier rushes in.*)

COURIER: A personal letter from Yi Kŭnt'aek.

(*He hands over the letter. At the same time,* **KOJONG** *is seen with the* **CHAMBERLAIN** *in another part of the stage. The setting now shows both Cheju Island and a palace room in Hanyang.*)

CHAMBERLAIN: Your Royal Highness, Hong Chong-u, the governor of Cheju, has sent fifty horses.

KOJONG: Who?

CHAMBERLAIN: He eliminated Kim Okkyun, the great traitor.

KOJONG: Hong who?

CHAMBERLAIN: Hong Chong-u.

KOJONG: I don't know who Hong Chong-u is.

(*An invisible dagger is struck into* **CHONG-U**'s *heart, and the scene returns to Cheju Island.*)

COURIER: Queen Minbi was assassinated. Now all of Hanyang seethes with rumors that Japanese scum did it.

CHONG-U: Prepare a ferry for me immediately! His Royal Highness is in grave danger. (*He departs in haste.*)

IN THE PRESENCE OF THE KING AT CH'ANGDŎK PALACE

(**YI TOJAE** *and* **YI MINSHIK** *review the contents of the secret letter from* **KOJONG** *that will be sent to The Hague International Peace Conference. The* **CHAMBERLAIN**, **YI JUN**, *and* **YI SANGSŎL** *appear.*)

CHAMBERLAIN (*to* **YI JUN** *and* **YI SANGSŎL**): His Royal Highness is growing impatient.

TOJAE and **MINSHIK** (*calling out to* **KOJONG**, *who is in an inner chamber*): Your Royal Highness!

CHAMBERLAIN: What brought you here?

MINSHIK: We have orders from His Royal Highness.

TOJAE: His Royal Highness ordered us to prepare a secret letter to be sent to world leaders. (**KOJONG** *enters*.)

CHAMBERLAIN: Your Royal Highness. This is the secret letter.

(*Everyone bows deeply.* **KOJONG** *comes forward.*)

KOJONG: What does it say?

TOJAE: "We are faced with an unprecedented critical situation because Japanese aggression has become so fierce that now they have deprived us of diplomatic rights and abused our sovereignty. Thus I and the entire nation shed tears of mortification, and there is no one who does not clamor at the sky and cry his heart out, all while his hands pound the ground in fury. I now beg you to consider the righteousness of mutual relationships among nations, and the righteousness of championing the weak against the strong. We will righteously discuss the matter with each of our allies, and, with legislation, announce our independence."

KOJONG: Too many "righteous" here! Cut it down to one.

(*As the embarrassed court subjects glance at the* **KING**, *he dozes off.* **YI TOJAE** *continues to read*.)

TOJAE: "We beseech you to help maintain the status of our independence, thereby helping me and the entire people of the country abide in sincere appreciation, and to help us lead virtuous lives for the next thousand years."

CHAMBERLAIN: Yi Jun and Yi Sangsŏl, you two take this letter to The Hague peace conference and announce it publicly to the whole world.

JUN YI: We will make sure everything is as you order.

TOJAE: Take a ship from Wŏnsan City to Vladivostok and then a train to Moscow. Go with Yi Pŏmjin seek an audience with Czar Nicholas II. Then go with Yi Pŏmjin's son to The Hague. Since we are deprived of diplomatic rights, it will be difficult for us to make an official appearance at the conference hall. Try to gain admission by appealing to the local newspapers. Carry out this order with dispatch.

(*The two men exit with their order.*)

MINSHIK: If the letter is made known to world leaders, news of it will reach Itō here at home. As the Japanese resident general, he won't sit back quietly. We need to come up with a counterplan.

TOJAE: We'd better let be known that the letter was written without His Royal Highness's knowledge, an act committed solely by Koreans living abroad.

MINSHIK: But then His Royal Highness's communication will lose its formal credibility in the international arena. Instead, His Royal Highness should claim authorship with confidence.

TOJAE: Don't forget! The Japanese are barefaced robbers who plundered our sovereignty! When His Royal Highness comes forward as the author of this letter, he will be in grave danger. We have to make sure that he cannot be connected to this mission.

MINSHIK: Then why send those two to The Hague?

TOJAE: At the very least, the fact that we were forced to sign the Protectorate Treaty[25] will become known to all the world.

KOJONG (*who has overheard the previous discussion*): That's what matters most.

MINSHIK: Then Your Royal Highness should acknowledge that the letter was conveyed by royal order and take responsibility for it.

KOJONG (*flaring up, indignantly*): But the treaty was arbitrarily signed by court ministers coerced by the Japanese. When did I ever give my consent to it?

TOJAE: Yi Wan-yong and Song Pyŏngjun signed the treaty. Your Royal Highness had nothing to do with it.

KOJONG: You advised me then just to sit and listen to what they said, didn't you?

MINSHIK: I see . . . Then, in order to make this matter appear unrelated to Your Royal Highness, we need a scapegoat who will take the blame for fabricating the secret letter. One of the court ministers should come forward.

KOJONG: Yi Wan-yong and Song Byŏngjun are the masterminds.

MINSHIK (*to* TOJAE): It looks like one of us should claim responsibility.

KOJONG: It was I who sent those two to The Hague! Why do you keep concocting some story? Don't try to cover for me!

(*Silence.*)

IN THE HAGUE ON JUNE 5, 1907

(YI JUN *and* YI SANGSŎL *appear where a caption was projected, holding the Korean national flag. On the other side of the stage,* YI WAN-YONG *appears in the presence of* KOJONG.)

WAN-YONG: This is an inquiry from the chairman of The Hague International Peace Conference. Did Your Royal Highness send someone . . . a messenger to The Hague? Resident General Itō is much concerned about this.

KOJONG: I have nothing to do with it. A rebellious group in The Hague fabricated my royal order. Consult with the resident general and look into it.

WAN-YONG (*pressing the* KING): No messenger was sent, correct?

KOJONG: Yes. No messenger was sent.

WAN-YONG: Then, I will consult with the resident general and take the proper measures.

CONFERENCE HALL AT THE HAGUE INTERNATIONAL PEACE CONFERENCE

(YI SANGSŎL *unfurls the Korean national flag high around his shoulders.* YI JUN *points a six-chambered revolver under his chin, fires, and collapses.*)

YI TOJAE'S RECEPTION ROOM

(HONG CHONG-U *hands over a newspaper extra edition to* YI TOJAE.)

CHONG-U: "King's Secret Messenger Attends Hague Peace Conference"—All the townspeople are out and loitering in groups. The news threw the entire town into an uproar—people cheer and weep for joy, now claiming to have regained national sovereignty. What is the reaction from the Japanese resident general's office?

TOJAE: It's reported that a Japanese fleet entered the port at Inchŏn yesterday.

CHONG-U: Is that a threat?

TOJAE: That's what a thug like Itō would do. What purpose is served by calling in the fleet when we have no soldiers to fight them? They are mocking His Royal Highness.

CHONG-U: A rumor is going around that his abdication of the throne is inevitable.

TOJAE: That's nonsense.

CHONG-U: But His Royal Highness can't endure like this . . .

TOJAE: He'll hold out.
CHONG-U: Are we so helpless? Are we just going to let His Royal Highness be so humiliated!? Please . . . beg His Royal Highness to tell the whole truth, even now! Something like, "I sent the messengers—so what are you going to do to me?"
TOJAE: But the first priority should be protecting His Royal Highness's safety!
(*Silence.*)
CHONG-U: I myself will accept the full responsibility for dispatching the secret envoys. As a citizen of this nation, leaving domestic affairs in the hands of others and just watching . . . is not at all the right thing to do.
TOJAE: I will convey your thoughts, but because the matter is so urgent, let's proceed to the royal court together.

IN THE PRESENCE OF THE KING

(**KOJONG** *and the* **CHAMBERLAIN**. **YI TOJAE** *and* **HONG CHONG-U** *bow deeply.*)

TOJAE: Your Royal Highness, I am accompanied by Hong Chong-u.
KOJONG: Hong Chong-u . . . I don't know who he is.
TOJAE: He eliminated the great traitor Kim Okkyun and received royal favor in his appointment as the governor of Cheju. He later was promoted to a secretary at the royal court, subsequently becoming a chief judge, and . . .
KOJONG: Kim Okkyun has already died.
TOJAE: Hong Chong-u was in charge of the secret mission to The Hague International Peace Conference.
KOJONG (*knowing now that the responsibility for the secret letter will not be laid at his feet, he can be magnanimous*): What kind of government post do you want?
CHONG-U: The opportunity to see Your Royal Highness is reward enough.
(**YI WAN-YONG** *enters.*)
TOJAE (*to* WAN-YONG): This is Hong Chong-u.
WAN-YONG: Your Royal Highness, Yi Jun committed suicide. The case of the secret envoys is now closed.
KOJONG: Who killed him?[26]
WAN-YONG: Here is the letter of resolution from the royal cabinet.
(*The* **CHAMBERLAIN** *receives the letter of resolution and reads it aloud.*)
CHAMBERLAIN: "I hereby declare my abdication of the throne in favor of the Crown Prince, selecting Ŭn, eldest son of the Crown Prince, to succeed

his father. My title shall be Great Emperor. All court officials should remain steadfastly faithful to their duties."

KOJONG: What did you say my title will be?

WAN-YONG: It will be "Great Emperor."

(**TAKEMATSU** *enters as* **WAN-YONG** *and the* **CHAMBERLAIN** *exit*.)

TAKEMATSU: Your Majesty. Resident General Itō has sent Your Royal Highness this sweet rice punch.

(**KOJONG** *moves to accept the gift*. **HONG CHONG-U** *strangles* **KING KOJONG**. **TAKEMATSU** *exits*. **CHONG-U** *is left alone, crying and laughing*.)

SHINJO TEMPLE, LOCATED IN BUNKYŌ-KU, TŌKYŌ

(**KIM OKKYUN**'s *tombstone in the backyard of the temple*. **WADA** *is burning incense and ringing a small bell*. **OKKYUN** *appears in the form of a ghost. In his hand, he holds a head, his own when he was alive. He tries to raise himself up but rolls over to one side. He shakes the head held in his hand. Astonished at the sight of his own head, he throws it to* **WADA**.)

OKKYUN: What happened to my body? Am I having a terrible nightmare or . . . Why can't I move my body? (*He believes he is tied because he can't move*.) Untie me now. I have to go see Li Hongzhang. Are you listening to me? Untie me. (**WADA** *believes that the head he holds in his hands is speaking*.)

WADA: It's a resurrection! He's returned from the dead!

OKKYUN: I don't know where my body has gone. I feel like my limbs are no longer attached. Would you massage me a little bit? Because I feel so stiff . . . listen, I feel so stiff . . .

(*While he shakes his head side to side, he shouts, spits, rolls back his eyeballs, grinds his teeth, thrusts his tongue in and out, laughs, cries, shouts, whispers, and generally carries on, then is worn out*.)

WADA: Your limbs are scattered all over Chosŏn's eight provinces.

OKKYUN: What are you talking about? Don't you remember that we went to Shanghai together to meet Li Hongzhang?

WADA: But we now are at a Buddhist temple in Hon-Komagome in Tōkyō.

OKKYUN: What! Are you saying that my body is scattered here in Tōkyō as well as Shanghai and all eight provinces in Chosŏn? Please do something. I have to go meet Li Hongzhang.

WADA: Don't you remember that you were shot in Shanghai?

OKKYUN: Here. (*He pats his lower belly.*) Chosŏn is in great danger, like sitting on a keg of gunpowder. His Royal Highness is waiting for me. I promised to see him again on another bright day, to achieve this nation's independence, to improve the people's daily lives, to make our life dignified and worthy . . . Who shot me?

WADA: A man named Hong Chong-u—from Chosŏn.

OKKYUN: Why am I here and not in Chosŏn?

WADA: Your Japanese supporters' society has held a memorial service for you ever since you were killed.

OKKYUN: It was you! It was you bastards who orchestrated all this, you who fabricated the letter from Li! It was your black-hearted scheme to kill me in Shanghai, hack me to pieces, and scatter my remains. I know it all. You scattered my limbs all over Chosŏn, but you brought my head to Tōkyō and buried it here, and since then, you have guarded it day and night for fear that someday the head would find the limbs and all would be reunited. Didn't you? Were you afraid that the dead body with its limbs reattached would later come to haunt you? You bastard! (*Pause.*) So be it. All the while you were dragging me here and there like a dog to Hokkaidō and Ogasawara, I was so naïve I had no idea that things would come to this.

WADA: You knew that Hong Chong-u was an assassin. We kept a watchful eye on him, but you even toyed with him, keeping him close to you. Eventually, it was your overconfidence that brought misfortune on yourself. It's not right to blame your own failings on younger people. Remember that you are an enlightened spirit of Chosŏn.

OKKYUN: I've only made the situation worse—I've made a mess of it! (*In the distance a street vendor appeals to customers shouting "Carp!" and passes by.*) What's that?

WADA: It's a carp vendor.

OKKYUN: Please take me to the sea. There is an old folk tale in my country. A fisherman caught a fur seal and ate it up, dumping its bones into a seaside pool. Next day, he returned to the spot and saw eight baby fur seals putting their mouths on their mother's bones and sucking the breast in vain . . . Please leave my head in one of pools near the shore. Then my scattered limbs will come find me someday. Once I have my limbs back, I will go meet Li Hongzhang and . . .

(*He faints.* **WADA** *rings the bell.* **KIM OKKYUN** *does not move. Then* **WADA** *brings large, fresh radishes and arranges them under* **OKKYUN**'s *head as if they were body parts.*[27] *A children's song is heard.*)

"Bellflower, bellflower, white bellflower,
Bellflower in deep and deeper mountains.
I wish I could dig up just a couple of roots . . ."²⁸

Curtain

NOTES
1. The reader may wish to think of scene titles as an integral part of O T'aesŏk's dramaturgy, projected at the beginning of each scene to set the locale and remind the audiences of the theatrical, nonrealistic nature of the event. The king's and queen's sexual dalliances suggest the moral decay of the late Chosŏn court.
2. Okkyun refers obliquely to Queen Min in a formal, flowery language associated with court protocol.
3. The Sino-Japanese War took place on Korean soil in 1894 and 1895, with far-reaching consequences for both China and Chosŏn.
4. In Korea, as in Japan, a high score on civil-service exams could mean security, prestige, and even power. Thus relinquishing the right to sit for the exams was a significant act.
5. Taewŏn-gun was the official title given to Kojong's father (1820–1898). A popular de facto regent, he was active behind the scenes, favoring the Chinese and working against Russian interests in Korea. Following Queen Minbi's assassination, he was forced into retirement and died three years later.
6. Minbi was Taewŏn-gun's daughter-in-law. Expected to be a nonentity when she became queen, she was a force to be reckoned with. Taewŏn-gun treated her with contempt and was implicated in the attempt on her life during the "soldiers mutiny" on June 9, 1882.
7. At the end of the Chosŏn dynasty, when the bureaucratic system was about to break down, many poor aristocrats sold their inherited family registers. By buying a family register, the only thing that could verify their family relationship and social status, rich merchant-class people entered their names in the book and identified themselves as members of the aristocratic family. Although illegal at the time, it was a popular device. The purchased register book was taken to government offices to verify the change and get a new family ID to carry. The main purpose of issuing a family ID was effective tax collection. Although poor aristocratic family members were unable to pay their taxes, the surging merchant class who bought their higher social status did have enough money to pay them. Thus the government was conveniently blind to the illegal practice of selling and buying social status.
8. Because Mr. Ku is illiterate, he does not understand the Chinese characters for Hyoch'ang Park and the post title and thus does not comprehend at all the nature of Chong-u's family post.

9. A *nyang* was a coin with a high silver content. Determining its value in today's currency is difficult, but one Web source suggests that 1 *nyang* was worth $3,000; another sets the value of 5 *nyang* at $25,000.
10. This post office is linked to what is called the Kapsin coup, an attempt by supporters of modernization to seize power and reverse foreign influence in Korean affairs. The coup was quickly squelched by Chinese forces under the direction of Resident General Yuan Shikai. Kim and Sŏ escaped to Japan.
11. Min Yŏng-ik, the head of the Min clan, was a principal target of the Kapsin coup. Badly injured, he escaped, first sheltered by Dr. Horace Allen, a missionary, and then spending his exile years in Hong Kong before dying in Shanghai in 1914.
12. Yuan Shikai (1856–1916) was sent by Li Hongzhang to Chosŏn in 1882 with three thousand men to counter Japan's growing power. At one time, he may have been the most powerful man in Seoul.
13. The list handed to King Kojong announces the new ministers' names and, in a Korean stage production, is read aloud. The reading serves O T'ae-sŏk's dramaturgy because the Korean version takes on a theatrical musicality at the same time it provides a history lesson for audience members, but the list would serve little dramatic function in any English-language performance of the play and thus is omitted in the translation.
14. Namsan is a small mountain situated in the south-central area of Seoul, just north of the Han River, which runs through the city.
15. There seems to be some incongruity here: a Korean asking the owner of the Japanese drinking house for Korean money (wŏn) in order to gamble in Japan with Japanese. Perhaps the monetary exchange between the two countries was more relaxed then than it is now!
16. Called Port Hamilton in English, the group of small islands is situated between mainland Korea and Cheju Island to the south. They were occupied by the British between 1885 and 1887.
17. Li Hongzhang (1823–1901) was an outward-looking Chinese statesman, but his East Asian foreign policy collapsed with the Chinese defeat in the Sino-Japanese War.
18. In earlier days, a large straw head-covering was placed on prisoners when they were moved from place to place. While wearing the bamboo basket, Okkyun Kim looks like a prisoner, which, in exile, he is.
19. "Hyŏngga" is a Chinese story about an assassin sent by Prince Dan of the Yan dynasty to kill a prince of the Qin clan. That prince later unified China (221 B.C.E.) and became the First Emperor of the Qin dynasty (221–207 B.C.E.).
20. Japanese samurai believed that a sword held the soul of its owner; thus if the sword were lost or taken from the family, the loss would have spiritual, as well as material, implications. This shame, or "loss of face," could lead to *seppuku*, ritual self-disembowelment.

21. Pak Yŏngho (1869–1931) was a promoter of modernization in Chosŏn and later became an industrialist.
22. The lion dance (*saja-ch'um*) is a part of many regional mask dance dramas (*t'alch'um*) in South Korea, as well as a distinctive genre in the Pukch'ŏng area of North Korea. The dance that Okkyun teaches Wada has an important dramatic irony because the dance itself is often connected with desires for good health and longevity—none of which Kim will experience.
23. A punishment for treason in old Korea was to tie the head and limbs to five carts and whip the horses. Here Kim's body is cut up so that his ghost cannot return to haunt those responsible for his death. Even today, a person who inspires hatred or deserves severe punishment is known as a *yukshibal nom* (one who should be torn into six pieces).
24. Mokp'o is located on the southeastern tip of present-day South Korea, a bustling, scenically attractive seaport and gateway to the many nearby islands, the Yellow Sea to the west and Japan to the east. Cheju Island is the southernmost Korean province, now known as "Korea's Hawai'i," a large island lying in the South Sea, a day-long ferry ride from Mokp'o.
25. The Protectorate Treaty was signed in November 1905 when Yi Wan-yong was a major minister. He was the prime minister of Korea from 1907 to 1910. Fervently pro-Japanese, he argued when he became prime minister that it was in Korea's interest to serve Japan. He signed the Treaty of Annexation with Japan and later became known as one of the "five traitors" for having collaborated with the Japanese.
26. The savvy king transforms the suicide into a murder, suspecting that someone was behind Yi Jun's death.
27. Korean and Japanese radishes are long, with a pale, skinlike color, very unlike the round red radishes common in the West.
28. A complete translation of the "Bellflower Song" (Doraji taryung) may be found in *Korea Sings: Folk and Popular Music and Lyrics*, Korean Cultural Series, vol. 5 (Seoul: Yonsei University Press, 1997).

A FEELING, LIKE NIRVANA
(NŬGGIM KŬGNAK KAT'ŬN)

YI KANGBAEK

Considered by many to be the doyen of Korean playwrights, Yi Kangbaek has been awarded every prestigious Korean playwriting award, his works numbering more than forty plays published in seven volumes. Born in 1947 in Chŏnju City, North Chŏlla Province, Yi is largely self-educated. His debut play, *Five* (*Tasŏt*, 1971), won first prize in a newspaper literary contest. Yi acknowledged that he wrote the play at that time because he was impressed by Samuel Beckett's *Waiting for Godot*.

Yi Kangbaek is known as perhaps the premier writer of allegorical social criticism, a form that evolved during the 1970s and 1980s to skirt oppressive censorship. His *Five* and *Watchman* (*P'asuggun*, 1973) exemplify his use of allegory to criticize abusive political power. However, it would be a mistake to categorize Yi solely as an allegorist. His *Homo Separatus* (1983) faults government intransigence on both sides of the Thirty-eighth Parallel, suggesting that human love may bridge the divide. *Chilsan Town* (*Chilsan-ri*, 1989), in particular, targets the South Korean government's rigid rightist ideology at the time. Other works explore themes such as sacrifice, redemption, and human compassion. The motifs in *A Feeling, Like Nirvana* (*Nŭggim kŭgnak kat'ŭn*, 1998) are many: the Confucian relationship between parent and child, master and apprentice; the place of tradition in the contemporary world; Buddhism as a living presence in a materialistic society; and society's obsession with surface perfection in contemporary South Korea, where an estimated 50 percent of women under twenty have had at least one cosmetic surgery.

The likable and noncombative apprentice, Sŏ-yŏn, is obsessed with inner truth, but he ultimately rises above his obsession and reaches nirvana. Egocentric, combative Tong-yŏn is obsessed with perfect form, and it is his obsession, his mental or spiritual imbalance, that inevitably manifests itself in his physical affliction midway through the play. The Western reader may feel that the playwright sides with Sŏ-yŏn against Tong-yŏn, but it is through the opposing obsessions that Yi Kangbaek emphasizes a major motif: balance in life. Ham Yijŏng says that she was happiest when she had both men with her. Yet as the play suggests, because we are human, we give priority to one need over others, thereby remaining in an unbalanced state and, therefore, unhappy. As the child Cho Sung-in says, "Since I was born, all I've experienced is disharmony between form and content. My life has been quite a difficult one."

One may wonder whether Yi's *Nirvana*, recognizing that balance in all things is an ideal, is not also suggesting that paradoxically human imbalance is necessary to create great art. Who is the true artist, the play seems to ask: He with clear artistic intuition, purity of calling and perseverance, or he who momentarily is stylish, creating works intended only to gain the crowd's applause?

A FEELING, LIKE NIRVANA
(NŬGGIM KŬGNAK KAT'ŬN)

TRANSLATED BY ALYSSA KIM

Characters

HAM MYOJIN, a master sculptor
HAM YIJŎNG, Ham Myojin's daughter
TONG-YŎN, Ham Myojin's pupil
SŎ-YŎN, Ham Myojin's pupil
CHO SUNG-IN, the son of Ham Myojin and Tong-yŏn
A CHORUS OF WOMEN

(*The curtain rises. The dead of night. Stars and a full moon in the sky. In an open field, there is a tent. Inside the tent, two candles burn brightly. Behind the candles is placed a wooden casket containing* **SŎ-YŎN**'s *body. In front of the casket is* **HAM YIJŎNG** *in her mourning clothes. Sounds of wind and crickets . . .* **CHO SUNG-IN** *enters.*)

CHO SUNG-IN: It's me, Mother. Cho Sung-in is here.
HAM YIJŎNG (*happy to see her son*): It's good to see you.
CHO SUNG-IN (*he pays his respects, bowing twice in front of the casket*).
HAM YIJŎNG: I was sure that you would be here tonight.
CHO SUNG-IN (*gazing at the casket*): He was my spiritual father.
HAM YIJŎNG: Mmm . . . Now that I look at you, you've grown into a man.
CHO SUNG-IN: My father sent me. He also sends this money to help you pay for the funeral. (*He takes an envelope from his coat and offers it to his mother.*) Take it, Mother.
HAM YIJŎNG (*she hesitates for a second but takes the envelope*): Thank you. But there's no need to worry about the

funeral. The third night¹ ends with the dawn, and tomorrow his ashes will be scattered over the field as he wished. There are many kind people in the village. They lent me candles, incense, and even this tent. (*She remembers something funny and smiles.*) Yesterday, priests from Songdŏk Temple came by. And it was . . . funny the way they chanted and beat their woodblocks. When he was alive, they all called him crazy. Yesterday, it was as if they wanted to send his spirit as far away as possible.

CHO SUNG-IN (*he looks at his mother's smiling face*): Mother, are you happy?

HAM YIJŎNG: Why do you ask?

CHO SUNG-IN: Because you don't seem sad.

HAM YIJŎNG: Yes, I'm happy.

CHO SUNG-IN: I'm troubled.

HAM YIJŎNG: Are you still tormenting yourself?

CHO SUNG-IN: Yes.

HAM YIJŎNG: That's not good . . .

CHO SUNG-IN: My two fathers are constantly fighting in my heart.

HAM YIJŎNG: Cho Sung-in . . . my son . . .

CHO SUNG-IN: My heart hurts when they fight; it's never able to choose one over the other.

HAM YIJŎNG: Their battle in your heart will end, and there will be nirvana.

CHO SUNG-IN: Father still hasn't forgiven you. When you left the house, he screamed in rage. "Your so-called mother went to that guy. Even when we married and she was living with me, she wanted to be with him." And he would tell me: "You are a strange one. You look like me on the outside but you think like him." I . . . hated hearing that. Hated it more than any curse in this world. At the same time, I liked hearing it. Hearing it was better than any compliment that I was like him. (*He goes to the casket and, on his knees, strokes the casket.*) I really wanted to meet him, my spiritual father. My father despised him so. It's a pity he is no longer of this world.

HAM YIJŎNG: But the feeling of him is.

CHO SUNG-IN: Feeling . . . you mean *memories* of him?

HAM YIJŎNG: Don't laugh, even if it seems strange. Even from the sound of rocks rolling in the field, I can feel him. In streams, breeze, in everything, I can feel that he is here. (*She blushes and laughs.*) I told you not to laugh, but look at me, laughing. Why don't you laugh with me?

CHO SUNG-IN (*he smiles a little*): You loved him. That's why you can feel him even after he is gone.

HAM YIJŎNG: Cho Sung-in, don't you understand? I love them both.

CHO SUNG-IN: Yes, I know that, Mother.

HAM YIJŎNG: And I love you very much.

CHO SUNG-IN: Yes, I know.

HAM YIJŎNG: When I was young, I thought I would be so happy if I could have a smart, strong son like you . . . I could talk about my problems, share happy memories, anything with my son. And then, I had a feeling of you . . . I enjoyed talking with the feeling of you. People thought that I was constantly mumbling to myself. In fact, I was talking to you . . .

CHO SUNG-IN: Tell me again from the beginning, Mother.

HAM YIJŎNG: From the beginning?

CHO SUNG-IN: Yes, before I was born. When you were young. How were they with each other?

HAM YIJŎNG: They were friends. At that time, everything was fine. The two lived with us as family while they apprenticed to my father, learning to sculpt bodhisattva statues. One day, my father went to the workshop but could not find them. He was very angry. He came into the house and started shouting their names. "Tong-yŏn! Sŏ-yŏn!" His voice thundered so you could hear him from a thousand miles away.

(*The stage becomes bright. The tent is lifted out of sight. The scene changes to* HAM YIJŎNG's *house.* HAM MYOJIN *enters. He looks angry.* HAM YI-JŎNG *and* CHO SUNG-IN *exit carrying the casket, candles, and incense.*)

HAM MYOJIN: Tong-yŏn! Sŏ-yŏn! Where are you?

HAM YIJŎNG (*from offstage*): They aren't here, Papa.

HAM MYOJIN: They aren't in the house?

HAM YIJŎNG (*from offstage*): Should I go look for them?

HAM MYOJIN: You stay where you are. (*He calls for them again.*) Tong-yŏn! Sŏ-yŏn!

(HAM YIJŎNG *and* CHO SUNG-IN, *out of the mourning clothes worn in the previous scene, enter wearing brightly colored clothing.* CHO SUNG-IN *remains close to* HAM YIJŎNG *for the remainder of the scene, invisible to others but a tangible presence to his mother.*)

CHO SUNG-IN: Why is father's voice so loud?

HAM YIJŎNG: Even the deaf can hear him.

HAM MYOJIN: Tong-yŏn! Sŏ-yŏn!

(TONG-YŎN *and* SŎ-YŎN *enter hurriedly and stand in front of* HAM MYOJIN.)

TONG-YŎN and SŎ-YŎN: Did you call for us?

HAM MYOJIN: You weren't at the workshop!

TONG-YŎN: I'm sorry. We were outside for a while.

HAM MYOJIN: Outside? Why?

TONG-YŎN: We have different opinions . . . we were having an argument.

HAM MYOJIN: An argument?

TONG-YŎN: Yes.

HAM MYOJIN: Sŏ-yŏn, why don't you tell me what you were arguing about?

SŎ-YŎN: I'm sorry about the argument.

HAM MYOJIN: You two have seen eye to eye in everything. I'm surprised that you would have something to argue about, so what was it?

SŎ-YŎN: Tong-yŏn said that when you make a bodhisattva statue, the bodhisattva spirit is in that statue.[2]

HAM MYOJIN: And you?

SŎ-YŎN: But . . . I said even if you were to make a statue of a bodhisattva, what's the point if the spirit of Buddha isn't in it?

TONG-YŎN: Master, please reprimand him. His opinion is trash, meant only to torment me.

HAM MYOJIN: Both of you, go get the statues you've made.

(TONG-YŎN *and* SŎ-YŎN *exit to bring their statues.* HAM YIJŎNG *goes to her father.*)

HAM YIJŎNG: Dad, do me a favor . . .

HAM MYOJIN: What is it?

HAM YIJŎNG: Don't punish Sŏ-yŏn too much.

HAM MYOJIN: This is none of your business.

HAM YIJŎNG: He hasn't been well, lately. Tong-yŏn is eating well and sleeping well but Sŏ-yŏn isn't.

HAM MYOJIN: Don't be dense. You're all grown up but still chase them around like they're your brothers. There is a season for singing and holding hands, the three of you spending time together, but that season is over. They're no longer your brothers. Do you understand?

HAM YIJŎNG: Well, if that's so, what season is it, then?

HAM MYOJIN: Now is the time for the brothers to be men, and the sister to be a woman. Look at the two of them. The fact that they are having an argument means that they have become men. Pretty soon, they will be fighting over you. A fight to get the woman you've become.

HAM YIJŎNG: Daddy, that's not . . .

HAM MYOJIN: You have to be careful! You shouldn't spend time in a threesome anymore.

HAM YIJŎNG: I like Sŏ-yŏn and Tong-yŏn! They like me, too. We'll live together, always.

HAM MYOJIN: Three of you, live together? How?

HAM YIJŎNG: Like brothers and sister.

HAM MYOJIN: You're not going to get married? No marriage, then no husband!

HAM YIJŎNG: I don't need a husband.

HAM MYOJIN: No husband, then no children!

HAM YIJŎNG: Don't worry about that, Dad. I have a feeling I'll have a son who'll be strong and smart.

HAM MYOJIN: What? A feeling?

HAM YIJŎNG: Yes. I even have a name for him. (*She stands next to her son, who has been near her for the entire scene.*) It's Cho Sung-in, "Sung" meaning the peak of perfection and "In" meaning benevolence. Cho Sung-in.

HAM MYOJIN: You have to stop doing that! Stop daydreaming!

(TONG-YŎN *and* SŎ-YŎN *bring pedestals on which to place their identical statues of Avalokiteshvara.*[3] *Two* CHORUS WOMEN *who will be the statues follow them in. When* TONG-YŎN *and* SŎ-YŎN *have placed their pedestals and statues side by side, the* WOMEN *sit in the lotus position.* HAM MYOJIN *examines the figures and marvels at the young men's talent.*)

HAM MYOJIN: Wonderfully crafted, both of them!

TONG-YŎN: Figures of Avalokiteshvara . . .

HAM MYOJIN: Yes, the most beautiful form of bodhisattva. Tong-yŏn, why don't you explain the characteristics of this. (*Referring to the statue.*)

TONG-YŎN: You have taught us that Avalokiteshvara has perfect beauty and balance. The lower part of her body sustains the weight, so when you craft the right leg, you must make it straight across against the left leg, which should be placed straight down so that they are perpendicular to each other. This vertical and horizontal balance creates this perfect form.

HAM MYOJIN: That's exactly right! Sŏ-yŏn, what about the upper body?

SŎ-YŎN: In making this Avalokiteshvara, the positions of her hands are important. Her right hand should rise toward her face to suggest a vertical axis. Her left hand should be placed on the ankle of her right leg to counterbalance the vertical line. In this way, the vertical and horizontal balance in the lower part of her body is replicated in the upper part, creating perfect balance in the overall figure.

HAM MYOJIN: Absolutely right! Sŏ-yŏn and Tong-yŏn, you have already acquired the skills to make a perfect bodhisattva.

TONG-YŎN: Thank you, Master.

HAM YIJŎNG (*observing this exchange with* CHO SUNG-IN): My father is usually quite stingy with compliments, but today he has complimented both of them.

CHO SUNG-IN: But, their reactions are completely different. Tong-yŏn seems happy to hear the compliment, but Sŏ-yŏn seems depressed.

HAM MYOJIN: Sŏ-yŏn.

SŎ-YŎN: Yes, Master?

HAM MYOJIN: You're not happy?

SŎ-YŎN (*he is silent*).

TONG-YŎN (*to* **SŎ-YŎN**): Tell him the truth . . .

SŎ-YŎN: I don't know how to tell you this, but . . . I made the figure as well as I could, but what I made is just a figure with no spirit.

HAM MYOJIN: What are you saying? There is no spirit of a bodhisattva in this statue? Is that it?

SŎ-YŎN: That's what I've been agonizing over . . .

TONG-YŎN: Master, please punish him. No Buddha spirit in these figures! What kind of shameful sacrilege is that?

HAM MYOJIN (*he stops* **TONG-YŎN**'s *complaint with a lift of his hand*): Hold on. (*To* **SŎ-YŎN**.) Let's hear a bit more from you. Here are two figures of bodhisattvas, one made by you, the other by Tong-yŏn. But, you say, the one you made is just an empty figure, with no bodhisattva spirit. Why is that so?

SŎ-YŎN: I don't understand the spirit of the bodhisattva. I made this without understanding it, so what it this but an empty shell . . .

HAM MYOJIN: Then, what about Tong-yŏn's bodhisattva? Is there a bodhisattva spirit in his work—or not?

SŎ-YŎN (*he is silent*).

HAM MYOJIN: Answer me!

SŎ-YŎN: This is truly well made. But . . .

HAM MYOJIN (*referring to* **TONG-YŎN**'s work): So this also is an empty figure, is that it?

SŎ-YŎN: Yes, I don't feel the spirit.

TONG-YŎN: There is no spirit in the bodhisattvas that I made? Sŏ-yŏn! How can you insult me like that? (*To* **HAM MYOJIN**.) I don't agree with Sŏ-yŏn. If the figure is crafted unskillfully, then it has no spirit. But if the figure is crafted perfectly, the spirit is in that perfection. Sŏ-yŏn is still a child. His immature workmanship has led him to create immature figures, and his childish ideas torment himself, his friend, and even his teacher. Please punish him. Tell him to get down to work and pay attention to nothing but perfecting his skills.

HAM MYOJIN: I've been teaching you how to make bodhisattvas. No one knows better than I how to create such statuary. But what can I say about the spirit?

Sŏ-yŏn, if you want to know about the spirit, ask someone else.

(**HAM MYOJIN** *starts to exit in agitation. As he does so, his left leg has a sudden muscle spasm.* **TONG-YŎN** *helps him as they exit. The light changes. In the yard are many figures of bodhisattvas.* **CHORUS MEMBERS** *have lined up in different positions, some in the lotus position, the half lotus position, Egyptian to Burmese postures.* **CHO SUNG-IN** *looks at them.*)

CHO SUNG-IN: There are a lot of bodhisattvas here.
HAM YIJŎNG: They also have different names. Should I tell you what they are?
CHO SUNG-IN: Maybe later.
HAM YIJŎNG: My dad must think that I'm mumbling to myself again when I'm talking to you.
CHO SUNG-IN: Look at the apricot tree in the yard. There are so many apricots . . . Who eats them all when they are ripe?[4]
HAM YIJŎNG: The priests will visit us today.
CHO SUNG-IN: Tong-yŏn would eat some, and so would Sŏ-yŏn.
HAM YIJŎNG: Priests from Paegun Temple and the abbots from the Pohyŏn and Wŏlgye temples will all be here.
CHO SUNG-IN: Why? Why would they come to eat the apricots? They will be sour because they aren't ripe yet.
HAM YIJŎNG (*smiling*): You don't think they'll be here for the apricots, do you?
CHO SUNG-IN: Then why?
HAM YIJŎNG: To look at the bodhisattvas. When they build a new temple, they will need some. Priests are very picky. They want only the best and will not even bother to look at any others and will not even glance at anything inferior. But if they like one, they will pay a lot for it—the price of a temple for one bodhisattva—or, if it is really well made, one bodhisattva could cost ten times more than a temple itself.
CHO SUNG-IN: Ten times more than a temple . . . That's a lot. (*He takes another look at the bodhisattvas.*) I didn't know they could be that expensive. (*He points to the bodhisattva made by* TONG-YŎN.) Mother, look over here! Here's the one grandfather said was wonderfully crafted.
HAM YIJŎNG: I know. That one was made by Tong-yŏn.
CHO SUNG-IN: Where is the other one?
HAM YIJŎNG: Sŏ-yŏn didn't put his here. Except for Tong-yŏn's bodhisattvas, everything else was made by your grandpa.
CHO SUNG-IN: But this is strange. Why did Grandfather put his pupil's bodhisattvas in the middle of his, not at the side, but in the middle?
HAM YIJŎNG: Because it would be most noticeable in the middle. He wants to show off Tong-yŏn's statue to the priests. They are so unbending. They would never believe that a pupil's creation could be better than his teacher's. So your grandfather wants to change their way of thinking by placing this in the middle of his bodhisattvas.
CHO SUNG-IN: Wait. Someone is looking at us.
HAM YIJŎNG: Who could . . . ?

CHO SUNG-IN: I feel like someone is.

HAM YIJŎNG: You're right. Tong-yŏn's there behind the apricot tree.

CHO SUNG-IN: He's coming this way. I think I should go sit with the statues.

(CHO SUNG-IN *sits with the bodhisattvas, imitating their posture.* TONG-YŎN *walks over to* HAM YIJŎNG.)

TONG-YŎN: I came to take a look. (*Gazes at the statues.*) As I thought, my work is placed where it should be.

HAM YIJŎNG: Dad put it here.

TONG-YŎN: Mine will be sold for sure. You'll see. It would be good if the abbot from Pohyŏn Temple buys it. They have a lot of money, you know. And I should get at least a temple's worth from the start. Other temples don't have that kind of money. I won't accept anything less.

HAM YIJŎNG: I hope everything turns out the way you want.

TONG-YŎN: And today it would be great if only mine is sold. I don't want mine to be bought lumped in with others. (*Looking around at the other statues.*) I'm sorry to say this, but your father is not good as he used to be. His figures aren't perfect; they're not as detailed as they once were. He has reached his peak, and that means it's about time for him to retire. Do you know what I really want? I want to inherit your father's workshop and marry you.

HAM YIJŎNG: Marry me?

TONG-YŎN: Why are you so surprised?

HAM YIJŎNG: It is just the idea of getting married. I hadn't thought about it . . .

TONG-YŎN: Answer me. You don't want to marry me?

HAM YIJŎNG: It's not that.

TONG-YŎN (*pointing to the statues*): Take a look here. If Amitabha is masculine,[5] Avalokiteshvara is feminine. She has an oval face, voluptuous bosom, and slender waist. I made it thinking of you.

CHO SUNG-IN (*half to himself, half to the audience*): I can't believe what I'm hearing! (*He cups his mouth with his hands and shouts.*) There! The priests are coming! The rich ones from Pohyŏn Temple and the poor priests, too. They're coming!

(*Covering her face in embarrassment,* HAM YIJŎNG *runs off. All the bodhisattvas dance together, creating a collage of different forms. The light changes. The setting is* HAM MYOJIN's *house at night. He sits dejectedly under a single light.* HAM YIJŎNG *enters with an apron around her waist, bringing a small, wheeled serving trolley with food.*)

HAM YIJŎNG: It's time for dinner.

HAM MYOJIN: I have no appetite. Just get me some wine.

HAM YIJŎNG (*she takes a spoonful of food and brings it close to his lips*): Just make me believe that you ate some. Then I'll get you a drink.

HAM MYOJIN (*he swallows the food unwillingly*): It tastes like sand.

HAM YIJŎNG (*tentatively*): Which bodhisattva did the priests buy?

HAM MYOJIN: Tong-yŏn's.

HAM YIJŎNG: Really? And yours?

HAM MYOJIN: They didn't buy a single one I made. The abbot from Pohyŏn Temple has impeccable taste. He pointed to Tong-yŏn's bodhisattva and said, "This one is one in a million." He paid the price of a temple for it and took it away.

HAM YIJŎNG: Tong-yŏn must have been very happy.

HAM MYOJIN: I was happier. That's what being a teacher is. There is nothing more rewarding than to have a student who outshines you. (*He pushes away the spoon.*) No, I don't want anymore. Give me some wine.

HAM YIJŎNG: Dad . . .

HAM MYOJIN: What?

HAM YIJŎNG: I know.

HAM MYOJIN: Know what?

HAM YIJŎNG: You say you are happy but . . . you feel depressed.

HAM MYOJIN (*silent*).

HAM YIJŎNG: Tong-yŏn said you aren't what you used to be. Looking at your bodhisattva figures . . . he said that it was about time for you to retire. He said he wants to inherit your workshop and marry me.

HAM MYOJIN: That ungrateful . . .

HAM YIJŎNG: Dad, I don't want to get married.

HAM MYOJIN: No, you should be married. I'm old and sick. I should decide on my successor. Before I die, I want to hold my grandkids in my arms. Tong-yŏn is an ingrate, but he's also talented and ambitious. He could be a good husband to you. (*He stands up in an awkward motion.*) I'm going to go to my room. Bring me some more wine. I have to be drunk to fall asleep tonight. (HAM MYOJIN *exits leaning on a cane, dragging his feet.* HAM YIJŎNG *is alone on stage, left to think.* CHO SUNG-IN *enters.*)

CHO SUNG-IN: Mother, what are you thinking so hard about?

HAM YIJŎNG (*she is not aware of her son*).

CHO SUNG-IN (*half to himself, half to her*): She doesn't know I'm here.

HAM YIJŎNG: Hmm . . . ?

CHO SUNG-IN: You were lost in thought. About what?

HAM YIJŎNG: Oh no, it was nothing.

CHO SUNG-IN: Mother, you were blushing.

HAM YIJŎNG: When?

CHO SUNG-IN: This afternoon. When Tong-yŏn was so blunt about the oval face, voluptuous bosom, slender waist . . . You seemed quite taken by it.

HAM YIJŎNG: Did I seem in love with him?

CHO SUNG-IN: I'm not sure, but I am certain that he's in love with you.

HAM YIJŎNG: I'm not sure, no matter how hard I think about it. Sŏ-yŏn and Tong-yŏn and I, we always were together, played together, and grew up together. So I thought that we would always live together, for the rest of our lives.

CHO SUNG-IN: So you want both of them as your husbands?

HAM YIJŎNG: No, not as husbands . . . but like a family. I guess you can't understand it.

CHO SUNG-IN: You are saying that you like one, but also like the other, so you can't choose either, isn't that it?

HAM YIJŎNG: No, that's not it, either. If I must like one, I must not like the other. I am afraid to—

HAM MYOJIN (*shouts from his room*): Give me some wine. More wine!

CHO SUNG-IN: Grandfather is yelling.

HAM MYOJIN (*shouts*): You forgot to bring me more wine!

HAM YIJŎNG: Yes, Father! I'm on my way!

(*She exits, pushing the serving trolley. The light changes. Inside the workshop. A scroll with an image of Amitabha descends from the flies.* TONG-YŎN *enters. He is working on a three-dimensional figure of Amitabha from the suspended image.* SŎ-YŎN *enters. It is obvious from his appearance that he has been wandering for a long time. He takes a rucksack from his shoulder, looks at what* TONG-YŎN *has been working on, and clears his throat to let him know of his presence.*)

SŎ-YŎN: Hm . . . Hm . . .

TONG-YŎN (*he intentionally does not look around*).

SŎ-YŎN: It's me. I've come back.

TONG-YŎN (*he takes a glance at him and goes back to his work*): You left without telling anyone and now that you're back, you want to crow about it?

SŎ-YŎN: I'm sorry. I was just so frustrated that I left to get some fresh air.

TONG-YŎN: So, you got some fresh air in you. You must have a lot of time to kill.

SŎ-YŎN: What are you working so hard on?

TONG-YŎN: I'm very busy. I was commissioned to make this Amitabha, which is going to be magnificent! It'll be made mostly of gold mixed with copper.

SŎ-YŎN: Congratulations, Tong-yŏn.

TONG-YŎN: I sold my previous bodhisattva for a price equal to the cost of a temple. The abbot priest of Pohyŏn Temple just fell in love with it. He recognized my talent, and now he's commissioned this figure of Amitabha. You'll see. When this is finished, I'll be famous.

SŎ-YŎN: I'm sure you will be. You'll be famous.

TONG-YŎN: Listen carefully. Our teacher plans to name me as his successor. He has been wavering between you and me, but finally he has chosen me. You shouldn't have any regrets, since we both had equal chances. I grabbed my chance, but you, you slacked off and missed the boat. (TONG-YŎN *stops working for a while and looks at* SŎ-YŎN, *who seems contemplative.*)

SŎ-YŎN: I've been to Unjang Mountain, and it was great. There are rows of oak, pine, and ash . . . It was the best experience to walk along a quiet path in the middle of nothing but trees. Tong-yŏn, how about it? Why don't you just take off with me? In this small workshop, with nothing but pictures of Buddha around you, you're stifling your heart and mind. There, in the mountains, everything is open to everywhere. You can see Chiri Mountain and beyond is the faint silhouette of Mudŭng Mountain, and you can also see the two peaks of Ma'i Mountain. If you climb down, following the path near the valley, you can see rocks in all different shapes and they look more like Buddha than any man-made figures.

TONG-YŎN (*derisively*): Is that right? Those rocks are better than the figures I've made?

SŎ-YŎN: Tong-yŏn, listen.

TONG-YŎN: What?

SŎ-YŎN: No one knows who drew the picture that you are trying to copy and even that one could be a copy of someone else's drawing. But here you are, trying to copy a copy. Don't you have any doubts about that? Give it some more thought. This (*Referring to the image of Amitabha.*) probably isn't what Buddha really looked like.

TONG-YŎN: I have no doubts whatsoever.

SŎ-YŎN: No doubts whatsoever?

TONG-YŎN: Why should I waste my valuable time doubting the obvious?

SŎ-YŎN: Hmm . . .

TONG-YŎN: Study! Don't waste time in useless doubting! (*He points to the scroll hanging from the ceiling.*) How much have you studied this figure? This Amitabha has ten faces on his head. Have you studied each face in detail? The earring, the necklace, and the vase and dragon flower in his hands. Have you studied their delicate design? A lazy good-for-nothing like you questions the meaning in the design rather than studying it.

SŎ-YŎN: So you've studied it a lot. Then tell me where the spirit of Buddha is in all these? (*Referring to Amitabha's faces.*)

TONG-YŎN: Here we go again!

SŎ-YŎN: Maybe I'm dense... I saw many temples on the way to Unjang Mountain, and I saw bodhisattvas while seeking the spirit of Buddha, but I could not see it.

TONG-YŎN: I don't want to hear any more of your quibbling.

SŎ-YŎN: I'm just frustrated. I made figures of bodhisattvas alongside you, but all that time, I never felt the presence of Buddha. I don't know what I should do.

(**HAM MYOJIN** *enters limping, using a cane. He is very happy to see* **SŎ-YŎN**.)

HAM MYOJIN: Sŏ-yŏn, you're here. Sŏ-yŏn is here.

SŎ-YŎN (*he stands and pays his respects to his teacher*): Yes, Master.

HAM MYOJIN: These days, I'm not able to move my legs as I used to. I have to have this cane with me. Anyway... where have you been all this time?

SŎ-YŎN: I went down to Chŏlla Province to take a look at the mountains there.

HAM MYOJIN: Chŏlla Province... There are many famous temples. Since you left wondering about whether there is or isn't a spirit of Buddha, I thought you went ahead and became a monk.

SŎ-YŎN: I thought about becoming one, but...

HAM MYOJIN: But?

SŎ-YŎN: I didn't have what it takes to be one. I couldn't abide by all those rules, either.

TONG-YŎN: At least you know yourself.

HAM MYOJIN: Then what did you do all this time?

TONG-YŎN: He saw rocks in the valley of Unjang Mountain.

HAM MYOJIN: You saw rocks?

TONG-YŎN: He said that all figures of bodhisattvas are mirages but the rocks are true bodhisattvas. Can something like that come out of a sane person?

HAM MYOJIN: Tong-yŏn has good news, Sŏ-yŏng. Have you heard?

SŎ-YŎN: Yes, I heard.

HAM MYOJIN: The Amitabha commission is the chance of a lifetime. But, I hoped that you would also have good news.

SŎ-YŎN: To tell you the truth... I have given up creating any more bodhisattvas.

HAM MYOJIN: Even if you give up creating the forms, don't give up the heart of it. My thinking has changed lately. I used to believe that creating the perfect bodhisattva form was the way to attain its true spirit, but that's not all there is to it.

TONG-YŎN: What? What are you saying?

HAM MYOJIN: What I am saying is that . . . if you concentrate too much on the appearance of the matter, you may remove yourself from the true essence of it. That's what I mean.

TONG-YŎN: That's not what you said before . . .

HAM MYOJIN (*he points to* **TONG-YŎN** *with his cane*): It's clear that you have more talent than even I. The figures of bodhisattvas you make will become more famous than mine. But Tong-yŏn, don't become arrogant after attaining all the fame and money you have desired. Just because you are able to create figures of bodhisattvas doesn't mean you are able to create the spirit of bodhisattvas. Mark my words. (**HAM MYOJIN** *exits from the workshop.*)

TONG-YŎN: Now he's become jealous of me.

SŎ-YŎN: Jealous of you?

TONG-YŎN: Jealousy is the only explanation. When you weren't here, he pretended to hand over everything to me, but now with you around, he is playing some mind game and is siding with you.

SŎ-YŎN: Are you uncomfortable with me around?

TONG-YŎN: It's nothing to be happy about.

SŎ-YŎN: Then I should leave again.

TONG-YŎN: Where to?

SŎ-YŎN: I'll be gone for a couple months and be back.

TONG-YŎN: You must have been born under a lucky star! Wonder around as long as you want, a couple of months or even a couple of years!
(**SŎ-YŎN** *takes out a few rocks from his sack and leaves them on the floor. The Amitabha scroll flies out. The lights change and come up on* **HAM YIJŎNG**'s *room. She is at the piano by herself, playing melancholic music.* **CHO SUNG-IN** *comes in, calling for his mother.*)

CHO SUNG-IN: Mother! Mother!

HAM YIJŎNG: What?

CHO SUNG-IN (*he opens his hands*): Take a look at these!

HAM YIJŎNG: What are they?

CHO SUNG-IN (*he opens his hands wide*): Small rocks!

HAM YIJŎNG (*she moves each rock from his hands onto hers and examines them*): What pretty, tiny rocks! Sŏ-yŏn must have left them . . .

CHO SUNG-IN: But only the rocks. No letter. A letter would be a hundred times better than these rocks. No, being here in person would be a hundred times better than a letter. Do you miss him?

HAM YIJŎNG: Yes, I miss him. It was so much better before . . . I would play the piano, and Sŏ-yŏn and Tong-yŏn would sing next to me. I don't know how I ended up as lonely as this.

CHO SUNG-IN: Should I sing with you instead?

HAM YIJŎNG: I am not sure if you could sing as well . . .

(*She gives him the music score of "The Clouds" composed by Hong Nanp'a, a Korean composer.*[6] *She plays the piano and he sings with her.*)

CHO SUNG-IN:

> The clouds form white sheep in the sky
> quietly passing by me.
> Where did the calf go?
> A shepherd is always tending them
> but the sheep in the blue sky
> play as much as they want.

HAM YIJŎNG (*she shakes her head dispiritedly*): No, this isn't it. Not at all.

CHO SUNG-IN: Don't I sound like their voices put together?

HAM YIJŎNG: No, it doesn't come close.

CHO SUNG-IN: Don't be sad, mother. I'll try harder and sing like two of their voices put together.

(*There is a rough knocking on the door.* **HAM YIJŎNG** *and* **CHO SUNG-IN** *tense.*)

HAM YIJŎNG: Who is it?

TONG-YŎN: It's me. Can I come in?

CHO SUNG-IN: Tell him he can't. It's the middle of the night.

HAM YIJŎNG: It's the middle of the night.

TONG-YŎN (*knocking on the door*): There's something I must say to you tonight.

HAM YIJŎNG: Come in, then. (**TONG-YŎN** *enters.*)

TONG-YŎN: Sŏ-yŏn was here.

HAM YIJŎNG: I know.

TONG-YŎN: You know?

HAM YIJŎNG: Yes.

TONG-YŎN: What do you think of Sŏ-yŏn?

CHO SUNG-IN: Be careful. He looks pretty serious.

HAM YIJŎNG: What do I think of him?

CHO SUNG-IN: What do you think of him? Do you like him or not—it must be that kind of question.

TONG-YŎN: When you compare him with me, what do you think?

HAM YIJŎNG: I like you and I like Sŏ-yŏn.

SŎ-YŎN: That's not an answer.

HAM YIJŎNG: I like you both.

SŎ-YŎN: What do you mean, you like both? Can't you tell one from the other?

CHO SUNG-IN: He seems very angry, like he's been humiliated.

TONG-YŎN: I don't like to criticize him, and I'm not happy talking about him this way, but Sŏ-yŏn is a stupid, lazy, self-centered good-for-nothing. I don't like saying this. He was my friend; I lived with him like family for a long time.

CHO SUNG-IN: Try yawning, Mother.

HAM YIJŎNG: Yawning?

CHO SUNG-IN: Show him that you are sleepy and want to go to sleep.

HAM YIJŎNG (*she covers her mouth and tries yawning*).

TONG-YŎN: Am I boring you, is that it?

HAM YIJŎNG: I'm sorry, Tong-yŏn. But can we talk tomorrow?

TONG-YŎN: I have something very important to tell you. I'm talking about how you can tell the difference between us. This world is what? A place filled with things, things we can see and are pleasing to our eyes. In order to succeed in life, one must produce things that are pleasing in form. In other words, a person who can create pleasing forms will succeed, and those who cannot will fail.

CHO SUNG-IN: I don't know why he is talking about the world all of a sudden.

TONG-YŎN: I see life as it is and know what is important, things Sŏ-yŏn would disregard! In the end, I will succeed and he will fail! That's how this world works. But his complete failure dares to rebuke and laugh at me, telling me garbage like my bodhisattvas figures are meaningless rocks! Adding insult to injury is your father's response to the whole thing. Instead of treating it as nonsense, he sided with Sŏ-yŏn. I hated it but said nothing. Why? Because I have a sense of responsibility. Your father is old and sick, and Sŏ-yŏn is a wandering tramp! If I don't take responsibility, who will?

CHO SUNG-IN: Mother, try yawning one more time.

HAM YIJŎNG (*yawning*): We don't have to worry about that yet.

TONG-YŎN: Not yet? You know your father is getting sicker by day. I'm not just talking about the paralysis of his legs. He does things he never did before and says this one minute and that the next. (*He grabs her shoulders.*) Now that I have explained this much—do you understand? Between Sŏ-yŏn and me, isn't it obvious who could take care of you in the future?

CHO SUNG-IN: Tell him to let go of your shoulders.

HAM YIJŎNG: Let go of my shoulders.

TONG-YŎN (*he grabs her tighter on her shoulders and begins to shake her*): You yawned twice when I was talking to you! Twice!

HAM YIJŎNG: I won't do it again; let go of me!

TONG-YŎN: If I let go of you, you'll just go to sleep. You don't know how crucial this moment in time is, and like an idiot, you'd just sleep like a log. (*He pushes her down on the floor and gets on top of her.*) I will decide for you! A woman cannot make a rational decision!

CHO SUNG-IN: Tell him to behave himself! Scream!

HAM YIJŎNG: Stop it! I'll call for father!

TONG-YŎN (*he starts to take off her clothes against her will*): Call him! He's too drunk to hear you! I love you! I will take care of you and make you happy!

CHO SUNG-IN: Mother, resist him. Scream your lungs out, scratch his eyes, and bite him.

HAM YIJŎNG (*she is breathing hard*): This is strange, really strange.

CHO SUNG-IN: What's strange? Hurry up, scratch and bite him!

HAM YIJŎNG: It's as if my whole body is melting.

CHO SUNG-IN: Because he told you he loves you and will take care of you?

HAM YIJŎNG: I can't breathe . . .

CHO SUNG-IN: Mother, don't do this! Love is fine. Responsibility, too, but the way this was done, the form is not perfect—it's flawed.

(*Lights dim. There is the heavy breathing of lovers having intercourse. Slowly, the stage brightens.* **HAM YIJŎNG** *is wearing a transparent skirt that is large enough to cover the entire stage. Naked* **CHO SUNG-IN** *is in a fetal position inside* **HAM YIJŎNG**'s *skirt. He looks quite unhappy.*)

CHO SUNG-IN: Tell me, Mother. Are you happy?

HAM YIJŎNG: Oh, yes I am!

CHO SUNG-IN: Well, I'm not.

HAM YIJŎNG: I can't hear you. Say it again.

CHO SUNG-IN: I said I am *not* happy!

HAM YIJŎNG (*lovingly caresses her pregnant belly*): *I'm* happy. I'm happy to be pregnant with you. When I touch my stomach, I can feel you wiggling about in there.

CHO SUNG-IN: I'm all cramped up in here. And I'm worried.

HAM YIJŎNG: What are you worried about?

CHO SUNG-IN: The form of it was bad. If the form was bad, then the content can't be good.

HAM YIJŎNG: Don't you worry your little head.

CHO SUNG-IN: I don't like the way I was conceived. My father made you have me by force. What did Grandfather say?

HAM YIJŎNG: He was . . . quite happy about it.

CHO SUNG-IN: Really?

HAM YIJŎNG: Really. He said it was a blessing.

CHO SUNG-IN: I'm sure he didn't know what to say. Father didn't even ask him for your hand in marriage but went ahead and produced a grandchild out of wedlock.

HAM YIJŎNG: What are you so unhappy about?

CHO SUNG-IN (*silent*).

HAM YIJŎNG: What is it? You don't want to come into this world?

CHO SUNG-IN: No, I don't want to.

HAM YIJŎNG: Why not?

CHO SUNG-IN: I liked it much better when I was just a feeling. I didn't even think about taking on a form before.

HAM YIJŎNG: When your mom and dad are married, you'll change your tune. We decided on the date, too: the fourteenth of next month, the day that Tong-yŏn exhibits his statue of Amitabha for the priests. It's a great statue with ten faces on his head. Everybody knows about it already. We expect throngs of people will come to the temple to take a look at the statue and attend our wedding afterward.

CHO SUNG-IN: Wait, wait a minute, Mother. You're going to have the wedding on the day of the exhibition?

HAM YIJŎNG: We'll have the blessings of that many people; the exhibition in the morning and our wedding in the afternoon. The day will be so festive; more festive than the birthday of Buddha himself.

CHO SUNG-IN: I can see it now. Father will be so proud of himself, showing off his statue, plus the fact that he has taken his teacher's daughter as his bride. That way, he gets what he wants: everyone will know that he is the best. But have you thought about what you will look like, Mother, on that day?

HAM YIJŎNG: What's wrong with the way I look?

CHO SUNG-IN: Mother, you're eight months pregnant. Even now, your stomach is bulging out like a mountain. Next month, on your wedding day, your stomach will be bigger. People will laugh at the way you look. I can't bear to think about it sitting here inside you. Tell Father. Delay the exhibition day or delay the wedding.

HAM YIJŎNG: You know what Tong-yŏn—I mean, your father—is like. He'd never delay the exhibition day or the wedding. The abbot at Pohyŏn Temple didn't like the idea at first and told him to set different dates for the exhibition and our wedding. But your father insisted that it was important, that they be held on the same day. (*She caresses her abdomen.*) I'm also worried a bit about my stomach . . . I'll have it bound. If I can bind it tight enough, it'll look a little better.

CHO SUNG-IN: You're going to have me bound?
HAM YIJŎNG: I know. You'll find it a bit stuffy.
CHO SUNG-IN: Oh, my God!
HAM YIJŎNG: But this is the only way. (*She begins to put tight band around her stomach.*) Just for a month, try to be patient.
CHO SUNG-IN: OK, Mother! If that's the way you're going to do it, I have an idea of my own! (CHO SUNG-IN *begins to stretch and move.* HAM YIJŎNG *begins to feel the labor pains.*)
HAM YIJŎNG: What are you doing? What are you doing, all of a sudden?
CHO SUNG-IN: I'm being born.
HAM YIJŎNG: No. Wait! You'll be two months early, and this is dangerous!
CHO SUNG-IN: No! I'm going to be born now!

(CHO SUNG-IN *begins to move faster. In haste,* HAM YIJŎNG *removes the tight band around her stomach and her skirt and screams because of her labor pains.* CHO SUNG-IN *manages to come out of his mother's skirt and rolls the skirt all around him.* HAM YIJŎNG *exits.* CHO SUNG-IN *sits like a baby and cries as if he is having a temper tantrum.* HAM MYOJIN, *in his wheelchair, goes to the baby. He is shaking a rattle to calm him down.* SŎ-YŎN *enters.*)

SŎ-YŎN: Master, Sŏ-yŏn has come back.
HAM MYOJIN (*he is shaking the rattle in agitation*): Stop crying! Please, stop!
SŎ-YŎN: I've come back!
HAM MYOJIN: Please, stop crying!
SŎ-YŎN: Master!
HAM MYOJIN: Who . . . Who is it?
SŎ-YŎN (*he pays his respects to him*): It's been a long time.
HAM MYOJIN: Sŏ-yŏn . . . It's you, Sŏ-yŏn.
SŎ-YŎN: Yes.
HAM MYOJIN: Tong-yŏn and Yijŏng went to Pohyŏn Temple.
SŎ-YŎN: What's going on at Pohyŏn Temple?
HAM MYOJIN: Today is their wedding.
SŎ-YŎN: Wedding? Truly?
HAM MYOJIN (*pointing to* CHO SUNG-IN): If you don't believe it, come here and take a look at him, my grandson. She got pregnant even before the wedding. He was born two months early, and we thought we'd lose him. But because his mother did her best, he survived.
SŎ-YŎN (*he draws close to* CHO SUNG-IN *and stares at him*): He looks very smart.
HAM MYOJIN: At first, he couldn't even cry, but now all he does is cry at the top of his voice. (*He shakes the rattle in front of the crying* CHO SUNG-IN.) My body's becoming numb. It's not just my legs anymore; it's my upper

body, too. I can't even move my hands. (*He drops the rattle.*) Stop it! For heaven's sake, stop crying!

SŎ-YŎN: Let me try?

(**SŎ-YŎN** *picks up the rattle and shakes it.* **CHO SUNG-IN** *cries louder.* **SŎ-YŎN** *seems to understand why the baby is crying and stops shaking the rattle.*)

SŎ-YŎN: I see, I see, my little one. I'll stop the rattling.

HAM MYOJIN: Ahhh . . . he stopped crying.

SŎ-YŎN: He's very sensitive to sound.

HAM MYOJIN: Sensitive? To sound?

SŎ-YŎN: Yes. He was crying because he didn't like the sound of the rattle.

HAM MYOJIN: He cried every time I rattled this . . . no wonder.

SŎ-YŎN: Do you have a name for him?

HAM MYOJIN: His mother named him. Sung-in. Since his father's last name is Cho, he is Cho Sung-in.

SŎ-YŎN (*he looks at* **CHO SUNG-IN**): Cho Sung-in. He looks just like Tong-yŏn.

HAM MYOJIN: From the moment he was born. He's the spitting image of his father. Tong-yŏn was petrified when his child was born too early. He was worried that a premature baby would have some physical defect. He examined him once, twice, probably a hundred times or more.

SŎ-YŎN (*smiles*): Appearance is important to Tong-yŏn.

HAM MYOJIN: I had hoped that he would take after me. (*Pause.*) I'm sure you aren't at all happy about this. Am I right?

SŎ-YŎN (*silent*).

HAM MYOJIN: I know that both you and Tong-yŏn liked my daughter. But since Tong-yŏn took her, I can imagine how upset you are.

SŎ-YŎN: I . . . I don't have the right.

HAM MYOJIN: Have the right?

SŎ-YŎN: Yes.

HAM MYOJIN: Why?

SŎ-YŎN: I lack talent. Nowadays . . . I feel incompetent more than ever . . .

HAM MYOJIN (*takes a closer look at* **SŎ-YŎN**): You do look worn out. Your search for the spirit of Buddha, what happened to that?

SŎ-YŎN (*silent*).

HAM MYOJIN: There's no good news yet?

SŎ-YŎN: No . . . It was good that you chose Tong-yŏn as your successor.

HAM MYOJIN: Tong-yŏn did the choosing! I didn't! Of course, I thought about making him my son-in-law and successor. But, how can I say this . . . It feels like he stole it from me even before I could give it to him. If he had waited a bit, everything would have been his, anyway. I don't understand what the hurry was!

SŎ-YŎN: Master, please lower your voice! The baby is just about to fall asleep.

HAM MYOJIN (*he lowers his voice but is unable to hide his anger*): Anyway, Tong-yŏn has become one conceited bastard. Now that he is the chosen successor, he wants the key to the workshop. He has no sense of decency. Isn't it right that he should at least pretend to refuse when I offer it? What good is it if I feel like I've been forced to give it to him? Take today, for example. On his wedding day, shouldn't he express his gratitude to me, his teacher and father-in-law? I've been depressed about all that he stole from me. Now he has forbidden me to go to my daughter's wedding. Since I'm sick and unable to move, he said it would be better for me to stay home and babysit Sung-in. Actually, I didn't want to go. It's not a family wedding, since they invited everyone from everywhere. I'd just look pathetic being there.

SŎ-YŎN: Nobody thinks you look pathetic.

HAM MYOJIN: No, that's not true. Even the priests think of no one but Tong-yŏn and his statues.

SŎ-YŎN: Why don't we go to the wedding now?

HAM MYOJIN: No, I won't go!

SŎ-YŎN: I'll go with you.

HAM MYOJIN: No, I won't. I won't be treated like a has-been.

SŎ-YŎN: Please try to be more generous to Tong-yŏn?

HAM MYOJIN: Even you . . . you are siding with him?

SŎ-YŎN: Tong-yŏn has the talent to create wonderful forms. You are angry because he took over even before you had the chance to give it to him, but please just think that he was too talented and forgive him.

HAM MYOJIN: You want me to be forgiving when he took my daughter before I could give him my blessing and my workshop before I could name him as my successor?

SŎ-YŎN: Master . . .

HAM MYOJIN: Say it, why can't you say it?

SŎ-YŎN: At first, I wasn't happy with Tong-yŏn's obsession over mere appearance. But now I understand. I have been to where life begins and ends, and it seems that appearance does decide everything. The fault does not lie with him but with the world.

HAM MYOJIN: So it's my fault, is it? Since I taught him about appearance! (*He realizes that he has raised his voice.*) Oh, no. My shouting may wake the baby.

SŎ-YŎN: Master, I'll put the baby in his room to sleep.

(HAM MYOJIN *and* SŎ-YŎN *exit with* CHO SUNG-IN, *who walks out like a duck walking with bent knees.* TONG-YŎN *and* HAM YIJŎNG *enter. Like bride and bridegroom, wearing festive clothes and with flowers in their hair, they dance together.* TONG-YŎN *is proud of himself, and* HAM YIJŎNG *looks happy. The* CHORUS, *which has entered dancing, looks like gold-painted figures of bodhisattvas. When they stop dancing, their arms and legs look intertwined to invoke an image of Buddha with a thousand arms and eyes.* HAM MYOJIN *and* SŎ-YŎN *enter.*)

SŎ-YŎN: Tong-yŏn, congratulations!

TONG-YŎN: Oh, you came.

SŎ-YŎN (*to* HAM YIJŎNG): Congratulations! I'm very happy for you.

HAM YIJŎNG: Thank you, Sŏ-yŏn.

TONG-YŎN: How did you hear about it? It's a wonder how you came on our wedding day when there is a world out there you haven't seen yet.

SŎ-YŎN: I didn't know. If I had, I wouldn't be here empty-handed. I'm sorry.

TONG-YŎN: Don't worry about it. We already have more than enough presents from people. You should have seen Pohyŏn Temple today. Almost all the famous priests from the country were there, devoted followers, the rich and the powerful, even the people who'd never set foot in a temple were there. It was so crowded. Everyone couldn't help but be mystified and awed by my Amitabha. Our exhibition took place in the midst of their praise, followed by our wedding. Ha, hahahahaha. It was exactly what I wanted. (*To* HAM MYOJIN.) Be happy for us. Many disciples diminish their teacher's esteemed reputation, but I have elevated that reputation and placed it on a pedestal.

HAM YIJŎNG: Dad, everyone had nothing but praises for him, and we received countless orders to fill.

HAM MYOJIN (*he shakes the rattle*): I'm happy. I'm so happy that I could cry.

TONG-YŎN: What?

HAM MYOJIN: If you shake this, you'll be so happy that you cry.

(HAM MYOJIN *turns his wheelchair around and exits, shaking the rattle.*)

TONG-YŎN: Why is he acting that way?

SŎ-YŎN: Tong-yŏn.

TONG-YŎN: What?

SŎ-YŎN: I hope you won't misunderstand me. It seems the master has some misgivings about you.

TONG-YŎN: It's nothing I did.

SŎ-YŎN: Why didn't you take him to the wedding?

TONG-YŎN: I asked him again and again, but he refused! What did he say to you? Did he complain that I wouldn't let him come?

SŎ-YŎN: I'm not saying you did anything wrong. Just try to be more understanding; try not to hurry things so much.

TONG-YŎN: Not to hurry things so much? What are you really getting at? Are you jealous?

HAM YIJŎNG: Sŏ-yŏn's not like that.

TONG-YŎN: You keep quiet.

HAM YIJŎNG: Tong-yŏn . . .[7]

TONG-YŎN: I am not Tong-yŏn. I'm your husband!

HAM YIJŎNG: Husband . . .

TONG-YŎN (*he points at the door*): Get out! Get out of my house now!

HAM YIJŎNG: Don't do this!

TONG-YŎN: You think I don't know what is going on here? Believe me, I do. (*To* **SŎ-YŎN**.) You also feel like you've lost everything to me, just like that old bastard claims he's been robbed.

SŎ-YŎN: Tong-yŏn . . . I don't feel that way about you.

TONG-YŎN: Same, you're all the same. Incompetent fools feel the same way! (*He again points to the door.*) Leave now! And don't set foot in this house again!

(**SŎ-YŎN** *bows to* **TONG-YŎN** *and takes off his shoes and puts them on his head.*[8] **TONG-YŎN** *explodes and grabs him by his collar. The light changes. The sides of the stage dim while the center slowly brightens.* **CHO SUNG-IN** *unfolds* **HAM YIJŎNG**'s *handkerchief, takes out the small rocks, and lines them up evenly. He takes a step back and examines them. Meanwhile,* **HAM YIJŎNG** *comes to stand next to him.*)

HAM YIJŎNG: What are you doing?

CHO SUNG-IN: Rocks. I'm looking at them.

HAM YIJŎNG: Why did you take them out? Put them back in the handkerchief.

CHO SUNG-IN: Why? *You* take them out time to time . . .

HAM YIJŎNG: Put back them before your father sees them.

CHO SUNG-IN: I think of him, Sŏ-yŏn, when I look at these rocks. I was very young, a month or two old, when he came by our house.

HAM YIJŎNG (*she picks up the rocks one by one*): You couldn't possibly remember him.

CHO SUNG-IN: I do remember him.

HAM YIJŎNG: Sung-in . . . Sŏ-yŏn came by more than ten years ago, and after that he never came again.

CHO SUNG-IN: He saw me and said, "He seems very sensitive to sound."

HAM YIJŎNG: Really? He said that?

CHO SUNG-IN: Yes, Mother. I even remember things before I was born, things you and I talked about, and at that time, I made a promise to you. I will try hard to put the two voices—Sŏ-yŏn's and Father's—together. So I've decided to become a composer.

HAM YIJŎNG (*she is taken aback by what he has just said*): What? A composer?

CHO SUNG-IN: Yes. I know. Their voices are so different that it will be very difficult to make music with them. But I feel that's what I was born to do, my fate and my karma in life.

HAM YIJŎNG: But do you think your father will let you? He wants you to continue his work . . .

CHO SUNG-IN: He doesn't understand me. What I am good at, what I want to do, he doesn't try at all to understand. He doesn't understand you, either, whether you are happy or unhappy . . . He's interested only in his work.

HAM YIJŎNG: Creating statues is a difficult job. You have to be perfect . . .

CHO SUNG-IN: Obsessing over forms will make you narrow-minded, always tense . . .

HAM YIJŎNG (*she wraps the rocks in her handkerchief*): I have a favor to ask, all right? Please don't hate your father.

CHO SUNG-IN: But Mother, why do you keep those rocks?

HAM YIJŎNG: Keep the rocks . . . ?

CHO SUNG-IN: You think of him even now, don't you?

HAM YIJŎNG: No, no. I just couldn't throw them away.

CHO SUNG-IN: Don't deny it. Even though you are afraid that Father might see them, you still keep them with you.

HAM YIJŎNG (*silent*).

CHO SUNG-IN: I wonder about Sŏ-yŏn . . . where would he be and what he might be doing . . . Have you heard anything about him?

HAM YIJŎNG: By chance, I did. He's somewhere in Chŏlla Province. A priest came by to buy a statue, and he told us the news. That he is insane.

CHO SUNG-IN: Insane?

HAM YIJŎNG: Mmmm . . . He goes around doing crazy things. He walks around the field collecting rocks and makes stone statues.

CHO SUNG-IN: Stone statues?

HAM YIJŎNG: A big rock is the body and a small rock becomes the head. It's just putting a small rock on top of a big rock. According to him, there is a line of them in the field. What is interesting is the people there. They go to pray and chant in front of those stone statues. The priest shook his head, saying that Sŏ-yŏn made even those simple people crazy.

CHO SUNG-IN: How strange. I just lined up his rocks without thinking. But it turns out that I was imitating him.

(**TONG-YŎN** *enters. He is very angry.*)

TONG-YŎN: This will not do!

HAM YIJŎNG: What is it?

TONG-YŎN: He comes in to the workshop and just nags about nothing! Paralysis must have gotten to his head, too. He is completely senile!

HAM YIJŎNG: You have be patient with him. Dad is . . .

TONG-YŎN (*he cuts off* **HAM YIJŎNG**): There's a limit to my patience! You know very well what Bhaisajyaguru looks like!⁹ The blaze and nimbus behind the body of the statue, you need great concentration to make each burning ray. But his senile himself comes in the morning and says the fire is bigger than the body, and at night, he says the body is bigger than the fire! Bigger, smaller, bigger, smaller. I'm going to go out of my mind this way!

HAM YIJŎNG: I'm so sorry. I didn't know that he was that bad.

TONG-YŎN: Starting today, the workshop is off-limits to him.

HAM YIJŎNG: What?

TONG-YŎN: I cannot allow your father to come into the workshop starting today.

CHO SUNG-IN: Off-limits, to Grandfather?

TONG-YŎN: That's what I said. Absolutely off-limits.

CHO SUNG-IN: But it was Grandfather's workshop.

HAM YIJŎNG: If you do that, he'll be brokenhearted.

TONG-YŎN: Nothing I can do about it.

CHO SUNG-IN: If he comes in the morning and says it is too big, just think he means that it is too small and at night he says it is too small, just think he means that it is too big. Then you won't lose your mind over Grandfather.

TONG-YŎN: You. Are you playing word games with me?

CHO SUNG-IN: No.

TONG-YŎN: If it's nothing, then what?

CHO SUNG-IN: I'm trying to make you laugh.

TONG-YŎN: Make me laugh?

CHO SUNG-IN: Yes. You're always so tense. You need to laugh once in a while.

TONG-YŎN (*he stares at* **CHO SUNG-IN** *for a while*): Are you really *my* son?

CHO SUNG-IN: What do you mean?

SŎ-YŎN: You look like me, but you are nothing like me.

(**HAM MYOJIN** *comes in, laboring to turn the wheels on his wheelchair. His face looks distorted by facial paralysis, and his hands have muscle spasms.*)

HAM MYOJIN: Tong-yŏn! Tong-yŏn! You make what should be bigger, small, and what should be smaller, too big. The body of it is too big and the fire is too small! It looks monstrous. Tong-yŏn! Tong-yŏn! You've created a monster!

TONG-YŎN: Don't think that I'm being cruel, but the workshop is off-limits to him. I'll lock the door from now on.

CHO SUNG-IN: Don't take it that way, Father. Grandfather is just trying to make you laugh, too.

TONG-YŎN (*he slaps* CHO SUNG-IN's *face*): You laugh all you want.

(TONG-YŎN *turns and exits.* HAM YIJŎNG, *not knowing what to do, looks at her son, who has his hand over his cheek.* CHO SUNG-IN *begins to speak in a very calm voice.*)

CHO SUNG-IN: Don't worry, Mother. I'm fine.

HAM MYOJIN: Me, too. (*With his trembling hand, he points to a key under his hips.*) Look. It doesn't matter if he locks the door. I can open it.

HAM YIJŎNG: Dad, no. You shouldn't.

HAM MYOJIN: Tong-yŏn isn't the only one with a key. I have one, too. I knew this day would come, so I had a copy made.

HAM YIJŎNG (*she goes to her father*): Give it to me. The key. Dad, you can't go there!

HAM MYOJIN (*he wheels himself backward*): No. This is mine!

HAM YIJŎNG: Please, Dad.

(HAM MYOJIN *hides the key under his hips and wheels off the stage.* HAM YIJŎNG *chases him out.* CHO SUNG-IN *is left alone on stage. He goes to the piano, puts his hands on the piano keys, and loudly plays discordant notes. Between the loud sounds, there is a distinct awareness of heavy silence.* HAM YIJŎNG *comes back empty-handed.*)

HAM YIJŎNG: What should I do? He won't give me the key.

CHO SUNG-IN: Mother, listen. I just composed this.

HAM YIJŎNG: I don't feel good about this. It feels like something bad will happen because of this . . .

CHO SUNG-IN: After I was slapped, I made up my mind. (*He creates a loud sound by pressing all his fingers on the piano keys.*) This is my father's voice. Visible, tangible, this is how my father is manifested. (*He takes his fingers off the keys.*) But this silence is Tong-yŏn. Invisible, intangible; he can't be captured in forms. (*He repeats the sound and silence as if to compare them.*) Listen carefully, Mother. Sound and silence are waging a war inside me.

HAM YIJŎNG: Stop it, Cho Sung-in. I don't like hearing it.

CHO SUNG-IN: Me, neither! I don't like hearing such discord, either.

HAM YIJŎNG: Please, stop this. (*She grabs his hands to stop him.*) You don't know anything about music yet. You don't know how to play the piano; you've learned nothing about composing music.

CHO SUNG-IN: So I know nothing. Is that what you're saying?

HAM YIJŎNG: Yes.

CHO SUNG-IN: But I know that life is full of jarring sounds. The question is, how can we make it sound harmonious?

(HAM YIJŎNG *looks worried and anxious. The stage lights fade to black and then come up on the area between the house and the workshop.* CHO SUNG-IN *is under an apricot tree reading a book about musical composition.*)

CHO SUNG-IN: "Composition is the act of lining up different sounds in a certain pattern. In addition, composition is used to express certain feelings in musical melodies and to mold melodies into a certain form." Form? Then form is important in music, too? "Composition is written into a musical score, which is the language of music. Therefore, in order to become a composer, one must be able to write musical scores. In addition, one must understand structural techniques and the rules in music in order to complete one's work." Oh, my. It talks about forms and rules over and over again. But why is form so important? I think instead my feelings should be more important. Hmm . . . The apricots hang in the tree, high and low. Just like musical notes. When I look at those notes, my mouth waters; I have a feeling that the apricots are sour. So to express apricots, a sour feeling is more important than form. I should think about this more and compare it to composition. (*He goes under the apricot tree and opens his mouth waiting for an apricot to fall.*) I'm waiting and thinking, waiting for a ripe note to fall into my mouth. I should open it a little bigger . . . ahhhh . . . bigger . . . ahhhhh . . .

(*In another part of the stage,* HAM MYOJIN, *with the key in his hand, wheels himself to the workshop. He unlocks the door and enters. There is a spotlight on the statues.* HAM MYOJIN *touches one, which is thrown off balance and falls, all the statues following in a domino effect, with* HAM MYOJIN *underneath them.* TONG-YŎN *brings out the fatally injured* HAM MYOJIN *in the wheelchair.*)

TONG-YŎN: Something terrible happened there. Your grandpa is dead.

CHO SUNG-IN: What do you mean Grandfather is dead?

TONG-YŎN: He unlocked the door to the workshop. He went in and something happened. I found him there underneath the statues.

CHO SUNG-IN: Grandpa, Grandpa!

TONG-YŎN: There's no use calling him!

CHO SUNG-IN: His neck isn't straight. It must be broken . . . Mother's feeling was right. She said something bad would happen because of the key.

TONG-YŎN: If she knew beforehand, she should have taken it away!

CHO SUNG-IN: She tried, but he wouldn't give it to her, no matter what.

TONG-YŎN: Stand aside, now. I have to go tell your mother what happened. (*Begins to push the wheelchair.*)

CHO SUNG-IN: Don't go like that.

TONG-YŎN: Like what?

CHO SUNG-IN: Leave Grandpa here and go to Mom by yourself. When you tell her what happened, talk to her quietly and gently; console her first.

TONG-YŎN: Talk quietly and gently?

CHO SUNG-IN: Yes.

TONG-YŎN: This isn't my fault! He did it to himself. Your mother shares the blame, too. She knew this would happen and did nothing to stop it!

(TONG-YŎN *pushes the wheelchair, and* CHO SUNG-IN *steps aside. There is blood where the wheelchair stood.* CHO SUNG-IN *looks as if he would vomit from the smell of the blood.*)

CHO SUNG-IN: The smell of the blood . . . I feel like throwing up.

(*The dead* HAM MYOJIN *enters in a wheelchair, propelling himself. On his back is what looks like the nimbus from a Buddhist statue,*[10] *but because it has not been securely fastened, it is dangling on his back.*)

HAM MYOJIN: This doesn't fit me.

CHO SUNG-IN: Grandfather . . .

HAM MYOJIN: It feels too big, no, maybe too small. It keeps dangling like this; it's uncomfortable.

CHO SUNG-IN: Your neck is the same way.

HAM MYOJIN: Mmm . . . I know. When your mother saw me, she fainted. (*He shows him a key to nirvana in his hand.*) Sung-in, I am going to go open the gate to nirvana. But I'm worried the key might not fit. It could be too big or too small . . . If I can't open the gate to nirvana, I'll try the gate to hell.

(*The dead* HAM MYOJIN *exits. The fire on his back dangles and his head droops from his broken neck.* CHO SUNG-IN *looks worried as he watches him exit. The stage is dark and gloomy. Change to inside* HAM YIJŎNG's *room.* TONG-YŎN *stands beside a small, delicately designed golden figure of a bodhisattva on a table.*)

TONG-YŎN: I made this. I made this just for you.

HAM YIJŎNG (*she raises her head and looks at the bodhisattva*).

TONG-YŎN: You haven't been yourself lately. It's as if you've lost your spirit to a ghost or devil. You can't get a grip on yourself. Take a good look at this bodhisattva. This is the image of the enlightened Buddha under the banyan tree. Imitate this position and meditate. Empty your mind of any other thoughts and don't let your heart waver. First, sit in the right position. (*Pause.*) Sit in the lotus position!

HAM YIJŎNG (*she stares at the bodhisattvas and does not move a muscle*).

TONG-YŎN: Do you hear what I said?

HAM YIJŎNG: What?

TONG-YŎN: Lotus position! Don't you know the lotus position? (*He goes to* HAM YIJŎNG *and crosses her legs into a lotus position.*) There are two different forms of the lotus position. One is to place your right leg over your left. The other is to place to your left leg over the right. Placing the left leg over the right one represents your acceptance of devil surrender. (*He grasps her hands and places them in her lap.*) Your hands, too. Meaning varies depending on the position of your hands. Open your left hand and place it on your legs, palm up, and put your right hand over the left one. Like this, your two thumbs should meet and this is the correct position. When you are in this position, all the raving demons will surrender. Are you listening to me?

HAM YIJŎNG: Yes . . . I am . . .

TONG-YŎN: In breathing, form is important. Inhale deeply all the way into your abdomen and exhale slowly through your nose. (*He shows her how to do it.*) Like this!

HAM YIJŎNG (*she inhales and exhales as* TONG-YŎN *showed her*).

TONG-YŎN: Good. Now meditate exactly the way I showed you.

(*The dead* HAM MYOJIN *enters in the wheelchair with the dangling fire on his back. He is holding onto the key to nirvana with trembling hands and looks as if he doesn't know what to do.*)

HAM MYOJIN: It won't open, the gate to nirvana . . .

HAM YIJŎNG: Dad . . .

HAM MYOJIN: I tried the gate to hell. It wouldn't open. I don't care where. I just want to go somewhere and rest . . . But I can't get into heaven or hell.

HAM YIJŎNG: Dad . . .

HAM MYOJIN: The key is either too big or too small. It wouldn't open anything.

(HAM MYOJIN *turns his wheelchair around and exits.* HAM YIJŎNG *stretches out her arms as if to stop her father.*)

HAM YIJŎNG: Dad, where are you going?

HAM MYOJIN: I'll try again to open the gate to heaven and, if I can't, I'll try the gate to hell.

TONG-YŎN: What's wrong?

HAM YIJŎNG: Dad . . . over there, my dad . . .

TONG-YŎN: There's no one there. We buried him, in a casket—in the ground! Priests chanted and burned incense to wish him a safe journey to nirvana. You were there, at the funeral!

HAM YIJŎNG: But I keep seeing him. Unable to enter heaven or hell . . .

TONG-YŎN: That's your mind. Your mind wanders and plays tricks on you and that's why you keep seeing your father. Just how long are you going to continue like this?

HAM YIJŎNG (*tears roll down her cheeks*): I'm sorry . . .

TONG-YŎN (*he wipes her tears away*): Don't cry. I love you. I love you very much. Don't you know that?

HAM YIJŎNG: I know. I know.

TONG-YŎN: If you know, why are you acting so . . . I can't work because of you. There are so many orders to complete, but I can't do anything because you are like this. (*He puts his hands on* HAM YIJŎNG's *cheeks and kisses her.*) Your lips are dry like a desolate desert. On this fragile face, your eyes have become ocean of water and your lips, a desert. You cannot meditate in this state. Get up! Stand up right now and bow three thousand times in front of the bodhisattvas.

HAM YIJŎNG: Three thousand bows?

TONG-YŎN: Fall prostrate on the ground, with your face down! Like this, make three thousand bows. Afterward, you'll return to your senses, and your complex worries and questions will merge into one simplified answer. (*He commands* HAM YIJŎNG *to do as he says.*) Hurry! Stand up! Stand and begin!

HAM YIJŎNG (*she stands up with difficulty*).

TONG-YŎN: I will count for you. (*Counting like a soldier.*) One!

HAM YIJŎNG (*she throws herself on the ground in front of the bodhisattvas and makes her first bow*).

TONG-YŎN: Two!

HAM YIJŎNG (*she stands and makes her second bow*).

TONG-YŎN: Three! My statue is perfect. So your prayers will be answered!

HAM YIJŎNG (*she stands up with difficulty and makes her fourth bow*).

TONG-YŎN: Four!

HAM YIJŎNG: Husband . . .

TONG-YŎN: Aren't you tired?

HAM YIJŎNG: Why don't you go? I'll do it by myself. You have work to do.

TONG-YŎN: By yourself?

HAM YIJŎNG: Yes.

TONG-YŎN: But if I'm not here, you won't finish it, will you?

HAM YIJŎNG: Yes, I will.

TONG-YŎN: Don't forget, three thousand. You'll be punished if you stop in the middle.

(TONG-YŎN *exits.* HAM YIJŎNG *throws her body on the ground and bows.* CHO SUNG-IN *enters. He counts the last numbers to three thousand.*)

CHO SUNG-IN: 2,998! 2,999! 3,000!

HAM YIJŎNG: Sung-in . . .

CHO SUNG-IN: You finished three thousand, Mother.

HAM YIJŎNG: No, I just started.

CHO SUNG-IN: Men are tangled by the forms they've created so they count only one by one, but Buddha is different. Merciful Buddha will count one, ten, one hundred, one thousand. His math doesn't follow human equations. (*He helps his mother to stand.*) You've already done a lot of bowing. After Grandfather's funeral, you bowed thousands of times in front of the famous Amitabha. Now, you want to do another three thousand?

HAM YIJŎNG: Buddha will not accept my bows . . . No matter how many times I bow . . . my mind cannot rest.

CHO SUNG-IN: You will kill yourself this way. Like your mother. Like Grandmother who hanged herself from that apricot tree.

HAM YIJŎNG (*she nods her head helplessly*): Maybe, yes . . .

CHO SUNG-IN: When she died, how did you feel? How did you cope with the shock?

HAM YIJŎNG: Then . . . it wasn't like this . . .

CHO SUNG-IN: Why not? You were young, then. You must have been more distressed.

HAM YIJŎNG: I had Sŏ-yŏn and Tong-yŏn then. I was sad but I was OK. I had the two of them with me and was able to find my balance. But now it's different. It's as if something is swaying me to one side and I'm not able to find my balance.

Sung-in, what should I do?

CHO SUNG-IN: What do you think you should do, Mother?

HAM YIJŎNG: I don't know.

CHO SUNG-IN: Think it over carefully and then tell me.

HAM YIJŎNG: You tell me first.

CHO SUNG-IN: What *you* think is more important.

HAM YIJŎNG: I . . . want to return to the past.

CHO SUNG-IN: That's impossible.

HAM YIJŎNG: If I could have both Sŏ-yŏn and Tong-yŏn with me, I could calm my mind.

CHO SUNG-IN: I think you are right. You have lost your balance. But you can't go back to the past. Don't look behind you; look ahead of you.

HAM YIJŎNG: Ahead . . . look ahead?

CHO SUNG-IN: Yes. Look to the future and reclaim your balance. (*He encourages her.*) I know you can do it. You've experienced that balance in your life. Just bring back that experience and you will know what to do. I don't have the experience. I was born when you found yourself leaning toward one over the other. I was born because you lost your balance. So since I was born, all I've experienced has been an imbalance between form and content. My life has been quite difficult. I've tried to match things together, but I don't have the experience of how things should be. But for you, it's easy. Just shift your balance and lean the other way round, and you will find your way again.

HAM YIJŎNG: You talk as if . . . you're telling me that I should go to Sŏ-yŏn.
CHO SUNG-IN: Mother . . .
HAM YIJŎNG: Yes?
CHO SUNG-IN: You always trusted me through thick and thin.
HAM YIJŎNG: True, that's true. We always shared everything.
CHO SUNG-IN: Mother, go and look for Sŏ-yŏn.
HAM YIJŎNG: Sung-in . . . my son . . .
CHO SUNG-IN: Yes, Mother.
HAM YIJŎNG: I can't bear to go without you.
CHO SUNG-IN: Don't worry about me. I'm all grown up. And don't worry about Father. I'll take care of him. Mother, hurry! Leave now.

(CHO SUNG-IN *goes to the piano. He opens the cover and puts his hands over the keys. He meditates momentarily as if to put his thoughts into order and starts to play impromptu.* HAM YIJŎNG *looks at* CHO SUNG-IN *for a while and then turns and exits.* TONG-YŎN *enters. He's taken aback by* CHO SUNG-IN'S *playing on the piano.*)

TONG-YŎN: You play the piano? Sung-in, you . . . ?
CHO SUNG-IN: You didn't know, Father?
TONG-YŎN: Did your mother teach you?
CHO SUNG-IN: No.
TONG-YŎN: Then, where did you learn?
CHO SUNG-IN: By myself. I bought some books on composition and taught myself to play the piano.
TONG-YŎN: The piano is for women, something trivial to pass the time away.
CHO SUNG-IN: I'm going to become a composer.
TONG-YŎN: What, a composer?
CHO SUNG-IN: Yes, I am playing what I composed.
TONG-YŎN: This is nothing but a racket to my ears. (*He shows his disappointment in his son.*) You must inherit the workshop and follow in my footsteps. You must become the most famous sculptor.
CHO SUNG-IN: I like music more than making statues.
TONG-YŎN: Are you in your right mind?
CHO SUNG-IN: I'm telling you this in my right mind.

TONG-YŎN (*he walks over to the piano, and although* **CHO SUNG-IN**'s *hands are still on the piano keys, he closes the cover on* **CHO SUNG-IN**'s *hands*): The piano is off-limits.

CHO SUNG-IN (*he removes his hands with a hurt look*): Father . . .

TONG-YŎN: Starting tomorrow, you must show up at the workshop! And you will learn how to make statues.

CHO SUNG-IN: I'm going to go to a music school.

TONG-YŎN: Music school?

CHO SUNG-IN: Yes. It's not enough to study at home by myself.

TONG-YŎN (*he calls to* **HAM YIJŎNG**): Wife, come here, right now! Your brat is talking nonsense.

CHO SUNG-IN: Mother ran away.

TONG-YŎN: Wife, come here! Now!

CHO SUNG-IN: It's because of your statues. They were too perfect. It's hard to talk to a perfectly beautiful woman. Likewise, you cannot talk to a Buddha that is too well made. He wouldn't accept bows, no matter how many. Mother couldn't take it anymore and left.

TONG-YŎN: She left? That's not true! (*He goes to the area in front of the statue of Buddha Sakyamuni*[11] *and looks around.*) What's . . . what's going on here? Your mother should be here making three thousand bows. Where did she go?

CHO SUNG-IN: She went to the stone Buddha. To the one who does not care about forms and makes Buddha out of rocks.

TONG-YŎN: Buddha . . . out of rocks?

CHO SUNG-IN: Yes.

TONG-YŎN: Not to Sŏ-yŏn . . . to that . . .

CHO SUNG-IN: There's a dormitory at the music school, but I'm going live at home while I'm in school. That way, I'll be able to cook and do laundry for you. You can concentrate on making statues.

TONG-YŎN: She's fooled herself. You think he could make her happy? That irresponsible, incompetent fool! He's a beggar, for God's sake! He's homeless, without a penny to his name!

CHO SUNG-IN: Could be. But I don't think they'll starve to death.

TONG-YŎN: Your mother is a whore. She married me but always thought about that bastard.

(**TONG-YŎN** *is still fuming as he exits. When he walks, he shows a slight sign of paralysis in his legs. He walks uncomfortably. The stage darkens. There are stars everywhere. In an open field, the wind blows.* **HAM MYOJIN** *enters in his wheelchair looking exhausted, worn out. The dangling fire on his back gives off a bluish light.*)

HAM MYOJIN: Tired. I'm tired. None of the gates will open, not to heaven, not to hell. I just want to get in somewhere, but this damned key won't work. I go to this door hoping, but it doesn't fit, so, to that door . . . and I go back and forth . . . As I shuttle back and forth, day changes into night. I'm less tired during the day when I go to try the gate of heaven. But when I go to the gate of hell at night, I'm completely beat. How long do I have to do this . . . a hundred years? A thousand years? Forever? Oh, God, I am tired, so very tired. (*He stops muttering to himself and stares into the darkness.*) There is someone besides me going back and forth. (*He questions the darkness.*) Who goes there? Who on earth wanders around this field in the middle of night?

HAM YIJŎNG (*she is not seen but her voice is heard*): Dad?

HAM MYOJIN: What do you mean, "Dad"?

HAM YIJŎNG (*her voice is heard*): It sounds like Dad.

HAM MYOJIN: I can't see you. Come closer!

(**HAM YIJŎNG** *appears next to her father.*)

HAM MYOJIN: It's you! (*He scrutinizes* **HAM YIJŎNG** *and clucks his tongue.*) What the hell happened to you? You're nothing but skin and bone—and look at your clothes.

HAM YIJŎNG: Dad, have you seen Sŏ-yŏn?

HAM MYOJIN: Sŏ-yŏn?

HAM YIJŎNG: Yes.

HAM MYOJIN: Why are you looking for him?

HAM YIJŎNG: Tell me if you saw him. I have to find him.

HAM MYOJIN: Are you looking for him because Tong-yŏn kicked you out of the house?

HAM YIJŎNG: People say that he's somewhere here in the fields. He wanders here and there making statues out of rocks.

HAM MYOJIN: So you, too, are wandering aimlessly in this field?

HAM YIJŎNG: I saw many stone bodhisattvas, but he was nowhere to be found.

HAM MYOJIN: I see. Maybe you were chasing where he had been. If you don't see him where the stone bodhisattvas were, then wait for him where there are none. That way you'll be able to find him. It's no use looking for him where he was in the past.

HAM YIJŎNG: I see. I didn't think about waiting for him where he would be, not where he had been in the past.

HAM MYOJIN: I am tired, really tired. (*The roosters crow.*) The roosters are crowing already. (**HAM MYOJIN** *turns his wheelchair around and heads off as if he is being chased by that sound.* **HAM YIJŎNG** *calls after him.*)

HAM YIJŎNG: Wait, Dad!

HAM MYOJIN: I don't have time. I have to get to the gate of hell before the day breaks.

HAM YIJŎNG: I will open the gate of nirvana for you.

HAM MYOJIN (*he turns his wheelchair around and looks at her*): How? You have the right key?

HAM YIJŎNG: I don't have the key, but I have the heart!

HAM MYOJIN: Heart?

HAM YIJŎNG: If I can feel nirvana, the gate of nirvana will open, but if I feel hell, then the gate to hell will open. When I see Sŏ-yŏn, I'll feel nirvana. Then the gate of nirvana will open wide and you can enter.

HAM MYOJIN: Tsk, tsk. Don't be so sure. We will see whether you'll feel nirvana or hell. (**HAM MYOJIN** *exits hurriedly. The day slowly breaks.* **HAM YIJŎNG** *leans on a wooden cane and looks around.*)

HAM YIJŎNG: Is it because of the daybreak . . . or is it because of my own feelings . . . I am here in the middle of darkness, in the middle of endless fields, but there is a path shining brightly in front of me. Cho Sung-in, Cho Sung-in, my son, I wish I could show you this. When I was wondering aimlessly, my heart and the path were separate. But now that I'm standing here and waiting, this path and my heart have become intertwined. (*She closes her eyes, opens her arms, and speaks in a quivering voice.*) I can feel it even with my eyes closed. I can feel everything that passes by this path. People pass by here. Animals pass by here. Even tiny insects pass by here. Coming . . . Sŏ-yŏn is coming. He's making stone statues as he comes this way.

(*The light changes.* **CHO SUNG-IN** *enters, pushing the serving trolley. He shouts to* **TONG-YŎN**.)

CHO SUNG-IN: Father, breakfast.

TONG-YŎN (*his voice is heard*): I don't want any. I'm not hungry.

CHO SUNG-IN: Still, you should try to eat something.

TONG-YŎN (*only his voice*): You eat all you want.

CHO SUNG-IN: Hurry up! If you don't, I'll stand here and yell until you do.

TONG-YŎN (*only his voice*): All right, all right! I'll be there!

CHO SUNG-IN: Now. Can you come now? (**TONG-YŎN** *enters in a wheelchair. He looks as if he had not slept. He stops in front of the trolley.*) I made some porridge for breakfast today.

TONG-YŎN: Porridge?

CHO SUNG-IN: Porridge. I made it especially for you, since you don't have much appetite. (*He points to the trolley.*) Do you remember this?

TONG-YŎN (*he looks at the trolley*): This is . . .

CHO SUNG-IN: Grandfather used to use this.

TONG-YŎN: I remember.

CHO SUNG-IN: Mother used to bring food to him on this trolley. I realized this is very convenient.

TONG-YŎN (*quiet*).

CHO SUNG-IN: You should eat before it gets cold.

TONG-YŎN (*reluctantly, he takes the spoon and has a bite*): Nowadays, I can't tell what anything tastes like. Whatever I eat.

CHO SUNG-IN (*he looks at* TONG-YŎN's *hand as it trembles holding the spoon*): Your hand is trembling.

TONG-YŎN: Can't tell whether this porridge is salty or not.

CHO SUNG-IN: Be careful. You might spill it.

TONG-YŎN: I couldn't get a wink of sleep. Last night I was wide awake . . . and in the darkness I saw your mother.

CHO SUNG-IN: I saw her, too.

TONG-YŎN: You, too?

CHO SUNG-IN: Yes. She was talking about something with Grandfather.

TONG-YŎN: Sung-in . . .

CHO SUNG-IN: Yes?

TONG-YŎN: Please, take over my workshop. Stop fiddling around with music composition and whatnot—study the making of statues.

CHO SUNG-IN: You have many students.

TONG-YŎN: I have students, but every one of them is stupid.

CHO SUNG-IN: Why?

TONG-YŎN: They're empty-headed, each one making the figures exactly alike, time after time.

CHO SUNG-IN: You make them exactly the same, too.

TONG-YŎN: I teach them that only perfect external form can have perfect internal content! But the fools can't understand my meaning. They're like robots making ten, twenty figures exactly alike, one after another. Sung-in, you're different. You think about things, you ponder. If you start now, you'll be a master sculptor. With the recognition comes fame and fortune. Music? Do you think you'll ever be successful making music?

CHO SUNG-IN: No, Father. But . . . music will be my life.

TONG-YŎN: I don't know anything about music but I have ears to hear. What you make is nothing but noisy discord, and it's painful for people to listen to your music.

CHO SUNG-IN: It's more painful for me.

TONG-YŎN: I'd think it would be!

CHO SUNG-IN: Sound and silence are constantly at odds with each other. There must be a way to bring them into accord . . .

TONG-YŎN: They don't teach you that at school?!

CHO SUNG-IN: They teach a lot of things. Like harmonics, counterpoint, and so on. But these theories are no help for the kind of music I want to make. There is silence in sound, and sound in silence . . . the most beautiful music there is . . . I want to make the music of nirvana.

TONG-YŎN (*he sets down his spoon on the table with a loud bang*): That's impossible.

CHO SUNG-IN: Are you done eating?

TONG-YŎN: Don't waste your life on something that's impossible!

CHO SUNG-IN: You should finish everything up.

TONG-YŎN: You're a strange one! Ever since you were young! You look exactly like me, but you're nothing like me. Even now! You look like my son, but the way you talk and think, who would believe I'm your father.

CHO SUNG-IN: I'm your son.

TONG-YŎN: You're just like Sŏ-yŏn. (*He takes out a letter from his pocket and puts it on the table.*) I got this letter yesterday.

CHO SUNG-IN: What kind of letter?

TONG-YŎN: Read it and you'll see. (*He turns the wheelchair around and exits.*

CHO SUNG-IN *takes out the letter from the envelope and starts to read.*)

CHO SUNG-IN: "Dear Ham Myojin, I hope everything is well with you. I am the abbot at Songdŏk Temple. I think you will remember me, since we met once when I went to your workshop to place an order for a statue." Songdŏk Temple? It sounds familiar . . . "Let me get to the point. A couple days ago, my disciples and I were going to a lake nearby to free a number of fish. We were surprised to see the crazy one, the one who used to study with you but now goes around making stone statues that beguile simple folks who live around here." Ah, it's him. Sŏ-yŏn! "There is a woman from the village who claims that she conceived a son after praying in front of the crazy one's stone Buddha, a stupid farmer who says his parents were cured because of it, a widow who claims that talking to the stone Buddha cured her depression, and some people are even saying that cows and horses stop by there and pay respect to it. All these rumors are causing financial problems for us." Hahaha, this is very interesting! "But to the point. It used to be that the crazy one went around by himself making the stone Buddha, but now he is doing it together with your wife." Mother, Mother is with him.

(*The light changes. The stage is empty but a light shows a winding path. An empty field.* **SŎ-YŎN**, *thin and sickly, enters followed by* **HAM YIJŎNG**. *They both wear ragged clothes. They pick up rocks on their way and make stone statues. The one who has picked up a larger stone puts it down first and the one who picked up a smaller rock puts it on top of the larger one. Rolling brooks, birds singing, and a breeze can be heard. At the side of the winding path, they continue to make statues. The* **CHORUS** *lines up as stone Buddhas along the winding path.* **SŎ-YŎN** *and* **HAM YIJŎNG** *joke around and laugh. They are like little children.*)

HAM YIJŎNG: I'm hungry. Aren't you?
SŎ-YŎN: I'm always hungry.
HAM YIJŎNG: Why don't we eat these potatoes? (*She picks up the potatoes from in front of a stone statue.*) Two for you and one for me. Someone left boiled potatoes in front of the bodhisattvas.
SŎ-YŎN (*he sits next to* HAM YIJŎNG *and eats a potato*): It's delicious, awfully delicious. It tastes better because we have stolen them from the bodhisattvas.
HAM YIJŎNG (*she laughs*): It's good as honey.
(SŎ-YŎN *has a sudden spasm of coughing and must stop eating. The sound of his cough indicates the seriousness of his illness.* HAM YIJŎNG *stops laughing and struggles to hold back her tears.* SŎ-YŎN *finally stops coughing; he gives back one of the potatoes to* HAM YIJŎNG.)
SŎ-YŎN: One for me and two for you.
HAM YIJŎNG: You should have one more, since you aren't well.
SŎ-YŎN: I've had enough.
HAM YIJŎNG: Sŏ-yŏn . . . my Sŏ-yŏn . . .
SŎ-YŎN: Yes?
HAM YIJŎNG: When you die, what should I do?
SŎ-YŎN: What should you do?
HAM YIJŎNG: If you aren't here, I'll be sad.
(SŎ-YŎN *coughs again.* HAM YIJŎNG, *worried and agitated, waits for his coughing to stop.*)
HAM YIJŎNG: Sŏ-yŏn, my Sŏ-yŏn . . .
SŎ-YŎN: A long time ago . . . I went to see the Master . . . He said you were marrying Tong-yŏn, that you also had a smart boy named Cho Sung-in . . . That day Tong-yŏn told me never to come back. That day I was at the end of my strength. The whole world was filled with empty shells of bodhisattvas . . . Nowhere was I able to see Buddha's spirit . . . I regretted . . . If I just continued making statues, I could have been spared this hardship . . . So I went back to the Master.
HAM YIJŎNG: That day Tong-yŏn kicked you out, and I just stood there and watched him do it . . .
SŎ-YŎN: It was a blessing that he did . . . Because he did that, I was able to fulfill my karma. I wondered around in the fields. My heart felt empty as if everything was bled out of me and I didn't know what I should fill it with. Then . . . it was a winter day. It snowed that day. I haven't seen that much snow before . . . the sky was all white . . . so was everything on the ground . . . Everything became a void, it was nothing but white emptiness. I . . . I . . . was terrified of the white vacuum. I called your name . . .

called your name again and again. I called your name until my heart would burst . . . to fill that emptiness with your name . . . When spring came, it melted all the snow . . . little buds and flowers blossomed . . . all looking like you. I was happy . . . truly happy . . . So, I wanted to leave a sign . . . that here is the nirvana. So, I collected the stones nearby . . . and created Buddhas.

HAM YIJŎNG: But Sŏ-yŏn, it was very windy last night; all the heads were knocked off the Buddhas.

SŎ-YŎN: I saw that, too. But does that take the spirit of Buddha with it?

HAM YIJŎNG: Sŏ-yŏn . . . Sŏ-yŏn . . .

SŎ-YŎN: Yes?

HAM YIJŎNG: Will you hold me?

SŎ-YŎN (*he holds* **HAM YIJŎNG** *and caresses her*): Don't cry. You're not little anymore.

HAM YIJŎNG: When I was little, I had both you and Tong-yŏn, and I was happy. I didn't know anything but I was happy. Now, I think I know a little about life, what happiness is, what sadness is . . .

SŎ-YŎN: You were happy without knowing it, so you should be happier now that you do know.

(**HAM YIJŎNG** *and* **SŎ-YŎN** *stand up. They walk along the path, making statues. The sound of a stream becomes closer. Light shows the stream.*)[12]

HAM YIJŎNG: This stream is where the road ends.

SŎ-YŎN (*he goes to the stream and drinks with his hands*): Why don't you have some, too? You must be thirsty.

HAM YIJŎNG (*she goes closer to* **SŎ-YŎN** *and looks into the water*): We can see ourselves in the water. Here are our faces . . . behind them are the clouds . . . behind them is the sky . . . (*She drinks water with her hands.*) The water is clean and refreshing.

(**SŎ-YŎN** *plays with the water, pretending to make a snowball with it.*)

HAM YIJŎNG: What are you doing?

SŎ-YŎN: Making a water Buddha.

HAM YIJŎNG: With water?

SŎ-YŎN: We can make it with rocks, then why not with water?

(**SŎ-YŎN** *goes into the stream and goes through the motion of scooping water in his hand and spraying it. It vanishes, leaving behind only a feeling of the presence of Buddha.*)

HAM YIJŎNG: Sŏ-yŏn, come this way.

SŎ-YŎN (*he crosses the water*): No. I'm going this way now.

HAM YIJŎNG: Sŏ-yŏn, Sŏ-yŏn.

SŎ-YŎN: You can come later.

HAM YIJŎNG (*she waves to him*): All right. Go ahead. I'll come later.

(**SŎ-YŎN** and **HAM YIJŎNG** *pause and look at each other.* **CHO SUNG-IN** *is composing a song on his piano. Across the stream, where* **SŎ-YŎN** *is, the stage becomes very bright. As if not to miss his chance,* **HAM MYOJIN** *hurries in on his wheelchair. The stage where* **SŎ-YŎN** *is becomes very bright.*)

CHO SUNG-IN: Grandpa, where are you going in such a hurry?

HAM MYOJIN: It opened. The gate to nirvana opened up.

(**HAM MYOJIN** *stands up from his wheelchair. He follows* **SŎ-YŎN** *into the light. The stage lights change.* **TONG-YŎN** *enters. He goes to* **CHO SUNG-IN** *and hands him a telegram.*)

TONG-YŎN: This is a telegram from the abbot at Songdŏk Temple. Sŏ-yŏn passed away.

CHO SUNG-IN (*he plays one low note for a long time*): And Mother?

TONG-YŎN: Why don't you go see her?

CHO SUNG-IN (*he stands up and closes the piano cover*): Yes, Father.

TONG-YŎN: I'll give you enough money for the funeral.

(*A tent opens up on the stage. It is the middle of night with stars and a full moon in the sky. Inside the tent, two candles are burning brightly. Behind the candles is a wooden casket containing* **SŎ-YŎN**'s *body.* **HAM YIJŎNG** *is in her mourning clothes sitting in front of the casket. There is a sound of wind and crickets.* **CHO SUNG-IN** *comes in.*)

CHO SUNG-IN: It's me, Mother. Cho Sung-in is here.

HAM YIJŎNG (*happy to see her son*): It's good to see you.

CHO SUNG-IN (*he pays his respects, bowing twice in front of the casket*).

HAM YIJŎNG: I was sure that you'd be here tonight.

CHO SUNG-IN (*gazing at the casket*): He was my spiritual father.

HAM YIJŎNG: Mmm . . . Now that I look at you, you've grown into a man.

CHO SUNG-IN: My father sent me. He also sends this money to help you pay for the funeral. (*He takes an envelope from his coat and offers it to his mother.*) Take it, Mother.

HAM YIJŎNG (*she hesitates for a second but takes the envelope*): Thank you. But there's no need to worry about the funeral. The third night ends with the dawn, and tomorrow his ashes will be scattered over the field as he wished. There are many kind people in the village. They lent me candles, incense, and even this tent. (*She remembers something funny and smiles.*) Yesterday, priests from Songdŏk Temple came by. And it was . . . funny the way they chanted and beat their woodblocks. When he was alive, they all called him crazy. Yesterday, it was as if they wanted to send his spirit as far away as possible.

CHO SUNG-IN (*he looks at his mother's smiling face*): Mother, are you happy?

HAM YIJŎNG: Why do you ask?

CHO SUNG-IN: Because you don't seem sad.

HAM YIJŎNG: Yes, I'm happy.

CHO SUNG-IN: I'm troubled.

HAM YIJŎNG: Are you still tormenting yourself?

CHO SUNG-IN: Yes.

HAM YIJŎNG: That's not good . . .

CHO SUNG-IN: My two fathers are constantly fighting in my heart.

HAM YIJŎNG: Cho Sung-in . . . my son . . .

CHO SUNG-IN: My heart hurts when they fight; it's never able to choose one over the other.

HAM YIJŎNG: Their battle in your heart will end, and there will be nirvana.

CHO SUNG-IN: Father still hasn't forgiven you. When you left the house, he screamed in rage. "Your so-called mother went to that guy. Even when we married and she was living with me, she wanted to be with him." And he would tell me: "You are a strange one. You look like me on the outside but you think like him." I . . . hated hearing that. Hated it more than any curse in this world. At the same time, I liked hearing it. Hearing it was better than any compliment that I was like him. (*He goes to the casket and, on his knees, strokes the casket.*) I really wanted to meet him, my spiritual father. My father despised him so. It's a pity he is no longer of this world.

HAM YIJŎNG: But the feeling of him is.

CHO SUNG-IN: Feeling . . . you mean *memories* of him?

HAM YIJŎNG: Don't laugh, even if it seems strange. Even from the sound of rocks rolling in the field, I can feel him. In streams, breeze, in everything, I can feel that he is here. (*She blushes and laughs.*) I told you not to laugh, but look at me, laughing. Why don't you laugh with me?

(*From afar, a bell tolls to announce the morning, followed by the crowing of the village roosters. The sound of the roosters seems like the voice of* **HAM MYOJIN** *calling out the names of* **TONG-YŎN** *and* **SŎ-YŎN**.)

Curtain

NOTES

1. Ham Yijŏng refers to three days of mourning for the deceased, during which time she has remained near the casket. The rigid codes of the earlier Chosŏn dynasty (1392–1910) could require up to three years of mourning. Even in today's South Korea, extended mourning periods are not uncommon when a parent or spouse dies.

2. A bodhisattva is a being who, although not yet enlightened, is working toward that goal. Believers often pray to a particular bodhisattva. They are popular subjects in Buddhist art, and statues and paintings of them surrounding some manifestation of Buddha are prominent in Buddhist temples. The bodhisattva most prominent in this play is Avalokiteshvara (Kannon in Japanese), the bodhisattva associated with compassion.
3. Avalokiteshvara is generally depicted as a male in India and Tibet and as a female in East Asia. Among the various depictions of Avalokiteshvara throughout Asia, an eleven-face version is common in Korea. The form praised by Ham Myojin is called, in Korean, *ban-gajwa* (half-seated posture), a pose taken by a bodhisattva in meditation. Buddha is never represented in this posture.
4. The apricot is commonly mentioned in Korean poetry. Note that in O T'aesŏk's *Bellflower* is this line: "Now I long to pluck an apricot flower and send it to my lover."
5. Amitabha (variously, in Korea, Amitabul) reigns over the Land of Bliss, a source of boundless light in the darkness of ignorance. Avalokiteshvara is a manifestation of the eternal Buddha.
6. Hong Nanp'a (1897–1941) was a major Korean composer whose works are often performed by Western artists.
7. Ham Yijŏng inadvertently uses the Korean word *oppa* (big brother), a term of affection, but not the word a wife would use when addressing her husband. Tong-yŏn hears *oppa* as an insult, thus the tone of his rebuke.
8. Putting the shoes on his head represents Sŏ-yŏn's abject humility, and it is only abject humility, the obliteration of one's ego, that offers a way out of an impasse like the one in which Sŏ-yŏn and Tong-yŏn find themselves. Tong-yŏn explodes with rage because he takes this as Sŏ-yŏn's refusal or indifference to what Tong-yŏn believes to be important.
9. Bhaisajyaguru (Yaksayŏrae in Korean) is the Buddha of Healing, invoked to care for the ill. He is often depicted in blue tones, with a bowl of medicinal herbs in his left hand and the right hand making the sign of "assurance from fear."
10. The nimbus is the light emanating from a Buddha or bodhisattva, symbolizing a kind of spiritual fire.
11. Sakyamuni (Sŏkgyŏrae in Korean) is the historical Buddha, shown seated, sometimes reclining, often just before his enlightenment.
12. Water as a purifier is commonly used in religions around the world, and the light connected with the stream in this instance is doubly meaningful, first as the image of enlightenment and, second, as the light that, anecdotally, beckoned many who were near death, but brought back to life.

IN PRAISE OF YOUTH
(CH'ŎNGCH'UN YECH'AN)

PAK KŬNHYŎNG

Pak Kŭnhyŏng received the Korean Ministry of Culture and Tourism's "Today's Young Artist" award in 1999, was named the "number one theater director for the next generation" by the *Dong-a Ilbo* newspaper (2003), and has received prestigious playwriting awards for *In Praise of Youth* (*Ch'ŏngch'un yech'an*, 1999) and *Kyŏng-suk, Kyŏng-suk's Father* (*Kyŏng-suk i Kyŏng-suk abŏji*, 2006). He represents a growing number of Korean theater artists who combine playwriting and directing, staging their own plays as well as the works of others.

Born in Seoul in 1963, Pak joined the Theater Company 76 in 1986. By the time he entered Taejin University in Pojŏn City (Kyŏnggi Province), he was an established director of other playwrights' works. *Aspirin* (*Asŭp'irin*, 1994) is the first work he both wrote and directed, a tale about a drug-abusing psychiatric patient and his family, followed by *Rats* (*Chwi*, 1998), in which humans who have no food become cannibals in order to survive. The works that Pak has written and directed since then, including *In Praise of Youth*, often feature a marginalized father figure and a dramatic world seen through the eyes of commoners, outsiders without power. In *Generations to Generations* (*Taedae sonson*, 2000) and *Kyŏng-suk, Kyŏng-suk's Father*, Pak interweaves family history with Korea's painful past (the colonial period and the Vietnam War in the case of *Generations to Generations*, and the Korean War in *Kyŏng-suk, Kyŏng-suk's Father*) in order to illuminate aspects of contemporary Korean society. In particular, in *Kyŏng-suk* and *In Praise of Youth*, Pak's dramatic fathers are alienated from the family and are capable of hardness, even cruelty, yet also of surprising acts of kindness or love. An example can be found in *Youth*, in the father's moving "memory" scene with his former wife, whom he blinded in a fit of rage. Pak never preaches in these plays and scrupulously avoids melodrama. His dramaturgy and his directing combine sparse language, minimal settings, fluid chronology, and unexpected humor (even slapstick) in moments of emotional disturbance. Despite the dark tone in Pak's works, hope flows under the surface. To paraphrase Pak, although his plays may depict lives seemingly condemned to meaningless activity, his effort to bring hopes to fruition gives one's life meaning. *Youth*'s conclusion urges both readers and audience to hold onto hope. Since its debut, the play continues to draw audiences, with three reprise runs in Seoul, the most recent in 2006.

Pak Kŭnhyŏng is a professor of playwriting at the Seoul Institute of the Arts.

IN PRAISE OF YOUTH
(CH'ŎNGCH'UN YECH'AN)

TRANSLATED BY YI HYEKYŎNG

Characters

YOUTH
FATHER
TEACHER
YONGP'IL
GIRL
SNAKE
EPILEPTIC
MOTHER

(*A room. As the lights come up on stage, the* **FATHER** *is drinking* soju *with kimchi. The* **YOUTH** *enters in his school uniform.*)[1]

YOUTH: What's up?
FATHER: Can't you tell? I'm watching TV.
YOUTH: Any good?
FATHER: Not really.
YOUTH: Then why are you watching?
FATHER: I'm just watching.
YOUTH: At least go out and lay bricks if you're going to sit around at home. (*Pause.*) Turn on *Unshili*.[2]
FATHER: It's over. Don't you know what time it is? Where are you coming from?
YOUTH: School.
FATHER: They say they're kicking you out. Your teacher came by when the 9 o'clock news ended. (*Gives* **YOUTH** *an envelope.*) He said to at least call if you don't want to go to school. By this week.

YOUTH: Where'd the money come from?
FATHER: Go and beg. You should at least complete *high school*. Once you graduate, enlist. They say the food is best at the front lines.
YOUTH: Father! You went to see Mom again, didn't you? Stop going! Aren't you even embarrassed? (*Pause.*) She still living with that bastard?
FATHER: It looks like it. Didn't ask.
YOUTH: Buncha retards. Dad . . . We should go live in Japan.
FATHER: As if just anyone can go? Did Japan say they'd take you in?
YOUTH: I heard a friend's dad made it big with *pachinko* in Japan.
FATHER: *Yakuza*, huh?
YOUTH: Is every *pachinko* joint run by *yakuza*?
FATHER: Then he's a *yakuza*'s goon?
YOUTH: Why do you always see the bad side of things?
FATHER: Which friend?
YOUTH: Yongp'il.
FATHER: So when did his old man move from Hong Kong to Japan? Bonehead! Choose your friends wisely. Meet just one good human being, then you won't fall on hard times when you're old. Like me! (*Pause.*) How 'bout a drink? (*The two face each other and drink.*)
YOUTH: Save your money. And don't go throwing money around just 'cause you got some.
FATHER: This is pretty good, right? Goes down smooth.
YOUTH: Why do you have to be so classless? Possessed by alcohol.
FATHER: Possessed?
YOUTH: Look, you have no soul. Jinro is a better brand by far.[3]
FATHER: Don't be so damn picky about what you drink. It's bad karma. (*Pause.*) Ya! sing me a song.
YOUTH: Sing a song? Don't be pathetic.
FATHER: Just one, please.
YOUTH: Would you stop pestering me when I come home? (*Pause.*) Whose?
FATHER: Anyone's. You know . . . that one. The one that goes like this. (*Stands up.*) Lalalala lalalaaaa lalala lala. Be happy . . .
YOUTH: You want to be happy?
FATHER: What about you?
YOUTH: Don't answer with a question! Don't you have any friends or anyone? Somewhere to sleep?
FATHER: Are you kicking me out? Where to?
YOUTH: It's a hassle for both of us when we live together.
FATHER: Am I a hassle for you?

YOUTH: Some. What's a grown man doing not working? You have arms and legs.
FATHER: Then you go out and work! You've got those, too!
YOUTH: I'm a student!
FATHER: You crazy bastard! Honestly, can you call yourself a student? If you have a problem living here, then take off! Why should I leave my own house?
YOUTH: Is this house really yours?
(*Pause.*)
FATHER: It's the same for me, you know.
YOUTH: What's the same?
FATHER: You're a pain in the ass for me, too. You have a lot of friends—and I won't go around looking for you, so if you don't like it here, get out!
YOUTH: Ah, what's wrong with you? You can't wait to chew up your only son.
FATHER: You stop thinking about chewing up your only father first!
(*Pause.*)
YOUTH: Did you eat?
FATHER: No.
YOUTH: Want me to get something for you?
FATHER: I don't care . . .
YOUTH: How about ramen, then?
FATHER: I'm sick of the taste of ramen flour. (*Pause.*) You have any?
YOUTH: I'll go buy some.
FATHER: Never mind. It's OK.
YOUTH: Come on, let's eat together! (*On his way out.*)
FATHER: Get the Shin-ramen brand! (*The phone rings.* FATHER *hastily picks up the phone.*) Hello? It's for you. Your teacher . . .
(YOUTH *just walks out. The television glow brightens, filling the room.* FATHER *pours himself a drink. As the lights go out, music softly plays. When the lights come up again, we see a classroom.*)
TEACHER: Efforts to connect the East and the West began in the mid-sixteenth century, as many aimed to make a profit through merchant trading, bringing goods from the East to Europe. Then the Industrial Revolution led to the mass production of goods from factories. The European powers, especially Great Britain, came to see the East as more than just trade partners. They saw the East as a market for their goods and a source of raw materials. The Opium War of 1839 was a result of the events stemming from that background. Speaking of that, although

I don't know who made it, there was a movie by this Chinese director. It's even called *The Opium War*, and there's a scene where a mountain of opium is burned . . .[4] You should see it sometime. Things haven't changed much from then. A nation and a people without strength will collapse. Can anyone tell me the source of that strength? (YONGP'IL *enters from the side of the stage.*)

YONGP'IL: Godzilla's ugly jaws. (*Spews cigarette smoke from his mouth, making roaring sounds.*)

TEACHER: Strength doesn't just pop up in front of your eyes. You! (*To the students.*) Did you see *Godzilla*?

YONGP'IL: Bullshit. (*He exits.*)

TEACHER: Students! I don't know why I even bother saying this to the likes of you, but don't be fooled! If you're fooled, you will become the fool. (*As the rest of the stage lights come up, we see the* YOUTH.)

YOUTH: Teacher!

TEACHER: You selfish pup!! You've never kept a promise. Do you really want to be like that?

YOUTH: I'm sorry.

TEACHER: Didn't I hammer it into your head that you had one week? But now, after three weeks and all the trouble I went through to visit your home, you finally show up!!

YOUTH: I'm sorry.

TEACHER: Sorry's not good enough. I know I teach kids only so I can pay the rent, but you're making me lose my hair nonetheless.

YOUTH: It's all my fault, sir.

TEACHER: Even you can tell how crappy my life is, right?

YOUTH: Yes sir!

TEACHER: Why did I have to be your teacher for four years, and you still a sophomore? Aren't you embarrassed when you see your friends on their way to college, walking around full of themselves? No answer, huh. Go vegetate at home! That's best for both of us. What do you think of that?

YOUTH: I think you're right, sir.

TEACHER: Bring the cane! You still haven't got your act together. The way I see it, you need to be taught a lesson. Forget teacher and student. All that aside, you need to be taught a lesson. We can talk after.

YOUTH: Yes sir. (*Brings the cane.*)

TEACHER: Think about your behavior while I hit you ten times. Come to school regularly starting tomorrow, OK? You don't even have to open a book.

YOUTH: Teacher, I'll get hit, but coming to school—can I think about it for one more week?
TEACHER: You bastard! (*Flings away the cane.*) I won't hit you—just never show me your face again, you bastard!
YOUTH: I still don't know for sure. What I have to do . . .
TEACHER: Is what? What? What? This is straight talk, you son of a bitch, I don't care if it's hard—graduate first! Then you can whine about your hardships afterward! Don't always have them on your mind, get it? Things that you can't even begin to imagine will start happening once you graduate, you fucking son of bitch!
YOUTH: I'm sorry.
TEACHER: "Sorry" doesn't cut it. What about the book report? Did you write it?
YOUTH: Well, not yet. I haven't read it all yet.
TEACHER: If you don't like reading, then rip it up! A book is a book, you bastard. If you don't read it, it's just a pile of paper. School is some dance club for you? You come by whenever you have money? Been drinking a lot nowadays, haven't you.
YOUTH: No.
TEACHER: Don't lie to me! Once I get paid, I'll get you your booze and visit every day; I won't even go home. Just stay at home. Just don't show up at school. You're an unteachable bastard, you know that?
YOUTH: Are you kicking me out?
TEACHER: Yeah, you're getting kicked out. I can't reason with you. Can't do anything with you. I give up! Get lost! I don't want to see you.
YOUTH: I understand. I'll leave, sir. Be well.
TEACHER: Come here! Come here and get hit before you go. I can't just send you away! (YOUTH *picks up the cane and hands it to* TEACHER.) OK, today's gonna be the big day. You can handle one hundred blows?
YOUTH: Yes, sir!
TEACHER: I'm not kidding around.
YOUTH: Yes, sir!
TEACHER: Count! (*Starts striking* YOUTH.)
YOUTH: One, two, three . . .
  (*The stage lights fade as the sounds of counting and hitting continue. When the lights come back up . . .*)
YONGP'IL: Four, five, six, *siete*, eight . . . nineteen, twenty.[5] Ah, fuck. Why twenty a pack? There's thirty days in a month. (*Puts a cigarette in his mouth.*)

GIRL: Hey, where is that asshole, Snake? Did he jet?
YONGP'IL: Jet where? Like he has anywhere to go! He'll get as far as a flea. Let's have another smoke.
GIRL: Smoke domestic! It's not like you have money, you poor shit.
YONGP'IL: So what? It's all good. Camel! (*To* GIRL.) C'mon, lady. Let's raise some kiddie Camels in our pockets. Ah fuck! Just smack this up! Tastes good. Price's all right. Fuckin' cool. Three birds with one stone! Domestic! That's just bullshit. Power comes from my ugly jaws! (*Spews out smoke.*)
GIRL: Crazy bastard! Your bones will rot! You like them smokes that much?
YONGP'IL: 'Course. I like smokes. Smoking and learning how to drive were my two wishes as a kid. Ninth grade, going home in the winter, I always sat right behind the driver whenever I got on the bus. You know, to learn how the pros shift gears. Then whenever he would crack open the window and smoke, man, inside I was practicing that and only that. Walking home, I'd make my breath go *huuuu huuuu*.
GIRL: Snake, that loser, where is he?
YONGP'IL: So weird. Just close my eyes, and put this in my mouth. Feels just like I'm dancing on MTV. Dancing somewhere with a fuckload of little teenyboppers. Wearing nasty shades and tight white pants—damn! (*Suddenly, a Pak Chin-yŏng track plays,*[6] *and* YONGP'IL *starts to dance and sing along with it.*)
YOUTH (*entering*): Yongp'il, what's up?
YONGP'IL: All right! You OK?
YOUTH: Who do you think I am?
    Pak Hae'il, the human being,
    Pak Hae'il, the youth, ain't that who I am?
GIRL (*embracing* YOUTH): Hey, baby!
YOUTH (*to the* GIRL): You're disgusting, creep.[7]
GIRL: Whatcha been up to, babe? It's been a while.
YOUTH: What else. Just doing whatever. Drifting here and there.
GIRL: Just drifting?
YOUTH: What's this "just drifting," creep? You're supposed to think while you drift.
YONGP'IL: What kind of thinking?
YOUTH: Like you would know if I told you. The deep thoughts of this youth.
GIRL: Did you drift a lot?
YOUTH: Yeah, I drifted a lot. Ah, shit, but you know, Kŭmgang Mountain[8] didn't go as planned . . . Expensive! I knew it! Let's go together next time. (*All laugh.*)

GIRL: What's happening now? Are you gonna start coming to school?
YOUTH: Well, we'll see. Probably starting next week.
YONGP'IL: One-week break?
YOUTH: I guess that's what happened. Anyways, anything fun?
YONGP'IL: Fun? Of course. Let's knock back some shots tonight.
GIRL: Babe? I got hit on today.
YOUTH: Hit on?
GIRL: Damn spring fling, those losers coming at me from all directions, trying to make me look cheap.
YONGP'IL: Hey, it's Snake! Snake's coming! (SNAKE *enters, mumbling to himself as if he is memorizing something.*)
GIRL: Hey, Snake! Ca va?⁹
SNAKE: What's up?
GIRL: Hey! You got some nerve, huh? (*Slaps* SNAKE's *face.*)
YOUTH: Been a while.
SNAKE: Huh? (*To* YOUTH.) Were you at school today?
GIRL (*to* SNAKE): Hey! Why're you talking to him? He's your better.¹⁰ So, I heard you've been bad-mouthing me.
SNAKE: Who? What did they say?
GIRL: Don't weasel, you motherfucker! You! You slept with me?
SNAKE: Me?
GIRL: Yeah you! You took advantage of me, and I heard you're running your mouth like a little bitch.
SNAKE: I never said nothing like that.
GIRL: Ha! Fucking headache. Wanna interrogation? I got witnesses.
SNAKE: Witness? Who?
GIRL: Yongp'il! Tell me right now what you said!
YONGP'IL (*to* SNAKE): That's what you said a day before. That you ran into each other at the Popeye's in front of HongDae U. By coincidence.¹¹
SNAKE: You son of a bitch!
GIRL: And?
YONGP'IL: And . . . You guys took some lemon *soju* shots; you took her to your friend's place and fooled around till morning.
SNAKE: Fool what, fucker?
GIRL: That's enough! I wanna live a decent life, Snake. An honest life. So why are you making up stories every chance you get. Why are you breaking the hearts of likable girls?
SNAKE: Break your heart? We *did* go to my friend's place!
GIRL: Did go? Man, you got a thick skull. And then what?
SNAKE: You wanted to sleep with me.

GIRL: Me?
SNAKE: Yeah, all drunk on your ass.
GIRL: Go on.
SNAKE: And I wasn't doing anything, but you were crawling all over me.
GIRL: This kid is really pissing me off today. And then?
SNAKE: So I started to ride the mood, and I'm about to take off my clothes when you puked all over. All over their blankets.
GIRL: Stop! That's it! You're dead today, by my hands. You know, even bullshit has its limits. You totally crushed my pride. On your knees! Kneel! (SNAKE *looks around, gauges the situation, and then kneels.*) Yongp'il, gimme a knife.
YONGP'IL: Knife?
GIRL: That Swiss Army knife?
YONGP'IL: It's a bit dull. (*Gives the knife to* GIRL.)
GIRL: If I had my way, I'd just rip your mouth apart, but I care about your future. Due to a shortage of time, I'll just peel off some fingernails. Just two. Any complaints?
SNAKE: All right, my bad, my bad! Please!
GIRL: It's all right, punk. It's all right. You won't die.
(GIRL *rubs* SNAKE's *head, then smacks him, and grabs his hand.*)
SNAKE: Aaaaahhh aaack!
GIRL: The knife's barely touching you!
(*Trying to cut the nails.*)
SNAKE: Aaaaahhh aaack!
GIRL: Hey babe! Fucker must be a turtle. The knife doesn't work.
YOUTH: Hurry up. What's taking you so long? Gimme that. (YOUTH *snatches the knife from* GIRL's *hands.*) Did you say two fingernails?
(*Suddenly* YONGP'IL *enters, bringing a table.*)
YONGP'IL: Ah, fuck. Why's the lighting so bright?
(*As* YONGP'IL *puts down the table, music comes up and the lights change. Now we are in a room at a coffee shop.*)
GIRL: Hey, Snake! Be good. Next time you get funny, money won't handle it. I'll pull 'em for real.
SNAKE: I know. I'm buying tonight, aren't I?
GIRL: Babe, whatcha up to? All this time.
YOUTH: Homework.
GIRL: Homework?
SNAKE: Fuck that!
YONGP'IL: Mr. History did him in, remember? Don't you know? His homework is to read that book and write a report. You still not done?

YOUTH: Well, I read it . . . But the report, well, you know . . .

GIRL: Was the book fun, babe?

YOUTH: Creep! You read books for fun? Well the words were easy, but the book was hard. I don't know.

GIRL: What was hard?

YOUTH: Just stuff.

YONGP'IL: Mr. History, that fucker plays favorites too much. We all screw up, but some kids are in and some kids are out. Sure he's not a spy?[12] That fucker.

YOUTH: Don't be a dumb shit.

SNAKE: Just copy the introduction. Change a few words around.

YOUTH: Hey, you think old History is an idiot?

YONGP'IL: Whatever. What is this place? Smells all moldy and shit. What kind of bar is this? Makes some money. Sells coffee, sells girls . . . sells alcohol, too.

GIRL: So, the girl here, who is she?

SNAKE: My big sister.

YONGP'IL: Why the hell would your sister be hanging around here for? Real sister?

She earn a lot?

SNAKE: No. Real sister? They say there's some connection with my mother's father. You know, some old complicated shit. Different last name, different everything. I really dunno.

YONGP'IL: She pretty? (*Sticks up his middle finger.*) Does she go out on calls too?

SNAKE: No, fucker. Just stays in the kitchen. She's ugly. And nowhere to go. She's nice though. But she . . . (**EPILEPTIC** *enters.*)

EPILEPTIC: You came. Can I get you anything?

SNAKE: Ah, booze! And anything else. Are you done for today?

EPILEPTIC: Yeah I'm alone now. I'll turn off the shop sign and be back.

SNAKE: Hey, sis? You sleep here alone?

EPILEPTIC: Yeah. You have no place to stay?

YONGP'IL: Well, I wouldn't put it that way . . .

EPILEPTIC: You guys can't stay here. Have to leave before 4:00. (*Pause.*) I have to look for somewhere else, too. I'm staying just through this week.

SNAKE: Why?

EPILEPTIC (*silence*).

SNAKE: Did you fight?

EPILEPTIC: Fight? Why would I fight with those little kids? (*Pause.*) They said they didn't like me.

SNAKE: Why?

EPILEPTIC: They'll come back in the morning. The girls.

YONGP'IL: How many? Are they pretty?

SNAKE: This is a friend. Yongp'il. His whole family is part of the Cho Yongp'il fan club.

YONGP'IL: Hey, what kind of introduction is that? (*In a parody of himself.*) Hello, ladies and gentlemen. This is Cho Yongp'il.

SNAKE (*pointing at* **YOUTH**): He's much older than me.

YONGP'IL: Was held back only two years.

EPILEPTIC: Hold on. You guys want to sing?[13]

YOUTH (*politely*): No. It's OK. (**EPILEPTIC** *exits.*)

YONGP'IL: Hey she's a total hippo, a hippo.

SNAKE: She can hear you, man!

YONGP'IL: Tell her to hear me. Anything I say untrue?

GIRL: Doesn't look a single bit like you.

SNAKE: I told you, my mother's side. They said that her mom was fucking hot. But she was part of this affair with a married man when she suddenly had this seizure. When she was pregnant.

YONGP'IL: Seizure?

SNAKE: You know, epilepsy.

GIRL: Is that contagious?

YOUTH: Not contagious—inherited!

SNAKE: She was pregnant, and it spooked out the guy's family so they fed her this strong herbal medicine—some vile shit. But her stomach got larger and larger. Yeah, so she has this kid. Her mom has nowhere to go, wanders, then this baby pops out, so you can imagine, huh.

YONGP'IL: Motherfucker, this is all bullshit.

SNAKE: It's true. My mom said so. When she gets excited this goes off.

YONGP'IL: You seen it?

SNAKE: When she flips, her eyes get all white, man, she just goes off.

GIRL: Ah, this is crap! Hey, babe, let's leave. You loser, when you said you'd buy, I should've known. Fuck, you little turd, how does the booze go down? In this shitty atmosphere.

YONGP'IL: Makes no diff. It's just us drinking

SNAKE: Yeah. Drink first. If you feel weird, we can leave after.

GIRL: Babe, let's leave. Let's le-eave! (**EPILEPTIC** *brings in a tray with drinks and snacks.* **GIRL** *gets up from her seat.*)

EPILEPTIC: There isn't much to eat. Let's have a few shots. I was feeling pretty closed in anyway . . . (*To* **GIRL**, *who is standing.*) Sit down. Why, you leaving?

GIRL: Shit, would you listen to her talk?[14]
EPILEPTIC: What's wrong?
GIRL: Why don't you beat it while I'm still nice!
SNAKE: What's wrong with you?
GIRL: Snake! You stay out of this. Get outta here, you fucking bitch!
EPILEPTIC: What's with her? Did I do something wrong?
GIRL: What makes you think you can just talk to me like that? Am I your pal? What a shitty day today!
YOUTH (*to* GIRL): At least Snake has poison. Yongp'il! Give me that knife.
YONGP'IL: Why?
SNAKE: Hae'il!
GIRL (*hanging onto* YOUTH): Bitch, you don't know what my babe is like. You're dead now.
YOUTH: Bitch?
GIRL: Babe!
YOUTH: Don't call me babe!
GIRL: Babe!
YOUTH: You still can't remember? How I got this scar? You know what I can't stand the most? People with their nose in the air! It's called self-importance in fancy words. Bitch? Why the bullshit? Bullshit! If you don't love your own mouth, who's gonna respect it then? You little bitch!

(*As* YOUTH, *raising knife, approaches* GIRL's *mouth, the stage goes black. Music can be heard—from the 1976 live performance of the Sex Pistols. When the lights come back up, we are in a massage parlor. A man is lying face down, and next to him stands* MOTHER.)

MOTHER: No . . . It hasn't been long since I started. I wasn't always like this. I was a fool. If I had just stayed quiet . . . (*Pause.*) I fought with my husband. Everyone does. You fight, and a few days later you make up. And then you live like you did before . . . I was glaring at him when we argued, just because. So in the heat of anger, he reaches out and his hands find cleaning acid. I should have backed off. Shouting at the top of my lungs, screaming, "Spray it, huh, spray it you asshole!" I kept talking back. Still glaring straight at him. Everything became white. Like a great snowfall . . . While I was being doused by acid, I kept my eyes open. My rashness . . . No we don't live together right now. After that he felt so sorry. Would always yell at me or throw something at the slightest reason. I guess it was hard for him, the way I went on with my life, quietly enduring. I looked for work I could do with my eyes closed and ended up like this. The man I live with now also can't see. It worked out,

I guess. Everyone has their own fate. I'm sorry. (*Pause.*) Are you sleeping? Sir!

(**MOTHER** *starts to massage the man's body again.* **FATHER** *walks in at this moment. He takes off his shoes.*)

FATHER: Hon . . .

MOTHER: Why did you come again?

FATHER: Sorry. I was around for work and I had something to say

MOTHER: You're killing me.

FATHER: Sorry. It's for work, for real. I didn't come for money. I still have some left.

MOTHER: I only have five minutes.

FATHER: I think I'll end up going to Japan. With Hae'il.

MOTHER: Japan where?

FATHER: You know, there. That place on TV all the time. With that big castle.

MOTHER: Where? Osaka?

FATHER: Yeah, there.

MOTHER: When?

FATHER: I can't come by anymore, even if I want to. I think we'll leave soon. Within three months. I'm coming back from the embassy right now.

MOTHER: You can't even speak Japanese. Who said they would send you?

FATHER: My squad-mate, from the army . . . Said he made it big with *pachinko* there. Says all his workers are Koreans. Told me that the Korean *yakuza* have the whole territory. I'll write from there, don't worry. Sad, huh? Makes you a little disappointed? I'll wait until your work is over. Want to drink some, like old times?

MOTHER: You should go home. I'm going in. No money right now. Later, come with Hae'il once before you go to Japan. Call before you come.

FATHER: Want me to go?

MOTHER: I'm busy. People are waiting in line. (**MOTHER** *leaves to start massaging again.*)

FATHER: Hey. How tall are you?

MOTHER: Four feet eleven and a half inches.

FATHER: Were you always so short? (*Pause.*) Should I wait out front?

MOTHER: We're divorced. Please don't be like this. I'm going in. (*She goes in.*)

FATHER (*picks up his shoes*): Where should I go? To Japan? For real.

(*Music comes up and the lights dim. As the lights come up again, the locale is a cheap inn. A naked man and woman lie together.*)[15]

EPILEPTIC: Sorry. It's that time for me.

YOUTH: That time?

EPILEPTIC: Ovulating cycle.
YOUTH: Ovulating cycle?
EPILEPTIC: The time to get pregnant!
YOUTH: Ha! My! So?
EPILEPTIC: I'll never forget how you were yesterday! Thanks. (*Pause.*) I love you! For understanding.
YOUTH: I don't love you. I don't understand you. I don't even know you!
EPILEPTIC: Don't lie. Once I have a seizure, everyone looks at me differently.
YOUTH: Me, too! You, you're disgusting. I was just drunk. Right? Now get dressed! Now!
EPILEPTIC: You're my first—
YOUTH: First? Filthy . . . Get dressed now, you bitch!
EPILEPTIC: Person who got angry for me.
YOUTH: It wasn't for you. What does you being sick have to do with me? Fuck, bitch, you're making me puke.
EPILEPTIC: Don't curse! We made love during the night.
YOUTH: When people drink they go mad! They go! Without thinking! It's not love. It just happened when we got drunk. You bitch!
EPILEPTIC: Father was like that, too. To my mother.
YOUTH: Are you retarded?
EPILEPTIC: No.
YOUTH: Then why don't you get what I'm saying?
EPILEPTIC: They say this is inherited.
YOUTH: Ah! Shit! What a fuckup! If you don't shut up, I'll smack you.
EPILEPTIC: I . . . I don't care if you don't believe it, but you're my first.
YOUTH: First for what?
EPILEPTIC: I wasn't sent out like the other girls.
YOUTH: Who would call for a fat bitch like you, you psycho!
EPILEPTIC: You don't know. My kind of body. A lot of people like it.
YOUTH: So . . .
EPILEPTIC: Last month some guy came to and tore up the bar because he called for me and I didn't go. He said he'd burn the place down.
YOUTH: So? Then you should have gone last month, you bitch. Why are you trying to rip me off, you whore! Just a bitch!
EPILEPTIC: Don't swear. I won't have a fit.
YOUTH: Crazy bitch! You afraid of fits? Retard! People don't care about you. The world gets along just fine. You retard!
EPILEPTIC: Can't I live with you?
YOUTH: Where?

EPILEPTIC: At your place. (*Pause.*) Or anywhere.
YOUTH: Am I some kind of gypsy?
EPILEPTIC: Honestly, I think I'm a nice girl.
YOUTH: My father's nice, too.
EPILEPTIC (*pause*): So maybe, so maybe if I don't get a baby, then I'll leave you. So can't we live together?
YOUTH: Just blabber all you want.
EPILEPTIC: I have a period, too, every month.
YOUTH: So?
EPILEPTIC: They'll close down the shop anytime now.
YOUTH: You said that before, too! That you're fired!
EPILEPTIC: I'll be good to you.
YOUTH: Don't talk like that!
EPILEPTIC: It's my first time being naked in front of someone else.
YOUTH: Great. Today must be your lucky day.
EPILEPTIC: It's my first time, but it's not embarrassing. (*Pause.*) You saw how people hate me, right?
YOUTH: Stop acting like we're married.
EPILEPTIC: Why not? I'm old enough to be your big sister.
YOUTH: Let me ask you one thing: Have you ever been beaten in your panties?
EPILEPTIC: No . . .
YOUTH: Then shut up.
EPILEPTIC: Then how should I talk to you?
YOUTH: Bloody hell. Look, fatty, just—Ah, phew . . . Fucking hell. You don't know it, but my life is pretty out there itself, and I've never met a bitch as screwed up as you.
EPILEPTIC: I'll sort myself out.
YOUTH: You're crazy. Huh?
EPILEPTIC: So what if I am crazy?
YOUTH: Heheheh. You ready to be crazy together?
EPILEPTIC: Yeah.
YOUTH: Really?
EPILEPTIC: I'll be good to you.
YOUTH: Anyone'd see this, they'd cry. They'd cry then bitch us out. Bitch us out.

   Ah, she's killing me.
EPILEPTIC: How am I killing you?
YOUTH: 'Cause we're a pathetic girl and guy. (*Puts a cigarette in his mouth.* **EPILEPTIC** *tries to light it, but he snatches away her lighter.*) Don't put on airs!

(*Pause.*) Fine—let's go. Let's go. Let's go nuts together! But you should know: It's fucking hard. By the way. My mom's blind. She lives with some other bastard now. Met him through the massage place. Guess she's happy now. My father is a dog. You'll figure out just how when you see him. And I'm a dog too! Why you jumping into this shit? You think it's gonna change things? Change life? Fine, let's try each other out. Wanna taste some dog meat? Hahahahaha. Crazy broad. (*Caresses her face.*) Oh, you messed-up broad! (**EPILEPTIC** *leans into* **YOUTH**'s *embrace.*)

(*Lights go out. When lights return, we're at* **YOUTH**'s *house.*)

YOUTH: Say hi. This is Dad.
EPILEPTIC: Hello.
FATHER: Who's this?
YOUTH: She's going to live with us.
FATHER: Who?
YOUTH: Her.
FATHER: Why?
YOUTH: Has no home. She has fits.
FATHER: So?
YOUTH: What do you mean, "so"?
FATHER: Has no home, has fits—and why does she have to live with us?
YOUTH: She worked at the coffee shop, but the girls teased her and kicked her out 'cause she foams up all the time.
FATHER: Who lets her stay here?
YOUTH: What do you mean by "who lets her"? She just lives here. Says she likes me.
FATHER: Why?
YOUTH: She's going to cook and do the laundry from now on. You know, she's older than me.
FATHER: How much?
YOUTH: She's five years older.
EPILEPTIC: I'll be good, Father!
FATHER: Father? You two been rubbing around?
YOUTH: I don't know.
FATHER: If you don't know, who does?
YOUTH: She asked me to be responsible. To take care of her.
FATHER (*to* **EPILEPTIC**): Already set your mind on living together, huh? Why would this kid take care of you?
YOUTH: Look who's talking. (*To* **EPILEPTIC**.) Hey, you can see for yourself, we have no money, nothing. You'll have to scrounge what you're gonna eat.
FATHER: Looks like she'd eat a lot.

YOUTH: Why are you always putting people down? (*To* **EPILEPTIC**.) Our phone only works for incoming calls.

FATHER: Even that doesn't work now. You be the father from now on, OK? I'll go to the district office and tell them I'm dead.[16]

YOUTH: Are you angry?

FATHER: Yeah, of course. Wouldn't you be?

YOUTH: Come on, let it be, just this once. Damn, what's wrong with that? (*When* **YOUTH** *sits down,* **FATHER** *stands up. From here on, they speak in an exaggerated polite tone.*)

YOUTH: Say hello. This is Father.

EPILEPTIC: Hello.

FATHER: And who might this be?

YOUTH: She'll be living with us, sir.

FATHER: Who?

YOUTH: Her.

FATHER: Why?

YOUTH: She has no home, sir. She has fits, sir.

FATHER: Well, since she has no home and she has fits, then surely she must live together with us.

YOUTH: She worked at the coffee shoppe, sir, but the girls teased her and kicked her out because she foamed up all the time.

FATHER: Tsk tsk tsk, how unfortunate!

YOUTH: She says she fancies me, sir.

FATHER: Why?

YOUTH: She's going to cook and do the laundry from now on. Sir, she's older than I.

FATHER: If you don't mind me asking, what is your age?

YOUTH: She's five years older.

EPILEPTIC: I'll be good, Father!

FATHER: Father? Please, no need to call me that. Have you two been intimate?

YOUTH: I don't know, sir.

FATHER: Well if you don't know, I don't see who would.

YOUTH: She expects me to take care of her, sir.

FATHER: I see you've made up your mind, to throw your lives away.

YOUTH: Look who's talking, sir. (*To* **EPILEPTIC**.) Well, you can see for yourself, we have no money, nothing. You'll have to find what you're going eat.

FATHER: Young lady, it seems like you'd eat a lot.

YOUTH: Why must you demean people, sir? (*To* **EPILEPTIC**.) Our phone only rings in.

FATHER: It no longer does even that. You should be the father from now on. I'll go to the district offices and tell them I'm deceased.

YOUTH: Are you angry, sir?

FATHER: Why of course I am. Wouldn't you be? (*Sits down.*)

YOUTH: Just this one request, all right? We'll make dinner. (*End of mock politeness. To* **EPILEPTIC**.) Hey!

EPILEPTIC: Yes?

FATHER: Food go down easy? In this shitty situation?

YOUTH: Do you want ramen?

FATHER: You two go ahead. Be a cute little couple and eat by yourselves. (*Pours himself* soju.)

YOUTH: Do you want me to drink with you? (*Picking up* soju *bottle to pour himself a drink.*)

FATHER: Leave it. If you want it, go buy your own. On your own.

YOUTH: Do you want me to sing for you? (*Pause.*)

FATHER: Life passes quickly. (*Pause. To* **EPILEPTIC**.) You sing some? Pour me a drink, will you? (**EPILEPTIC** *pours a drink.*) You know T'ae Chin-a?

EPILEPTIC: Yes.

FATHER: T'ae Chin-a!

(**EPILEPTIC** *stands and sings T'ae Chin-a's "Yellow Handkerchief."*[17] **FATHER** *drinks while keeping beat with a spoon.* **YOUTH** *drinks straight from the bottle. A long time passes. Then, as he flips over the small table the drinks were on,*)

YOUTH: So what are you happy about? Like a fucking retard! You should be thankful that I didn't kill you already, that I let you leech off me. What kind of human being are you? Trying to be a father or something? Is that why you're acting like a big shot now?

FATHER: Sit!

YOUTH: Fuck that!

FATHER (*slaps* **YOUTH** *on the cheek*): You come to your senses? You're crazy, you little punk!

YOUTH: Yeah, I'm like this 'cause I'm fucking crazy. And you know what? I ain't getting any better. Actually. Actually, no, today it's all becoming clear.

FATHER: Acting up when you're sober is one thing. You pull this shit while you're plastered, after drinking like that, and you're a fucking dog, a dog. Once you're a dog, life's over right then and there, you pathetic shit.

YOUTH: Don't become a dog yourself, you sad excuse for a father. Fuck, I should just!

EPILEPTIC (*shaking*): Please don't fight.

YOUTH: Shut the fuck up, you bitch! You gonna act up like you did last time?

FATHER (*to* **YOUTH**): You make sure *you* don't act up, punk.

YOUTH (*to* **EPILEPTIC**): If you have a fit, I'm gonna fucking kill you.

FATHER: I'll kill you before that, you little shit.

EPILEPTIC (*shaking*): Don't swear!

YOUTH: Don't sweat it! Stop shaking, little bitch. Stop that comic act! Hey, Dad, she's a fucking comedienne, huh?

FATHER: You're worse. You're fucking hilarious, you son of a bitch!

EPILEPTIC: Don't fight! Don't curse! Can't you see me shaking? I'll collapse. Father, please stop! If I collapse, they don't know what to do with me. I messed my pants last time. It's usually only ten minutes, but sometimes I go for an hour.

YOUTH (*fed up with hearing this, he begins to blow on the bottleneck, "playing" the bottle*).

EPILEPTIC: That's embarrassing for everybody, right? I crap in my pants. Please stop! Don't swear! (**EPILEPTIC** *really starts shaking, her eyes become unfocused, and she starts to foam at the mouth.*)

YOUTH: All right, I'm sorry. It's my fault. Stop. Stop, OK?

(*The climax of the* **EPILEPTIC**'s *fit.* **EPILEPTIC** *falls over, and the fit continues. Music can be heard now. The lights go out. A pause. Lights come up again, and we're in the same room as before.* **YOUTH**, **FATHER**, **EPILEPTIC** *lie on the floor, asleep.* **YONGP'IL** *is in a corner of the room, speaking—*)

YONGP'IL: Fuck, I totally dozed through that shit. What kind of play has no humor? What's a play or a flick about anyway? Fun! Action and spectacle! Why, huh, why would people pay shitloads of money to watch all that? 'Cause life is stuffy and life is boring, ain't that why people go to the theater? You know, to see something new, right? Then why the hell is this play just weepy shit from beginning to end. Blabbering with no meaning. Title was good enough. *The Cherry Orchard*.[18] You know, then the plot should be clear, it's not like it's "Corn Fields"! . . . It's fucking *Cherry Orchard*, man, shouldn't they at least do it there once? You know, all romantically, take it all off. Shit, the audience wants it. Pea-brains got no crowd-pleasing mentality! Should've gone to the ball game or caught a flick. Motherfuckers! You think a field trip audience is shit? You think money for tickets grows on trees? (*Pause.*) You sleeping? Hae'il? Hae'il! (*No response.*) Shit, what kind of host invites a guest and does this? Sleeping all by themselves.

FATHER: I'm not sleeping.

YONGP'IL: You weren't sleeping?

FATHER: No, I was, but I woke up 'cause you were too loud.
YONGP'IL: Did you hear everything?
FATHER: Sorry for hearing everything. Have you been that loud for a long time?
YONGP'IL: I'm sorry. You were sleeping . . .
FATHER: If you're sorry, then go to sleep.
YONGP'IL: There's no room to lie down.
FATHER: You know how people are. People share even the smallest beans. We can make space.
YONGP'IL: Then, if you'll excuse me . . . (*He crawls under the edge of the blanket covering the three.*)
FATHER: Sorry we're not much of a host.
YONGP'IL: Sir? Do you have any spare pillows?
FATHER: Sorry, I'll have a heap of pillows for you next time.
YONGP'IL: Heh heh heh . . .
FATHER: What's so funny?
YONGP'IL: The way you said "heap." How's hippo doing? What is she up to during the day?
FATHER: She does things.
YONGP'IL: What does she do?
FATHER: Dunno. What is your father up to? Is he still raking in the money?
YONGP'IL: Well, money, yeah he's always bringing some in. But what is he gonna do with just money?
FATHER: Nothing wrong with having money. Your mother must be happy. He sends it in every month, every month, from Japan.
YONGP'IL: Japan?
FATHER: Did he go somewhere else already?
YONGP'IL: Of course. It's been a while. He's coming back to Korea the day after . . .
FATHER: Where is he?
YONGP'IL: We got a letter the day before. Says he's catching tuna. Somewhere in the South Pacific or something. Says that it's half water, half tuna down there. Says that some are bigger than a grown man.
FATHER: Yeah, right.
YONGP'IL: It's for real.
FATHER: D'you see it?
YONGP'IL: Do I have to see it to know? It's common knowledge. How can you have so little common knowledge, sir?
FATHER: Sorry I don't know anything. Why'd he quit the *pachinko*?

YONGP'IL: He said the police come down pretty hard. Every time the government changes, it happens. You know, Korea, Japan, that shit is all the same. Sir? Do you want to meet my father while you're at it? He's coming to Pusan or somewhere.

FATHER: Yeah, let's meet up. (*Pause.*) Let's sleep.

YONGP'IL: OK. Sweet dreams. (*He pulls the covers over himself, but immediately it's pulled away.* **YONGP'IL** *sits up.*)

FATHER: Do you like comics?

YONGP'IL: Nah. I did when I was little, though. I'm all grown up now. I'm not some kid, am I? Why?

FATHER: What do you mean by "why"? I still read comics once in a while. Makes time go quickly. Yongp'il! You ever think you're just like some character in the comics? (**FATHER**, *looking up at* **YONGP'IL**.) Let's sleep. (*Pause.*) Yongp'il! Wanna know some common knowledge?

YONGP'IL: Sure.

FATHER: Who gave birth to you?

YONGP'IL: My mom, of course!

FATHER: Wrong. It was your father. (*Pause.*) Go visit your father in prison once in a while.[19]

YONGP'IL (*becomes lost in thought*).

(*Lights out. As the lights come up again, the setting is a classroom. We can see only* **TEACHER**.)

TEACHER: At first the socialist revolutionaries, the Mensheviks, had the upper hand, but Bolshevik leaders were returning from exile one by one. In April, Lenin, and, in May, Trotsky, returned and supported the Bolsheviks. The temporary government, looking for a big victory, mounted a huge attack in June but instead ended up losing to the Germans. When reports of this great loss reached Moscow, the people of the Soviet Union became more restless. In July, the workers and farmers of St. Petersburg attempted to overthrow the government with the help of the Bolsheviks, but they were suppressed. Many Bolsheviks, including Trotsky, were arrested, and Lenin fled to Finland. Later, he returned to his motherland by hiding in the cargo of a mail truck.

(*All the stage lights come up and we can see* **YOUTH**.)

YOUTH: Teacher! I'm sorry. I was wrong. I'll be hit one hundred times.

TEACHER: Hey, you came!

YOUTH: I'm sorry, sir. I was wrong.

TEACHER: It's been a while.

YOUTH: Teacher! I'll come to school everyday, starting tomorrow.

TEACHER: Why?

YOUTH: I was wrong, sir. Please, hit me.

TEACHER: Hae'il!

YOUTH: I'm sorry for the way I acted, sir. (*Pause.*) I wrote the book review.

TEACHER: Did you read it all?

YOUTH: Yes, sir.

TEACHER: Hae'il! You've been kicked out. Completely. You don't have to put up with this pain anymore. Later when you grow up, you can study. Study, then. Take the GED exam. (*Pause.*) Are you all right?

YOUTH: Yes, sir

TEACHER: Ha! (*Pause.*) I quit. I want to study. We're leaving here, my wife and I. Going overseas.

YOUTH: Studying abroad?

TEACHER: Studying, whatever. Heard there're a lot of log cabins in New Zealand. Going to raise cows and play all day down there. Going to live without a care, like you.

YOUTH: Teacher . . .

TEACHER: This place stinks. I can tell, 'cause you said so.

YOUTH: Teacher!

TEACHER: Shut up. Don't fool around. Going to be a carpenter. Going to study to be a carpenter. (*Pause.*) Hey, beat it, you little punk. You make me sick.

YOUTH: When?

TEACHER: You don't need to know.

YOUTH: Zorba? But, what about Zorba, sir?

TEACHER: Crazy son of a bitch (*Pause. Then, referring to the book report.*) Read it.

YOUTH (*reads from his book report*): The man who chopped off his finger with an ax, because it got in the way of spinning. The man who collected women's hair and made it into a pillow. Of all the men yet to be separated from the umbilical chord to Mother Earth, his soul is the most open, his body exudes the most confidence, and he freely examines his own soul—Zorba!

TEACHER: Hae'il! If you want to, go walk through the reed fields whenever you like, without regard for the season. (*Pause.*) Tear that up. (*Pause.*) This is going to sound insolent and arrogant, but I give up on this country. History has no power. It wasn't supposed to be this way . . . (*Pause.*) Be happy. You should be. You're young.

(**TEACHER** *exits.* **YOUTH** *is left alone. The location changes to the massage parlor.* **MOTHER** *is massaging a patron. As* **FATHER** *comes in,* **MOTHER** *moves to one side.*)

MOTHER: I'm sorry. What can I do? I tried to save up some spending money . . . When are you leaving?
FATHER: To where?
MOTHER: Japan.
FATHER: I'm not going anymore.
MOTHER: Because of money?
FATHER: No. That was all a lie. I made it all up. (*Pause.*) Actually, I'm going off to the far seas. To catch tuna.
MOTHER: Tuna?
FATHER: They say some place down in the South Pacific is filled with it. Say it's half water, half tuna down there. Say that some are bigger than a grown man.
MOTHER: Liar. Did you ever see it yourself?
FATHER: Do I have see it to know? It's common knowledge. How can you have so little common knowledge? (*Pause.*) The family's grown, at home.
MOTHER: Your family?
FATHER: No, Hae'il's family. And we might get one more, too.
MOTHER: Then why do you seem so down? You grew old.
FATHER: And you're the same as ever. Hae'il's girl looks really funny. She's mild mannered, and she's healthy, too.
MOTHER: That's good.
FATHER: Yeah, very good. But she's sick.
MOTHER: Where?
FATHER: Just, you know, a little. Sometimes. Sometimes, only once in a long while. It's OK.
MOTHER: Remember how we went to the Han River when Hae'il entered middle school?
FATHER: Yeah, we did.
MOTHER: We took a cab, and at the riverside park we rode that three-sided or four-sided, or whatever-sided cruise boat. We played all day. And you had a box of *soju* in your pocket, and we drank, even on the boat, through a straw, and the guide would tell us which bridge we were under, and it started to rain. It rained until we went home . . . (*Pause.*) I'll go in now.
FATHER: Should I wait for you outside?
MOTHER: Just leave. (*Takes money from her pocket.*) Would fifty thousand wŏn be enough?[20]
FATHER: But I have money . . . (*Takes the money.*) Come by home some time. We stuck stars on the ceiling. Glow-in-the-dark stars! Come see the baby. It'll be pretty. (*Pause.*) Ah! You can't see.
MOTHER: Still, I'd like to see it, just once.

FATHER (*pause*): When the three of us lie down, the room is so crowded. It's so warm. It feels just like lying in a coffin. (*Laughs. Pause.*) I'll go now. Next time I'll call before.
(*The two stand facing each other. Music flows on while the lights go out.*)

Curtain

Notes

1. Even though the play's action takes place in the present day, the actual chronological time in the play is fluid. The time of day is generally not important. The setting is simple and stark, perhaps not much more than a bare platform to which are added the minimal, necessary props that are taken away when no longer needed.
2. *Unshili* is a popular television drama.
3. A ten-ounce bottle of *soju* costs about $1.50; Jinro is a brand that costs a bit more.
4. There are two films to which the Teacher may be referring. One is the 1943 pro-Japanese version by Bu Wangcang, and the other, more likely, one is the 1997 award-winning version by Yapian Zhangheng.
5. The Korean script has the English word *seven* in the sequence of numbers: *net, tasŏt, yŏsŏt,* seven, *yŏdŏl* . . .
6. Pak Chin-yŏng (Park Jin-young) is a singer/entertainer popular with South Korea's young set.
7. As in American slang, the seemingly derogatory term used by the Youth has no negative connotation here.
8. It is not clear which of at least two mountains named Kŭmgang (Diamond Mountain) is the subject here. The more likely mountain is located in the far southeastern corner of North Korea, in some of the most beautiful scenery on the entire Korean Peninsula. Depending on the political climate, South Koreans may travel to limited areas in North Korea, but generally as part of an expensive group package tour.
9. The original dialogue uses "Come on!" in Koreanized English.
10. Awareness of social levels is a central element in Korean culture and language. The Girl seems particularly aware of distinctions between those "above" and those "below," as we shall see later when the Girl castigates the Epileptic for using familiar language when speaking to Youth and her.
11. The American fast-food chain Popeye's is popular in Korea. HongDae U is Hongik University, in an area of Seoul known for its artists and popular bars.
12. It is not clear whether Yongp'il is referring to a North Korean or a South Korean spy.
13. The Korean version of karaoke.

14. The Epileptic addressed the Girl in terms that were too familiar for the Girl's taste.
15. In Korean productions, the actors were not nude but appeared in underwear.
16. Koreans have a national identity card and also must register with their local district offices. The head of each household is listed in the rolls, and all information is updated as the family's composition changes. The Father is being sarcastic here, as he has no intention of relinquishing his place as head of the household.
17. T'ae Chin-a (Tae Jin-a) is a crooner in his fifties, a singer in the older, "big-band" style enjoyed by older Korean audiences, especially women.
18. Anton Chekhov's plays are often translated and performed in Korea.
19. For a brief moment, Father sees the reality of Yongp'il's life—and his own.
20. Fifty thousand wŏn is about $50.

CH'OE SŬNGHŬI (CH'OE SŬNGHŬI)

PAE SAMSHIK

Born in 1970 in Chŏnju City, North Chŏlla Province, Pae graduated from Seoul National University, where he majored in humanities and then studied playwriting under Pak Choyŏl and Yi Kangbaek at the Korean National University of Arts. Considered to be one of Korea's most promising young playwrights, Pae gained recognition in 1999 for his first play, *November* (*11 wŏl*). Since then, he has written two or three plays a year, among them a musical, *Jungle Story* (*Chŏnggŭl iyagi*, 2004), *The Life of Sir Chu* (*Chu-kong haengjang*, 2006), and *Inching Toward Yŏlha* (*Yŏlha ilgi manbo*, 2007), for which he received a Daesan Literary Award. He also worked closely with the Mich'u Theater Company, famous for its annual production of *madangnori*, a modernized version of Korean folk theater, and has written *madangnori* scripts: *The Story of Three Kingdoms* (*Samkukchi*, 2004), *Wealthy Man, Mr. Hwang* (*Map'o Hwang puja*, 2005), *Mr. Byŏn, a Stud* (*Byŏn kangsoe*, 2006), and *Mrs. Pak, Who Wears the Pants* (*K'waegŏl Pakssi*, 2007).

Pae is known for his carefully structured plots. He is a master craftsman of Korean language and its dialects, even in his adaptations of foreign plays, among them Fukuda Yoshiyuki's *A Fairy in the Wall* (2005), Noda Hideki's *Red Demon* (2005), and Pedro Calderón de la Barca's *Life Is a Dream* (2004). Pae's adaptation of the Chinese novel by Yu Hua, *Chronicle of a Blood Merchant* (2003), was selected as one of the three best plays of the year in 2003 by the Korean Association of Theater Critics.

Ch'oe Sŭnghŭi, known as Sai Shōki during the Japanese colonial era, was an internationally recognized dancer who went to North Korea before the Korean War. For that reason, for decades it was illegal for South Koreans to discuss her career publicly, let alone stage a play about her. The version of the play presented here was written in 2004 but has yet to be staged in Korea. A musical version of *Ch'oe Sŭnghŭi*, directed by Son Chinch'aek and performed by the Mich'u Theater Company, premiered at the Seoul Arts Center in September 2003.

CH'OE SŬNGHŬI
(CH'OE SŬNGHŬI)

TRANSLATED BY ALYSSA KIM

CHARACTERS

CH'OE SŬNGHŬI
AN MAK, Ch'oe Sŭnghŭi's husband
AN SŬNGHŬI, daughter of Ch'oe Sŭnghŭi and An Mak
CHORUS (five members)
PIANO PLAYER

(*Empty stage.*[1] *A piano is at one corner of the stage.* PIANIST *enters the stage holding some music scores and sits down at the piano. He plays a couple of exercises on the piano for practice. The* CHORUS *enters. Dressed in leotards and tights, they run around the stage with cleaning equipment, cleaning the floor and placing chairs on the stage. Then,* CHORUS 1 *and* CHORUS 2 *enter downstage and cross the stage, speaking.*)

CHORUS 1 (*entering the stage*): Why? Don't ask me such a question. Anyhow, there were red shoes in front of the girl. Shining, shimmering red shoes. The girl put on the shoes. The shoes began to dance. Lalalala talalala . . .
(CHORUS 1 *and* 2 *clean the floor as they dance across the stage.* CHORUS 3, 4, *and* 5 *do the same from the opposite direction, and the piano music takes on the rhythm of a waltz.*)

CHORUS 3: . . . talalalalala lala . . . The red shoes danced. Day and night, lalalala lalala, without stopping. The red shoes took away the girl. Across a plain and a river, over the mountains, and beyond the sea, lalalala talalala . . . Dancing and dancing, they went to the end of the world.

CHORUS 4: And?

CHORUS 3: And? They still must be dancing. The red shoes will never stop.
CHORUS 5: She must be worn out by now.
CHORUS 4: She could just take them off.
CHORUS 3: She can't.
CHORUS 4: Why not?
CHORUS 3: I told you not to ask me such a question! That's just the way it is with the red shoes. Once you put them on, you can't take them off. Talalalala lalalala . . .

(CHORUS *dances as they clean the floor, and each takes a chair and sits. The sound of the waltz music slowly fades. A light shines on two women upstage. The woman in her mid-fifties is* CH'OE SŬNGHŬI, *and the other woman in her mid-thirties is* AN SŬNGHŬI. *Wearing a traditional Korean dress,*[2] CH'OE SŬNGHŬI *is holding a suitcase. Also holding a suitcase,* AN SŬNGHŬI *is dressed in Western-style clothes. They look as if they have just returned from a trip or are just about to go on a trip. Silence.*)

AN SŬNGHŬI: Flowers are blooming.
CH'OE SŬNGHŬI: They are.
AN SŬNGHŬI: I still can't understand it.
CH'OE SŬNGHŬI: Our time has passed.
AN SŬNGHŬI: Some questions linger on. Even after we're gone. They're still left behind.
CH'OE SŬNGHŬI: . . .
AN SŬNGHŬI: Did you really believe it was possible?
CH'OE SŬNGHŬI: The tree blossoms are withering away.
AN SŬNGHŬI: Did you think it was possible to escape from this place?
CH'OE SŬNGHŬI: Like that day.
AN SŬNGHŬI: I still can't tell.
CH'OE SŬNGHŬI: Are the blossoms trying to escape from the tree?
AN SŬNGHŬI: That day, just what was in your heart?
CH'OE SŬNGHŬI: They must be dancing in place of the tree. In that short moment of being airborne between the branches and the ground, they dance their last dance.
AN SŬNGHŬI: I still can't understand it.
CH'OE SŬNGHŬI: It's too bright.
AN SŬNGHŬI: I still can't forgive you, Mother.
CH'OE SŬNGHŬI: I can't forgive myself, either. I can't forgive myself for being this far away from those beautiful things. But my dear Sŭnghŭi, our time has passed.
AN SŬNGHŬI: Mother.

CH'OE SŬNGHŬI: It has passed.
(*Piano music. The light on* CH'OE SŬNGHŬI *and* AN SŬNGHŬI *fades.* AN MAK *stands in the middle of the* CHORUS. *The* CHORUS *and* AN MAK *wear long coats and felt top hats. With the downlight on* AN MAK, *the* CHORUS *looks like his silhouettes.*)

AN MAK: One summer night in 1957, I was walking along the bank of Taedong River,[3] coming home from a Cultural Committee conference. In the twilight, cicadas sounded like air-raid sirens.[4] Just then, across the river, between the pine trees, I saw a light go on at Ch'oe Sŭnghŭi's dance studio. Doong . . . doong, I could hear the carefree sound of a drum.

CHORUS 1 (*speaks as* AN MAK): It had been four years since the war ended. Along the river, places here and there reveal their scarlet skin from having been bombed earlier. The river below me quietly flows by. A bombshell is lodged in the river.

AN MAK: One night at the end of summer, I gazed at the corroding red bombshell in the lukewarm river as if I were dreaming. The war and the roads we traveled were like a dream.

CHORUS 2 (*speaks as* AN MAK): The war has ended. But a new war has just begun, one muted and clandestine. I have no means whatsoever to fight in this war. I can neither fend off my enemy nor make an escape. Because my enemy is my own past.

CHORUS 3 (*speaks as* AN MAK): The days gone by are raining down on me like a bombardment.

AN MAK: I was gazing at the corroding red bombshell in the lukewarm river.

CHORUS 4 (*speaks as* AN MAK): How long would I be able to avoid them?

AN MAK: I was gazing at the corroding red bombshell.

CHORUS 5 (*speaks as* AN MAK): A school of small fish swim through the bombshell. The hard iron shell gave itself up to the soft current, and now it's at peace.

AN MAK: Night falls. I am walking up the hill.

CHORUS 1: I walk up the steps between the pine trees, past the front yard, and stand in front of the door.

CHORUS 2: I am just about to ring the bell, but I hesitate for a moment.
(*The sound of door opening.* AN SŬNGHŬI *comes out opening the front door.* CH'OE SŬNGHŬI *is not seen.*)

AN SŬNGHŬI: Father.

AN MAK: It's me, Sŭnghŭi.

AN SŬNGHŬI: Why are you standing there? Come in.

(AN MAK *turns to face the river below. Wind blows.* AN SŬNGHŬI *walks over to her father and stands next to him. The* CHORUS *does not exit but remains onstage as active spectators or invisible observers upstage.*)

AN MAK: The breeze is cooler tonight.

AN SŬNGHŬI: Summer is almost over.

AN MAK: Is it?

AN SŬNGHŬI: Yes.

AN MAK: So, how was Moscow?

AN SŬNGHŬI: It was good.

AN MAK: I see.

AN SŬNGHŬI: They have white nights right now.[5]

AN MAK: I see. I guess it must be that time of the year.

AN SŬNGHŬI: I couldn't sleep at all.

AN MAK: Did you see your old friends?

AN SŬNGHŬI: Yes.

AN MAK: I heard that they liked your Dance of Gypsies the most, is that right?

AN SŬNGHŬI: Yes.

AN MAK: I would love to have seen it.

AN SŬNGHŬI: But you don't like that dance. You said, "Why does it have be about gypsies, of all things? It seems too gloomy and smells of decadence."

AN MAK: Did I?

AN SŬNGHŬI: Yes.

AN MAK: . . . I must have been afraid that you might really become a gypsy and one day just pack up and leave with a circus.

AN SŬNGHŬI (*laughs*): So, it's true that you don't like that dance. (*They both laugh.*)

AN MAK: Did you already start practicing today? You still must be tired from your traveling.

AN SŬNGHŬI: I have to go on tour in Eastern Europe this coming September.

AN MAK: You're too thin.

AN SŬNGHŬI: But I still like being on tour. This place here doesn't feel like home . . .

(*While looking at his daughter,* AN MAK *becomes lost for words. He has a sudden muscle spasm in his right cheek. He hides it by covering the cheek with his hand.*)

AN SŬNGHŬI: Dad?

AN MAK: I'm all right. It has been giving me trouble lately. It must be lonely for the bombshell fragment that used to be there.

AN SŬNGHŬI: Let's go in, Dad.

AN MAK: Sŭnghŭi . . .
AN SŬNGHŬI: Yes?
AN MAK: You're twenty-six years old now?
AN SŬNGHŬI: Yes.
AN MAK: Twenty-six . . . You're young.
AN SŬNGHŬI: Dad, that's nothing new. (*Pause.*)
AN MAK: Sŭnghŭi?
AN SŬNGHŬI: Yes?
AN MAK: This is your house. You're different from me or your mother. Your place is here. This is your house.
AN SŬNGHŬI: . . . Dad.
AN MAK: Let's go in.
(AN MAK *and* AN SŬNGHŬI *go into the house. The light changes.* CH'OE SŬNGHŬI *enters looking quite stiff. Taken aback,* AN MAK *looks at* AN SŬNGHŬI.)
AN SŬNGHŬI: We heard.
AN MAK: Ah, I see . . . So, that's what happened.
CH'OE SŬNGHŬI: So, that's what happened!? What did happen exactly?
AN MAK: I know you wanted to go, but you should forget about it this time. Now is not a good time. After all, Japan is so close that if you were to tip over, it would be right under your nose. You should be able to go anytime you want. When things improve . . .
CH'OE SŬNGHŬI: I asked you to tell me exactly happened.
AN SŬNGHŬI: Mother.
CH'OE SŬNGHŬI: Sŭnghŭi, you stay out of it. (AN SŬNGHŬI *walks away from her parents.*)
AN MAK: Yes. The Cultural Affairs Committee met to discuss permitting you to perform in Japan. After a long, intense debate, we couldn't reach a consensus, so we had to vote. And as you've already been told, permission was denied.
CH'OE SŬNGHŬI: I just can not understand those people. I'm a dancer! And there are people who would like to see my dance. I should be able to go anywhere there are people who want to see my dance. I must!!
AN MAK: Even if we were to approve your visit, the Japanese government wouldn't give you permission to enter Japan. They have prohibited any ship or anybody from entering their country from North Korea.
CH'OE SŬNGHŬI: A Japanese committee is inviting my dance company to Japan. What about their petition?
AN MAK: That's all that they can do.
CH'OE SŬNGHŬI: Which is exactly why you have to give me permission! That would give them more support.

AN MAK: Listen, this problem is not that simple.

CH'OE SŬNGHŬI: What's so complicated about it?

AN MAK: Too many political agendas are mixed up in this problem. There is the issue of repatriating Korean Japanese, and there are other problems as well. This isn't only about you. During the liberation war,[6] Japan was our enemy. It still is.

CH'OE SŬNGHŬI: What's that got to do with my dance? Even during the Pacific War, I danced in the United States. In New York, the center of our enemy nation.

AN MAK: Now is not then.

CH'OE SŬNGHŬI: That's true. Then, An Mak, you were by my side. Are you still? (*Pause.*)

AN MAK: Let's just drop it. It's all over.

CH'OE SŬNGHŬI: Just what did you do? You are the vice head of the Committee for Cultural Affairs. but you have no power to make this work? Tell me, just who was against this, and why?

AN MAK: . . . People who opposed the tour were the ones who care about you. The people who care about the people's dancer of the Democratic Republic of North Korea.

CH'OE SŬNGHŬI: Does that include you, too?

AN MAK: Yes.

CH'OE SŬNGHŬI: How could you?

AN MAK: I'm sorry. But I had to.

CH'OE SŬNGHŬI: I don't know about others, but I thought you would have approved it.

AN MAK: Some people did. But do you think that they did that for your sake?

CH'OE SŬNGHŬI: You were against granting permission because of me?

AN MAK: It was a game . . . a trap. I couldn't put my foot in that trap. You must know it, too. How the party has been watching you and me. They aren't stupid. They know very well what your visit to Japan would mean.

CH'OE SŬNGHŬI: It's true. I wasn't going to come back.

AN MAK: Let me ask you one more time. Do you have to do this?

CH'OE SŬNGHŬI: Yes, I have to.

AN MAK: Can't you do it here?

CH'OE SŬNGHŬI: No, not here.

AN MAK: But what about Sŭnghŭi? Did you think about our Sŭnghŭi?

CH'OE SŬNGHŬI: For her, too. It's also for the dances that she will dance.

AN MAK: She's not like us.

CH'OE SŬNGHŬI: How is she different? What do you know about our Sŭnghŭi?

AN SŬNGHŬI (*from offstage*): Mom, what do *you* know about me?
AN MAK: Her roots are here. She can be free here.
CH'OE SŬNGHŬI: Do you really think that's true?
AN MAK: . . . She doesn't have a past like we do.
CH'OE SŬNGHŬI: We are her past and her roots.
AN MAK: . . . She is young. She should be able to . . .
CH'OE SŬNGHŬI: Still, she won't be able to get away from it.
AN SŬNGHŬI (*from offstage*): Yes. That's true.
AN MAK: But no matter where we go . . .
CH'OE SŬNGHŬI: It would be better than here. I want to dance my dance. What good is it to have one's chest full of medals? I am still one of the soldiers who march in a line. Why? Are you going to lecture me again about the party, the people, the loyalty to the republic, and duty and responsibilities?
AN MAK: . . . No matter what, we will never be free of them. The freedom you dream of does not exist in this world.
CH'OE SŬNGHŬI: You must think I'm one of the girls with her head in a book dreaming of some fairyland. You were the one who said it. "Freedom can be obtained only by struggle." So we have to struggle. What I want to do is, at least, go to a place where I can fight against the things that stand in my way. Here, I can't even do that. I am being bred like a pig. My dance will be buried in my bloated fat. Then I'll be dragged to a slaughter house to be butchered. (*Pause.*)
AN MAK: In order to fight back, we have to survive. You should have been more careful. You made too many enemies. You must realize what a precarious situation we're in.
CH'OE SŬNGHŬI: How much more! How much more do I have to suck up to them?
AN MAK: Wait just a little longer. How many times have I told you this is not a good time? But in spite of everything, you sent a letter to Mr. Ishii,[7] making things more difficult. You threw your cards down way too early, and everybody read them. This was a game we couldn't win! I had to salvage the situation so at least we won't lose everything.
CH'OE SŬNGHŬI: How long? How long do I have wait? I, I . . . I'm getting older. My body, my body is getting older. Dances embedded in this body are slipping away one by one. I should wait?! I don't have time to wait! If I wait, will things improve? I know very well how things have been developing. If not now, we won't have another chance. You know it as well as I do. (*Pause.*)
AN MAK: You know, not everything is bad news. I have good news, too.

CH'OE SŬNGHŬI: What is it?

AN MAK: You will be able to see Mr. Ishii . . . soon.

CH'OE SŬNGHŬI: Mr. Ishii? How? You said I won't be able to go to Japan.

AN MAK: Since you can't go, he'll come here.

CH'OE SŬNGHŬI: Mr. Ishii, in P'yŏngyang?

AN MAK: Yes. Mr. and Mrs. Ishii will be here in P'yŏngyang on September 9, to celebrate the ninth anniversary of the republic. They were very happy to hear the news. They can't wait to see you. I know you're scheduled to leave for your Eastern European tour, but you could postpone that in order to see them before you leave.

CH'OE SŬNGHŬI: I will leave according to my own schedule.

AN MAK: What?

CH'OE SŬNGHŬI: If I were to see Mr. Ishii here in P'yŏngyang, then I'd no longer have a reason to visit Japan, would I?

AN MAK: That's not it.

CH'OE SŬNGHŬI: You're trying to rob me of the last card I have left.

AN MAK: I made this difficult arrangement possible only for you.

CH'OE SŬNGHŬI: Thank you, but no thank you. I can't see Mr. Ishii—not here in P'yŏngyang.

AN MAK: It wasn't easy to get him invited. He will be heartbroken not to see you after making the difficult trip here.

CH'OE SŬNGHŬI: I want to see him, too. But not here! I must go to Japan to see him. If you won't join me, I will go by myself.

AN SŬNGHŬI (*from offstage*): Mom, did you really believe that that would be possible?

AN MAK: I said just wait a little longer.

CH'OE SŬNGHŬI: An Mak, how did you get so weak? What happened to the courageous and decisive man who brought me here on a fishing boat from Inchŏn? When everybody was telling me to become a housewife, you were the one who told me to join you in Tōkyō. Do you remember? That winter? Every day that winter, you went to the train station to sweep snow. Our family of four lived on that pittance. Do you remember? One day you went to your friend's house and took his piano keys and sold them at a pawn shop. Without giving it a thought to what you did, you reprimanded me at the top of your voice for not practicing enough when you came back home. I practiced at the studio all night without any heater, but I didn't feel tired. Because we had a dream. I was happy because we were fighting together.

AN MAK: . . .

CH'OE SŬNGHŬI: An Mak... Why did you bring me here? Why did you bring me here...⁸

(*The sonorous sound of piano. The light on* AN MAK *dims, and simultaneously the light on* AN SŬNGHŬI *brightens. Only a silhouette of* AN MAK *is visible.*)

AN SŬNGHŬI: It was a late summer night in 1957. On that day, when the Committee for Cultural Affairs denied Ch'oe Sŭnghŭi's dance company permission to perform in Japan, my mother was asking, "Why did you bring me here?" Dad couldn't say a word, but he stood there for a long time. He turned his head to hide the spasm in his right cheek. With her words, it was as if my mother put a stake into his heart. To my dad, who sacrificed everything for her.

CH'OE SŬNGHŬI: I just wanted to help him decide.

AN SŬNGHŬI: You were forcing him.

CH'OE SŬNGHŬI: You can call it whatever you want. But in the end, I was right. The chance to go to Japan was the only one we had. But we couldn't take it.

AN SŬNGHŬI: A chance? It was only chaos that came afterward—all because of you. It was a crisis that you brought about. Everything had been peaceful. Everything was going along as we wanted it to.

CH'OE SŬNGHŬI: Only on the surface. I couldn't stand that peace. Because it was fake. I was staring into the political storm that would engulf us.

AN SŬNGHŬI: Yes. You knew it. You knew what was happening to Dad at the time. Some time ago, his friends and the people around him started to disappear one by one.

CH'OE SŬNGHŬI: Your father filled those empty places one step at a time and was being promoted. He knew well what lay ahead at the end of those steps.

AN SŬNGHŬI: For whom do you think he climbed those steps?

CH'OE SŬNGHŬI: That was not what I wanted. In that year of liberation when your father came to me in Beijing and said he was going to Yŏnan,⁹ I tried to talk him out of it. But he wouldn't listen. He shouldn't have gone to Yŏnan. He shouldn't have gone down the path of politics.

AN SŬNGHŬI: If he didn't, do you think you could have continued to dance?

CH'OE SŬNGHŬI: Hungry, poor, and desperate, I would have danced my dances.

AN SŬNGHŬI: People who are truly hungry, poor, and desperate wouldn't be able to say that. Mother, do you know how I lived after the day you left? I became a farm worker. They told me to work shoulder to shoulder with farmers, and they told me to dance with muscles built from productive labor. And that's what happened. I got muscles from my labor. I was reborn with hard and knotted muscles! And the dances left me forever. Sometimes the cultural affairs people would come to our farm, and they would sing and dance in front of us. Do you know what I thought about while looking at them? My dance? Don't make me laugh. If only I could follow their movements. But I couldn't even do that because my hand had been cut off by a rice cutter! My dance? You want to talk about my dance? That's rich. And the person who made it possible for you to say something that rich was my father!

CH'OE SŬNGHŬI: That's cruel.

AN SŬNGHŬI: Yes. Reality is cruel. And what you called "my dance" was not able to escape from it, either.

CH'OE SŬNGHŬI: You could try to get away from it, but if you don't even try, it is not a dance.

AN SŬNGHŬI: You can't dance in midair. You need ground for your feet.

CH'OE SŬNGHŬI: We kick it to lift off.

AN SŬNGHŬI: In the end, we have no choice but to come back down.

(*Pause.*)

CH'OE SŬNGHŬI: I had hoped that your father wouldn't go to the end of those steps. I was trying to help your father, you, and myself.

AN SŬNGHŬI: That was not it. You were just lost in midair. You had no idea what was going on under you. Dad had to climb those steps because you were like that, and you were the one who pushed him over when he got to the end of those steps. And you left me alone in that darkness.

(*Pause. The light on* **CH'OE SŬNGHŬI** *dims.*)

AN SŬNGHŬI: On that night in 1957, Dad stood there without a word. With his head turned to hide the spasm in his right cheek, the ripples of a bombshell left behind in his cheek by an American bomber.

(*The sound of a distant explosion is heard. The* **CHORUS**, *in the costumes of* **SOLDIERS**, *slowly approaches* **AN SŬNGHŬI**.)

CHORUS 1: The same is left behind in my leg.

AN SŬNGHŬI: When the Korean War broke out in June 1950, we were performing in Moscow.

CHORUS 2: A sharp pain shoots through every part of my leg.

AN SŬNGHŬI: When I came back to P'yŏngyang, I became a member of an entertainment troop and headed to Kwangju and then Mokp'o.

CHORUS 3: The war will end soon.

AN SŬNGHŬI: The south is famous for its food. And the beach is nice for a swim.

CHORUS 4: On September 15, 1950, the Americans landed at Inchŏn.

CHORUS 5: We were left behind enemy lines.

CHORUS 1: In September 1950, the *Proletarian* newspaper reported that An Sŭnghŭi, a member of the third entertainment unit of the People's Democratic Republic of North Korea, was killed in action.

CHORUS 2: I was following a trail back to the north somewhere on Mount Taebaek.[10]

(*Two* **CHORUS** *members help the feverish* **AN SŬNGHŬI**, *who limps and moans. The sound of explosions gets gradually louder, and when it reaches its loudest, it suddenly stops. Silence.*)

CHORUS 1: As I wander around the dark hillside with a wounded leg, I ask myself a question.

AN SŬNGHŬI: Why did you bring me here?

CHORUS 2: Suffering from malaria and high fever, I ask myself a question.

AN SŬNGHŬI: Why did you bring me here?

CHORUS 1: Comrade An Sŭnghŭi, wake up. You mustn't fall asleep here.

AN SŬNGHŬI: Leave me alone. Just let me rest.

(*The sound of loud gunshots. The* **CHORUS** *falls.* **AN SŬNGHŬI** *collapses, looks down at the corpses, and looks up to the sky.*)

AN SŬNGHŬI: Ah, there are so many stars in the sky.

(*The* **CHORUS** *slowly stands and then sits next to* **AN SŬNGHŬI**. *They look up at the sky.*)

CHORUS 3: Because it's fall now. Because we're in the midst of mountains.

CHORUS 4: I look up to the night sky in the midst of these corpses.

CHORUS 5: Why is it so cold when I feel so hot?

CHORUS 1 (**AN SŬNGHŬI** *feels the face of* **CHORUS 1**): Your body is freezing to my touch, but I guess you can't feel any of it.

CHORUS 2: This cold body lying next to me was my comrade who, only a moment ago, was singing and dancing with so much life.

CHORUS 3: I stand face to face with death. That cold, shapeless face.

CHORUS 4: Soon you will become one, too.

CHORUS 5: Soon you will be at peace.

CHORUS 1: I look up to the night sky.

AN SŬNGHŬI: Ah, there's a falling star. (*The light comes up on* **CH'OE SŬNGHŬI** *and* **AN MAK**.)

CH'OE SŬNGHŬI: No. Our Sŭnghŭi is not dead.

AN SŬNGHŬI: It fell too fast. I couldn't even make a wish.

CH'OE SŬNGHŬI: Our Sŭnghŭi is not dead.

AN SŬNGHŬI: Mom.

CH'OE SŬNGHŬI: Our Sŭnghŭi is not dead.

AN SŬNGHŬI: You said it will be over soon, soon.

CH'OE SŬNGHŬI: Stand up, Sŭnghŭi.
AN SŬNGHŬI: You left me alone.
CH'OE SŬNGHŬI: Now!
AN SŬNGHŬI: You left me alone, and again where did you go?
CH'OE SŬNGHŬI: Now!
CHORUS 2: Comrade An! Comrade An! (AN SŬNGHŬI *stands with the help of the* CHORUS.)
AN SŬNGHŬI: Ah, there were so many stars in the sky.
CHORUS 1: Like bullets.
CHORUS 2: Stars like scattered rice.
AN SŬNGHŬI: Somebody put a ladder between those stars. I don't know how to read their signals.
CHORUS 3: Without knowing where I was headed, I walk in the mountains without any trails.
CHORUS 4: Something hotter than malaria is making me walk.
CHORUS 5: Passing P'yŏngyang desolated from bombardment.
CHORUS 1: Headed to Shinuiju.[11]
CHORUS 2: I walk and walk again.
CHORUS 3: Mother. If my mother won't come for me, I'll go to her.
CHORUS 4: Mom was in Beijing.

(*The sound of a whistle is followed by the sound of train entering a platform. One* CHORUS *member stands in front of* AN SŬNGHŬI *with a file in her or his hands.*)

SOLDIER (*searches through the file*): You're not on the list. Who did you say you were?
AN SŬNGHŬI (*feeling very faint*): An Sŭnghŭi, a member of the third entertainment unit of the People's Democratic Republic of North Korea.
SOLDIER: It's not here. Did you fall behind?
AN SŬNGHŬI: Yes.
SOLDIER: Report to headquarters and return to your station.
AN SŬNGHŬI: I have to go to Beijing.
SOLDIER: I told you, your name isn't here. Not everyone can ride on this train.
AN SŬNGHŬI: My name is An Sŭnghŭi.
SOLDIER: So?
AN SŬNGHŬI: . . . I'm An Sŭnghŭi, the daughter of Ch'oe Sŭnghŭi, committee head of the Association of Comrade Dancers and an honored member of the Communist Party of the People's Democratic Republic of North Korea!

(AN SŬNGHŬI *faints. The* SOLDIER *hurries to help her. At the same time, the sound of a departing train is heard. It fades away. In the darkness, the sound of train gets louder, and when it dies down, a light piano melody is heard. The lights go up.* CH'OE SŬNGHŬI *and* AN SŬNGHŬI *are on the stage. The* CHORUS *is dancing behind* CH'OE SŬNGHŬI. AN MAK *stands a little apart from them.*)

AN SŬNGHŬI: I waited for my mother at our house in Beijing. Until late into the night.

CH'OE SŬNGHŬI: I told you already. I had a class.

AN SŬNGHŬI: In the alley, Chinese men in their underwear were gawking and laughing at me.

CH'OE SŬNGHŬI: Why didn't you come directly to the studio?

AN SŬNGHŬI: Bastards.

CH'OE SŬNGHŬI: I knew you'd come back alive.

AN SŬNGHŬI: Yes, Mother. I did come back.

CH'OE SŬNGHŬI: I knew.

AN SŬNGHŬI: Mother hugged me and shed tears. Words that felt like they would explode in my heart became all tangled up and muddled.

CH'OE SŬNGHŬI: You were quiet. I kept asking you questions, but all you said was, "It was a close call. But I'm OK now." That was all.

AN SŬNGHŬI: It wasn't a pleasant trip to talk about.

CH'OE SŬNGHŬI: Your face had a veiled look.

AN SŬNGHŬI: You were exactly the same. You taught students and performed on stage. Well, as you said, you knew.

CH'OE SŬNGHŬI: Every night I had a dream about you. I worried so much because of you. But what could I have changed? If I hadn't worked or danced, I would have gone insane.

AN SŬNGHŬI: Which is why you also had an affair.

CH'OE SŬNGHŬI: Sŭnghŭi . . .

AN SŬNGHŬI: The love that was conceived in wartime shellings. Falling in love with an Indian dancer—that transcends nationality or race. She abandoned everything that tied her down and headed toward a new world of possibilities where her world of art will blossom once again. Very romantic. Wonderful. You're really something.

CH'OE SŬNGHŬI: Sneer all you want. How could you possibly understand what's in my heart?

AN SŬNGHŬI: Do *you* understand? (*Pause.*) How could you? Because you knew you could enjoy a little romance while I was at death's door. Because you knew I would come back, you went to Shanghai with that black Indian dancer? To be on a ship on a quest for your ideals?

CH'OE SŬNGHŬI: Shut up.

AN SŬNGHŬI: OK. Let's just say that I died. But how about Father? How could you even think about abandoning him? He sacrificed his entire life for you. Just what are we in your life?

CH'OE SŬNGHŬI: . . . All right. That's me. I still miss it. That body. Yes. This is me. I liked that body of his. What are you going to do about it? Yes. I liked his black eyes. In his eyes, there was no war. No ethics, no responsibilities. There was no right or wrong. There was nothing but the sun from a southern nation. My heart started to beat. In front of him, I was a woman. Even after I turned forty, I was a woman. A fire started inside me. With no qualms or fear of losing face, I would blush. I wanted to dance. Dances just came out of me . . . Yes. That was me, too. Inside me, there was someone that I didn't even know about. I followed her. I wanted to go and see the end with her. What are you going to do about it?

AN SŬNGHŬI: I can't forgive you.

CH'OE SŬNGHŬI: Forgive!? Who is going to forgive whom? Forgive what? The only person who can forgive me is me. Only my dance can be the judge of my life.

AN SŬNGHŬI: Mother.

CH'OE SŬNGHŬI: Go ahead, throw stones to your heart's content. Spit at me and laugh!

AN SŬNGHŬI: It's useless. If I threw a stone at you, you would already be gone.

(*The sound of waves.* **AN SŬNGHŬI** *disappears into the darkness.* **CH'OE SŬNGHŬI** *is left alone. The sound of waves becomes loud and violent. The* **CHORUS** *stands on the stage holding a newspaper.*)

CHORUS: Sai Shōki.

CH'OE SŬNGHŬI: Go ahead, come on! Throw stones at me all you want.

CHORUS: Jap collaborator.

CH'OE SŬNGHŬI: Spit at me and laugh at me!

CHORUS: Traitor.

CH'OE SŬNGHŬI: You won't be able to hit my dance with your stones.

CHORUS: Traitor! Turncoat!

CH'OE SŬNGHŬI: You won't be able to smear my dance.

CHORUS: Opportunist! Whore!

CH'OE SŬNGHŬI: Go ahead. Where do you feel the itch? Nation? Country? Ethics? Morality? Is that all? Is that all? Are they the scabs that are bothering you? OK. I will lick them for you. I will lick them as much as you want. Come. You have been my guests for a long time. Long ago, you came to me, grappled with me, and found comfort on top of this body. Now you're calling those nights a filthy wicked sin. Are you ashamed? That you were seduced by this body? Like the male animals leaving the red light district in the morning? Beat me all you want. Spit at me all you want. I know nothing about shame. Anything is fine. Just let me open my body one more time. I will take out my liver and give it you. If I could just dance. I will open myself and offer you my lungs. I will offer you my soul. If I could just dance.

(CHORUS *reads the newspaper.*)

CHORUS 1: "Dancer Ch'oe Sŭnghŭi goes over the Thirty-eighth Parallel."

CHORUS 2: "On July 20, 1946, Ch'oe Sŭnghŭi goes to the North from Inchŏn Port."

(*When the sound of waves gradually subsides, the light on* CHORUS *dims.*)

AN MAK: We faced a rough sea that night.

CH'OE SŬNGHŬI: Waves we couldn't even see tossed our boat close to the sky and then dropped us back to the ocean.

AN MAK: The small eight-ton boat spun around in the ocean like a fallen leaf.

CH'OE SŬNGHŬI: Everybody was vomiting, their bodies bent in half.

AN MAK: Until the Big Dipper became all yellow.

CH'OE SŬNGHŬI: The engine groaned as if it would die at any moment.

AN MAK: I found out why Shimch'ŏng[12] had to be offered as a sacrifice.

CH'OE SŬNGHŬI: The sunburned face of the captain paled. But you stood tall in the front of the boat.

AN MAK: I was afraid. I wondered if we ever again would be able to set foot on solid ground.

CH'OE SŬNGHŬI: Maybe it would have been better for us not to have landed anywhere.

AN MAK: No, that's not true. You held onto me and asked me where we were going to and whether we were headed in the right direction.

CH'OE SŬNGHŬI: I asked you if we could turn back even then.

AN MAK: There was no place for you in the south. (*Pause.*)

CH'OE SŬNGHŬI: That night on the sea you wrote a poem, "I Ask the Big Dipper." So what did the Big Dipper tell you?

AN MAK: Well . . . it was there. That was the answer.

CH'OE SŬNGHŬI: Why didn't I see it?

AN MAK: It was really there.

CH'OE SŬNGHŬI: You lie. There was nothing but clouds in the sky that night.

AN MAK: No, the sky was clear. The sea rose and fell as if it were crazed, but the sky was clear like a glass ball.

CH'OE SŬNGHŬI: No. There were no stars or moonlight. I couldn't see anything remotely like the Big Dipper.

AN MAK: When it showed itself off the bow of the boat, the waves became calm.

CH'OE SŬNGHŬI: You saw an illusion. Because you were too frightened.

AN MAK: Yes, I was frightened. We had no choice but to go to the north.

CH'OE SŬNGHŬI: Since we had no choice, we did not choose to go. You made it so we had no choice. That day in 1945. When you left me in Beijing and went to Yŏnan . . . You shouldn't have gone to Yŏnan.

AN MAK: Even I had beliefs.

CH'OE SŬNGHŬI: There is nothing more dangerous than beliefs. They are illusions created out of fear. Like the Big Dipper you found in the cloudy sky that night.

AN MAK: Your dance was just as dangerous. It was dangerous enough for me to throw away my beliefs.

CH'OE SŬNGHŬI: You never threw them away.

AN MAK: Just as you were never able to throw your dance away. (*Pause.*)

CH'OE SŬNGHŬI: Where was that?

AN MAK: Mmmmm?

CH'OE SŬNGHŬI: We were buffeted by wave after wave. Finally we docked someplace and spent the night there.

AN MAK: It was right before Haeju somewhere.

CH'OE SŬNGHŬI: It was an island.

AN MAK: I don't think it was.

CH'OE SŬNGHŬI: I'm right. It was an island. It couldn't have looked that peaceful if it weren't an island.

AN MAK: It seemed that way because we had suffered so much at sea that night.

CH'OE SŬNGHŬI: When we got off the boat, we held hands.

AN MAK: It had been a long time.

CH'OE SŬNGHŬI: Just like a long time ago.

AN MAK: A long time ago at the Sugwang temple.

AN SŬNGHŬI: Now they have found one moment in time when they were happy together. Holding hands, they walk into days of shimmering light. But where should I go?

(*The sound of nature. The sound of a stream and the chirping of birds, the sunlight shining down between the tree branches.*)

AN MAK: It was May.

CH'OE SŬNGHŬI: We took a train to a village just below Sugwang temple.

AN MAK: Cherry orchards were still in bloom, even though they all were wilted at Kyŏngsŏng City.

CH'OE SŬNGHŬI: Trees were alive in hues of green. There were red oaks, apricot and pear flowers.

AN MAK: The whole mountain was white. Just like you in that white bridal veil.

CH'OE SŬNGHŬI: Birds were singing.

AN MAK: When I woke up in the morning, you weren't there. I took the trail to the temple. You were sitting by the valley stream in the middle of the forest.

CH'OE SŬNGHŬI (*she hums*).

AN MAK: I stood there for a long time just taking you in. The wind blew, shaking the forest and sunlight, and the trees shook off their blossoms. Suddenly I was dizzy. I felt like you would soon disappear. You would fade into that dizzying array of sunlight. I called your name. "What are you looking at?" I said.

CH'OE SŬNGHŬI (*she turns around to find* **AN MAK**).

AN MAK: You turned around to find me. That glance. I was more lost for words. A moment went by that was like an eternity. You started giggling.

CH'OE SŬNGHŬI: Why are you standing there? Come over here.

AN MAK: Stomping and galumphing, I went down the slope.

CH'OE SŬNGHŬI: There're a lot of fish here.

AN MAK: They're sweetfish.

CH'OE SŬNGHŬI: They are?

AN MAK: They are.

CH'OE SŬNGHŬI: Are you sure?

AN MAK: I think so.

CH'OE SŬNGHŬI: I already decided to name them after me—Sŭngfish! But they had a name. That doesn't matter. I'm going to call them Sŭngfish.

AN MAK: They're sweetfish!

CH'OE SŬNGHŬI: Sŭngfish! (*Talking to the fish.*) You don't want to be still even for a second.

AN MAK: Because they are in the current. They're trying not to flow downstream.

CH'OE SŬNGHŬI: You there. That's a petal. You can't eat that.

AN MAK: They go all the way down to the sea.

CH'OE SŬNGHŬI: Really?

AN MAK: And then they'll return to this place to lay their eggs.

CH'OE SŬNGHŬI: These small things? But why?

AN MAK: Why? They are born that way.

CH'OE SŬNGHŬI: But if they're only going to come back, why leave?

AN MAK: Because they can't get big here. They go to sea to grow up and then come back to this place.

CH'OE SŬNGHŬI: To sea. Oh, that's some feat. You really are Sŭngfish.

AN MAK: That's right. You went to Japan for the same reasons.

CH'OE SŬNGHŬI: Don't mention Japan.
AN MAK: We have to go back.
CH'OE SŬNGHŬI: That's all in the past. No one appreciates my dance, anyway.
AN MAK: That's why we have to go. To a bigger place.
CH'OE SŬNGHŬI: I just want to live here and be your comfort like any other housewife.
AN MAK: You could never do that. You know that better than anyone.
CH'OE SŬNGHŬI: And then you held my hand tightly.
AN MAK: And you became the faraway expression that was in your eyes.
CH'OE SŬNGHŬI: Your hands were sweaty.
AN MAK: You were off again to a faraway place.
CH'OE SŬNGHŬI: If you hadn't called me back then.
AN MAK: You still would have gone to the sea. Sweetfish are born that way.
CH'OE SŬNGHŬI: Sŭngfish.
AN MAK: Yes, Sŭngfish.

(*The sounds of nature. The sound of a stream and the chirping of birds. When the sound fades away, the light on* CH'OE SŬNGHŬI *and* AN MAK *dims. At the same time, the light on* AN SŬNGHŬI *brightens.*)

AN SŬNGHŬI: There was no me in those shining days. There was no place for me to sneak in. When my parents held hands and went to the end of this world together, I was at home alone . . . (*A faint sound of a hornpipe is heard.*) It was one day after my mother came back from her tour in America. I woke from my sleep in the early morning, I felt like crying. I went looking for Mother at her studio. She used to lock the studio door so no one could see her practicing. The sound of a pipe was coming from the studio. The door was locked that day, too. I knocked on the door crying. But she wouldn't open the door for me. I screamed and kicked the door. I didn't know when the door opened, but she was there looking down at me. After a while, she said, "Go back to your room and sleep." And the door closed again. I heard the sound of the pipe again. I went back to my room . . . Soon after that she left for Manchuria to entertain Japanese soldiers.

(*The light on* AN SŬNGHŬI *dims. The sound of the pipe becomes mixed with the sound of wind. The pipe sound fades, but the sound of wind remains. The light on* CH'OE SŬNGHŬI *and* AN MAK *brightens.*)

CHORUS 2: We crossed the desert.
CHORUS 3: After Manchuria, we crossed the desert in swirling Mongolian winds.
CHORUS 4: We went to this platoon and that platoon, covered in sand, dust everywhere.

CHORUS 5: We walked and walked but couldn't catch a glimpse of blue sky.
CH'OE SŬNGHŬI: How long do I have to dance this dance?
AN MAK: The soldiers need some comfort.
CH'OE SŬNGHŬI: Where can I get comfort for myself?
AN MAK: . . . There isn't anything we can do. We're in the middle of a war.
CH'OE SŬNGHŬI: Why are there always so many things we can't do anything about?
AN MAK: At least we can breathe here. If we were in Japan right now, you would be dancing to a marching song. (*Pause.*)
CH'OE SŬNGHŬI: I can't open my eyes in this dust storm.
AN MAK: Close your eyes. I'll lead the way.
CH'OE SŬNGHŬI: I sense something strange from you.
AN MAK: From me?
CH'OE SŬNGHŬI: When I am dancing, what do you do?
AN MAK: I watch you.
CH'OE SŬNGHŬI: You do? (*Pause. The sound of wind.*) In that desert. An Mak, you were overflowing with life. Did the desert sun excite you? I sensed a strange passion in you. You wouldn't return until late at night.
(*The light on* AN MAK *gradually dims.*)
AN MAK: Close your eyes. I'll lead the way. (AN MAK *fades into the darkness.*)
CH'OE SŬNGHŬI: You kept disappearing in the dusty wind over the dunes. We walked and walked but couldn't catch a glimpse of blue sky. Even the sand that blanketed the whole world couldn't cover my shame . . . We crossed the desert. At the end of that desert, I came upon the statues of bodhisattvas. (*One of the* CHORUS *members stands like a bodhisattva statue.*) I stood in front of it like a grain of sand that was carried there by wind. Those rocks were quietly smiling and telling me that it was nothing, just nothing. I cried. Because I was so small. Because the eternal silence, the emptiness yet tender comfort were too overwhelming.
(*Music begins and the* CHORUS/*bodhisattvas slowly starts to move and dance.* CH'OE SŬNGHŬI *slowly follows the* CHORUS, *and she also begins to dance. The two dance together for a while. The* CHORUS/*bodhisattvas slowly disappears into the darkness.* CH'OE SŬNGHŬI *reaches out her hand into the darkness. The light on* AN SŬNGHŬI *comes up.*)
AN SŬNGHŬI: What was there? What did you see?
CH'OE SŬNGHŬI: Something that blinded my eyes.
AN SŬNGHŬI: What?
CH'OE SŬNGHŬI: It made me dance.
AN SŬNGHŬI: What was it?
CH'OE SŬNGHŬI: I don't know.

AN SŬNGHŬI: I know what it was.
CH'OE SŬNGHŬI: You do? I don't even know.
AN SŬNGHŬI: It was you. (*Pause.*)
AN SŬNGHŬI: You were always looking at yourself, no matter what you were looking at. There was only the dance. It was only your body that shone in your dance. Nothing in the world could make you take your eyes off it. You were intoxicated with yourself. You were blinded by yourself.
CH'OE SŬNGHŬI: Thank you for opening my eyes.
AN SŬNGHŬI: I still remember. At night you would get a massage from your dancers. You would lie with a look full of indolence and nonchalance. As if you were a queen. As if you were some kind of goddess. You know what? You were a goddess. Gods never look at mortals. No matter where they are or what they are looking at, they see only themselves.
CH'OE SŬNGHŬI: Is that what made you so angry?
AN SŬNGHŬI: Yes! That expression in your eyes would make anyone angry. More appalling than that is the fact that you still cannot take your eyes off yourself.
CH'OE SŬNGHŬI: I wanted you to take my hand.
AN SŬNGHŬI: No. You pushed me away.
CH'OE SŬNGHŬI: You were the one who pushed my hand away.
AN SŬNGHŬI: You were the one who closed the door. I begged you. To please look my way. To stop just for a moment. To please take a look at me. To wait just for my sake. But you didn't stop. (*Pause.*)
AN SŬNGHŬI: Just where did you plan to go?
CH'OE SŬNGHŬI: Outside.
AN SŬNGHŬI: There is no outside.
CH'OE SŬNGHŬI: Really?
AN SŬNGHŬI: I saw that clearly on that day somewhere at the foot of Mount Taebaek. The expressionless stars that darkened the already dark sky.
CH'OE SŬNGHŬI: You saw that way too early. Even before your eyes had matured.
AN SŬNGHŬI: I was grateful that I still had pain in my leg. There was nothing I could grab onto except for the feverish, shaky leg of mine. There was nothing else.
CH'OE SŬNGHŬI: Sŭnghŭi.

(*Standing away from her daughter,* CH'OE SŬNGHŬI *reaches out to her as if to embrace her. But* AN SŬNGHŬI *refuses.*)

AN SŬNGHŬI: Outside . . . That could be it. Maybe that's where you've always been.

CH'OE SŬNGHŬI: My heart always rattled. Like a window that was opened to the outside world. Not here, but not there, either. Somewhere in between, it would rattle on.

(*"The Dancer of Nostalgia" is played on the piano.* CHORUS 1 *and* CHORUS 2 *are on the stage.* CHORUS 1 [CH'OE SŬNGHŬI*'s mother*] *is braiding the hair of* CHORUS 2 [*the young* CH'OE SŬNGHŬI].)

CHORUS 2: Mom, I don't like the wind.
CHORUS 1: Why not?
CHORUS 2: It takes away the flowers.
CHORUS 1: You silly girl.
CHORUS 2: Why won't it just leave the flowers alone?
CHORUS 1: They wilt away because it's their time to do so.
CHORUS 2: Ah . . . They wilt away so fast.
CHORUS 1: They'll come back next year.
CHORUS 2: I can't wait that long.
CHORUS 1: It'll be soon enough.
CHORUS 2: Mom.
CHORUS 1: What?
CHORUS 2: Why do you think I'm here?
CHORUS 1: What do you mean?
CHORUS 2: What I mean is, why did you have me in this place?
CHORUS 1: What's wrong with this place?
CHORUS 2: Why didn't you have me in Japan or America or Europe? Then I wouldn't have had to go very far and I wouldn't have had to leave you.
CHORUS 1: . . . That would have been better.
CHORUS 2 (*referring to her hair*): Just have it tied up. When I go to Japan, I'm going to cut it all off.
CHORUS 1: Really? That's not a pleasant sight on a girl.
CHORUS 2: I can't dance with braided hair dangling on my head.
CHORUS 1: Why not?
CHORUS 2: That's just how modern dance is. It's not like geisha dance.
CHORUS 1: All dances are alike.
CHORUS 2: They're different. Mom, when will you understand?
CHORUS 1: Anyhow, what about your beautiful hair! This beautiful hair.
CHORUS 2: It will be cooler for me.
CHORUS 1: Sŭnghŭi.
CHORUS 2: Uh?
CHORUS 1: Do you have to go?
CHORUS 2: Not again.
CHORUS 1: . . . Never mind.

CHORUS 2: Aren't you done yet? My, why are you so slow today?
CHORUS 1: All done.
CHORUS 2 (*set free from her mother's hands, she jumps around*): Shall I show you something nice?
CHORUS 1: What?
CHORUS 2: This is the dance I saw Mr. Ishii do at the music hall. (*She imitates Ishii Baku's dance from "The Captives."*) With your hands tied in the back like this, you dance like this, and like that . . . What do you think? Isn't it fantastic?
CHORUS 1: That's not a dance. You look like a frog after it has been hit by a stone. Stop flopping around. Someone might see you.
CHORUS 2: Mom . . . you don't know anything about art.
CHORUS 1: That's right. Your mother knows nothing about art. But since you're so insistent on going . . .
CHORUS 2: Mom. (*She runs to her mother's arms.*)
CHORUS 1: No matter where you go, you are a Korean. You are my daughter. Don't forget that. (*She caresses her daughter's head.*) Anyhow, this beautiful hair. Can you not cut it off?
CHORUS 2: Three years. When those flowers will have bloomed and died three times.
CHORUS 1: How can I wait that long?
CHORUS 2: It's not that long.
CHORUS 1: Not that long. (*The light on* CHORUS 1 *and* 2 *dims.*)
CH'OE SŬNGHŬI: I saw my mom crying, and as she was following my train leaving Kyŏngsŏng Station,
CHORUS 3: I called out for her and cried.
CH'OE SŬNGHŬI: But by the time my train passed Yongsan Station, I was humming and looking out the window.
CHORUS 4: My poor mother.
CH'OE SŬNGHŬI: But I didn't have time to look back.
CHORUS 5: There was an endless road ahead of me.
CH'OE SŬNGHŬI: I didn't have time to think about the past.
CHORUS 3: I ran and ran toward what lay ahead. (*The sounds of explosion and marching soldiers.*)
CH'OE SŬNGHŬI: In the midst of war and revolutions,
CHORUS 4: In the midst of those cold and impenetrable forces,
CH'OE SŬNGHŬI: To grab hold of those dances that would slip away like smoke,
CHORUS 5: I ran and I ran again.
CH'OE SŬNGHŬI: In the midst of burning fire,

CHORUS 3: Across the dead bodies,
CHORUS 4: On the bleeding foothill,
CHORUS 5: At the moaning beachside,
CHORUS 3: On the starving hillside,
CH'OE SŬNGHŬI: I danced!
CHORUS 4: Bomb smoke was my stage lights.
CHORUS 5: Barbed wires were my costumes.
CHORUS 5: Explosions were my music.
CHORUS 3: In the land of desolation,
CH'OE SŬNGHŬI: I wanted to make a flower bloom.
CHORUS 4: With the desolation as my mirror, I wanted to make a bright flower bloom.
CH'OE SŬNGHŬI: I wanted to open a way to the outside, to a different world.
CHORUS 5: Away from all the misery and abomination,
CH'OE SŬNGHŬI: I wanted to take the people.
CHORUS 3: I wanted to take myself away.
CH'OE SŬNGHŬI: Only there could I be free.

(*The light on* **CH'OE SŬNGHŬI** *dims, and the light on* **AN SŬNGHŬI** *brightens.*)

AN SŬNGHŬI: But Mother, flowers fade away soon. We needed something more tangible. Something we could have in our hands. Flowers bloom so that they will die. They die for their fruit. But you didn't want to accept that . . . Freedom. Because of that, you were trapped. You trapped yourself. The stage was your prison . . . Flowers, yes. You were a blossom. But did you ever think? About the tree that was holding onto that hollow blossom?

(*Piano music. The light on* **AN SŬNGHŬI** *dims, and the light on* **AN MAK** *brightens.*)

AN MAK: It was spring. I was sent to work on the railroad. I saw some of my comrades from Yŏnan. We pretended not to have seen one another. As I leveled the ground with my pickaxe and carried logs, I mulled over the meaning of the word *purge*. In Chinese, it means "solemnity" and "purity." Solemn and pure. Pure. Out of the blue, it reminded me of what you were looking at, that clean water of the valley and the sweetfish swimming there.

CH'OE SŬNGHŬI: You vanished. Just like when you left for Yŏnan leaving me behind in Beijing. Only this time, without a word or a letter.

AN MAK: A traitor to the party. An American spy. An Mak. I thought about it long and hard. Our days gone by. We went all over the place. Japan, China, Mongolia, Taiwan, West Europe, East Europe, Russia . . .

CH'OE SŬNGHŬI: From America to the faraway Andes.

AN MAK: It occurred to me that it could be true. Without realizing it, I could have acted as an American spy.
(*For the next few lines,* AN MAK *and* CH'OE SŬNGHŬI *continue in their separate, though related, reveries.*)
CH'OE SŬNGHŬI: Like how we were seen as Japanese collaborators but worked for the independence at the same time.
AN MAK: Out of all the people we met, we might have come across at least one American spy.
CH'OE SŬNGHŬI: What are you looking at?
AN MAK: Yes. It could be true.
CH'OE SŬNGHŬI: Are you still looking at the Big Dipper?
AN MAK: Perhaps I will never leave this place.
CH'OE SŬNGHŬI: Are you at peace with yourself now?
AN MAK: Like the sunken bombshell in the river. Nothing to do but to slowly rust away.
CH'OE SŬNGHŬI: Where are you? (*The light on* CH'OE SŬNGHŬI *slowly dims.*)
AN MAK: As I leveled the land and carried logs, the vision of that clear stream was always before me. That clear blue water. Your eyes. That faraway look in your eyes. Afraid that they will soon disappear, I call your name . . .
(CH'OE SŬNGHŬI *disappears into darkness, no longer visible.*)
AN MAK: The sweetfish return to freshwater from the ocean. When they come back, they lay their eggs. And they die. Purge. Solemnity and purity. For the sweetfish that came back from the sea, the water is too clean. That's it. It's that simple . . . But what about their eggs? What about the baby sweetfish that never made it to the sea? Sŭnghŭi and Pyŏnggŏn?
(AN MAK *fades into darkness as* AN SŬNGHŬI *becomes visible onstage.*)
AN SŬNGHŬI: As a traitor to the party, An Mak perniciously collaborated with the Japanese from the very beginning, and when the liberation became imminent, he, working as an American spy, infiltrated the so-called Yŏnan Party and did nothing but prove himself to be an opportunist and a turncoat. It has been a blessing to the people and the party that the crimes committed by An Mak and his conspirators have now been revealed as clearly as daylight. I, An Sŭnghŭi, will wash away every ideological flaw that I inherited, and with my art, I swear to work only for the advancement of the party and the people. Unfortunately, even after being given numerous opportunities—thanks to her artistic talent—comrade Ch'oe Sŭnghŭi, heavily influenced by An Mak's ideologies, was unable to cast off the dregs of imperial and colonialist ideas about art. She behaves arbitrarily rather than following the party's teach-

ings regarding dance company operations and cleaning one's self of stagnant bourgeois ideas, not to mention that she allows herself to wallow in megalomania and self-promotion. As a result, her productions are nothing but a showcase of idiosyncratic dances that fail to earn the people's support.

CH'OE SŬNGHŬI: It was a very passionate and moving speech.
AN SŬNGHŬI: . . .
CH'OE SŬNGHŬI: You were full of energy. It was the first time I saw your eyes shine like that.
AN SŬNGHŬI: You were sitting below the podium.
CH'OE SŬNGHŬI: With my hands quite demurely folded.
AN SŬNGHŬI: You gazed at me, with self-composure. I couldn't look right at you.
CH'OE SŬNGHŬI: There was no need to pity me.
AN SŬNGHŬI: And suddenly you smiled at me. You sneered at me. And at everyone there.
CH'OE SŬNGHŬI: I was choreographing.
AN SŬNGHŬI: No. You were sneering at me.
CH'OE SŬNGHŬI: At that moment, I had a revelation.
AN SŬNGHŬI: When that many people were looking at you! I was so angry I didn't know what to do.
CH'OE SŬNGHŬI: I told you it was a great speech.
AN SŬNGHŬI: Do you have any idea how I felt?
CH'OE SŬNGHŬI: I understood somewhat.
AN SŬNGHŬI: Mother.
CH'OE SŬNGHŬI: I don't care. Now can I be on stage?
AN SŬNGHŬI: Not yet. It was hard enough just to bring you back to P'yŏngyang. You have to wait little longer . . .
CH'OE SŬNGHŬI: I waited long enough! Just how long do I have to wait? I learned my lesson from the people and did enough repenting. What more do you expect? There are some ideas for the stage I prepared when I was in the country.
AN SŬNGHŬI: I read them.
CH'OE SŬNGHŬI: Did you? What do you think? I don't see how anyone could criticize them because of ideology or beliefs, do you?
AN SŬNGHŬI: I don't know.
CH'OE SŬNGHŬI: What do you mean, you don't know?
AN SŬNGHŬI: Your dances are not yet militant or revolutionary enough.
CH'OE SŬNGHŬI: What? Which part of my dances do you mean?
AN SŬNGHŬI: I mean overall.

CH'OE SŬNGHŬI: A woman suffering under the persecution of feudalism fights for her rights and freedom in the face of unjust sexism. What could be more militant or revolutionary than that?

AN SŬNGHŬI: The problem is that it's about only one woman. What makes it dangerous is that she's acting on her own, not following the direction of the party.

CH'OE SŬNGHŬI: What?

AN SŬNGHŬI: If everyone fights for what only he or she believes in, then the whole idea of a unified order is true only in name. When an individual's belief contradicts the order of the party and the individual fights according to his or her own belief, then the party becomes the enemy.

CH'OE SŬNGHŬI: Sŭnghŭi, I can't believe I am hearing this from you.

AN SŬNGHŬI: I'm just telling you how other people will see your dances. Because I'm worried about you. If you stage this dance, it will be like seeing if fire is hot. "Ch'oe Sŭnghŭi is still wallowing in her individual megalomania." (*Pause.*)

CH'OE SŬNGHŬI: The order of the party . . . Even the party is, in the end, only one entity, isn't it?

AN SŬNGHŬI: Be careful what you say. (*Pause.*)

CH'OE SŬNGHŬI: Sŭnghŭi.

AN SŬNGHŬI: I'm sorry. Please try to understand my position.

CH'OE SŬNGHŬI: Have you forgotten your "Dance of the Gypsies"?

AN SŬNGHŬI: I criticized myself and repented more than enough for that dance.

CH'OE SŬNGHŬI: When I saw that dance, my heart trembled so with crazy jealousy that I wanted to tear my hair out.

AN SŬNGHŬI: I've forgotten it.

CH'OE SŬNGHŬI: No. That dance is still inside you.

AN SŬNGHŬI: I have to go now. I have to go to a rehearsal. Don't ever discuss this dance with anyone. Just this one time, please.

CH'OE SŬNGHŬI: Sŭnghŭi.

AN SŬNGHŬI: Yes?

CH'OE SŬNGHŬI: What about you?

AN SŬNGHŬI: What about me?

CH'OE SŬNGHŬI: Are you free?

AN SŬNGHŬI: Free . . . freedom is obtained when I accomplish the grand order of our great leader and our party in a militant and revolutionary spirit.

CH'OE SŬNGHŬI: Does your heart tremble when you're on stage?

AN SŬNGHŬI: . . . (*Pause.*)

AN SŬNGHŬI: However, in spite of everything, you submitted that dance to the party and were given permission to stage it. That dance ended your career.

CH'OE SŬNGHŬI: You criticized me more harshly than anyone.

AN SŬNGHŬI: Since they already were suspicious of you, that dance was like gasoline being poured on smoldering embers. Can you imagine what I had to do to stop that fire from . . .

CH'OE SŬNGHŬI: "The True Daughter of the Party" was your production the following year. As if you were crying out to say you weren't Ch'oe Sŭnghŭi's daughter but the daughter of the party.

AN SŬNGHŬI: Because I had to survive. I thought surviving was the only way to protect you. For the sake of Pyŏnggŏn . . . For Dad . . . I couldn't surrender like that. But you . . . you didn't stop. Like a train heading toward a cliff, you *wouldn't* stop.

(*Piano music is heard.* AN SŬNGHŬI *disappears into darkness, and* AN MAK *is seen on the stage.*)

AN MAK: What are you looking at?

CH'OE SŬNGHŬI: The trees have blossomed.

AN MAK: . . . Hmm, there are lots.

CH'OE SŬNGHŬI: That's not interesting. You write poetry, but all you can say is that there are lots?

AN MAK: There are lots, so I said, there are lots.

CH'OE SŬNGHŬI: When I left Kyŏngsŏng and got to Tōkyō, there were this many blossoms.

AN MAK: Because it was March.

CH'OE SŬNGHŬI: When I stood under the shade of all those white petals, can you believe it? I felt dizzy. I didn't get dizzy even on that ship coming to Tōkyō . . . March 24, 1926, I was fifteen years old then.

AN MAK: I saw you for the first time at Kokubuji Station on the Chūō Line.

CH'OE SŬNGHŬI: Instead of studying, you spent all your time chasing girls, didn't you?

AN MAK: You were on a train with your hair braided.

CH'OE SŬNGHŬI: Taking a peek at me, you sly old dog.

AN MAK: You were standing there.

CH'OE SŬNGHŬI: How was it, your first impression of me?

AN MAK: Well . . .

CH'OE SŬNGHŬI: It must have been so-so.

AN MAK: No. No matter how many times I saw you, it was always like seeing you for the first time.

CH'OE SŬNGHŬI: What do you mean?

AN MAK: That handbag you always carried with you. I wondered if you made yourself several faces and kept them there, putting on a different face each time. I was very curious about the inside of that bag.

CH'OE SŬNGHŬI (*pause. Referring to* AN MAK's *imagery*): Better this time. Not bad at all.

AN MAK: Thanks.

CH'OE SŬNGHŬI: Fifteen. I was still growing and changing.

AN MAK: Yes. Every time I saw you, you seemed to have grown by a foot.

CH'OE SŬNGHŬI: Ah, those days. Everything I saw and touched made its way inside and became my dances. I practiced ten or more hours a day, but I didn't know I was tired. I was ecstatic as my muscles found a way to move in my body, and the dances were carved onto my muscles. I would leap and leap again because I didn't want them to slip away. I would carve them on my body again and again to hold onto those dances that wanted to scatter away like smoke.

AN MAK: You put on a face again. Like when you were fifteen.

CH'OE SŬNGHŬI: You know the saying: The body ages but the heart doesn't.

AN MAK: The body ages but the heart doesn't.

CH'OE SŬNGHŬI: The problem is that your body does age. My heart hasn't changed, but my body has abandoned me. Dances have forsaken me and left me one by one. Like smoke. My muscles don't have the strength to hang onto them.

AN MAK: But, I remember every one of your dances.

CH'OE SŬNGHŬI: Remember? Yes. My body remembers those dances. It remembers what I don't have anymore. It is the cruelest thing in the world.

AN MAK: . . .

CH'OE SŬNGHŬI: I should have been a sculptor.

AN MAK: A sculptor?

CH'OE SŬNGHŬI: Because rocks are hard. Is there any material more ephemeral than the human body? Like the ripples on sand sculpted by the wind. No, it's more fleeting even than that.

AN MAK: . . .

CH'OE SŬNGHŬI: Do you suppose the bodhisattva statues are still there?

AN MAK: I'm sure.

CH'OE SŬNGHŬI: Eternally?

AN MAK: At least for now.

CH'OE SŬNGHŬI: Sculptors must be happy. At least, they don't have to see the sculptures they carved soften and dissolve in front of their eyes.

AN MAK: One day they, too, will disappear.

CH'OE SŬNGHŬI: I chose the wrong material. So I am being punished for it. (*Pause.*)

I curse that moment. I curse the moment when I saw Mr. Ishii's dance for the first time, curse that Kyŏngsŏng music hall, curse my brother who took me there. I curse those dances that blinded me and took away my soul . . . But if I could feel my body trembling as it did on that day. If I could only go back to that place where my legs wouldn't stop shaking and I held my breath to keep from screaming . . . (*Pause.*)

AN MAK: I guess it's time for you to leave again?
CH'OE SŬNGHŬI: Yes. I've had enough of it here.
AN MAK: Why don't you rest a bit now?
CH'OE SŬNGHŬI: I want to live!
AN MAK: . . .
CH'OE SŬNGHŬI: Live like a maniac.
AN MAK: . . .
CH'OE SŬNGHŬI: I don't want to live as if I were dead.
AN MAK: Sŭnghŭi . . .
CH'OE SŬNGHŬI: I don't want to feebly waste away!
AN MAK: That's being too selfish.
CH'OE SŬNGHŬI: We had too many things in our lives that were beyond our control. I've had enough of them now.
AN MAK: . . .
CH'OE SŬNGHŬI: I want to do what I want to do. Just this once.
AN MAK: What if . . .
CH'OE SŬNGHŬI: I don't care! My heart is still beating. I'm alive now. That's enough for me.
AN MAK (*he smiles*): Ah, you're incorrigible. Like a child without a care.
CH'OE SŬNGHŬI: But this time I am alone.
AN MAK: I'm sorry.
CH'OE SŬNGHŬI: I want to dance.
AN MAK: You always do.
CH'OE SŬNGHŬI: With you!
AN MAK: With me?
CH'OE SŬNGHŬI: Yes.
AN MAK: I don't know how to dance.
CH'OE SŬNGHŬI: And you nagged me all this time?
AN MAK: That was my job.
CH'OE SŬNGHŬI: Come here.
AN MAK (*he hesitates*).
CH'OE SŬNGHŬI: Now.

(*A waltz is played on the piano. Standing where they are,* **AN MAK** *and* **CH'OE SŬNGHŬI** *take positions to waltz. Although they stand apart, they dance together.*)

CH'OE SŬNGHŬI: One, two, three. One, two, three. Ta talalalala ta tata. Give your body to the music and just follow my lead.

AN MAK: It's too fast.

CH'OE SŬNGHŬI: Ouch!

AN MAK: Oops. I'm sorry I stepped on you.

CH'OE SŬNGHŬI: You are so stiff. How can you call yourself the husband of the world-renowned dancer Ch'oe Sŭnghŭi?

AN MAK: I'm trying.

CH'OE SŬNGHŬI: Let's try again. One, two, three. One, two, three. Ta talalalala . . .

(*Taking the cue from the piano, the orchestra plays the waltz, which continues as if they were in a grand ballroom. As they continue to dance, enjoying themselves, the light dims, and the dancing couple disappears into the darkness. When the light comes up again,* **AN SŬNGHŬI** *and* **CH'OE SŬNGHŬI** *are onstage.*)

AN SŬNGHŬI: That day in 1967 . . . did you really believe it would be possible?

CH'OE SŬNGHŬI (*she hums to herself*).

AN SŬNGHŬI: You went out for a walk on the banks of Taedong River. And that day, you didn't return home until very late.

CH'OE SŬNGHŬI: That day in 1957, you were standing there.[13]

AN SŬNGHŬI: I went to the top of the hill.

CH'OE SŬNGHŬI: What were you looking at?

AN SŬNGHŬI: You were standing at the river. I was looking at the back of you from the hill. There were two men standing a little away from you.

CH'OE SŬNGHŬI: What were you staring at for so long? There is nothing but water.

AN SŬNGHŬI: In that soft sunset shining on the river, you seemed peaceful.

CH'OE SŬNGHŬI: I was looking at you by the window of my dance studio.

AN SŬNGHŬI: From behind, you suddenly seemed to lose your balance.

CH'OE SŬNGHŬI: Like a lost boy. You were standing there.

AN SŬNGHŬI: It seemed like you would be sucked in by the river.

CH'OE SŬNGHŬI: I wanted to call out to you.

AN SŬNGHŬI: I called out to you. Mother!

CH'OE SŬNGHŬI: But I couldn't.

AN SŬNGHŬI: Mother!

CH'OE SŬNGHŬI: . . .

AN SŬNGHŬI: Mom . . . ! Only then, you slowly turned around and saw me.

CH'OE SŬNGHŬI: . . .
AN SŬNGHŬI: Because of the sunset behind you, I couldn't see your face. But I could feel your eyes on me. Your eyes, as if you saw me for the very first time. (*Reverie ends.*)
CH'OE SŬNGHŬI: Ah, Sŭnghŭi!
AN SŬNGHŬI: Your walk lasted longer today.
CH'OE SŬNGHŬI: The breeze was very refreshing.
AN SŬNGHŬI: What were you staring at for so long?
CH'OE SŬNGHŬI: I don't know.
AN SŬNGHŬI: There wasn't anything.
CH'OE SŬNGHŬI: I know.
AN SŬNGHŬI: Let's go in. It's gotten dark.
CH'OE SŬNGHŬI: It has gotten dark already.
AN SŬNGHŬI: They have to go home, too.
CH'OE SŬNGHŬI: Yes. (*To* MEN.) Thank you. Why don't you go home? I'm going to go home now.
MEN: Thank you for the walk, Mrs. Ch'oe. You're going to Chagang Province tomorrow?
CH'OE SŬNGHŬI: I'll leave by the night train tonight.
MEN: We see. We can't go with you there, so we'll wait and see you when you come back to P'yŏngyang.
CH'OE SŬNGHŬI: Thank you for everything.
MEN: Oh, no. It was our pleasure. Well, have a safe trip. (*The* MEN *exit.*)
AN SŬNGHŬI: Just be patient and wait a little longer. Soon . . .
CH'OE SŬNGHŬI: I'm fine. I like being with the little ones. Some of them have real talent.
AN SŬNGHŬI: I'm trying my best, but things are not getting any better yet.
CH'OE SŬNGHŬI: Thank you, but don't try so hard.
AN SŬNGHŬI: Are you all packed?
CH'OE SŬNGHŬI: Yes. Let's stay here just a little longer and then we'll go. Today is the last day for the Taedong River.
AN SŬNGHŬI: What do you mean?
CH'OE SŬNGHŬI: Sŭnghŭi . . .
AN SŬNGHŬI: Yes?
CH'OE SŬNGHŬI: I'm leaving. (*Pause.*)
AN SŬNGHŬI: As you spoke those words, you looked so mischievous. Like a child playing a trick. I nearly asked you: "To where?"
CH'OE SŬNGHŬI: Come with me.
AN SŬNGHŬI: What are you talking about?
CH'OE SŬNGHŬI: I have everything prepared.

AN SŬNGHŬI: Mother . . .

CH'OE SŬNGHŬI: I can't wait any longer.

AN SŬNGHŬI: I'll pretend that I didn't hear anything.

CH'OE SŬNGHŬI: I know you want to come, too.

AN SŬNGHŬI: Mother, please! You're saying this now! After thinking about what it is you've planned to do!?

CH'OE SŬNGHŬI: I thought about it too long.

AN SŬNGHŬI: You just don't think about your effect on others, do you? You think only about yourself!

CH'OE SŬNGHŬI: It's also for you.

AN SŬNGHŬI: I don't want it.

CH'OE SŬNGHŬI: How long will you go on lying to yourself?

AN SŬNGHŬI: The one who is lying to oneself is you! Leaving is impossible. Insane. You are insane. You will stand out no matter where you are. How do you think you can avoid being seen by so many others? How do you plan to elude so many eyes?

CH'OE SŬNGHŬI: Yes. I'm insane. Which is why I can leave.

AN SŬNGHŬI: I won't let you go.

CH'OE SŬNGHŬI: What? You?

AN SŬNGHŬI: Please, for my sake, don't do this! For Pyŏnggŏn's sake!

CH'OE SŬNGHŬI: If you won't come with me, I'll go alone. It's time for my train. (**CH'OE SŬNGHŬI** *picks up her suitcase.*)

AN SŬNGHŬI: We went to P'yŏngyang Station together. I can't remember how we got there, but on the way we didn't say a word.

CH'OE SŬNGHŬI (*she hums to herself*).

AN SŬNGHŬI: As we were entering the station, someone greeted us. He was a very old man with a bent waist. I went to pass by him as quickly as I could, but my mother smiled brightly and after saying hello, she stood there holding hands and chatting with him.

CH'OE SŬNGHŬI: You know what? He saw my performance in Tōkyō!

AN SŬNGHŬI: I thought that my heart would freeze right there. but my mother, her face all rosy and pink, was so at ease with herself—as if she was about to go on a picnic.

CH'OE SŬNGHŬI: Oh, no! The way I'm going, I might miss my train!

AN SŬNGHŬI: If only that would happen . . . We stood there at the platform. Under the blinking platform lights, I was picking lint from my mother's coat. I kept taking off the lint, not saying a word.

CH'OE SŬNGHŬI: The train is late.

AN SŬNGHŬI: But the train arrived at the platform. Mother got on it. At the end, I couldn't say a word. (*The sound of a train coming into the station.*)

AN SŬNGHŬI: Before she got on the train, she gave me her hand.
CH'OE SŬNGHŬI: Think it over one more time tonight. It's tomorrow night.
AN SŬNGHŬI: In my hand was a tiny note that she gave me. A note with a name of a small hotel at a city near the border.
CH'OE SŬNGHŬI: I'll wait.
AN SŬNGHŬI: Mom. I couldn't even say that short word, so I just held her hand. (*Whistle sound.*)
AN SŬNGHŬI: At that moment, at that moment, she smiled at me. She winked and smiled at me. Like the nonchalant light of the star that I saw somewhere on Mount Taebaek. And somehow I let go of her hand.
(*The sound of a train moving.* CH'OE SŬNGHŬI *waves out the window. The sound of the train gets louder and then fades away.* CH'OE SŬNGHŬI *disappears into the darkness.*)
AN SŬNGHŬI: . . . The train disappeared into darkness. With that, everything came to an end . . .
(*Piano music fills the stage.* AN SŬNGHŬI *looks at the note in her hand. The stage slowly darkens. The music continues to play. The lights go out and then on, and* AN SŬNGHŬI, CH'OE SŬNGHŬI, *and* AN MAK *stand downstage. Their faces are not visible. Behind them at center stage, the* CHORUS *crisscrosses the stage, clearing away things. Light and playful music is played on the piano.*)
CHORUS 1: The red shoes were talking to the red shoes as they were dancing. "My dear red shoes, my dear red shoes. Can you please put me down?"
CHORUS 2: When the dance changes from a waltz to a tango, the red shoes said, "For some time now, that's what I wanted say. Why won't you take me off and come down?"
CHORUS 1: Because you won't stop.
CHORUS 2: Because you won't leave me alone.
CHORUS 1: Just stop for a moment.
CHORUS 2: I stopped.
CHORUS 1: I stopped, too.
CHORUS 2: Then why are we still dancing?
CHORUS 1: What's going on?
CHORUS 2: Who's the one who's dancing here?
(CHORUS *exits. The faces of* AN SŬNGHŬI, CH'OE SŬNGHŬI, *and* AN MAK *are now visible.*)
AN SŬNGHŬI: Listen. To these sounds . . . The sound of our footsteps, the stomping and reverberating sound of time as we walked and ran to get to now . . . Listen to the ever slightly creaking sound of our bodies. In every nook and cranny of this floor, our hair and bits of ourselves mingle with dust . . .

AN MAK: You were sitting by the valley stream.

CH'OE SŬNGHŬI: Like a lost boy, you were standing there for a long time.

AN SŬNGHŬI: This glossy floor was worn smooth with our own bodies. The scent of sweat mixed with tears poured into this . . .

AN MAK: The trees, sunlight, and petals that were waving in the wind. That crystal water. And the sweetfish swimming in that crystal water.

CH'OE SŬNGHŬI: What were you looking at? At the river, what were you trying to find?

AN SŬNGHŬI: After we are gone, who would remember these?

(AN MAK *turns around and, with his back to the audience, looks at the stage as if seeking something.*)

AN SŬNGHŬI: The trees are in bloom.

CH'OE SŬNGHŬI: Yes, they are.

AN SŬNGHŬI: Like that day.

CH'OE SŬNGHŬI: The sun is in my eyes. (*Pause.*)

AN SŬNGHŬI: Mother, did you really believe it?

CH'OE SŬNGHŬI: . . .

AN SŬNGHŬI: That it was possible to escape from this place?

CH'OE SŬNGHŬI: Yes. And I also knew that it could be the end.

AN SŬNGHŬI: Then, why?

CH'OE SŬNGHŬI: I always danced as if it were my last dance. I wanted to dance to the very end. I wanted to stay alive.

AN SŬNGHŬI: You wanted to fade away like that.

CH'OE SŬNGHŬI: . . .

AN SŬNGHŬI: You chose that voluntarily.

CH'OE SŬNGHŬI: Was that a choice?

AN SŬNGHŬI: You did what you set out to do. You won. But why did you? Why in my hand did you have to . . .

CH'OE SŬNGHŬI (*she stops her*): Sŭnghŭi, stop.

AN SŬNGHŬI: Look at this hand, Mother. This is the hand that held onto you. This is the hand that you thrust aside. That day with this hand I . . .

CH'OE SŬNGHŬI (*she holds her hand*): Stop. Sŭnghŭi . . . (CH'OE SŬNGHŬI *caresses* AN SŬNGHŬI'*s hand.*)

CH'OE SŬNGHŬI: It's gone. Our time has passed.

AN SŬNGHŬI: Yes. Everything passes away. It disappeared. But I still can't understand. I can't forgive.

CH'OE SŬNGHŬI: I won't ask for your forgiveness.

AN SŬNGHŬI: Because the only one who can forgive you is yourself. Only your dances could do that.

CH'OE SŬNGHŬI: But would they?

AN SŬNGHŬI: Show me your dance just one more time. The light in your eyes that you have never saw me with, your eyes that had me seduced. That laughter. So I can hate you. So I can fight.

CH'OE SŬNGHŬI: I can't forgive myself, either. The fact that I am this far away from those beautiful things. (*Meaning the blossoms.*) But my dear Sŭnghŭi, our time has passed.

AN SŬNGHŬI: Mother.

CH'OE SŬNGHŬI: But, my Sŭnghŭi . . . It was I who worried to death because of you. It was I who cried over your father's loneliness.

AN SŬNGHŬI: . . . (*Pause.*)

CH'OE SŬNGHŬI: What are you doing?

AN MAK: Did you see it?

CH'OE SŬNGHŬI: See what?

AN MAK: A box. A pine box with a bat-shaped hinge.

CH'OE SŬNGHŬI: Why are you looking for that?

AN MAK: I put something in it.

CH'OE SŬNGHŬI: What?

AN MAK: My old notes that I scribbled for practice.

CH'OE SŬNGHŬI: Why are you looking for them?

AN MAK: To throw them away.

CH'OE SŬNGHŬI: Why?

AN MAK: Because I'm ashamed of them. Things you're ashamed of are hard to get rid of. They hide in some corner and hang on. I have to get rid of those notes. Where did they go? (*Pause.*)

CH'OE SŬNGHŬI: We should go now.

AN MAK: Yes.

CH'OE SŬNGHŬI: Blossoms are dying.

AN MAK: Like that day.

CH'OE SŬNGHŬI: It's too bright.

AN MAK: I feel like dancing.

(CH'OE SŬNGHŬI *and* AN SŬNGHŬI *look at him in surprise.*)

AN MAK: Why are you surprised? I like dancing, too. I was born in the wrong era. Of all the times in the world, I was born in the same time as your mother. To make matters worse—I met your mother! (*They laugh.*)

AN MAK (*to* AN SŬNGHŬI): I'd like to see your "Dance of Gypsies" one more time.

AN SŬNGHŬI: But you don't like that dance.

AN MAK: No, I like that dance most of all.

CH'OE SŬNGHŬI: Enough to make me jealous. (*Piano music begins again.*)

AN SŬNGHŬI: When did the blossoms die . . .

CH'OE SŬNGHŬI: They will bloom again.
AN SŬNGHŬI: When?
CH'OE SŬNGHŬI: Soon.

(*The music becomes louder, and the three people disappear into darkness upstage. The* **CHORUS** *and the* **PIANIST** *look on as they walk into the darkness. Spotlight on the* **PIANIST**. *A male actor can play the pianist to imply that he is An Pyŏnggŏn,* **CH'OE SŬNGHŬI***'s son.*)

Curtain

NOTES

1. Despite the historical reality of the characters and many of the events mentioned in this work, it still is a "memory play." The images may have soft edges in some places, but the inner life of the characters must be truthful, and the conflicts among and in them must have depth. Giving in to melodrama and emotional excess will be a mistake. A warning: like our memories, the play's chronology is fluid, and there are moments in which two characters seemingly speak directly to each other when they are in fact in individual moments years apart, as in the scene between An Sŭnghŭi and Ch'oe Sŭnghŭi late in the play when they discuss events that took place at the river.
2. The dress is called a *hanbok*.
3. The Taedong is an important river with its origins in central North Korea, flowing past P'yŏngyang on its way to the Yellow Sea.
4. In late July and August, cicadas in East Asia make a piercing racket, a sure sign that autumn is approaching.
5. Late May to early July is the period of "white nights" (*beliye nochi*). In northern Russia, especially in St. Petersburg, the sun never dips below the horizon, making day and night nearly indistinguishable.
6. An Mak is referring to World War II. The terms "war of liberation" and "liberation war" often appear often in Korean scholars' writings.
7. Ishii Baku (1886–1962) was a Japanese modern dancer and impresario.
8. Ch'oe Sŭnghŭi is referring to North Korea.
9. The year of liberation was 1945. Yŏnan (in Korean; Yan'an in Chinese) is in northwestern China, a stop on Mao Zedong's Long March of the 1930s and the site of his lectures on art in 1942.
10. Mount Taebaek is in east-central South Korea.
11. Shinuiju is a town in the far western corner of North Korea, on the border with China.

12. Shimch'ŏng is a fictional heroine who dived into the sea as a sacrifice in order for her father's sight to be restored.
13. Ch'oe and An are speaking in reverie: Ch'oe is talking to the absent An Mak, and An Sŭnghŭi is speaking to her mother.

APPENDIX
THEATER IN SEOUL

Unlike poets or novelists, whose artistic productions are conveyed directly to the audience (reader) with no intermediary save print, playwrights must rely on a variety of intermediaries to transfer the written word to the stage and audience: actors, designers, directors, technicians, accountants, and even poster designers and ticket sellers. A playwright's work may be conceived as though it were to be staged in ideal conditions—indeed, the artistic vision expressed in words may exceed the limits of available performance methods or technology—but that same work is not immune from influences emanating from the surrounding world of theater: the auditorium's size and form, the audience's maturity and sophistication, the actors' ability and age, financial resources, and so on. Acknowledging that musical theater now is the dominant artistic and economic force in the Korean theater, one with its own production environment, this appendix focuses on those aspects of staging drama in Seoul that may help the reader better apprehend, or appreciate, the works in this anthology and the theater world they represent.

The locus of the multifaceted, complex contemporary theater world in South Korea is Taehangno (University Avenue), a popular entertainment center in north-central Seoul that is about a half mile long and not much more than two hundred yards wide on the eastern side of the avenue. Including a few recently added and well-appointed small theaters built into new university satellite campus buildings, seventy-three theaters intended for stage productions compete for attention in a jumble of coffee shops, teahouses, book stores, pizza parlors, fast-food eateries

(Asian and American), upscale foreign cuisine restaurants, trendy clothing stores, bars, game parlors, noodle shops, Korean barbecue establishments, *norae-bang* (karaoke rooms), and convenience stores. Seating between 150 and 200 patrons, most theaters are belowground, and their entrances are marked not by blazing marquees but by simple signs and a makeshift ticket booth on the street, their surface impression belying the rich variety of theater staged underground.

Two imposing edifices with larger auditoriums stand as the aesthetic anchors of Taehangno. In the northeast is the modern Tongsung Art Center, with a 450-seat auditorium belowground and a 150-seat theater on the fifth floor. On the south side, facing the basketball courts and band shell in Marronier Park, is the older Arco Arts Center (formerly known as the Munye), with a 710-seat auditorium on the first floor and a 200-seat flexible theater belowground.

Scattered across the city beyond Taehangno are thirty-eight venues, many of which, such as the LG Arts Center (1,050 seats) and the Sejong Cultural Center (large hall: 3,895 seats; small hall: 522 seats), hold only concerts or musicals. The imposing National Theater of Korea and the architecturally impressive Seoul Performing Arts Center have venues accommodating opera, musicals, drama, and folk performances. Of the small theaters presenting dramas outside Taehangno, perhaps the best known are the aboveground Sanullim Theater and the Theater Cecil (200 to 250 seats).[1]

It might seem that dramatists have access to a wide variety of venues in which to produce their works, but such is not the case. If one removes the venues dedicated to music concerts, musicals, opera, or the popular theater for young audiences, then discounts the growing number of theaters in Taehangno offering standup comedy or soft-porn shows, and finally subtracts those theaters staging translations of Western plays, the number of affordable venues available and suitable for domestic, artistically serious dramatic works is limited, especially in light of the two hundred registered theater companies competing for performance space in Seoul.

Over the past two decades, Korean critics have repeatedly observed that despite improvements, Korean drama and theater face many challenges, including production obstacles, financial solvency, theater size, stage shape, and actors. Noting that most dramas and comedies are staged in small theaters and that high-quality drama and theater are indeed produced in such settings, in what ways are the small theaters a challenge?

Access to a typical Taehangno underground theater like the Taehangno Theater, the Guerrilla Theater, or Arungguji Theater is not easy. One, sometimes two, flights of narrow, dimly lit stairs must be navigated. At the bottom, the "foyer" may accommodate twenty people (frequently fewer), so audience members often have to stand in the stairwell or in the street until the house is opened. The dimly lit seating area holds between one hundred and two hundred backless bench seats with thin seat cushions.

The stage generally is small, not much more than twenty-five to thirty feet wide by twenty-five feet deep, often with no architectural feature separating the "auditorium" and the stage. Wing space right and left generally is nonexistent, and there is no fly loft to move scenery in and out. Because of the low ceilings in both the "house" and stage areas, stage lighting is limited (although O T'aesŏk's Arungguji Theater seems to accommodate complex lighting designs). These cramped stages suggest a paradox: Korea's many internationally recognized designers—such as Kim Hyŏn-suk, Shin Sŏnhŭi, Yi T'aesŏp, and Yu Chŏngsŏp—create visually stunning works, but they often cannot practice their craft to the fullest in such conditions. It is only in the large theaters that space and perhaps budget permit fully realized designs, thus offering the writer more help in attaining his artistic vision.

In the underground theaters, the sets tend to be sparse and often lack finishing details or high-quality painting because the funds necessary to mount productions frequently are inadequate (despite any governmental subsidies). Too, the designer and assistants have little time in the theater to set up and detail the set, and the sets must be removed quickly when the show closes in two weeks or less. Some productions do indeed run for more than two weeks, but the fierce competition for performance space brought on by the sheer number of theater companies and the more than 140 professional productions offered each year (including musicals and a significant portion of new works) make long runs the exception rather than the rule.

The two-week runs, low ticket prices ($10 to $15 for students), and limited seating capacity make it unlikely that production costs can be recouped through the box office even if the production has been subsidized and the actors are paid minimal wages. Economic considerations aside, the small houses and limited runs affect playwrights and actors (and, to a lesser degree, the director), who need repeated exposure to audiences in order to evaluate their own work and develop artistically. Time affects artistry in other ways as well.

Performances in Seoul's small theaters usually last ninety minutes or less. For the dramatist, ninety minutes may not be enough to present and explore significant characters and themes, but intermissions are feasible only in theaters with lobbies (and restrooms) or in small theaters with easy access to the street. Dramas that require intermissions generally are staged at one of the medium-size houses (such as the Arco Arts Center and the National Theater), but *Please Turn Off the Lights* was staged at the underground Taehangno Theater. Clearly, some performances last longer than ninety minutes without an intermission, but they test an audience's comfort and ability to focus.

Even when time is not a factor, the playwright's work is viewed by audiences largely consisting of high-school and university students whose developing aesthetics are shaped not by a history of active theatergoing but by television and other media. Korean male workers spend their after-work hours eating and drinking with their colleagues (perhaps even in Taehangno). Furthermore, a married woman's lifestyle does not usually include going to the theater (unless the play is a musical), especially if there are children at home. For older patrons, just getting into and out of the small theaters may present significant obstacles. A particular playwright's or director's reputation can draw a demographically varied audience into the theater for a particular production, but performances in the small theaters generally are attended by students, intellectuals, and theater artists (or would-be artists). Still, whatever drawbacks might be found in this kind of audience, the positive energy and enthusiasm for the event that flow from the audience to the performers must be very much like the atmosphere present in Off-Off Broadway experimental theaters in the 1970s.

Advertisements in entertainment magazines or on the poster boards lining Taehangno generally feature young casts. Make no mistake: there *are* talented, mature stage actors performing in Seoul, actors who have given transcendent performances in distinguished careers, among them actresses Kim Sohŭi, Kim Sŏngnyŏ, and Ch'ae Chinhŭi and actors Kim Chong-yŏp, Pak Yongsu, and Sŏ Hŭi-sŭng. Unfortunately, many older actors have left the theater to earn a living in television and film. Consequently, it is common to see younger stage actors playing characters older than they, but with neither the experience nor the gravitas that real maturity offers.

Korea now has more than forty theater departments, a marked increase over the past two decades. But because of the popularity of television dramas and the draw of film stardom, many, if not most, of the acting students in those departments are drawn to either the musical theater or television and film, not to serious drama. For many reasons, including the structure of Korean high-school and university education, most students entering actor-training programs with an eye toward a career as "legitimate" stage actors have relatively minimal precollege experience, and many graduate without a cohesive, ingrained, and reliable stage technique. Moreover, if they cannot join a major acting company with its own training regimen, they are on their own, unable to practice their craft consistently and, often, acting only in the small theaters in which their psychophysical technique is slow to mature because of the confined space and the young audiences. In these circumstances, actors must rely heavily on stage directors, the most powerful presence in the Korean theater.

While a certain tension between dramatist and director can foster creativity, a director's cavalier treatment of playwrights and their work can result in changed dialogue, altered scenarios, and added visual elements seemingly at odds with the playwright's expressed wishes or the script itself. As in the American theater, where many directors no longer treat the playwright's work as sacrosanct, in Seoul there recently have been legendary battles between directors and playwrights for artistic control. To ensure artistic control over the production of the drama, more than a few playwrights are now directing their own plays—and directors are writing their own plays. Recently, perhaps 20 percent of stage productions in Seoul were by director-playwrights. In some instances, like works by Han T'aesuk, Ki Kuksŏ, Kim A-ra, and Yang Chŏng-ung, the director does not interpret a written script; rather, the director *is* the script, the source of artistically provocative kinesthetic and audiovisual concepts combined with nonrealistic verbal communication. The traditional director of realistic plays no longer dominates the Korean theater.

Korea's contemporary theater—and its dramas—are alive with change. For example, linguistically minimalist productions relying on movement rather than linear dialogue are represented by Yun Yŏngsŏn's *Kiss* (*K'isu*, 1996):

MAN: I am here.
WOMAN: I am here, too.
MAN: There? (*Pause.*) There, where?
WOMAN: Just here.
MAN: Just there?
WOMAN: No, here.
MAN: So, there.
WOMAN: No, not there but here, I mean. (*Pause.*) Here.
MAN: So, there.
WOMAN: No. (*Pause.*) Here, here, here. (*Pause.*) I am here. (*Long pause.*)

Translated by Yi Hyŏngjin

Updated adaptations of traditional Korean tales or adaptations of Shakespearean plays incorporate shamanistic rituals (*kut*), mask dances (*t'alch'um*), farmer's music, and martial arts. Casts composed of Korean and Japanese or Korean and Chinese actors are increasingly common. Adaptations of Chinese, Japanese, and other foreign novels also blur lines between genres and challenge performance boundaries. An example is the incorporation of *p'ansori*-like songs in the 2008 adaptation of the book *The Time Seller: A Business Satire* (2006), by Fernando Trías de Bes.

Broad domestic comedy has become more popular, with an element of nostalgia is seen in revivals of *shinp'a*-like works from the 1930s. Portrayals of life during the colonial period now seem gentler, and some even offer comic relief. Revivals of earlier works by living icons in the Korean theater are common. Female playwrights still may be underrepresented in the Korean theater world, but the recognition given to such writers as Ko Yŏn-ok, Kim Myŏnghwa, and Kim Yunmi suggests advances over the last decade. To productions of domestic works have been added productions of translations of American and European works, giving Taehangno a truly international flavor through much of the year.

Over the last two decades, Seoul has become a major theater center in Asia and served, for example, as a site of the BeSeTo (Beijing-Seoul-Tōkyō) Theater Festival. Taehangno itself was transformed seemingly overnight in the wake of investment and construction in the area, and major university buildings added in the past few years attest to the Korean theater's maturation and cultural legitimacy. World-class actors, designers, directors, and writers intermingle easily in Seoul, the cultural, economic, political, and artistic capital of the nation. The streets of Taehangno are like a theater buffet featuring a great variety of choices, evincing a palpable youthful optimism and energy that feeds both mature and maturing artists' passion for theater as an art and social force. Moreover, the importance of family in Korean culture is mirrored in the compact scope of the theater "family" in Seoul and in the intimate small theaters, where "oneness" in the audience and the approachability of Korean dramatists and theater artists permit and sustain a special physical and psychological interplay between the artists and the audience. From the stage manager's warmly applauded precurtain appearance on stage to request that cell phones be silenced to the inclusion of the performers' e-mail addresses in the production program, productions in the small theaters of Seoul truly are remarkably personalized events.

Korean drama and theater still face challenges. But while some artists are moving on to other endeavors, perhaps theater still matters to many writers and artists because freedom of expression has been a rare gift throughout the history of modern Korean drama and theater. At the same time, Koreans have remained an expressive, resilient people with a great life force in the face of hardships. Despite the many obstacles—or perhaps because of them—Korean playwrights and theater artists have become leaders and visionaries in the contemporary Asian theater world and have earned respect and accolades from their European and British counterparts. Whatever the challenges faced, wherever the unpredictable Korean theater and drama are headed, one thing is certain: on any given night in Seoul one may find examples of drama and theater to grace stages anywhere in the world.

NOTE

1. This overview of theater performance spaces does not include permanent outdoor venues for the performance of traditional mask dances (*t'alch'um*) or the temporary, large tents, seating three thousand or more patrons, erected to house the popular *madangnori* (a revuelike family entertainment blending traditional Korean dance and music with warm-hearted satire of contemporary Korean life).

BIBLIOGRAPHY

GENERAL WORKS

Breen, Michael. *The Koreans: Who They Are, What They Want, Where Their Future Lies*. London: Orion, 1998.

Cumings, Bruce. *Korea's Place in the Sun: A Modern History*. Updated ed. New York: Norton, 2005.

Koo, John H., and Andrew C. Nahm, eds. *An Introduction to Korean Culture*. Seoul: Hollym, 1997.

Macdonald, Donald Stone. *The Koreans: Contemporary Politics and Society*. Edited and revised by Donald N. Clark. Boulder, Colo.: Westview Press, 1996.

Meijer, Maarten. *What's So Good About Korea, Maarten?* Seoul: Hyeonamsa, 2005.

Pratt, Keith, and Richard Rutt. *A Historical and Cultural Dictionary*. Richmond: Curzon Press, 1999.

Robinson, Michael E. *Korea's Twentieth-Century Odyssey*. Honolulu: University of Hawai'i Press, 2007.

WORKS ON KOREAN DRAMA, THEATER, AND LITERATURE

Brandon, James, ed. *The Cambridge Guide to Asian Theatre*. Cambridge: Cambridge University Press, 1993.

Chung Jin-soo. "Korean Theater, Past and Present." *Korea Journal* 20, no. 3 (1980): 4–9.

Fulton, Bruce, and Youngmin Kwon, eds. *Modern Korean Fiction: An Anthology*. New York: Columbia University Press, 2005.

Han Sang-chul. "Trends in Postwar Theatre." In *Korean Cultural Heritage: Performing Arts*, edited by Korea Foundation, 3:196–206. Seoul: Samsung Moonwha, 1997.

Jang, Won-jae. *Irish Influences on Korean Theatre During the 1920s and 1930s*. Gerrads Cross: Colin Smythe, 2003.

Kim Hunggyu. *Understanding Korean Literature*. Translated by Robert J. Fouser. Armonk, N.Y.: Sharpe, 1997.
Kim Yun-cheol. "The Influence of Western Drama on Contemporary Korean Theatre." *European Cultural Review*. Available at http://www.c3. hu/~eufuzetek/ en/eng/15/ index. php?mit=yunceol (accessed November 2007).
Kim Yun-cheol. "Theatre in the 1990s." *Koreana* 11, no. 2 (1997): 32–35.
Kim Yun-cheol and Kim Miy-He, eds. *Contemporary Korean Theatre: Playwrights, Directors, Stage-Designers*. Seoul: Theatre and Man Press, 2000.
Lee, Meewon. "Korean Modern Theatre Seeking for Its National and Cultural Identity." Available at http://www. twscholl. net/ASTR/Docs/ASTR%20Lee. doc (accessed November 2007).
Lee, Peter H., ed. *Modern Korean Literature: An Anthology*. Honolulu: University of Hawai'i Press, 1990.
Leiter, Samuel, ed. *Encyclopedia of Asian Theatre*. Westport, Conn.: Greenwood Press, 2007.
Seo Yeun-ho. "Korean Playwrights of the 1960s and 1970s." *Korea Journal* 20, no. 3 (1980): 10–17.
Yang Hye-suk, ed. *Korean Performing Arts: Drama, Dance, and Music Theatre*. Seoul: Jipmoondang, 1997.
Yoo Min-young. "Fifty Years of Korean Drama Since Liberation." *Korea Journal* 36, no. 1 (1996): 114–43.

ANTHOLOGIES

Ham Se-dŏk. *Plays of Colonial Korea: Se-Dŏk Ham*. Translated and edited by Jin-hee Kim. Norwalk, Conn.: EastBridge Press, 2007.
Kang Seong-hui. *Kang Seong Hui higok cheonjip* [Collected Works by Kang Seong-hui]. Vol. 4. Seoul: Hanuri Media, 1996.
Kim, Jinhee, trans. *Korean Drama Under Japanese Occupation: Plays by Ch'i-jin Yu and Man-sik Ch'ae*. Paramus, N.J.: Homa and Sekey Books, 2004.
Korean National Commission for UNESCO, ed. *Wedding Day and Other Korean Plays*. Seoul: Si-sa-yong-o-sa, 1983.
Korean PEN, ed. *Modern Korean Short Stories and Plays*. Seoul: Korean Centre, International PEN, 1970.
Lee Kang-baek (Yi Kangbaek). *Allegory of Survival: The Theatre of Kang-Baek Lee*. Translated by Alyssa Kim and Hyung-jin Lee. Youngstown, N.Y.: Cambria Press, 2008.
Lee Yun-t'aek (Yi Yunt'aek). *Four Contemporary Korean Plays by Lee Yun-Taek*. Translated by Dongwook Kim and Richard Nichols. Lanham, Md.: University Press of America, 2007.
Oh T'ae-sŏk (O T'aesŏk). *The Metacultural Theatre of Oh T'ae-Sŏk: Five Plays from the Korean Avante-Garde*. Translated by Ah-jeong Kim and R. B. Graves. Honolulu: University of Hawai'i Press, 1999.

Yu Ch'ijin. *Three Plays by Chi-Jin Yoo*. Translated by Won-jae Jang. Gerrads Cross: Colin Smythe, 2005.
Zong In-sob, ed. *Plays from Korea*. Seoul: Korean Language School, 1968.

WORKS BY PLAYWRIGHTS REPRESENTED IN THIS VOLUME

Ch'a Bŏm-sŏk (Ch'a Pŏmsŏk). *The Angry Machine*. Translated by Zong In-sob, in *Plays from Korea*, edited by Zong In-sob. Seoul: Korean Language School, 1968.
Ch'a Bŏm-sŏk (Ch'a Pŏmsŏk). *Barren Land*. Translated by Song Yo-in, in *Modern Korean Short Stories and Plays*, edited by Korean PEN. Seoul: Korean Centre, International PEN, 1970.
Ch'a Bŏm-sŏk (Ch'a Pŏmsŏk). *Burning Mountain*. Translated by Janet Poole. *Korean Literature Today* 4, no. 4 (1999): 175; and 5, no. 1 (2000): 153.
Ch'a Bŏm-sŏk (Ch'a Pŏmsŏk). *The Fourth Class Car*. Translated by Edward D. Rockstein, in *Wedding Day and Other Korean Plays*, edited by Korean National Commission for UNESCO. Seoul: Si-sa-yong-o-sa, 1983.
Lee Kang-baek (Yi Kangbaek). *Chaos and Order at a Gallery*. Translated by Alyssa Kim and Hyung-jin Lee, in *Allegory of Survival: The Theatre of Kang-Baek Lee*. Youngstown, N.Y.: Cambria Press, 2008.
Lee Kang-baek (Yi Kangbaek). *Five*. Translated by Alyssa Kim and Hyung-jin Lee, in *Allegory of Survival: The Theatre of Kang-Baek Lee*. Youngstown, N.Y.: Cambria Press, 2008.
Lee Kang-baek (Yi Kangbaek). *A Gem and a Woman*. Translated by Hanguk University of Foreign Studies. Seoul: Hanguk University of Foreign Studies, 1991.
Lee Kang-baek (Yi Kangbaek). *Getting Married*. Translated by Sŏ Chi-mun, in *Wedding Day and Other Korean Plays*, edited by Korean National Commission for UNESCO. Seoul: Si-sa-yong-o-sa, 1983.
Lee Kang-baek (Yi Kangbaek). *Homo Seperatus*. Translated by Koh Myung-shik. *Korea Journal* 24, no. 1 (1984): 62–78; and 24, no. 2 (1984): 33–47.
Lee Kang-baek (Yi Kangbaek). *The Marriage*. Translated by Ryu Yŏng-kyun. Available at http://www. drama21c. net/text/marriage. htm (accessed November 2007).
Lee Kang-baek (Yi Kangbaek). *Spring Day*. Translated by Alyssa Kim and Hyung-jin Lee, in *Allegory of Survival: The Theatre of Kang-Baek Lee*. Youngstown, N.Y.: Cambria Press, 2008.
Lee Kang-baek (Yi Kangbaek). *Watchman*. Translated by Alyssa Kim and Hyung-jin Lee, in *Allegory of Survival: The Theatre of Kang-Baek Lee*. Youngstown, N.Y.: Cambria Press, 2008.
Lee Kang-baek (Yi Kangbaek). *Wedding*. Translated by Alyssa Kim and Hyung-jin Lee, in *Allegory of Survival: The Theatre of Kang-Baek Lee*. Youngstown, N.Y.: Cambria Press, 2008.

Lee Man-hŭi (Yi Manhŭi). *It Was a Small Hole Inside the Darkness of a Buddhist Woodblock*. Anonymous translator. Script in possession of Lee Man-hŭi and Richard Nichols.

Oh T'ae-sŏk (O T'aesŏk). *The Bicycle*. Translated by Ah-jeong Kim and R. B. Graves, in *The Metacultural Theatre of Oh T'ae-Sŏk: Five Plays from the Korean Avante-Garde*. Honolulu: University of Hawai'i Press, 1999.

Oh T'ae-sŏk (O T'aesŏk). *Ch'un-p'ung's Wife*. Translated by Ah-jeong Kim and R. B. Graves, in *The Metacultural Theatre of Oh T'ae-Sŏk: Five Plays from the Korean Avante-Garde*. Honolulu: University of Hawai'i Press, 1999.

Oh T'ae-sŏk (O T'aesŏk). *The Drug Peddler*. Translated by Sŏl Sun-bong. *Korea Journal* 20, no. 3 (1980): 44–54.

Oh T'ae-sŏk (O T'aesŏk). *The Drug Peddler*. Translated by Sŏl Sun-bong, in *Wedding Day and Other Korean Plays*, edited by Korean National Commission for UNESCO. Seoul: Si-sa-yong-o-sa, 1983.

Oh T'ae-sŏk (O T'aesŏk). *The Grass Tomb*. Translated by Ryu Yung-kyun. Available at http://www.drama21c.net/writers/ohtaesok/grasstombtxt.html (accessed May 2008).

Oh T'ae-sŏk (O T'aesŏk). *Intimacy Between Father and Son*. Translated by Ah-jeong Kim. *Asian Theatre Journal* 12, no. 1 (1995): 1–36.

Oh T'ae-sŏk (O T'aesŏk). *Intimacy Between Father and Son*. Translated by Ah-jeong Kim and R. B. Graves, in *The Metacultural Theatre of Oh T'ae-Sŏk: Five Plays from the Korean Avante-Garde*. Honolulu: University of Hawai'i Press, 1999.

Oh T'ae-sŏk (O T'aesŏk). *Lifecord*. Translated by Ah-jeong Kim and R. B. Graves, in *The Metacultural Theatre of Oh T'ae-Sŏk: Five Plays from the Korean Avante-Garde*. Honolulu: University of Hawai'i Press, 1999.

Oh T'ae-sŏk (O T'aesŏk). *Why Did Shim Ch'ŏng Plunge into the Sea Twice?* Translated by Ah-jeong Kim and R. B. Graves, in *The Metacultural Theatre of Oh T'ae-Sŏk: Five Plays from the Korean Avante-Garde*. Honolulu: University of Hawai'i Press, 1999.

Park Joh-yeol (Pak Choyŏl). *O Chang-gun's Toenail*. Translated by Bruce Fulton and Ju-Chan Fulton. *Korea Journal* 30, no. 6 (1990): 56–72; and 30, no. 7 (1990): 49–59.

WORKS BY OTHER PLAYWRIGHTS

Ch'ae Mansik. *Memorial Day*. Translated by Jinhee Kim, in *Korean Drama Under Japanese Occupation: Plays by Ch'i-jin Yu and Man-sik Ch'ae*. Paramus, N.J.: Homa and Sekey Books, 2004.

Chang Cheong-il (Jang Jung-il). *Mother*. Translated by Bruce Fulton and Ju-Chan Fulton. *Korea Journal* 29, no. 10 (1989): 56–62.

Chang (Jang) Wang-rok. *Strangers in the Night*. *Korea Journal* 7, no. 11 (1964): 31–38.

Ch'oe Inhun. *Away, Away, Long Time Ago*. Translated by Park Hui-jin, in *Modern Korean Literature: An Anthology*, edited by Peter H. Lee. Honolulu: University of Hawai'i Press, 1990.

Ch'oe Inhun. *Hans and Gretel*. Translated by Ryu Yŏng-kyun. Available at http://www.drama21c.net/text/3plays/5-009a.html (accessed November 2007).

Ch'oe Inhun. *A Sonata of Lost Spring*. Translated by Ryu Yŏng-kyun. *Korea Journal* 29, no. 12 (1989): 60–74.

Ch'oe Inhun. *Shoo—oo Shoo Once upon a Time*. Translated by Ryu Yŏng-kyun. Available at http://www.drama21c.net/text/3plays/awyact1.html (accessed November 2007).

Ch'oe Inhun. *Wha . . . i, Whai, a Long Long Time Ago*. Translated by Cho Oh-gon (Cho Oh Kon), in *Wedding Day and Other Korean Plays*, edited by Korean National Commission for UNESCO. Seoul: Si-sa-yong-o-sa, 1983.

Ch'oe Inhun. *Wha . . . i, Whai, a Long Long Time Ago*. Translated by Cho Oh Kon. *Korea Journal* 20, no. 4 (1980): 42–56.

[The preceding three citations are translations of the same play.]

Ch'oe Inhun. *When Spring Comes to Hills and Dales*. Translated by Ryu Yŏng-kyun. Available at http://www.drama21c.net/eda/playscripts.html (accessed November 2007).

Ch'oe Man-shik, *Memories of the Dong-Hag*. Translated by Zong In-sob, in *Plays from Korea*, edited by Zong In-sob. Seoul: Korean Language School, 1968.

Ham Se-dŏk. *Child Monk*. Translated by Jinhee Kim, in *Plays of Colonial Korea: Se-Dŏk Ham*, edited by Jinhee Kim. Norwalk, Conn.: EastBridge Press, 2007.

Ham Se-dŏk. *Mountain Cove*. Translated by Jinhee Kim, in *Plays of Colonial Korea: Se-Dŏk Ham*, edited by Jinhee Kim. Norwalk, Conn.: EastBridge Press, 2007.

Ham Se-dŏk. *Potatoes, a Weasel and the Schoolmistress*. Translated by Jinhee Kim, in *Plays of Colonial Korea: Se-Dŏk Ham*, edited by Jinhee Kim. Norwalk, Conn.: EastBridge Press, 2007.

Jin U-chŏn. *Waves*. Translated by Zong In-sob, in *Plays from Korea*, edited by Zong In-sob. Seoul: Korean Language School, 1968.

Kang Soeng-hui. *Freedom, as Large as This World*. Translated by Sukcha Lee Kennel, in *Kang Seong Hui higok cheonjip* [*Collected Works by Kang Seong-hui*]. Vol. 4. Seoul: Hanuri Media, 1996.

Kang Seong-hui. *The Lost*. Translated by N. M. Pankaj, in *Kang Seong Hui higok cheonjip* [*Collected Works by Kang Seong-hui*]. Vol. 4. Seoul: Hanuri Media, 1996.

Kang Seong-hui. *A Night in Harlem*. Translated by N. M. Pankaj, in *Kang Seong Hui higok cheonjip* [*Collected Works by Kang Seong-hui*]. Vol. 4. Seoul: Hanuri Media, 1996.

Kim, Cha-rim. *The Inheritance*. Translated by Zong In-sob, in *Plays from Korea*, edited by Zong In-sob. Seoul: Korean Language School, 1968.

Kim, Jinsu. *Pleasure Ground*. Translated by Zong In-sob, in *Plays from Korea*, edited by Zong In-sob. Seoul: Korean Language School, 1968.
Kim Jongjin. *Fifteen Minutes*. Translated by Zong In-sob, in *Plays from Korea*, edited by Zong In-sob. Seoul: Korean Language School, 1968.
Kim Kwang-lim. *In Quest of Love*. Translated by Howard Blanning and Jinbae Park, 2005. Script in possession of Howard Blanning and Jinbae Park, Miami University of Ohio.
Kim, Yong-ik. *Village Moon: A Comedy in One Act. Korea Journal* 23, no. 12 (1983): 46–55.
Kim, Yong-ik. *Village Wine: A Play in One Act. Korea Journal* 23, no. 12 (1983): 56–66.
Kim Yongsu. *The Pig*. Translated by Zong In-sob, in *Plays from Korea*, edited by Zong In-sob. Seoul: Korean Language School, 1968.
Lee Kunsam. *Manuscript Paper*. Translated by Zong In-sob, in *Plays from Korea*, edited by Zong In-sob. Seoul: Korean Language School, 1968.
Lee Kunsam. *A New Common Sense*. Translated by Lee T'ae-dong and Greggar Sletteland. *Korea Journal* 14, no. 8 (1974): 42–56; and 14, no. 9 (1974): 57–69.
Lee Kunsam. *A New Common Sense*. Translated by Lee T'aedong and Greggar Sletteland, in *Wedding Day and Other Korean Plays*, edited by Korean National Commission for UNESCO. Seoul: Si-sa-yong-o-sa, 1983.
Lee Kunsam. *A Respectful Profession*. Translated by Song Yo-in. *Korea Journal* 20, no. 3 (1980): 25–35.
Lee Kunsam. *A Respectful Profession*. Translated by Song Yo-in, in *Modern Korean Short Stories and Plays*, edited by Korean PEN. Seoul: Korean Centre, International PEN, 1970.
Lee Yun-t'aek (Yi Yunt'aek). *Citizen K*. Translated by Dongwook Kim and Richard Nichols, in *Four Contemporary Korean Plays by Lee Yun-Taek*. Lanham, Md.: University Press of America, 2007.
Lee Yun-t'aek (Yi Yunt'aek). *Dummy Bride*. Translated by Dongwook Kim and Richard Nichols, in *Four Contemporary Korean Plays by Lee Yun-Taek*. Lanham, Md.: University Press of America, 2007.
Lee Yun-t'aek (Yi Yunt'aek). *Mask of Fire*. Translated by Dongwook Kim and Richard Nichols, in *Four Contemporary Korean Plays by Lee Yun-Taek*. Lanham, Md.: University Press of America, 2007.
Lee Yun-t'aek (Yi Yunt'aek). *O-Gu: A Ceremony of Death*. Translated by Dongwook Kim and Richard Nichols, in *Four Contemporary Korean Plays by Lee Yun-Taek*. Lanham, Md.: University Press of America, 2007.
O Yŏng-jin. *Wedding Day*. Translated by Song Yo-in. *Korea Journal* 11, no. 12 (1971): 36–50; and 12, no. 1 (1972): 39–47.
O Yŏng-jin. *Wedding Day*. Translated by Song Yo-in, in *Wedding Day and Other Korean Plays*, edited by Korean National Commission for UNESCO. Seoul: Si-sa-yong-o-sa, 1983.

Oh Hak-yong. *Bridge of the Abyss*. Translated by Kim Mija and Frank Tedesco. *Korea Journal* 30, no. 9 (1990): 36–50.
Park Hyŏnsuk. *On Foot Again*. Translated by Zong In-sob, in *Plays from Korea*, edited by Zong In-sob. Seoul: Korean Language School, 1968.
Song Yong. *Mr. Gum-San Hwang*. Translated by Zong In-sob, in *Plays from Korea*, edited by Zong In-sob. Seoul: Korean Language School, 1968.
Yu Ch'ijin. *The Cow*. Translated by Won-Jae Jang, in *Three Plays by Chi-Jin Yoo*. Gerrads Cross: Colin Smythe, 2005.
Yu Ch'ijin. *The Ox*. Translated by Jinhee Kim, in *Korean Drama Under Japanese Occupation: Plays by Ch'i-jin Yu and Man-sik Ch'ae*. Paramus, N.J.: Homa and Sekey Books, 2004.
[The preceding two citations are translations of the same play.]
Yu Ch'ijin. *The Donkey*. Translated by Won-Jae Jang, in *Three Plays by Chi-Jin Yoo*. Gerrads Cross: Colin Smythe, 2005.
Yu Ch'ijin. *Fatherland*. Translated by Song Yo-in, in *Modern Korean Short Stories and Plays*, edited by Korean PEN. Seoul: Korean Centre, International PEN, 1970.
Yu Ch'ijin. *The Memorial Service*. Translated by Zong In-sob, in *Plays from Korea*, edited by Zong In-sob. Seoul: Korean Language School, 1968.
Yu Ch'ijin. *The Mud Hut*. Translated by Won-Jae Jang, in *Three Plays by Chi-Jin Yoo*. Gerrads Cross: Colin Smythe, 2005.
Yu Ch'ijin. *The Shack*. Translated by Jinhee Kim, in *Korean Drama Under Japanese Occupation: Plays by Ch'i-jin Yu and Man-sik Ch'ae*. Paramus, N.J.: Homa and Sekey Books, 2004.
[The preceding two citations are translations of the same play.}
Zong In-sob. *The Diamond Mountains*. Translated by Graham Weakley, in *Plays from Korea*, edited by Zong In-sob. Seoul: Korean Language School, 1968.

TRANSLATORS

Bruce Fulton and Ju-Chan Fulton are internationally recognized, award-winning translators of Korean literature. Bruce Fulton (Ph.D., Seoul National University) holds the Young-Bin Min Chair in Korean Literature and Literary Translation at the University of British Columbia.

Lee Hye-kyoung / Yi Hyekyŏng (Ph.D., University of Michigan) is an active theater critic and the chair of the Department of Theater, Kookmin University, Seoul.

Lee Hyung-jin / Yi Hyŏngjin (Ph.D., Pennsylvania State University) is a cotranslator of *Allegory of Survival: The Theatre of Kang-Baek Lee* (2008) and an assistant professor of English language and literature at Sookmyung Women's University, Seoul.

Alyssa Kim (Ph.D., Korea University) is a lecturer in English at Hongik University, a freelance translator for leading theater and film companies in Seoul, and a cotranslator of *Allegory of Survival: The Theatre of Kang-Baek Lee* (2008).

Jinhee Kim / Kim Chinhŭi (Ph.D., Indiana University) is the translator of *Korean Drama Under Japanese Occupation* (2004) and *Plays of Colonial Korea* (2007).

Richard Nichols (Ph.D., University of Washington) is an emeritus professor of theater at Pennsylvania State University and a cotranslator, with Dongwook Kim, of *Four Contemporary Korean Plays by Lee Yun-Taek* (2007).

Janet Poole (Ph.D., Columbia University) is an assistant professor in the Department of East Asian Studies at the University of Toronto. Her most recent translation is *Eastern Sentiments*, a collection of anecdotal essays by Yi T'aejun, from the Pacific War period, to be published by Columbia University Press.

PERMISSIONS

The editor and publisher acknowledge with thanks permission granted to publish the following plays.

Ch'a Pŏmsŏk. *Burning Mountain* (*Sanbul*). Translated by Janet Poole and published by permission of the estate of Ch'a Pŏmsŏk and Bumwoo Publishing Company.

O T'aesŏk. *Bellflower* (*Toraji*). Translated by Yi Hyŏngjin and Richard Nichols and published by permission of O T'aesŏk and Pyungminsa.

Pae Samshik. *Ch'oe Sŭnghŭi*. Translated by Alyssa Kim and published by permission of Pae Samshik.

Pak Choyŏl. *O Chang-gun's Toenail* (*O Chang-gun ŭi palt'op*). Translated by Bruce Fulton and Ju-Chan Fulton and published by permission of Pak Choyŏl and *Korea Journal*.

Pak Kŭnhyŏng. *In Praise of Youth* (*Ch'ŏngch'un yech'an*). Translated by Yi Hyekyŏng and published by permission of Pak Kŭnhyŏng and Theatre and Man Press.

Yi Kangbaek. *A Feeling, Like Nirvana* (*Nŭggim kŭgnak kat'ŭn*). Translated by Alyssa Kim and published by permission of Yi Kangbaek and Pyungminsa.

Yi Manhŭi. *Please Turn Off the Lights* (*Pul chom kkŏ chuseyo*). Translated by Kim Chinhŭi and published by permission of Yi Manhŭi.

GPSR Authorized Representative: Easy Access System Europe, Mustamäe tee 50, 10621 Tallinn, Estonia, gpsr.requests@easproject.com